Schooling by DESIGN

Mission, Action, and Achievement

ALEXANDRIA, VIRGINIA USA

GRANT WIGGINS AND JAY MCTIGHE

1703 N. Beauregard St. • Alexandria, VA 22311-1714 USA
Phone: 800-933-2723 or 703-578-9600 • Fax: 703-575-5400
Web site: www.ascd.org • E-mail: member@ascd.org
Author guidelines: www.ascd.org/write

Gene R. Carter, *Executive Director;* Nancy Modrak, *Director of Publishing;* Julie Houtz, *Director of Book Editing & Production;* Darcie Russell, *Project Manager;* Georgia Park, *Senior Graphic Designer;* Barton Matheson Willse & Worthington, *Typesetter;* Dina Seamon, *Production Specialist/Team Lead*

All Web links in this book are correct as of the publication date below but may have become inactive or otherwise modified since that time. If you notice a deactivated or changed link, please e-mail books@ascd.org with the words "Link Update" in the subject line. In your message, please specify the Web link, the book title, and the page number on which the link appears.

PAPERBACK ISBN: 978-1-4166-0580-5   ASCD product #107018   s7/07
Also available as an e-book through ebrary, netLibrary, and many online booksellers (see Books in Print for the ISBNs).

Quantity discounts for the paperback edition only: 10–49 copies, 10%; 50+ copies, 15%; for 1,000 or more copies, call 800-933-2723, ext. 5634, or 703-575-5634. For desk copies: member@ascd.org.

Library of Congress Cataloging-in-Publication Data

Wiggins, Grant P., 1950–
Schooling by design : mission, action, and achievement / Grant Wiggins and Jay McTighe.
p. cm.
Includes bibliographical references and index.
ISBN 978-1-4166-0580-5 (pbk. : alk. paper) 1. Education—United States—Aims and objectives. 2. Educational change—United States. 3. Curriculum planning—United States. I. McTighe, Jay. II. Title.

LA217.2.W53 2007

370.1—dc22   2007004394

18 17 16 15   7 8 9 10 11 12

Acknowledgments iv

Introduction 1

Part I. A Vision of Schooling

1. What Is the Mission of Schooling? 9
2. What Should Curriculum Accomplish? 36
3. How Should Curriculum Be Re-Formed? 58
4. How Should Teaching Be Appropriately Depersonalized? 111
5. What Is the Teacher's Job When Teaching? 128
6. What Is the Teacher's Job When Not Teaching? 155
7. What Is the Job of an Academic Leader? 172

Part II. A Plan for Schooling by Design

8. How Should Backward Design Apply to School Reform? 199
9. What Are the Desired Results of School Reform? 210
10. What Evidence Should We Collect? 227
11. What Actions Should We Plan? 242
12. What Habits Must We Confront? 252

References 273

Index 278

About the Authors 286

Acknowledgments

Many individuals, far too numerous to mention, have helped us develop and refine the ideas and materials in this book. Nonetheless, a few are deserving of special acknowledgment.

First, we owe a debt of gratitude to the members of the Understanding by Design Training Cadre for their eagerly shared wisdom and experience: John Brown, Ann Cunningham-Morris, Marcella Emberger, Judith Hilton, Everett Kline, Elizabeth Rutherford, Elliott Seif, Janie Smith, and Allison Zmuda. We are especially appreciative for the helpful advice from Allison, John, and Elliott given over the course of countless hours of review and conversation. They gently but firmly pushed us beyond an earlier, less effective draft and provided great feedback as we finished.

We offer heartfelt thanks to the thousands of educators with whom we have worked and whose questions, struggles, suggestions, and creative approaches helped the ideas in this book develop and mature. More specifically, we wish to highlight a few individuals: Frank Champine, Susan Clayton, Alan Dichter, Pamela Francis, Elaine Gorman, Andy Greene, Peter Heaney, Dorothy Katauskus, Marcia Kramer, Ann Lewis, Kim Marshall, Hilde McGeehan, Ron Thomas, Diane VanAusdall, and Mark Wise were among many of our most helpful colleagues. Andy deserves special thanks for his constant willingness to both react to and contribute materials in spite of his endless duties as principal of Candlewood Middle School.

Indeed, whatever strengths educators recognize in this book, they are due to the many insights and practical tools that evolved as a result of our work with numerous schools and districts. Although it would be impossible to reference them all, we salute the following contributors of the practical examples and tools found in this book: Baltimore County Public Schools (MD), Candlewood Middle School (NY), Grand Island Public Schools (NE), Greece Central Schools (NY), Hinsdale Township High School District 86 (IL), Montgomery County Public Schools (MD), Nanuet Public Schools (NY), New Hope–Solebury School District (PA), District #9 in New York City, St. Charles Community Schools (IL), St. Tammany Parish Schools (LA), State College Area School District (PA), Tewksbury Schools (NJ), Virginia Beach City Public Schools (VA), and West Windsor–Plainsboro Schools (NJ).

Schooling by Design would never have come about had it not been for the support provided by Ann Cunningham-Morris at ASCD. Ann helped to craft the initial vision of *Schooling by Design* and sustain its evolution over the past several years.

We are also thankful to Darcie Russell and her editorial colleagues for their helpful queries, suggestions, and shepherding of a rough draft to a polished publication. Finally, we once again thank our families for tolerating the endless phone calls, trips back and forth between Maryland and New Jersey, and hours spent on the road using and refining these materials. Grant is especially grateful to Denise for her substantive contributions and edits to the first four chapters, her tolerance of his endless doubts and brainstorms, and her cheerful willingness to help him think through or clarify key issues in the book. We trust that Daisy, Denise, and all the kids—once again—understand.

Introduction

> To accomplish great things, we must not only act, but also dream; not only plan, but also believe.
>
> —Anatole France

Volumes have been written on education and school reform. So what do we offer that is fresh and perhaps useful? Simply put, a clear and powerful conception of a mission-driven approach to schooling and a practical strategy for realizing that mission. Although many people have written about mission, few have described how mission should be honored by informing schooling and its structure. Using mission to inform schooling and its structures is what we set out to do here.

What is true of school mission? Regardless of the particulars, schooling should enable learners to achieve worthy intellectual accomplishments, as reflected in (1) their ability to transfer their learning with understanding to worthy tasks and (2) their mature habits of mind. What, then, must be true of genuine reform? That we find and root out the myriad ways in which mission is ignored or overlooked in day-to-day teaching, and that we derive curriculum, assessment, job descriptions, and policies "backward" from what the mission requires. Without a constant focus on teaching that is meant to culminate in meaning and transfer, schooling will likely remain mired in timeless, unexamined habits and rituals, and limited by incoherent practices and structures.

Throughout *Schooling by Design*, we use an architectural analogy: if "schooling" is an existing building, how should we think about its renovation? We envision a (re-)building resting upon six pillars:

• A clear and constant focus on the long-term mission of all schooling: enabling learners to achieve worthy intellectual accomplishment, as reflected in their ability to transfer their learning with understanding to worthy tasks and in their habits of mind.

- A curriculum and assessment framework that honors the overall mission as well as the explicit long-term goals of academic programs, to ensure that content coverage is no longer the de facto approach to lesson planning and instruction.
- A set of explicit principles of learning and instructional design, based on research and the wisdom of the profession, to which all decisions about pedagogy and planning are referred.
- Structures, policies, job descriptions, practices, and use of resources consistent with mission and learning principles.
- An overall strategy of reform centered on the constant exploration of the gap between the explicit vision of reform versus the current reality of schooling; in other words, a feedback and adjustment system that is ongoing, timely, and robust enough to enable all teachers and students to change course en route, as needed, to achieve the desired results.
- A set of tactics linked to the strategy and a straightforward process of planning for orchestrating the key work of schooling and school reform "backward" from the mission and the desired results.

The book offers an explanation of these elements, the rationale for them, and practical tools and processes for making such renovation focused and feasible. In short, the book is about getting beyond mere intentions, endless complaints, and naive dreams. We provide a plan of action that is driven not by vague values or random criticisms but by what any legitimate school mission statement implies for the practice and structure of schooling. We also include a plan for overcoming long-standing bad habits.

The challenge is not to invent some ideal school that is unmoored from reality (as many reforms have implied) or to presume that the current core functions of school are adequate to the task (they aren't), but rather to build exemplary schooling "backward" from its long-term goal of making students thoughtful, productive, and accomplished at worthy tasks. We offer new ideas, yes; but more important, the book is built upon a commonsense method for clarifying local goals and what they require of us, and for rooting out the blind spots and habits that run counter to those goals.

The logic is simple: if X is our mission, then what follows for curriculum, teaching, and school organization? We refer to such engineering from the mission as "schooling *by design*."

The point of education can be captured in a single phrase: *worthy accomplishment, achieved by causing thoughtful and effective understanding that enables transfer*. Any education, regardless of content or philosophy, should help learners, right from the start, to "come to understanding" in two senses: (1) to enable them to constantly *make meaning* from their schoolwork and (2) to equip them to *apply* their learning to new situations not only in school but also beyond it—that is, to transfer. Both goals are worked on now, in the present, not in some distant future after students have *first* learned all possible "stuff worth knowing." When such understanding is the aim, the habits of mind we most value will be fostered. Thus, schooling should be judged by what students have genuinely accomplished, not whether they have become good at "school." The point of school is to learn *in school* how to make sense of learnings in order to lead better lives *out of school;* to learn *now* to apply lessons to *later* challenges, effectively and thoughtfully.

At the center of the book (literally and figuratively) is thus a plan for reinventing the key embodiment of schooling—the curriculum—in a way that meets school goals and undercuts our habit of thinking of "teaching" as "covering content." To put it bluntly, the traditional curriculum and the view of teaching attached to it are dysfunctional and have been for centuries. A list of content and activities is not a plan; marching through material can never ensure habits of mind and genuine ability. Content mastery is not the ultimate goal of a school; it is a *by-product* of a successful education. To invoke the architectural analogy, mastering state standards is *not* the primary outcome of an educational renovation. The standards are like the building code that any reform blueprint has to honor, but they are not the blueprint itself. In short, schooling is random and school change becomes chaotic without a curriculum, assessment, and instructional framework derived from the mission and grounded in valid learning principles.

From the mission of achieving successful student *use* of learning, all other educational practices, policies, and structures must follow. This is the practical implication of the phrase *backward design* used throughout the book. Reform must be guided by a constant focus on the meaning of school mission and the analysis of that mission into aligned policies, structures, and practices.

Such a declaration about the importance of focusing on understanding and useful learning may perplex some readers. *Of course*, you might be thinking, *don't all educators want students to understand what is taught and to be able to apply what they have learned in their lives?* Well, yes and no. Yes, we *say* we value understanding and the particular habits of mind stated in our various program and mission statements, but when we look at how curricula are written, what gets assessed locally, and what happens day in and day out in classrooms, we see that the goals of thoughtfulness, meaning, and transfer get quickly lost and perpetually postponed so that the basics of "content" can *first* be taught by the teacher and then be tested on an easily scored paper-and-pencil assessment. As a result, genuine applications of learning (and the habits related to them) are all too frequently sacrificed.

Some of the reasons for the lack of constant focus on understanding and transfer are understandable. The textbooks we use reinforce a propensity to cover content superficially and out of context. Pressures to prepare for high-stakes tests (primarily using a selected-response format, in which content is again isolated from context of use) reinforce a local instructional focus on discrete knowledge and skills. State and federal accountability systems that define "success" narrowly (based on test results of material that can be efficiently tested using large-scale measures) seem to conspire against teaching for in-depth understanding and transfer. Despite such obvious culprits, we believe that subtler psychological and social forces of greater impact and long standing prevent us from a focus on our declared mission.

Lurking behind our book are vital but rarely asked questions: Why have well-intentioned, skilled, and hardworking educators, over the years, so often lost sight of the goal of causing understanding? Why do the majority of our students *not* end up understanding or becoming accomplished in the ways we hoped and often desired that they would? Why is it so *easy* for teachers to get sidetracked by content coverage, test prep, or engaging activities unmoored from worthier intellectual purposes? Why do so many students find school boring and unworthy of their best learning efforts, and why do we have a blind spot about their experience? Our answer, in brief: we argue that successful reform depends on each educator and staff person breaking a long-standing array of habits and attitudes that for centuries have held schooling back from entering a new era.

Our critique is structural, not personal. Many teachers, acting in good faith, have been led to believe *incorrectly* that their job is to march through content and to test for low-level knowledge and discrete skills (though that is not even what most state standards expect). This misunderstanding is not only the result of centuries of institutional habits and mental models of "teaching" and "testing," but also the inevitable effect of relying on typical curricula and textbooks.

A Flexible and Realistic Process

In addition to an understanding-oriented mission to guide school renovation, we need a realistic plan that presumes humility and the need to constantly adjust both individual teaching and schooling based on feedback and other results. We must ensure that there are constant inquiries into what is working and what isn't, leading to timely and effective alteration of practice. As it stands now, educators have few mechanisms for obtaining needed feedback and for making systemic adjustments once schooling is under way. We lack both troubleshooting guides and needed ongoing reviews of current performance against goals.

The reform process must therefore involve an ongoing three-step cycle:

- An increasingly clear and powerful vision of where we want to end up, based on our mission and agreed-upon learning principles.

- A constant and unflinching assessment of where we stand at present against the mission.
- Timely adjustments based on regular analysis of the gap between vision and reality, between goals and results.

When these conditions are met, both inertia and change for change's sake are overcome. The gap between a tangible and desirable result versus the current reality focuses our work to close the gap. The more we analyze the gap, the more we clarify the vision. The more we clarify the vision, the more it seems desirable and feasible. The more feasible it seems, the more we are unsatisfied with current results, and so on. In our view, educators in all positions must view this kind of work as being at the heart of their job.

In sum, though literally thousands of books address the subjects of school leadership and educational reform, we propose a more modest but highly focused approach. We ask readers to think through with us, in a backward-design way, what a commitment to learning for understanding and the long-term goals of mission require of schooling. If the aim is to make the classroom, the school, and the organization more understanding focused and true to the mission, which actions and plans will most likely get us there? What are the *mission-critical* tasks at which teachers, building leaders, and district staff must succeed in order to make the classroom, the school, and the system understanding based and mission focused?

A Preview of *Schooling by Design*

The book is divided into two parts. Part I (Chapters 1 through 7) sets forth a *vision* of schooling and its implications for curriculum and staff roles. Part II (Chapters 8 through 12) proposes a *plan* for achieving such schooling—by design. In fact, the book is organized around the logic of backward design; that is, given a clear and robust mission and guiding principles of learning, the particulars of schooling—curriculum, assessment, instruction, roles of staff, policies, structures, use of resources—are derived from the results desired. Figure A provides a graphic representation of the components we address.

In Chapter 1 we begin with an exploration of the primacy of educational mission and its influence on all aspects of schooling. We argue that all the many missions reflect a common goal: developing *understanding and transfer* ability in every subject and developing the key *habits of mind* that signify a mature and effective adult. Chapter 2 characterizes the nature of a curriculum for achieving the mission—by design. Chapter 3 describes the particular elements of this new curricular framework, with many examples of what is needed. Chapter 4 makes the case for adopting an explicit set of learning principles associated with the mission. Chapters 5, 6, and

Figure A

Schooling by Design—Key Elements

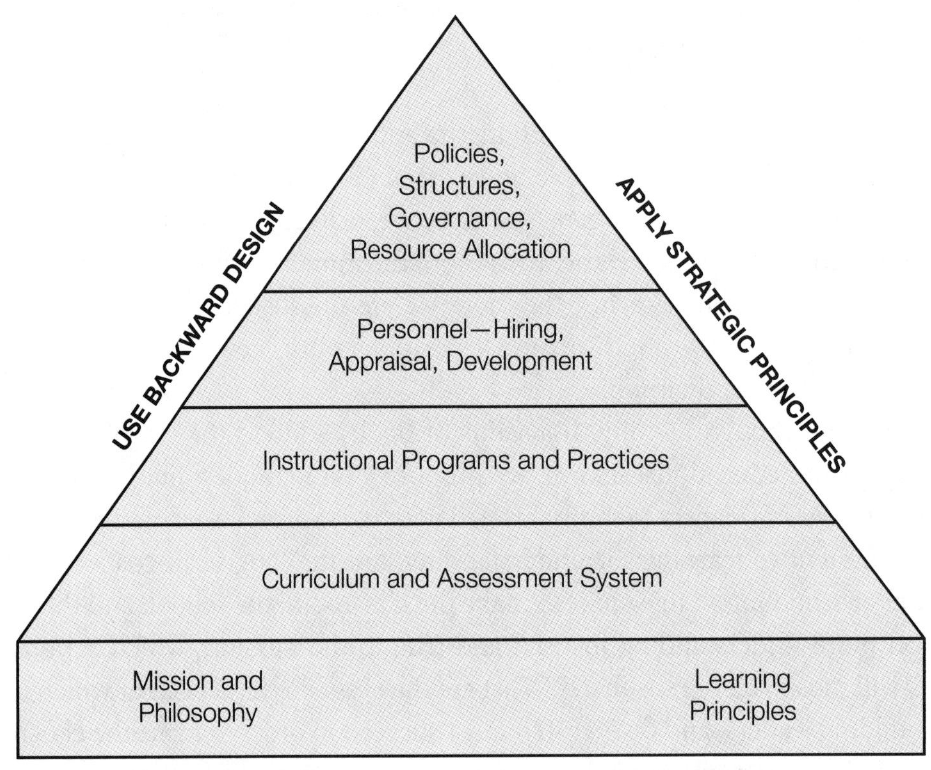

7 specify general roles and particular job descriptions for teachers and academic leaders in a school or district committed to such a mission.

In Part II, chapters 8–11, we describe a practical three-stage backward-design process for reform planning, with tactics for each stage. Chapter 12 looks at the reality of school change with an emphasis on habit as the key target of change.

Additionally, many chapters conclude with Ideas for Action—specific steps that educators may take to act on the ideas presented within the chapter.

Like our book *Understanding by Design,* its curriculum cousin *Schooling by Design* does not and cannot provide a quick fix. We don't believe in foolproof leadership approaches any more than we believe in teacher-proof curricula. What we think we offer here is a plan for more thoughtful, sustained, and ultimately effective results in the necessarily hard and time-consuming work of making schools honor their promise.

Part I

A Vision of Schooling

1

What Is the Mission of Schooling?

> No doubt some excellent educational work is being done by artistic teachers who do not have a clear conception of goals but do have an intuitive sense of what is good teaching. . . . Nevertheless, if an educational program is to be planned and if efforts for continued improvement are to be made, it is very necessary to have some conception of the goals that are being aimed at. These educational objectives become the criteria by which materials are selected, content is outlined, instructional procedures are developed, and tests and examinations are prepared.
>
> —Ralph Tyler, *Basic Principles of Curriculum and Instruction*

The title of this book is *Schooling by Design*. Schooling *by design* means that we develop school to achieve a learning-related mission. As the dictionary definitions remind us, to *design* or to *produce a design* is to aim to achieve a specific and explicit purpose:

- To formulate a plan for; devise.
- To create or contrive for a particular purpose or effect.
- To have as a goal or purpose; intend.
- To make or execute plans.
- To have a goal or purpose in mind.
- The purposeful or inventive arrangement of parts or details.
- A plan; a project.
- A reasoned purpose; an intent.
- Deliberate intention.

Thus, a school mission is the long-term goal in mind against which we design (and forever adjust) schooling. To design with a purpose in mind means to intend to achieve a clear and explicit goal, to be committed to achieving specific effects in learners. Schooling at its best reflects a purposeful arrangement of parts and details, organized with deliberate intention, for achieving the kinds of learning we seek. A mission summarizes what we are in business to accomplish in learners. To honor it, we have to ensure that schooling is organized to accomplish it. In our language, school must be designed backward from the mission.

This is not a new or offbeat idea. The New England Association of Schools and Colleges (NEASC) highlights this idea in its first current accreditation standard for high schools:

> Mission and Expectations for Student Learning
>
> The school's mission statement describes the essence of what the school as a community of learners is seeking to achieve. The expectations for student learning are based on and drawn from the school's mission statement. These expectations are the fundamental goals by which the school continually assesses the effectiveness of the teaching and learning process. Every component of the school community must focus on enabling all students to achieve the school's expectations for student learning.
>
> 1. The mission statement and expectations for student learning shall be developed by the school community and approved and supported by the professional staff, the school board, and any other schoolwide governing organization.
> 2. The school's mission statement shall represent the school community's fundamental values and beliefs about student learning.
> 3. The school shall define schoolwide academic, civic, and social learning expectations that
>   - are measurable;
>   - reflect the school's mission.
> 4. For each academic expectation in the mission the school shall have a targeted level of successful achievement identified in a rubric.
> 5. The school shall have indicators by which it assesses the school's progress in achieving schoolwide civic and social expectations.
> 6. The mission statement and the school's expectations for student learning shall guide the procedures, policies, and decisions of the school and shall be evident in the culture of the school.
> 7. The school shall review regularly the mission statement and expectations for student learning using a variety of data to ensure that they reflect student needs, community expectations, the district mission, and state and national standards. (Commission on Public Secondary Schools, 2005, p. 3)

So when we talk about schooling by design, we refer to a simple set of questions related to purpose that should guide the building, or especially the renovation, of school and the actions of every educator:

• What is the school's mission, its reason for being? What would successful graduates look like, be like, be capable of doing well with their learning?

• Given the school's mission, what follows for curriculum and assessment?

• Given its curriculum and assessment (and what we know about learning), what follows for instruction?

• Given such a system for causing mission-related learning, what follows for the jobs of teachers and administrators, school structures, policies, and action?

In other words, what does mission imply and obligate us to? What kind of schooling does mission demand? This is the inquiry and the logic of the book: schooling *by design,* not schooling by habit or impulse.

The Point of Schooling

What is the particular mission of school? What learning is school in business to achieve? There have been as many answers as educators throughout history, of course. But we narrow the responses dramatically if we ask a more practical analytic question: in general, how might we categorize the long-term educational accomplishments that schools have said historically they are in business to achieve? That question generates only a handful of categories and we summarize them as follows:

- Academic excellence and intellectual preparation for higher education.
- The development of mature habits of mind and attitudes.
- Artistic and aesthetic ability and sensitivity.
- Health, wellness, and athletic development.
- Character—mature social, civic, and ethical conduct.
- Personal skill development and professional direction.

More specifically, a scan of hundreds of mission statements reveals that three long-term aims predominate: "lifelong learning," "critical and creative thinking," and "productive contributions to society." Here are some typical mission statements:

> The mission of LaVace Stewart Elementary School is to form a partnership with parents and the community to prepare our diverse population of students to become lifelong learners in a nurturing, safe environment with high expectations so they will become responsible, productive citizens in an ever-changing society.

> Bremen High School aims to develop students who
> - Exhibit creative and critical thinking.
> - Develop self-esteem, pride, and respect for themselves and others.

- Find a balance between academic success and involvement in extracurricular activities.
- Adapt to a continually changing technological world.
- Demonstrate the democratic living skills of consensus building and group problem solving in order to become active citizens in their community.
- Span the transition from competent student to productive, responsible citizen.
- Understand the value of education and the need for lifelong learning.

The mission of the West Windsor–Plainsboro Regional School District, valuing our tradition of excellence, is to develop all of our students as passionate, confident, lifelong learners who have competence and strength of character to realize their aspirations and thoughtfully contribute to a diverse and changing world.

The mission of the Memphis City Schools is to prepare all children to be successful citizens and workers in the 21st century. This will include educating them to read with comprehension, write clearly, compute accurately, think, reason, and use information to solve problems.

These statements can be reduced to one encompassing sentence: Schools exist to cause learning that is intellectually vital, generative of future self-directed learning, personally meaningful and productive, and socially valuable.

Some readers may protest: "But schools don't have a coherent mission. They can't—there are too many diverse forces, values, and goals at work in education." Others may protest in the other direction: "You are trying to take away my professional freedom!" We think that both positions confuse the *idea* of having a clear and explicit purpose for an education with the defects of particular mission statements and school policies. We are not claiming that all schools should have the same mission, nor are we claiming that coherence comes easily. We are saying that the point of any school is meaningful, useful, and coherent learning derived from explicit and vital long-term purposes, regardless of content and pedagogical philosophy. Nor are we claiming that a mission statement should narrowly focus on one goal or mandate one form of pedagogy. We are claiming that what *any* valid mission statement should do is summarize what an education is meant to help the learner achieve over the long haul, in and beyond school. It should summarize the worthy student accomplishments we are *dedicated* to causing over time outside our individual classrooms above all else. A mission is a *commitment* to a few priority results, from which some concrete pedagogical implications logically follow.

We put the matter in terms of long-term commitment for a very practical reason. The problem with all conventional schools, we think, whether public or private (or whether we consider primary, secondary, or higher education), is that when we look closely at what students actually spend their time doing in school, we see that there is rarely a long-term, consistent commitment to *any* long-term intellectual result beyond a particular class and lesson. When we say schooling should have purpose, we mean simply this: no matter what the content or activity, the relationship between it and a long-term, worthy learning goal should be logical, built into curriculum and assessment, and transparent to students, teachers, and community.

A Focus on Understanding, Transfer, and Habits of Mind

In *Understanding by Design* (Wiggins & McTighe, 2005), we proposed that understanding can be thought of in two basic ways that shape our conception of the mission of schooling. We understand when we (1) learn to use powerful ideas to make schoolwork connected and meaningful and (2) are able to transfer our learning thoughtfully and effectively to novel situations and problems.

Accordingly, we contend that schools exist to develop and deepen students' understanding of important ideas and processes in the disciplines, equipping them to transfer their learning in meaningful and effective ways, and cultivating lifelong habits of mind. To accomplish this mission, curricula, courses, units, and lessons must be built backward from the meanings and the transfer that we seek. Failure to do so will ensure that the broader mission is lost.

The point of learning anything is to make it our own, to have it culminate in some new power and perspective. Teachers have always held this commonsense view: if we really "get it," we can make all sorts of meaningful connections—to other learning in school and to our own lives—and we can apply our learning. When we "understand" a subject, we possess more than a technical grab bag of official knowledge and skill, in other words. We have become capable of "disciplined" thought and action, in varied situations; we can make meaning of events and facts that strike others as unconnected or uninteresting; we can tap and wisely adapt all our prior learning to a quirky challenge at hand (think of the expert diplomat, jazz musician, orthopedist, or practitioner of karate). In short, understanding is never a passive possession of information or mere automaticity of skill, but the capacity to act wisely, decisively, and effectively. All learning must be designed, therefore, to develop our judgment and ability to act wisely in context.

A focus on understanding is, in fact, the only way to honor the diverse dispositional goals we summarized earlier. The point of school is not merely the attainment of technical expertise. School is in business to promote certain worthy habits, attitudes, and conduct that stand beyond subjects: critical thinking, civic responsibility, and lifelong learning, among others. Without stretching the meaning of the word *understand* too far, we think it helpful to note that one cannot truly understand without those habits of mind (see Costa & Kallick, 2000; Perkins, 1992). In fact, the very habits of mind we seek are best honored and developed when the curriculum and assessments make them the requisites for academic success *and* the desired effect of academic accomplishment. An education geared solely for knowledge acquisition bypasses the key habits of mind by making them unnecessary for short-term success.

In sum, we can best safeguard the long-term educational goals that perpetually fall through the cracks of "coverage" by ensuring that key lessons and assessments *demand* the habits of mind, character traits, and intellectual abilities we find in mission and program goal statements. Only an education framed to make content serve as a *means* to meaning making and transfer ability can yield the habits and attitudes that school is in business to accomplish.

What Would an Understanding-Focused Education Look Like?

Consider the difference between a typical unit of study and an understanding-focused curricular approach when applied to the same targeted content. Our examples address a common topic in secondary mathematics, "measures of central tendency"—mean, median, and mode. Notice how the second version focuses on meaning making, transfer, and worthwhile habits of mind—without sacrificing content.

Here is a familiar treatment of the topic from a major textbook (Burton et al., 1998):

1. The text defines the terms *mean, median,* and *mode,* with examples for each term. "When you want to summarize a set of data as one value, you can use one of the three measures of central tendency" (p. 248).
2. An example of the same data set is graphed and considered in light of each type of measure discussed.
3. The text provides independent practice via 15 problems (for example, completing a table in which all three measures are calculated for a data set).
4. The text poses three so-called problem-solving applications; for example, "Eight joggers ran the following number of miles: 8, 5, 6, 4, 8, 8, 7, and 10. Determine the mean, median, and mode of the miles jogged" (pp. 247–249).

The text presents the content as a discrete skill, taught and tested with no apparently larger purpose. The only hint that measures of central tendency have potentially interesting and important uses appears in one sidebar, called "Business Link":

> Television advertisers often use the median income of an audience as the basis for deciding what products to advertise during a particular show. Why would

> knowing the median income of the audience be better than knowing the mean income of the same group? (p. 248)

The authors also comment:

> Because of the two high scores of 30 [outliers compared with the rest of the data], the mean is much larger than the mode or median. So the mean is not a good measure of the data. Either the median or mode represents the data better. (p. 248)

The text offers no insight about what "represents the data better" means, or how the presentation of data is *invariably* reflective of purpose and audience. In short, the "why?" and "so what?" questions are not raised or considered. The test questions provided in the book only reinforce for teacher and students alike that the de facto goal is to learn to calculate answers related to each kind of measure, in isolation. Nowhere is there an emphasis on the real-world problem of transfer of this idea: *When* should students use or not use which measure of tendency and *why*? When do people *need* this idea? How do you begin to better judge when *which* measure is or is not called for?

How might the topic be treated differently in a curriculum designed for understanding and built backward with transfer in mind? Here's an alternative approach:

1. Begin with an essential question (considered across many topics, not just measures of central tendency), such as this: *What is a "valid" and "honest" answer to situations in which fairness is at stake, and how can mathematics help us determine it?* Discuss the following questions: *What do we mean by a "fair" solution and an "unfair" solution? What are examples, and why do we call them fair or unfair?*

2. Ask students to brainstorm and research various problems and challenges related to fairness: majority versus supermajority voting; comparisons of the scoring in cross-country running (add up the place of finish of the first five runners) with the scoring in diving (calculate the mean score, but throw out the high and low scores); progressive versus regressive income tax; misleading uses of mean and median in politics; best criteria for identifying the number one college football team in the nation; and so on. In short, present real problems and questions that require learning some related math content.

3. Introduce mean, median, and mode as helpful possible tools; do some of the same textbook exercises related to them. Quiz for knowledge and skill (but make clear that this is more like a sideline drill than the game).

4. Conduct a three-part final assessment for understanding:
   - Propose and defend the "fairest possible grading system in school" based on all the work done in the unit.
   - Generalize: When is each of the three measures of central tendency *most* useful and when is each *least* helpful/most misleading?
   - Reflect: What is your answer now to the essential question framing the unit?

Do you see the contrast? In the latter case, the same content is treated very differently, *as a means* for addressing inherently problematic situations and issues that students can relate to. Moreover, the assessments signal that thoughtfully making sense of, and using, content is the purpose. The habits of mind and long-term goals discussed earlier now come into play; the student *has* to be a critical thinker and *has* to be productive. To succeed at the tasks, the student is gaining practice in lifelong learning.

Now imagine if other units consistently sent the same message, and you begin to see the vision of what a constant focus on understanding would yield, particularly if we generalize our example:

1. Begin with an essential question related to real-world issues or problems (needing consideration across many topics).
2. Ask students to brainstorm and do preliminary research related to the question or issue. Introduce the content as a potentially helpful resource for solving the problems. Lecture and drill only as needed to equip students to address the challenge.
3. Frame the unit around a culminating assessment task requiring transfer. Use quizzes only to provide supplementary evidence related to discrete knowledge and skill. Then design the lessons backward from what students will need in order to do well at the task.
4. Frame additional units around other essential questions.

What Follows for Curriculum Design and Sequencing?

To achieve a coherent and coordinated curriculum made up of such understanding-focused units, we need to reconsider the nature of subject-matter content in relation to the larger mission. Here are two mission statements that address this point. Notice how they subsume subject-area expertise under broader intellectual goals:

> Salem High School is a student-focused community challenged by a rigorous curriculum that fosters both critical and creative thinking. Provided with a personalized, safe learning environment, students will demonstrate higher-order reasoning skills, service to the school and community, and tolerance toward all

individuals. Each student will leave Salem High School with the tools necessary for a lifelong commitment to citizenship, service, and learning.

The mission of the Loomis Chaffee School is to advance the development in spirit, mind, and body of boys and girls drawn from diverse cultural and social backgrounds and to inspire in them a commitment to the best self and the common good. The goal of the school's academic program is the formation of skilled and discerning minds in preparation for higher education and lifelong learning. Through its courses and community life, Loomis Chaffee also educates its students for service in the nation and in today's global civilization. In all things, the school aims to be, as its founders intended, "a shrine from which boys and girls shall take the highest inspirations for better and grander lives."

These mission statements describe specific long-term intellectual *accomplishments* by the learners in which academic content knowledge and skills are properly seen as *enablers* rather than the ultimate goals. Students are meant to leave school as not merely learned, but inquisitive; not merely knowledgeable, but capable of using their education for good ends; not merely with technical skills, but with the appropriate habits of mind that determine whether the skill is used wisely, unwisely, or not used at all when needed. Again, content mastery is not the primary point of teaching even when the mission refers to academic goals.

What may surprise readers is that many state content standards documents make the same point, especially in their introductory statements of purpose. Here are two typical examples, one from New Jersey and one from California. The vision of the mathematics standards in the New Jersey Core Curriculum Content Standards is focused on achieving one goal:

GOAL: To enable ALL of New Jersey's children to move into the twenty-first century with the mathematical skills, understandings, and attitudes that they will need to be successful in their careers and daily lives. (Rosenstein, Caldwell, & Crown, 1996, p. 10)

As teachers use the recommendations in their teaching, it is expected that among the results will be students who are excited by and interested in their activities and students who are learning important mathematical concepts rather than simply memorizing and practicing procedures (adapted from New Jersey Mathematics Coalition, 1994).

The vision of California's history and social science curriculum says:

As educators in the field of history–social science, we want our students to perceive the complexity of social, economic, and political problems. We want them to have the ability to differentiate between what is important and what is

> unimportant. . . . We want them to respect the right of others to differ with them. We want them to take an active role as citizens and to know how to work for change in a democratic society. We want them to understand the value, the importance, and the fragility of democratic institutions. . . . We want them to develop a keen sense of ethics and citizenship. And we want them to care deeply about the quality of life in their community, their nation, and their world. (History–Social Science Curriculum Framework and Criteria Committee, 2005, p. 2)

Even the states agree: the goal of school and of standards for each academic program is not to simply "get good at school" or "know stuff" in each subject. The goal is to leave school able to improve our lives and our society, based on accomplishments that prepare us to be effective, thoughtful, and engaged adults. The standards summarize not only the short-term content-related goals, but also the indicators of long-term success of schooling—pieces of the vision.

The subjects are "disciplines," and like all disciplines—karate, yoga, chess, or mathematics—they are mastered by "doing" the subject while learning it. As the authors of the now-famous SCANS (1991) report so artfully state,

> SCANS believes that teachers and schools must begin early to help students see the relationships between what they study and its applications in real-world contexts. It is not true that everything we need to know in life we learned in kindergarten; it is true, however, that we can begin that early to learn what life requires.
>
> We believe, after examining the findings of cognitive science, that the most effective way of teaching skills is "in context." Placing learning objectives within real environments is better than insisting that students first learn in the abstract what they will then be expected to apply. SCANS suggests three principles from cognitive science to guide real contextual learning in all our schools:
>
> - Students do not need to learn basic skills before they learn problem-solving skills. The two go together. They are not sequential but mutually reinforcing.
> - Learning should be reoriented away from mere mastery of information and toward encouraging students to recognize and solve problems.
> - Real know-how foundation and competencies cannot be taught in isolation; students need practice in the application of these skills. The foundation is best learned in the context of the competencies that it supports.
>
> Reading and mathematics become less abstract and more concrete when they are embedded in one or more of the competencies; that is, when the learning is "situated" in a systems or a technological problem. When skills are taught in the context of the competencies, students will learn the skill more rapidly and will be more likely to apply it in real situations. Personal characteristics such as self-esteem and responsibility, to use another example, are best developed in teamwork efforts. Choosing between teaching the foundation and the competencies

> is false; students usually become more proficient faster if they learn both simultaneously. In sum, learning in order "to know" must never be separated from learning in order "to do." Knowledge and its uses belong together.

This approach is the norm in many learning situations: first-year law students analyze real cases, Suzuki violinists learn to perform in recitals within weeks of beginning to play, foreign language students are immersed in listening and speaking the language right away, apprentice carpenters work on real buildings from the start, and beginning skiers traverse the (gentle) slopes on short skis on their first day. We believe that only old prejudices and habits block us from seeing that the same should be true in history or biology.

So we need a new kind of planning to help us design a more purposeful and transfer-focused approach to learning "stuff" from the start. Instead of seeing education as the teaching and learning of lengthy lists of knowledge and skills that are *somehow* meant to *eventually* be meaningful and useful, an education devoted to understanding helps learners see from the beginning why the content matters (that is, what vital tasks and questions it helps them address), what use it can be put to, and how to transfer their learning immediately. This approach parallels what athletic and artistic coaches (and good reading teachers) refer to as a "whole-part-whole" approach: we consider the larger performance challenge (such as the "game" and its demands), identify and work on needed skills and knowledge, and put them into immediate use in a realistic context. The math example reveals two other practical aspects: the use of essential questions to help "uncover" important content ideas, and a focus on learning to equip learners for important performances.

More specifically, because mission statements and academic standards typically highlight transfer goals, we need to ensure that local planning, instruction, and assessment are built backward from transfer tasks in each subject and that most assessments are not merely tests of recall and "plug-in." Such "doing" of the subject involves "testing" the student's ability to apply prior learning to a new challenge or an unfamiliar problem. As Gardner (1999) puts it,

> An individual understands a concept, skill, theory, or domain of knowledge to the extent that he or she can apply it appropriately in a new situation. . . . This formulation entails an acid test for understanding: posing to students a topic or theme or demonstration that they have never before encountered, and determining what sense they can make of those phenomena. (p. 119)

In other words, transfer requires that students learn quickly and often how to integrate their knowledge and skill, along with various mature habits of mind, to successfully perform in situations "that they have never before encountered." Schooling must be designed backward from such transfer in the same way that athletic and medical training are—*from the start and throughout* teaching and learning.

Again, common sense. We nod in agreement with what Madeline Hunter (1971) said more than 30 years ago: "Transfer is accurate generalization of learning to new situations and is sought as the end product of all formal instruction and schooling" (p. 2). Even E. D. Hirsch (Hirsch, Kett, & Trefil, 1988), the generator of the lists for cultural literacy, reminds us that the *point* of cultural literacy is transfer: "In modern life we need general knowledge that enables us to deal with new ideas, events, and challenges" (p. 11).

Needed: Perspective on Content

The preceding analysis reminds us that an educational purpose cannot derive solely from content knowledge objectives. Making "content" the focus of all teaching, learning, and assessing gets the matter backward. Decisions about what to teach and how it should be learned and assessed derive from long-term learning goals related to mission. Content and pedagogy are *means to ends*. Coherent and effective schooling requires that all educational decisions be considered from a vantage point *outside* of the content. Only then do we have a way to make decisions about what to keep and what to cut, how learning should be structured and how not.

This is an old idea. Indeed, it was Ralph Tyler's (1950) key point 60 years ago, but it has been routinely overlooked or ignored in educational reforms:

> The purpose of a statement of objectives is to indicate *the kinds of changes in the student to be brought about* so that the instructional activities can be planned and developed in a way likely to attain these objectives; that is, to bring about these changes in the student. Hence, it is clear that a statement of objectives in terms of content headings . . . is not a satisfactory basis for guiding the further development of the curriculum. (pp. 45–46) (emphasis added)

The point is to change the mind and conduct of learners, not to make them merely knowledgeable. As Tyler notes, this view of a statement of objectives, cast as it is in terms of changes of behavior, means that organizing and justifying a curriculum by content headings makes no logical sense. No wonder, then, that if a textbook becomes the de facto curriculum and coverage is the de facto goal, there is no way to relate content learning to long-term educational goals—there cannot even be palpable priorities. In the absence of clear performance goals related to a few key accomplishments sought, we have no way to stand *outside* the textbook to determine what we should emphasize and what we should skip to cause certain kinds of valid and worthy performances. Nor is there any basis on which to critique overly didactic and isolated teaching.

So the well-known "Tyler rationale" should be seen as a procedure for not just developing but also constantly critiquing a school to ensure its purpose is honored.

Here we provide the elements of the Tyler (1950) approach, with each step rephrased in brackets to relate to the arguments in our book:

> Four fundamental questions must be answered in developing any curriculum and plan of instruction. These are:
>
> 1. What educational purposes should the school seek to attain? [What is the school's mission?]
>
> 2. What educational experiences can be provided that are likely to attain these purposes? [What kind of learning is most likely to lead to achievement of the mission?]
>
> 3. How can these educational experiences be effectively organized? [What should the curriculum and assessment system be to make schooling maximally effective and efficient at achieving the mission?]
>
> 4. How can we determine whether these purposes are being attained? [By what process should we get feedback and adjust the system to make achievement of the mission most likely?] (p. 1)

Why Mission Matters

What, then, could be more logical? Establish and commit to a worthy educational goal—understanding reflected in genuine accomplishments and habits of mind—then design structures, policies, and practices to bring about that understanding.

However, as readers well know, schools have rarely been designed and run to achieve long-term results related to student understanding and dispositions for lifelong learning. Step back from routine and look carefully. Conventional schooling is fixated on coverage of discrete content; teachers work in isolation from other teachers; teachers work with textbooks relating only to their particular content, not the institution's goals; no mechanism exists to ensure that assessments and grades reflect coherent practice related to mission. In short, we see a hodgepodge of well-intended yet isolated content and activities—not purposeful schooling. From the learner's perspective over 12 years, school has no mission, regardless of what appears on wall plaques and Web sites.

That schools lack a self-conscious mission and a serious commitment to it is clear enough from answers to simple questions about purpose asked of learners and teachers. Few members of a school community have a good answer to the time-honored question about longer-term goals of short-term lessons: why are we studying this?

To check out our assertion, we encourage readers to ask learners in the midst of solo or group work the following four simple questions to better see for themselves that the problem is as fundamental as we describe it:

- What are we doing right now?
- Why are we doing it?

• How does it relate to what we have been doing in the last few days and weeks?

• What does doing it help us do in terms of our long-term goals and priorities for your learning?

It is rare for a student, at any level of learning, to provide satisfactory answers to these questions. Indeed, if all that students ever do in school is march on a long journey through content to no known destination, what could they possibly answer? The absence of good answers indicates at the very least that the learner is aware of no clear priority outcomes and long-term goals.

We also encourage teachers to write out *their* answers to these same questions for every unit they teach, in light of yearlong goals, and then compare their answers with those of their colleagues who teach the same subjects or grades. We predict that this exercise will illustrate how rarely we think about how our teaching connects with others' teaching to contribute to the overall mission.

Speaking on an institutional level, we can look at the current use of time to see the de facto learning priorities in a school. Ask yourself these questions—or better yet, do a formal time-use study that asks these questions:

• What are the actual priorities of school, as reflected by which goals and actions get the most time in (and out of) class?

• Is the minute-by-minute use of our time in school consistent with the mission or a focus on in-depth understanding? Or do teachers spend a good deal of time "teaching" with no goal beyond "learn what I am teaching"?

Then, once again, ask the vision question:

• What use of time in class and out of class would we see if the mission were being honored day in and day out? How would class time be used if transfer of learning and key habits of mind were the focus?

Even worse than the absence of clear priority outcomes and long-term goals is the fact that many teachers seem to believe that larger purpose is irrelevant to their jobs. How else should we understand the familiar phrase "I have to cover the content"? To a large extent, the entire body of work we, the authors, have produced over the years under the heading of *Understanding by Design,* and now in *Schooling by Design,* is an attempt to show why this all-too-common statement reflects a lack of commitment to a greater educational purpose and is thus a profound mistake (no matter how often said and believed).

Toward Clarifying and Honoring Mission

Making matters far worse is that we tend to confuse our noble intentions with our actual practices and results (what Argyris [1993] calls the inevitable gap between espoused theory and theory-in-action). So reform is far more difficult than we might imagine when exploring the straightforward logic of backward design. It obligates us to learn to see that our blind spots, unconscious bad habits, and resistance to exploring the potential disconnect between our words and deeds impede necessary changes. We must dedicate ourselves to rooting them out.

Schooling by design moves forward with constant if/then questioning: *if* this is our mission, *then* what would it look like in practice? What would day-to-day teaching and learning look like *if* we were to truly honor the goals of transfer, responsible citizenship, or lifelong learning? What content would we teach? And *how* would that content be taught and assessed *if* these goals (or goals like them) were the goals to which we were all committed?

Thus, the logic of this questioning is in part a demand for a more clear and robust "vision." A vision is what we would see *if* our goals were achieved. A vision in this sense is an essential component in turning an inherently abstract mission statement into concrete policy and practice. In other words, a vision is not a hopelessly idealistic dream of a world that will never be, but a picture of the world we seek to build—the equivalent of an architect's blueprint or an athlete's mental image of the upcoming performance. The graphic from the State College Area School District in Pennsylvania (Figure 1.1) makes this clearer.

We can see the potential usefulness of such envisioning if we try it with the mission statements presented earlier: How would language arts have to be *taught and assessed* to make students more passionate and confident as readers? What would assessment in social studies need to be to determine whether our students are critical or uncritical students of history? What would we see in classrooms and on assessments if we were successful in making math students more productive in using their math as citizens and lifelong learners? In general, we would expect to see constant instruction in and assessment of students' ability to go *beyond* the content and learn, without constant prodding or prompting. As part of the curriculum, we would expect learners to apply their learning *now,* in school, to be productive so as to thoughtfully contribute and gain vital practice in solving *present-day* school and social problems. Therefore, case-based/problem-based curriculum would be the norm, not the exception—as we find in medicine, law, and engineering. We say this not to be politically correct; we say this because such instruction is logically implied in the elements of the mission statements.

Figure 1.1

Characteristics of a State College Area High School Graduate

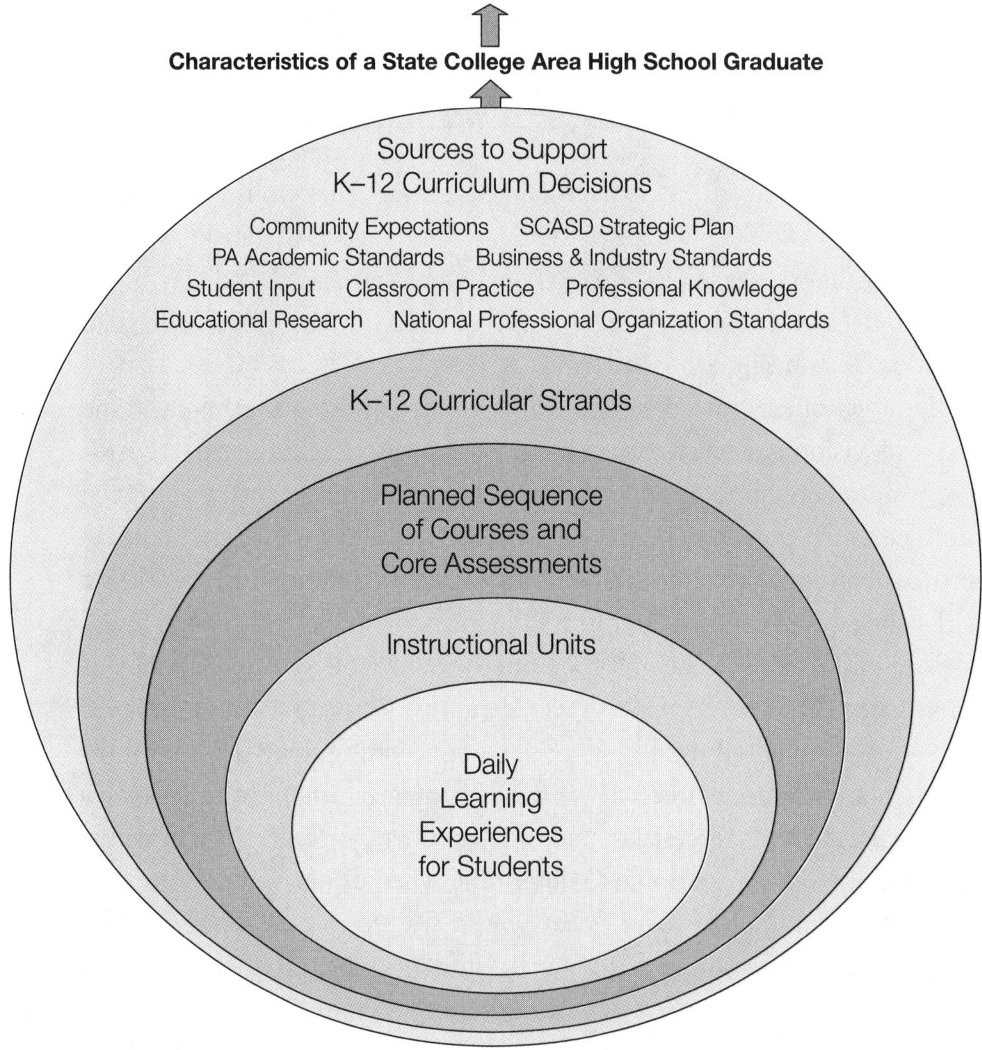

Characteristics of a State College Area High School Graduate

- A responsible and involved citizen
- A clear and effective communicator
- A competent problem solver who thinks critically and creatively
- A productive individual who works independently and collaboratively
- One who demonstrates respect for self and others in an increasingly diverse society
- A user of evolving technologies
- A knowledgeable practitioner of wellness behaviors
- An informed consumer and effective manager of personal and family resources
- A responsible steward of the environment
- A participant in the arts

Source: Adapted from concept by Pamela L. Francis; used by permission of SCASD K–12 Curriculum Council.

With answers to questions about "What would we see if . . . ?" we would next ask the key empirical questions: What is the current reality? How passionate and productive are our students now? How focused on critical thinking is our curriculum now? How successful are we in producing lifelong learners in our subjects? Finally, we would address the inevitable gaps that arise from comparing vision with reality: What can we do to improve our curriculum, instruction, and assessment to improve results against mission?

Again, logical. Set a goal, get feedback about where we stand and how we might improve, then take action to close the gap. This flow is the engine of all change, in any sphere; this is how the desire to change becomes intrinsic instead of extrinsic. The book elaborates on this process in later chapters.

Toward Institutional Purpose

Without a *commitment* to mission, we don't really have a school; we just have a home for freelance tutors of subjects. Without a shared commitment to a clear and worthy mission framed as desired accomplishments, we lack not only a common target but also a set of criteria for (1) evaluating how schoolwide learning should *best* occur, given our goals; (2) prioritizing content, instead of just indiscriminately marching through it; and (3) judging which of our practices as (isolated!) teachers and teams are most and least effective, and what must be changed in order to honor mission.

How is it possible for an entire school community to be active and engaged in hard work, in good faith, but without a clear purpose (as we claim)? No one has written more clearly on the general subject of purpose and purposeful behavior than Stephen Covey. In his well-known book *The Seven Habits of Highly Effective People*, Covey (1989) succinctly describes the result of purpose or its absence as the difference between being merely busy versus being effective:

> It's incredibly easy to get caught up in the activity trap, in the busy-ness of life. . . . It is possible to be busy, very busy, without being effective. . . . How different our lives are when we really know what is deeply important to us, and, keeping that picture in mind, we manage ourselves each day to be and to do what really matters most. If the ladder is not leaning against the right wall, every step we take just gets us to the wrong place faster. We may be busy, we may be very *efficient*, but we will also be truly *effective* only when we begin with the end in mind. (p. 98)

To "begin with the end in mind" is what we call "backward design." Let's take a simple driving example: wanting to arrive at a faraway destination by car. To make our trip effective, we have to plan the route "backward" from the destination (as opposed to starting out with only a list of sites and no sense of where we will end up and how). We can then say how far we have left to travel (as opposed to merely saying how far we have gone from home), and we have a clear sense of what it means to be off course. Without clarity about the destination—the intended *effect* (from which the word *effective* is derived)—we can't really plan for or accomplish a result "by design." All we can do is trust that the journey will be pleasant, wherever we end up. The old adage is apt: if you don't know where you are going, any road will get you there.

So any voyage can be "efficient" if it is running smoothly, with little time wasted. But it only makes sense to talk of being "effective" in reference to a sought-after destination. Many schools may well be efficient, smooth-running, and lovely places in which to work. Yet none of that has to do with effectiveness—honoring the school's purpose, its mission. We have observed that the typical teacher or principal functions more like an earnest tour guide who *hopes* that long-term goals will be met as a result of a well-paced journey through the content. By contrast, architects, moviemakers, cooks, lawyers, doctors, and software coders are *totally* focused on achieving very specific effects, and they keep adjusting their plans and actions to ensure the product, performance, or result sought.

The difficulty in thinking about long-term desired accomplishments is revealed by some (so-called) mission statements. As you read the following examples, consider what is lacking:

> East High School is a school where students are invited to meet the challenges of a rich and rigorous college preparatory program, where opportunities for performance, applied, and service learning are integrated into the daily structure, and where choice and variety are maintained as genuine options. Moreover, the program incorporates meaningful service learning experiences and entrepreneurial learning into its offerings at every grade level. Greater variety and rigor in the academic program, in the form of the proposed International Baccalaureate curriculum, will offer talented students the external validation and rigorous challenge they need to feed their aspirations and ensure future success.

> West Middle School will form a partnership with home and community to facilitate a positive and safe learning environment based on mutual trust, respect, and understanding. Each student will be provided educational opportunities that develop intellectual, social, emotional, and physical potential.

Neither statement describes a definitive learning result or desired effect. Each mostly states what schools and staff will provide, not what the school is in business to accomplish. This is the equivalent of coverage in teaching: too much emphasis on the inputs, but no clear destination and commitment to desired outcomes; no clear sense of what the inputs should specifically make happen in learners.

Thus, the hard work of schooling by design involves thinking through mission and what mission implies, with staff committed to identifying and closing the (never-ending) gap between vision and reality, to restructuring the educational structures to better achieve it.

Toward a Collective Commitment to Mission and True Professionalism

One implication of mission-driven schooling reflects backward design; that is, our desired results determine the content emphasis and the assessments and instructional approaches we use.

The challenge is not merely to analytically derive which *content* is appropriate or inappropriate, but also which *pedagogies* and *assessments* are appropriate or inappropriate, given the priority accomplishments sought. Instruction—process and content—flows from the goal. Our individual habits, comfort level, and personal beliefs about teaching and learning cannot be the primary source of, or criteria for, choosing our methods. The same is true for curriculum and assessment: without course designs and assessments that follow logically from our long-term learning goals, we remain trapped in the habit of framing curriculum around content instead of mission—and assessment follows accordingly.

At present, few schools operate in a coordinated fashion in pursuit of a common mission. Indeed, the culture and operation of many schools are reflected in a comment by a veteran high school principal. We were discussing with him the need for consensus around agreed-upon school and departmental goals, and he said that was impossible. When we said, "Well, you're the principal; you can use staff meetings to do something about it," he sarcastically replied, "Principal? No, I am not the principal. I rent space in an educational mall to self-employed entrepreneurs."

The idea of a school has no meaning if each teacher, even a hardworking and highly qualified one, is free to teach and assess as he wishes. The whole point of an institution with a mission is that, regardless of our differences, we are all obligated to work to cause some agreed-upon effects, in a coherent and coordinated manner. By being a teacher in a school or a college, we agree to agree about some fundamental ends and means. And working collaboratively (and selflessly) to achieve those common goals characterizes true professionalism.

Our own view is that educators are well intentioned but sometimes naive. We tend to think that we are doing the best anyone can possibly do with the kids we have in the school where we work (although we have never tested that assumption). By contrast, no athletic coaches or band leaders think that way; they are constantly making changes in light of feedback against goals and models that are public and widely held.

But how could it be otherwise for teachers, stuck as we are in isolated rooms, drawing upon only our habits and beliefs, divorced from the long-term effects of our teaching and a dispassionate analysis of results? We can simply teach our subject or use our favorite fun activities without worrying too much about lofty goals that seem beyond our abilities to achieve or irrelevant to our content. Worse, some teachers—especially at the secondary and collegiate levels—believe that academic freedom grants them complete autonomy to decide what to teach, how to teach, and what evidence to collect.

But even if we are effective in achieving our own personal objectives, that achievement is a far cry from honoring and meeting institutional goals. A key reason why so many schools and colleges are unwittingly less effective than they might be is that day-to-day teacher planning and instruction are rarely scrutinized against long-term organizational aims. In almost all schools, no effective feedback mechanism or validation process is available for comparing individual short-term actions with long-term institutional goals. In fact, many educators like it that way: we rarely have to justify what we teach, how we teach, or what we assess in the absence of an external set of objective criteria. An obligation to a mission and long-term goals requires something that most schools and colleges do not presently have to counteract this dysfunctional attitude: a governance system and set of criteria for determining what the mission-related accomplishments demand of us.

As we shall argue later, however, this view is not at odds with the belief that teachers deserve the freedom to innovate. In fact, we maintain that effective innovation is possible *only* when there are clear goals and results against which to judge practice, whether conventional or innovative. Essential questions in schooling by design, in fact, are these: Where *must* we agree to agree? And where can we happily agree to disagree? Given our shared obligations, how should we explore innovations to spur better performance? Given our areas of freedom, what innovations should we try out and share in the name of mission? Few staffs have ever considered these questions in depth (or been asked to by administrators), yet answers to the questions are key to making a school's purpose vital and the job description of teachers clear. (We take up the issue of job descriptions for teachers and leaders in later chapters.)

Missions and State Standards

"But aren't the state standards our mission?" Not exactly. Yes, they represent specific obligations, reflecting *some* of our goals. But standards in specific content areas rarely address the long-term purposes of schooling explicitly, nor do they pretend to cover every important educational aim. Beyond their often lofty introductory statements, many state standards take the form of long lists containing a typically unhelpful mixture of content, process, and performance indicators. The standards, for good or for ill, were deliberately built as analytic compilations of each separate subject's core content, not as images of how those lists might be formulated into a coherent goal-focused curriculum or how they should best be taught.

Indeed, many state standards documents offer explicit caveats about overreliance on the standards in their familiar list form. For example, here are warnings found in New Jersey's document (New Jersey Department of Education, 2004a):

> While New Jersey's Core Curriculum Content Standards and cumulative progress indicators have been developed in terms of separate academic disciplines, this familiar approach was chosen primarily for the sake of organizational convenience and simplicity of communication. The results expected of New Jersey's students *could have been described in more integrative terms which would have reflected more accurately how students would someday apply what they have learned in school*. Because students obtain knowledge and skills in a multiplicity of ways, it is most productive to concentrate on how we can best use resources to achieve higher order results across an array of content areas. . . . Although the *standards have been organized into separate academic disciplines, this is not meant to imply that each standard can only be met through content-specific courses*. The very nature of learning lends itself to an integrated approach with reinforcement through experiences beyond the school's walls, such as community service, mentorships, and structured learning experiences. (Introduction) (emphases added)

As we've said before, standards should be thought of as the building codes that new constructions must meet. They do not represent the blueprint or model of the desired result. Standards, in building or in education, are rules to be met, not the vision of success. Meeting standards is necessary but not sufficient: they must be met "by design," but they are not the purpose of the design. The architect and the contractor do not focus all their work on honoring building codes, and neither should educators. The key is to honor the code while constantly aiming to honor the vision of an excellent education.

We think that there is a need to do a better job of helping teachers and administrators understand the standards (and their inherent limits) and how to turn them into curriculum and—especially—high-quality local assessments. That is precisely what a new mission-focused curriculum framework at the local level must do, a point that we address in the following two chapters.

Many teachers erroneously believe that we face a dilemma: teaching to the standards *or* pursuing worthy long-term intellectual goals. This is a false choice, caused by our failure to write curricula that reflect our mission as well as subject matter. To see how this is so, let's return to one of our earlier sample mission statements, the one on social studies from California (History–Social Science Curriculum Framework and Criteria Committee, 2005) to see how we might work with standards while honoring mission statements:

> As educators in the field of history–social science, we want our students to perceive the complexity of social, economic, and political problems. We want them to have the ability to differentiate between what is important and what is unimportant. (p. 2)

What would we see *if* this mission were realized? What might we imagine students doing that would reflect this accomplishment? Here are a few examples. We would see local assessments in U.S. and world history requiring students, on their own, with minimal cues and hints, to do well on tasks such as these:

- Justify a rank ordering of the relative importance of events in a historical period.
- Provide an explanation of the complex causes of key events, without fixating on a single reason or the most blatant cause.
- Explain why certain historical interpretations are too simplistic.
- Create a graphic organizer showing social, economic, and political connections for a historical event or time period, and provide an oral explanation for the connections depicted.

We would see instruction that provides students with plenty of guided and unguided opportunities to identify, on their own, the important conclusions, arguments, and causes and effects for any historical account. Teaching would use resources beyond the textbook, because the text typically tells students what is important rather than helping them see the complexities and connections.

Recognizing the aforementioned weaknesses, a growing number of states have attached "mini" vision statements (typically called "performance indicators" or "indicators of success") to their standards, to help teachers fixate less on the content and its coverage and focus more on the desired accomplishment in the use of content (see, for example, New York and Georgia). Here is an example from Georgia's Language Arts Standards (Georgia Department of Education, 2007b) in which we learn what we would see *if* the 8th grade student has met the standard:

> The student demonstrates comprehension and shows evidence of a warranted and responsible explanation of a variety of literary and informational texts.
>
> For literary texts, the student identifies the characteristics of various genres and produces evidence of reading that:

> a. Identifies the difference between the concepts of theme in a literary work and author's purpose in an expository text.
>
> b. Compares and contrasts genre characteristics from two or more selections of literature.
>
> c. Analyzes a character's traits, emotions, or motivations and gives supporting evidence from the text(s).
>
> d. Compares and contrasts motivations and reactions of literary characters from different historical eras confronting similar situations or conflicts.
>
> e. Evaluates recurring or similar themes across a variety of selections, distinguishing theme from topic.
>
> f. Evaluates the structural elements of the plot (e.g., subplots, climax), the plot's development, and the way in which conflicts are (or are not) addressed and resolved.
>
> g. Analyzes and evaluates the effects of sound, form, figurative language, and graphics in order to uncover meaning in literature:
>
> i. Sound (e.g., alliteration, onomatopoeia, internal rhyme, rhyme scheme, meter)
>
> ii. Figurative language (e.g., simile, metaphor, personification, hyperbole, symbolism, imagery)
>
> h. Analyzes and evaluates how an author's use of words creates tone and mood and provides supporting details from text. (Grade 8 ELA Standards)

The addition of these indicators is designed to help teachers realize that the content standard is not and never was the point. In a document titled "Curriculum Frequently Asked Questions", the Georgia Department of Education (2007a) makes clear that the aim is to clarify the desired performance:

> 4. What IS a performance standard, and why does it represent an improvement upon the old content standards used in the previous curriculum?
>
> Performance standards go into much greater depth than the content standards used in the previous curriculum. The *performance standard* incorporates the *content standard,* which simply [told] the teacher what a student [was] expected to know (i.e., what concepts he or she is expected to master), [but] expands upon it by providing three additional items: *suggested tasks, sample student work,* and *teacher commentary on that work*.
>
> Performance standards provide clear expectations for assessment, instruction, and student work. They define the level of work that demonstrates achievement of the standards, enabling a teacher to know "how good is good enough." (emphasis added)

Departmental and Grade-Level Team Goals

The logic of backward design and the emphasis on a vision to make general goals more concrete and obligatory suggest that there should also be clear long-term goals and indicators for all program areas in school. Formulating statements of purpose and identifying evidence of goal-related accomplishments are especially critical at the departmental and team levels, because realistically this is where "the rubber meets the road." The mission is either honored or overlooked during day-to-day planning, teaching, and assessing within our subject-area slots.

Alverno College in Milwaukee is probably one of the best-known examples of an entire college focused on developing long-term achievements that incorporate and transcend subject-area knowledge objectives. For the past 30 years, Alverno staff members have worked within an "ability-based undergraduate education" framework in which each academic program identifies its priority goals within the larger context of eight institutional learning goals: (1) communication, (2) analysis, (3) problem solving, (4) valuing in decision making, (5) social interactions, (6) developing a global perspective, (7) effective citizenship, and (8) aesthetic engagement. Departmental faculty work on developing programs and assessments to achieve results related to each of those goals with each faculty member serving in two distinct roles: as a member of each academic department and as a member of one of the eight ability committees whose charge it is to develop the assessments and research related to their ability. This structure ensures that the overarching abilities are always kept in view and that departmental goals are always connected to the larger mission.

Now consider the mission of various departments at Alverno College. Here are two examples, in history and biology:

> History Department—We sit down as a department and try to determine what a graduate should be *able to do with what she knows about history*. In order to do that, we ask ourselves: what does it mean for us to think and act in a historically-minded way? . . . Departmental discussions such as these led to the articulation of the following advanced-level outcomes:
>
> The student—
>
> • Identifies culturally grounded assumptions that have influenced the perception and behavior of people in the past and identifies those that influence her own perception and behavior.
>
> • Identifies and critiques the theories, concepts, and assumptions that historians have used to create coherent interpretations in the past. . . .
>
> • Takes responsibility for her own interpretations of the past by explaining and defending them publicly in a variety of personal and professional contexts. (2001b, p. 2)

> Biology Team (Science Department)—We believe that a graduate of our program should demonstrate the following outcomes in biology, regardless of her specific professional goals. The student—
>
> • Accurately interprets biological information and demonstrates understanding of the limitations of scientific analysis.
>
> • Demonstrates proficient library, mathematical, and computer skills in biological data gathering and analysis.
>
> • Designs, conducts, and effectively communicates biological experiments.
>
> • Applies concepts of biology ethically to environmental and societal issues. (2001a, p. 3)

These examples show us how we might bridge content-related objectives with longer-term goals having to do with enduring intellectual accomplishments. Rather than merely stating the content to be learned, we must state what constitutes successful long-term use of and thought about content. In other words, we must frame goals in terms of learner habits of mind and performance in using content. Teachers and students must see content learning as the means of achieving broader goals, not the end in itself.

Here is an example of a departmental philosophy and goal statement from Scarsdale High School in New York that makes this point overtly:

> The primary objective of the social studies program is to prepare students to become thoughtful individuals whose academic background and skills will enable them to function successfully in an increasingly complex, multi-cultural, and changing world. The social studies program must provide students with an intellectual framework of knowledge, the skills necessary to process information, and the capacity to understand and appreciate people from backgrounds and cultures different from their own. . . .
>
> It is further understood that students can only learn history by "doing" history, that is to say, students must be active participants in the educational process, examining primary and secondary data, debating, role-playing, identifying and considering critical questions, and drawing their own conclusions through a process of critical thought. The desired end: to draw our students out into the world community, providing them with the capacity to live effective personal and public lives. (Scarsdale High School, n.d.)

Following this statement is a list of specific common objectives for knowledge, skills, and values.

A purposeful institution is one that transforms hundreds of seemingly discrete tasks, activities, and objectives into a few mission-critical goals and accomplishments. An effective school focuses on those goals to develop the methods and paths most likely to enable achieving them. In other words, to have a mission and to honor it means that we *never* lose sight of our priorities—as teachers or learners. We don't confuse the urgent with the important (in Covey's helpful phrase).

So in any effective educational institution, certain critical components guide actions and structures:

- Long-term goals for learner accomplishments (the mission).
- Specific performances and indicators of the varied ways in which those accomplishments can be embodied within and across content areas (the vision), and the assessment evidence by which we will gauge progress toward the vision.
- Guidelines for how to craft activity, using the means (that is, content, methods, and resources) to achieve the desired results.

Readers familiar with our book *Understanding by Design* (Wiggins & McTighe, 2005) will recognize that these three elements reflect the key stages of backward curriculum design: *identify the desired results; specify the evidence needed,* given those results; and *identify the requisite learning and teaching* for generating the evidence of achieving the results.

How is mission put into operation through curriculum writing so that it doesn't amount to a mere platitude? What must local assessment be to ensure that the key habits of mind are required for performance success? How do we make long-term intellectual goals more real, obligatory, and linked to content standards—without inducing or seeming to recommend coverage? We address that challenge in Chapter 2.

Ideas for Action

- Locate the current mission statement for your school or district. Distribute the statement at a faculty meeting or during a professional development day and discuss with staff. Questions such as the following may be used:
    - To what extent do we agree with this mission statement?
    - Do students and parents know that this is the mission? Do they understand and agree with it?
    - Are important educational goals missing? What should be added or changed?
    - To what extent does this mission influence our day-to-day work?
    - How are we doing in terms of achieving the mission? What evidence is needed to answer this question?
    - What could we do differently to make it more likely that the mission is achieved?

• Have *every* staff member agree to ask learners in the midst of solo or group work the following questions: Why are we studying this? What are we doing right now? Why are we doing it? How does it relate to what we have been doing in the last few days and weeks? What does doing it help us do in terms of our long-term goals and priorities for your learning? Ask staff to compile the student responses to share and discuss at a future staff meeting. What do the responses suggest?

• Lead staff through an exercise called "Picture the Graduate." Here's how it works. Individually, ask people to think about their vision of the ideal graduate after X years of schooling in their institution (for example, a K–12 school system, a university), and record their views in writing and symbolically. In other words, what would we like to see in our graduates in terms of knowledge, skills, and dispositions? What should they be like? How should they act and live? Then, form groups of four or five staff members and have them share and discuss their individual visions and compile (as much as possible) a consensus picture. Record these on chart paper and then share via a "gallery walk" so that the entire group can see all of the ideas. A synthesis from the larger group provides the beginnings of a collective vision.

• Analyze state/provincial/national standards (including their introductory statements) to identify the long-term goals and habits of mind.

2

What Should Curriculum Accomplish?

> Form follows function—that has been misunderstood. Form and function should be one, joined in a spiritual union.
>
> —Frank Lloyd Wright

In Chapter 1 we noted that curriculum is properly derived from mission. A curriculum is literally "the course to be run" for best reaching a desired result. In other words, any curriculum is implied by and derived from a prior decision about the destination. When we are clear on what should result, we design the best "course" for getting there. The curriculum is a means for achieving our goals and is therefore derived backward from what the goals imply. The NEASC Accreditation Standards highlight this very point in Standard 2:

> The curriculum, which includes coursework, co-curricular activities, and other school-approved educational experiences, is the school's formal plan to fulfill its mission statement and expectations for student learning. The curriculum links the school's beliefs, its expectations for student learning, and its instructional practices. The strength of that link is dependent upon the professional staff's commitment to and involvement in a comprehensive, ongoing review of the curriculum. (Commission on Public Secondary Schools, 2005, p. 4)

It sounds straightforward: derive the curriculum content and its requisite teaching—the "inputs"—from the performance goals—the "outputs." Logically, the curriculum emerges as a result of asking, "If that is what learners are supposed to accomplish in school and be prepared to accomplish in the future, what should the learning plan look like, and what methods of learning and instruction are most likely to help us achieve our goals?" We have also said that a primary aim of schooling is to develop student understanding—the ability to make meaning of and transfer the learning—and the related habits of mind that both permit and flow from such understanding. So it makes sense that curriculum framing must highlight the understanding and habits of mind at the heart of the purpose of schooling.

But typical college and K–12 school and district curricula are not developed that way, as readers are well aware. For many years now, curricula have been constructed around bulleted and hierarchical lists of the major topics of each subject area, such as the Civil War, the parts of a cell, long division, and the elements of fiction. We then put some verbs in front of such "content" and call it a curriculum: "Know the causes and effects of the Civil War," "Identify the parts of a cell," "Calculate using division," and "Describe and apply the elements of fiction." A list of content, even if preceded by verbs, is not a curriculum but an inventory of stuff.

Our claim in this and the next chapter is that this all-too-familiar way of conceiving and writing curriculum is fundamentally flawed. And this typical approach to writing curriculum is a major reason why coverage predominates, why habits of mind get ignored, and why understanding-focused goals fall through the cracks of schooling. Instead of writing curriculum backward from performance goals related to understanding, we typically derive lessons from discrete content (or favorite activities, textbooks, and other available resources). Content mastery, instead of being shaped into tools and processes for meeting worthy challenges related to mission, becomes an end in itself. By writing curriculum around content instead of desired performances requiring understanding, we ensure that uncritical thinking, inert knowledge, and lack of transfer will be the rule, not the exception.

A curriculum is not a list of places to visit, but an engaging and effective itinerary. It is not a list of the "input" to be taught, but a plan for causing the student "output" that would reflect successful understanding and habits of mind. For it to be a curriculum, in sum, it would have to be a plan for achieving performance purposes, for specifying how learners are to accomplish important understanding-related tasks *with* content, not just a plan for teaching content.

In this chapter we explain in greater detail why traditional curriculum writing is a chief impediment to effective schooling and school reform, and we provide a vision of a feasible alternative: a curriculum built upon a different foundation, with different categories, derived from considering the desired output of long-term accomplishment at the heart of mission and program goals. Concisely stated, the shift we propose is this: the key to reform is to write curriculum backward from transfer goals and worthy tasks that require students to use content wisely (with that use also requiring the key habits of mind, such as critical thinking and persistence, for task accomplishment). To use a phrase often associated with the reform of learning, the curriculum must be written to help students "do the subject," not just learn its findings. We have to start doing what athletics and performing arts coaches already do: write academic curricula based on the demands of the "game," not lists of isolated drills. We have to provide to teachers what architects provide builders:

a blueprint designed to show how parts relate to a whole and how a work plan can be inferred to ensure that the building ends up the way it was envisioned.

Needed: A Blueprint for Shaping Curriculum

A complex education, like a complex building, cannot be well built without a blueprint. Any blueprint fulfills two vital functions: it permits us to envision, in greater detail than just a verbal or visual model provides, what the desired results will look like in their interconnection; and it enables us to derive from it a logical and effective work plan. Architects develop blueprints to enable the contractor and all subcontractors and workers to logically plan for and successfully accomplish the construction of the building. The goal is to ensure that all discrete work adds up to a coherent realization of the big picture.

To design and build the schooling of students is no different. Working backward from the mission, it requires the equivalent of what the architect's blueprint provides: a plan by which everyone concerned can envision the end result and can develop coherent and logical work plans derived from and in support of a common long-term goal. The typical curriculum, as we currently understand and "write" it, lacks such a blueprint. In fact, almost all curricula fail to unite all educators in a common cause derived backward from mission. As presently written, most curricula encourage and enable teachers to do the worst possible thing: go off and work entirely on their own, with little regard for the long-term overarching goals that define a school's purpose. By emphasizing each short-term content goal in isolation from the others, and by focusing on content mastery instead of connected understanding, we cannot possibly produce a coherent and lasting "building."

The problem is not the individual choices about which content and activities should be in the so-called curriculum. Those choices in isolation may well be justified by the classroom teacher. Rather, the problem is the very meaning we assign to the word *curriculum*—the categories in the document that determine what goes in it, and the "curriculum writing" that districts and schools produce in its name.

To make clearer why the typical content-based curriculum enacted in the present structure of schools is *inherently* doomed to fail, let's extend the metaphor of architecture, blueprints, and building. Consider what home construction would look like if the renovators—the contractors and workers—had at their disposal only what many teachers now have to guide their "construction" work:

- There is no blueprint, only a crude image of a design sketched on the back of a napkin and a long list of many possible building materials and work activities.
- There are dozens of subcontractors who come and go. New subs take over but feel little obligation to continue the work of the others. They speak different languages and work in isolation from one another. Each makes any number of idiosyncratic

interpretations of the sketch on the napkin, and some teams disagree with one another about what the sketch really means or the methods by which the work should be done (but there is no attempt to resolve the disagreements).

• Subcontractors and their workers develop a plan for each part of the building without working with other builders, and they construct rooms in separate locations, hoping that when they return with their piecework it will somehow fit into the whole. Sadly, some of the subs don't really care if it will fit, as long as their own piece of work is completed satisfactorily.

• Work proceeds based only on the sketch and the list of materials on the napkin. The builders seldom, if ever, pause to consider the clients who will live in the house, what the clients need, or the clients' interests. No one talks to the clients except to give them tasks to do. When someone suggests that work might proceed more effectively with a blueprint and discussion with the clients, some contractors and workers become insulted and complain that their professionalism and creativity have been dishonored.

• Instead of working in partnership with the clients, teasing out the clients' needs and interests and educating the clients as to costs and benefits, the contractors mostly act on their own professional sense of what the building should be. Some subcontractors have their own ideas about what features might be nice, and they start building them.

• Some subcontractors believe that their work is done when they have piled their tools and materials at the site and given directions to the client about what each tool and building material does.

• Workers rarely measure along the way and are often frustrated when their pieces don't fit with other pieces.

• No one is sure what the building code requires, and some veteran workers do not care. Subcontractors are unable to anticipate whether they will pass or fail the building inspection. They blame the building inspector and curse the building code if they fail the inspections.

• Some subcontractors know that the materials are not up to par but use them anyway because they are the only materials that have been bought by the district construction company and delivered to the site.

• There is a pacing guide for making sure that all materials get used according to an arbitrary calendar, irrespective of weather delays or whether the construction is advancing logically or meeting the clients' needs.

• Near the end of the project, when the clients complain that the work doesn't meet their needs and interests, the contractors counter that they did their job and anything beyond that is not their responsibility.

• There are separate architects for each level of the three-story building and they don't confer.

Alas, we believe that the metaphor accurately describes the "building" of an education in the absence of a detailed blueprint and concomitant curriculum "work plan" deliberately designed to achieve a school's mission. The teacher "subcontractors" are provided with long lists of content and sent off into different rooms to build their piece of a whole in isolation. The teacher workers in one subject rarely discuss their work with the teacher workers on other floors (grade levels) of the building, and even more rarely with teachers in other sections of the building (other subject areas). The state standards are the building code that few know really well, and the state tests represent the summative building inspections. (Of course, building inspections provide immediate results, whereas external test results arrive many weeks or months later!)

By now, the point should be clear: a thorough, expertly drawn blueprint and a results-based work plan for achieving it are essential—in education as in architecture. Vague wishes, high energy, good intentions, long lists of "materials" (that is, content and activities), and a personal repertoire of construction procedures (instructional strategies) for piecemeal actions cannot, by themselves, ever yield a successful result. There must be a detailed plan for honoring what the mission implies and answering such key goal-related questions as these: *What kind and quality of performance and products signify accomplishment of the mission? What would we need to see in classroom instruction to cause that accomplishment?* Most current approaches to writing curriculum overlook this vital analysis of what long-term goals demand. Teachers do not work from model syllabi for every course designed backward from "misson accomplished." Consequently, many teachers end up "covering" grade-level content in discrete and isolated lessons, much like homeowners involved in random do-it-yourself projects.

No wonder massive local curriculum documents often gather dust on the bookshelves of supervisors and teachers! Instead of the curriculum providing teachers with a coherent and effective plan for achieving the mission together (with guidance on how to use the textbook as a resource to do so and how to integrate discrete content into purposeful work toward a performance goal), it merely outlines or states discrete and isolated topics and activities.

Educational researcher Robert Marzano (2003) concluded from a meta-analysis of numerous studies that a "guaranteed and viable curriculum is the #1 school-level factor impacting on student achievement" (pp. 23–24). Given the inadequacies of many existing curricula, is it any wonder that school and school reforms often yield disappointing results?

Toward a Mission-Focused Curriculum Blueprint

So what would a new kind of curriculum blueprint look like? What approach to curriculum framing and writing is needed to avoid even more long lists of isolated stuff and related activities? The educational blueprint, like the architect's, would first have to be based on a vision—the drawing of the ideal and a physical model of that dream. We first need to know, in other words, what success at our goals actually looks like. That's the vision of our mission. So, referring to the example of "critical thinking" that appears in many mission statements, we must first envision it: "If students were critical thinkers in history, math, science, reading, and so on, they would be able to handle such challenges as . . . and their products and performance would show such characteristics as . . ." Whatever the answers, the curriculum would be designed to honor this vision and make the achievement of it more likely.

Beyond the architect's model is the blueprint: the incredibly rich yet compact document of interrelated drawings detailing how the infrastructure forms an integrated whole. The blueprint not only gives us various pictures, from different perspectives, of the goal; it also summarizes how the separate work—plumbing, heating, carpentry—comes together in the final result. So any design for successful schooling must start with the equivalent of architectural blueprints: curriculum documents that are designed backward from the desired results. The curriculum documents must show how the learner is expected to use content to accomplish meaningful performances and how the work of individual teachers must come together.

What this approach means in practice is that before considering content and sequence of the curriculum, we must design the *assessment* framework for critical thinking in every subject. The assessment framework must allow for transfer and meaning making, or understanding. Why start with assessment? Because we first need to know what *mission accomplished* looks like in terms of the desired output of student learning before we say how we should teach for it. The curriculum only then lays out the work plan, the best route for causing such performance. To invoke a simple athletic analogy, you can only design an appropriate training regimen for success in the decathlon in the Olympics when you are crystal clear about the events that make up the decathlon. In sum, clarity about the ultimate performances desired—the desired results of teaching for understanding—is the only way to ensure purposeful teaching as opposed to aimless and uncritical coverage of content.

Because this idea is so at odds with habits and typical thought, let's say it a few different ways:

- The goal of curriculum is not to take a tour of content but to learn to use and investigate that content, right from the start. Curriculum is thus inseparable from the design of valid, recurring performance assessment tasks.
- If autonomous transfer and meaning making is the goal, then the curriculum must be designed from the start to give students practice in autonomous transfer and meaning making, and make clear via assessments that this is the goal.
- An academic curriculum must be more like the curriculum in law, design, medicine, music, athletics, and early literacy: focused from the start on masterful performance as the goal.

Such a performance-based curriculum requires not only prior clarity about key assessments and exemplars, but also a new framework for ensuring that lessons, units, and courses focus short-term work on long-term accomplishments related to mission. We require, in short, a new template for curricular documents so that teachers begin thinking more like coaches of transfer than purveyors of content.

The ideas underlying such an accomplishment-based curriculum are certainly not new. Indeed, performance- and competency-based programs have existed for years in technical education and the arts. Albert Shanker, illustrious former president of the American Federation of Teachers, proposed 20 years ago that the Boy Scout merit badge system be the model for school reform. More recently, the SCANS report (1991) similarly recommended reforms to make the curriculum more transfer-focused, as we noted in Chapter 1. Sizer's Coalition of Essential Schools (1984, p. 222*ff.*) and Schlechty's exhortation to "work on the work" (2001, p. 107) provided the core principles for identifying worthy work. But no one has yet put forth an approach to rebuilding mainstream K–12 schooling around these ideas in a feasible and comprehensive way. That's what we lay out in the following sections.

In the rest of this chapter, we provide an outline of this new framework; in the next chapter, we describe the recommended curriculum components in greater detail, with examples. Later chapters explore the supporting role definitions and job descriptions needed to enact such a curriculum for successful student accomplishment.

Designing Curriculum Backward from Desired Performances

As stated earlier, the most basic flaw in the writing of conventional school curriculum is that it is too often divorced from the ultimate accomplishments desired. Thus, when we advise educators to design the assessment system first, we are not referring to typical tests of mere content mastery. We are speaking of worthy authentic performances that embody the mission and program goals. Think of them as "cornerstone" performances—merit badge requirements—reflective of the key challenges and accomplishments in the subject, the essence of "doing" the subject with core content. Here are examples of such challenges in a number of disciplines:

- In science, the design and debugging of significant experiments.
- In history, the construction of a valid and insightful narrative of evidence and argument.
- In mathematics, the quantifying and solving of perplexing or messy real-world problems.
- In world language, the successful translation of complex idiomatic expressions.

• In communication, the successful writing for specific and demanding audiences and purposes.

• In the arts, the composing/performing/critiquing of a sophisticated piece.

Like the game in sports or the play in drama, these cornerstone performance demands are meant to embody key learning goals by requiring meaning making and transfer of prior learning. Furthermore, such challenges can only be accomplished with the requisite habits of mind highlighted in school and program mission statements.

To see the value of thinking of curriculum as transfer and meaningful understanding, let's look at an example of an accomplishment-focused course syllabus in a college business course, in marketing:

> Course Learning Goals
>
> We will emphasize doing rather than memorizing: in addition to learning the core concepts of consumer behavior, you will master the performance of specific analytic tasks in consumer behavior. The core understandings and their accompanying tasks include the following:
>
> 1. No marketer can successfully satisfy all consumers—given differences in background characteristics and consumption preferences—with the same product, so they must choose which consumers they can satisfy. This is the application of market segmentation, the core concept of marketing, to the analysis of consumer behavior.
>
> • Recognize the relevant background characteristics—culture and values, demographics, personality, lifestyle, psychographics, and reference groups—that affect consumers' purchase of a particular product.
>
> • Identify the most important background characteristics for the product.
>
> • Specify the most appropriate target market of consumers that can be satisfied by the product.
>
> 2. Consumption is the complex result of a variety of behavioral processes—both psychological and social—that allow the individual to satisfy his or her needs.
>
> • Analyze the psychological and social processes used by consumers to complete the consumer purchase process.
>
> • Determine the differences in psychological and social processes used by segments of consumers.
>
> 3. Any act of consumption is the result of a series of interactions between buyer and seller, but occurs in a context that is influenced by intended and unintended actions of others who are not parties in the transaction. This reflects the influence of the external environment on consumers and marketers in contemporary society.
>
> • Recognize the consumers, marketers, and public policy actors involved in consumer behavior.

• Identify the issues related to the purchase of a particular product that elicit action from public policy actors.

4. Because consumption is only one of the many activities of a consumer, marketers and public policy actors who want to influence consumption must understand the broad range of human behavior in order to most effectively influence a particular purchase.

• Analyze the effects of marketing communication and shopping environment on consumers' behavior.

• Identify the roles played by interpersonal communication on consumption of a particular product.

• Explore consumers' use of behavioral processes in the decision to adopt a new product. (From a former course syllabus, College of New Jersey)

Notice how the course is framed in terms of the desired results—understandings and authentic performances—rather than the typical list of inputs—the knowledge and skills the course will cover. The rest of the syllabus explains how the learning goals will be met, how work will be assessed and graded, and what the course calendar looks like in light of those goals. These are the kinds of documents that we think should be developed for every course in every school.

Keeping the End in Mind: Framing Curriculum Around Performance Goals

Until we grasp the idea that a curriculum has no coherence or power divorced from vital accomplishments related to transfer and meaning, we will not avoid aimless coverage of content objectives. Nor will we have a mechanism for doing what we so badly need in order to achieve our goals: an effective method for prioritizing and pruning content.

How does a constant focus on a long-term performance goal solve the problem of incoherence and too much indiscriminate content? Consider the challenge of learning to drive a car in preparation for getting one's license. The long-term goal is clear enough: learn to be an effective, courteous, and law-abiding driver. It is a clear example of an accomplishment involving transfer. We cannot prepare you for every possible driving event, but we can equip you with enough skill, knowledge, and savvy to earn a license and head down the road to becoming a capable driver. The goal, equivalent to state testing and accountability requirements, involves passing the written and road tests.

Now, we could say that to become a really good driver you first need to learn lots of information (for example, all the rules of the road or the name and function of every part of your automobile) and master a host of discrete skills (like how to use the brake, turn the steering wheel so it snaps back, respond to a skid on ice) before getting in a car. And we no doubt would do this if getting a license were based exclusively on an extensive written test. But we don't do this. Why? Because we are focused on accomplishing the desired performance from the start and throughout the learning. Is all "content" important? Of course! Should we wait 10 years to give you a license? No. Is the goal mastery of only the content as represented on a paper-and-pencil test? Of course not! The practical goal of preparation for real driving is key to prioritizing content knowledge and framing the learning around actual practice in the key challenges of driving.

Indeed, this is the critical point: the transfer goal of having students ready to drive a real car on real roads by the time they are 16 or 17 shapes our methods of teaching and compels us to pare down the content to a bare minimum and to translate it into useful information for driving. Too often in traditional academic curriculum design, however, we postpone the learners' need to try to apply their learning in genuine situations, claiming the belief that "you're not ready; you need more content." We don't have a method for paring and shaping content, either.

The propensity to cover lots of content before allowing students to use it in authentic situations may be well intentioned, but it reveals a fundamentally flawed (we believe) conception of learning. This view may be characterized as the "climbing the ladder" model of cognition. Subscribers to this belief assume that students must learn the important facts before they can address the more abstract concepts of a subject. Similarly, they think that learners must master all relevant discrete skills before they can be expected to apply them in more integrated, complex, and authentic ways.

Ironically, this view of teaching and learning may have been unwittingly reinforced by Bloom's Taxonomy (1956), an educational model originally proposed more than 50 years ago for categorizing degrees of cognitive complexity of assessment items and tasks on university exams. Although hierarchical in nature, Bloom's Taxonomy was never intended to serve as a model of learning or a guideline for instruction. Nonetheless, we have known many teachers who use it in this way.

One practical problem with the "climb the ladder" view directly affects lower-achieving students. Because they are less likely to have acquired the basics on the same schedule as more advanced learners, struggling learners are often confined to an educational regimen of low-level activities, rote memorization of discrete facts, and mind-numbing skill-drill worksheets. The unfortunate reality is that many of these students will *never* get beyond the first rung of the ladder and, therefore, have minimal opportunities to actually use what they are learning in a meaningful fashion. Who wouldn't be inclined to drop out under such conditions?

Cognitive psychologists have for some time rejected the "climb the ladder" view, based on research on learning. Lorrie Shepard, noted researcher and former leader of the American Educational Research Association, summarizes the contemporary view as follows:

> The notion that learning comes about by the accretion of little bits is outmoded learning theory. Current models of learning based on cognitive psychology contend that learners gain understanding when they construct their own knowledge and develop their own cognitive maps of the interconnections among facts and concepts. (1989, pp. 5–6)

Her view is echoed throughout the widely read book titled *How People Learn* (Bransford, Brown, & Cocking, 1999), published by the National Research Council of the National Academy of Sciences.

Confusing the Drills with the Game

Let's consider the practical implications of the theory via an athletic analogy. Coaches of many sports include drills as part of their practices. These drills are necessary to develop and refine the basic skills of the game. However, coaches also have their athletes actually play the game—early and often—so that the players apply the skills in realistic situations. How many football players would spend the weekday practices dutifully blocking a sled or practicing handoffs if they weren't going to play actual games on Saturdays? How many age-group swimmers would swim endless laps if they weren't going to participate in forthcoming swim meets? John Wooden, the great UCLA basketball coach often cited as an extraordinary teacher, summed up his approach to practice this way:

> Coach Wooden used a systematic pedagogical approach that he describes as the "whole-part" method. He did not teach and practice skills out of context. He always made sure players understood the whole of what they were learning, so as he introduced and drilled them on the parts, they understood how each related to the whole: "I would show them the whole thing to begin with (i.e., the entire play, based on a strategy). Then I am going to break it down into the parts and work on the individual parts and then eventually bring them together." He carefully explained the purpose of the play and the movement of the basketball and players. Then when the offense was broken down into its parts . . . the purpose of each part—how that part fit into the big picture, the play—became apparent. (Nater & Gallimore, 2005, p. 91)

Unfortunately, for too many students, much of their school experience involves the equivalent of decontextualized sideline drills, without the chance to ever play the game (to "do" the subject). We are certainly not suggesting that the basics are unimportant. Instead, we believe that meaningful learning is achieved through the interplay of drill and practice combined with authentic performances (playing the game). Indeed, it is in the very attempt to apply knowledge and skills within a relevant context that the learner comes to appreciate the need for the basics and marshals the motivation to learn them.

To generalize, without a firm commitment to clearly identified performance goals involving transfer, we have no way to avoid three problems of long standing in school: (1) an overloaded curriculum of discrete objectives, (2) teaching construed as "coverage" and isolated drill instead of transfer, and (3) the disengaged learning of "stuff" out of context. Without a focusing performance goal "outside" the content, we have no guiding principle for judging how to select, prioritize, and shape the content to ensure accomplishment and interest.

What Is a "Discipline"?

We can derive a different way to understand how curriculum must be reconceived and reframed by pondering the idea of a subject area. Often we refer to a subject as a discipline. *Discipline* is a useful word here. Think of yoga or the close reading of text: a "discipline" at its core is a set of habits of mind and behavior, not a list of findings. As Senge (2006) put it, a discipline is a "body of theory and technique that must be studied and mastered to put into practice. A discipline is a developmental path for acquiring certain . . . competencies" (p. 10). The dictionary reveals four related meanings that get to the heart of our ideas about accomplishment-based curriculum.

> Discipline:
>
> 1. Training expected to produce a specific character or pattern of behavior, especially training that produces moral or mental improvement.
> 2. Controlled behavior resulting from disciplinary training; self-control.
> 3. A set of rules or methods, as those regulating the practice of a church or monastic order.
> 4. A branch of knowledge or teaching.

This idea of accomplishment-based curriculum development may at first seem at odds with content standards and traditional academic goals and requirements. Indeed, some readers may reject the analogies with getting a driver's license or learning to play a sport. But this is a misunderstanding, due in part to confusion about the nature of academic goals. Many people erroneously think of academic disciplines as the "content," but that is not what a "discipline" is. A discipline is a regimen for achieving challenging ends. Both yoga and physics involve having "discipline" or "being disciplined" in this sense. A discipline is all about "doing" the work of the subject properly; avoiding the kinds of impulses, habits, and misunderstandings to which novices are most prone, so as to "produce a specific character or pattern of behavior—i.e., new, more mature habits of mind and behavior, based on understanding." (Note that it isn't until the fourth definition in the list that we get the more familiar connotation of the term *discipline*.)

Science is a "discipline" because the habit of jumping to conclusions based on prior beliefs runs deep in human beings (and novice scientists) and is overcome only through the discipline of trying to isolate key variables and methodically testing for them. You have to learn the discipline of carefully observing, gathering appropriate evidence, and weighing its limited implications while remaining skeptical. The so-called scientific method is not an isolated "skill" but a set of dispositions, skills, and transfer abilities in the use of content, learnable only by doing. Similarly, the goal in learning to "do" history is to avoid present-centeredness and simplistic causal reasoning. One must learn to think and act like a journalist/curator/historian to learn the discipline of history. Learning only the factual content or highly scripted skills is as little likely to make you "disciplined" as merely practicing discrete moves in basketball will equip you to be a successful game player.

Recall the revised math unit on fairness and measures of central tendency introduced in Chapter 1. The essential question ("What is fair, and how can math help us answer the question?") and the transfer task in which the learner proposes the fairest grading system involve not only the "doing" of mathematics, but also the "discipline" of looking carefully for patterns and answers related to the question instead of jumping to glib and unsupported conclusions and making sense of current experience via the content. This example gets at the essence of transfer as a goal: learning the (self-)discipline that permits prior learning to be effectively activated and used in new meaningful situations. And that's how habits of mind will find their proper way into the curriculum—as the needed habits for success at worthy, complex tasks.

Identifying the Key Challenges That Require Discipline

A simple way to envision the curriculum reform we are proposing, then, is to imagine that every subject area be defined not by its content but by its key (cornerstone) performances, the challenges that require not merely content and skill but great discipline and, thus, wise control over a wide-ranging repertoire of "moves." In other words, every subject area would be framed around its own version of the decathlon in the Olympics or the scout's merit badges: a set of worthy and diverse performances that concretely represent long-term, desired accomplishment—the "discipline" of doing all subjects well.

Assessment tasks demanding these habits of mind and embodying these key accomplishments would anchor the curriculum in two senses: (1) by shaping instruction to ensure that it prepares for transfer and (2) by recurring over the grades, as such tasks currently do in athletics, the arts, and professional training, varying only in terms of degree of difficulty of the particular tasks and abilities demanded. Rather than thinking of these increasingly complex tasks as grade-specific, we would think of them as levels of challenge, as in karate, diving, and vocational certification.

What are examples of such cornerstone performance challenges, to recur every year? Here are a few:

- In history, a key challenge is the ability to turn a messy batch of facts, gaps in the information, and different interpretations of the facts into a coherent, justifiable, and illuminating story with minimal bias and maximal insight—whether we are talking about an oral history of a playground fight in 1st grade or an Advanced Placement project using primary and secondary sources in 12th grade.
- In world language, a key task is to successfully communicate in the target language, in complicated and realistic situations, with an accent, rapidly, with speakers who speak no English.
- In mathematics, a key challenge is to take inherently messy data and find insightful patterns—without being stymied or led off track by the inevitable errors and outliers in the data.
- In science, a key challenge is to design and debug an experiment without being dishonest or self-deceiving about the data collected and analyzed.
- In language arts, a key challenge is to communicate an idea or a feeling to an audience that is inclined to not see it your way.
- In the performing arts, a key challenge is to place a personal stamp onto a scripted performance.

To distinguish a "challenge-and-discipline-based" curriculum from the more familiar "topic-and-activity-based" approach, we offer in Figure 2.1 some simple contrasts between key *accomplishments* based on long-term goals and isolated *learning activities* typically found in curriculum documents.

In some cases, these recurring performances and the specific tasks that embody them at various levels can be derived directly from existing state or provincial standards. For example, the *New Jersey Core Curriculum Content Standards for Social Studies* (New Jersey Department of Education, 2004b) present a list of broad competencies at the heart of the discipline:

1. Analyze how historical events shape the modern world.
2. Formulate questions and hypotheses from multiple perspectives, using multiple sources.
3. Gather, analyze, and reconcile information from primary and secondary sources to support or reject hypotheses.

4. Examine source data within the historical, social, political, geographic, or economic context in which it was created, testing credibility and evaluating bias.
5. Evaluate current issues, events, or themes and trace their evolution through historical periods.
6. Apply problem-solving skills to national, state, or local issues and propose reasoned solutions.

Figure 2.1
Accomplishments Versus Learning Activities

Key Accomplishments	Related, ***but Insufficient***, Learning Activities
Leave school with a personal direction based on valid information about your competence and interest; get hired accordingly.	Learn about careers, describe your goals.
Successfully solve a number of genuinely important, challenging, and complicated problems, with *minimal* prompts and cues and maximal self-direction and initiative.	Do textbook "problems" that are simplified and cued so that the learner simply "plugs in" previously learned facts and skills.
Get your writing published or successfully reviewed by expert readers.	Learn, use, and be assessed on "the writing process."
Critically identify questionable assumptions and conclusions in speech, texts, or symbol systems that most people do not think are problematic.	Learn and complete exercises on logical fallacies and grammatical errors.
Develop an insightful and supported account of a present issue, in light of history and the varied points of view.	Read the history text and pass tests on the content of history.
Leave school able to comprehend text beyond the 10th grade level (the level of newspapers of record in the United States).	Learn, use, and be tested in reading strategies via short passages.
Successfully defend your thesis.	Write a research paper following a prescribed format.
Make a difference by, for example, influencing local policy, improving the community, bettering someone's life.	Study civics, speak in an informed way about how laws are in theory made.
Truly achieve a purpose with an audience: engage, move, persuade them.	Play a musical piece or say a character's lines correctly.
Settle an argument; resolve a dispute.	Engage in discussion.
Identify the most salient variables and control for them in the design and debugging of experiments.	Complete science labs as designed and complete the structured lab sheets.

7. Analyze social, political, and cultural change and evaluate the impact of each on local, state, national, and international issues and events.

8. Evaluate historical and contemporary communications to identify factual accuracy, soundness of evidence, and absence of bias, and discuss strategies used by the government, political candidates, and the media to communicate with the public. (p. F-6)

Such a list can guide the development of a set of recurring tasks, tied to the particular history content for various grade levels.

The curricular goal, then, is to ensure that such performance demands recur and thus become the backbone of the curriculum—instead of just another standard among many. A successful curriculum shows teachers how to use the content (generally presented in standards documents as lists of discrete facts, concepts, and skills) in the service of grade-appropriate and content-appropriate tasks reflective of program goals and the overall mission. A curriculum focused on accomplishment would show teachers clearly how to transfer the standards into effective learning for worthy performance.

Safeguarding Accomplishment-Based Learning

> How did we get so far off the track in setting up our educational practices? The goal must be plain; one must have a sense of where one is trying to get to in any given instance of activity. For the exercise of skill is governed by an intention and feedback, and what one has achieved so far. . . . This means far more emphasis on making clear the purpose of every exercise, every lesson plan, every unit, every term, every education.
>
> —Jerome Bruner, *The Relevance of Education*

It is sobering to realize that more than 35 years after Bruner (1971) wrote these words, we are perhaps more off course than ever. In this era of prescribed content standards and narrowly focused (yet high-stakes) standardized testing, schoolwork that is true to the discipline and relevant to the needs and interests of learners is rarer than ever, as are long-term goals that are manifest in short-term work. We are sorely in need of practical models for how to re-form (in both senses) not only the curriculum but also approaches to instruction that make learning more effective and in the learner's interests.

Yet what has struck us for decades (and was repeatedly underscored by Goodlad [1984] in *A Place Called School*) is that athletics, the performing arts, and professional training in the workplace already supply us with working models from which to learn. Only habit and prejudice about "academics" keep us from seeing the matter clearly.

The Spiral: Recurring Questions and Performances

We are invoking, in other words, an old idea in a new guise. In an education for accomplishment (as the arts and athletics make so clear), the key ideas and transfer tasks spiral throughout the curriculum, just as Bruner, and Dewey before him, proposed. An educational curriculum can never be linear; it has to be recursive. Why? Because an education for understanding and self-discipline requires a constant revisiting of key ideas and challenges that are never mastered in one attempt. That's why understanding takes discipline. A sad legacy of behaviorism and other simplistic views of learning for understanding is that an inherently complex goal is reduced into a set of simplistic one-shot goals, as if mastery were just the sum of simple parts.

In an education for understanding and transfer, the curriculum would spiral in two ways: (1) courses and units would be organized around a few cornerstone disciplinary tasks, toward which all teaching and learning would be focused and prioritized; and (2) the same essential questions would recur, in different forms, over the course of the entire education. Although the *particulars* of a task might differ in terms of developmental complexity, the performance demands would basically be the same each time. For example, think of the game in soccer, the recital in music, or the genre in writing. The tasks recur from kindergarten through 12th grade. The same would be true for the overarching essential questions: What's the pattern? What are the key variables? What really happened and why? What is the author trying to say? These are questions that must be revisited each course, each year, at increasingly sophisticated levels of inquiry and performance.

Revisiting the same key essential questions and performances is not only desirable but critical to allow students to stay on course toward the complex accomplishments that can never be mastered in a single try. Known tasks and recurring performance demands remove the harmful "mystery" from schoolwork, making long-term obligations crystal clear for students and teachers alike. This factor is key for building confidence as well as competence in learners. Moreover, it is no more boring for students to revisit key performances and "big ideas" than it is boring for good musicians or soccer players to play anew. Finally, one of the most significant findings in recent educational research is that formative assessment causes the greatest gains in student achievement (Black & Wiliam, 1998).

Unfortunately, most typical curricula still parcel out work in a linear, one-shot manner. Instead of a few key tasks in a course (derived from recurring essential performances), students confront hundreds of discrete test questions that are asked only once. Feedback is generally isolated and related to a specific test or assignment instead of ongoing and related to genuine performance goals. Until curriculum is designed backward from recurring performances leading to genuine accomplishment, neither learners nor teachers have a way of knowing where they stand against exit goals in time to do anything about it. When we truly understand how to devise a results-based curriculum (and why), we will see far more of such recurring assessments with multiple opportunities to receive timely feedback.

A Plan to Adjust: Making Feedback More Central to Curriculum Design and Implementation

Almost 30 years ago, Thomas Gilbert (1978), a designer and consultant on results-based workplaces and learning, proposed a complete framework for learning to accomplish worthy tasks:

> The requirements of an information system sensibly designed to give maximum support to performance are absurdly simple, and they can be summarized in eight steps:
>
> 1. Identify the expected accomplishments: mission, responsibilities, and duties.
> 2. State the requirements of each accomplishment.
> 3. Describe how performance will be measured and why.
> 4. Set exemplary standards.
> 5. Identify exemplary performers and any other available resources that people can use to become exemplary performers.
> 6. Provide frequent and unequivocal feedback about how well each person is performing. This should be expressed as a comparison with an exemplary standard.
> 7. Supply as much backup information as needed to help people troubleshoot their own performance and that of the people for whom they are responsible.
> 8. Relate various aspects of poor performance to specific remedial actions. (pp. 178–179)

Gilbert notes sardonically that it "may be that their simplicity helps explain why they are so rarely followed" (pp. 178–179) and asks his readers to consider the information we present in Figure 2.2 as describing the opposite intent in a powerfully concise yet sadly recognizable way (our comments are inserted in brackets to help focus on schooling).

As a parting shot, Gilbert notes, "Then, ask yourself if these things aren't often done—almost as if there were a conspiracy to create incompetence. Anyone who studies the table and doesn't see that most of these tactics are the rule, not the exception . . . simply hasn't had much experience" (p. 86). In short, the table explains, in a simple but powerful way, why teachers and students alike lack the information, resources, and built-in incentives to improve their performance.

Figure 2.2

Why Students and Teachers Don't Improve Performance

Information	Resources	Motivation
(1) FEEDBACK: Don't let people know how well they are performing. Hide from people what is expected of them. Give people little or no guidance about how to perform well.	(2) TOOLS: Design resources without ever consulting the intended users [or without reference to the goals of the learning].	(3) INCENTIVES: Provide no intrinsic rewards; poor performers get rewarded as well as good ones.
(4) KNOW-HOW: Leave training to chance; make it irrelevant to mission.	(5) MAXIMIZED CAPACITY: [Schedule and organize learning in classes in a way that is convenient for the scheduler and teacher.]	(6) MOTIVES: Give pep talks rather than incentives.

Practically speaking, the essence of Gilbert's message is that a robust feedback system is a key to achieving performance goals. This idea is also echoed in the literature on instructional design as well as recent findings on learning, as documented by Black and Wiliam (1998) and summarized by Marzano, Pickering, and Pollock (2001). Yet we all know the reality of schooling once the curriculum is underway: even though the plans don't work out as initially designed, conventional curricula offer little or no help in dealing with this most basic reality of mass schooling. Although we know that ongoing feedback and adjustment lie at the heart of a robust performance-based system, mechanisms for acting on this knowledge are notably absent in existing curriculum materials.

Curricula rarely include troubleshooting guides or built-in diagnostic and formative assessment systems; in other words, they rarely provide for the *inevitable need to adjust* based on feedback. In the worst cases, districts use curriculum "pacing guides" to ensure that teachers won't "fall behind" in covering the content—*irrespective of results*. This amounts to "teach, test, hope for the best"—the antithesis of what we are advocating.

At the very least, an accomplishment-based curriculum honors the idea that once the course is underway, adjustments will *likely* be necessary. It might need to adjust in little ways: each syllabus leaves two days per month completely unplanned to allow midcourse corrections. It might need to adjust in major ways: teachers get together at midyear to plot changes to the syllabus, in light of midyear assessments. The ironic challenge, then, is to not overplan but to plan to adjust.

One of us heard Marv Levy, the coach of the Buffalo Bills football team, underscore the importance of changing well-laid plans, based on emerging results. During a postgame radio interview, a reporter asked Levy how he explained the Bills' surprising ability to come back from a few lackluster showings at the end of the regular season to handily beat the Pittsburgh Steelers in the first play-off game. Levy responded sarcastically: "What do you think we do out here? Develop a great playbook in July, wind it up, and pray? Coaching is about adjustment—constant adjustment in light of results against your goals." Too few teachers understand that they, too, must plan to aggressively adjust the curriculum, as needed, in light of the inevitable gap between results and goals.

The job is not to hope and assume that optimal learning will occur, based on our curriculum and initial teaching. The job is to ensure that learning occurs, and when it doesn't, to intervene in altering the syllabus and instruction decisively, quickly, and often. A key part of our job as coaches with a curriculum, in other words, is to learn, not just teach—to learn deeply from feedback about what kids actually do with their learning based on the results they produce. We must fixate not on written guides and time lines, but on the feedback against worthy goals: student work, student comments and reflections, and student attempts to make sense of their learning. The job is to ensure mission-related results manifested as deepening understanding and transfer, even if it means we must question and alter our "playbook" and "game plan" when the feedback tells us lots of learners aren't performing anywhere near well enough.

That's why the curriculum is not, and can never be, a script. The job of teaching is not to "execute" the paper curriculum irrespective of results, any more than it is the coach's job to execute the playbook irrespective of the score. The teacher's job is to flesh out the lessons in the curriculum and adjust instruction, whenever needed, to ensure optimal learning and performance. Given that purpose, teachers need a curriculum that provides troubleshooting advice and builds in opportunities to alter courses, as warranted. They need a curricular framework that designs in more pre-tests and ongoing formative tests against long-term desired results, with "free" days deliberately scheduled within the syllabus to accommodate the inevitable need to adjust once they look at results.

Consider the need presented by our constant struggle to get all students to pass algebra. For decades we have known that the failure rate in 9th grade algebra is unacceptably high—more than 30 percent in some districts. Why haven't we planned to adjust in light of this predictable bad result—*before* it is too late? Why haven't we developed in every high school a "Plan B" for handling this failure before it is no longer possible to save the student's year? Here are various ways to anticipate the trouble and do something about it in a timely manner:

• Give every incoming 9th grader a test on the enabling skills and ideas related to success in algebra, closely monitor in September and October the grades of students who do poorly on the test, and be prepared to set them up in an alternative algebra program that slows the pace way down (by providing a two-year course) in order to remediate the needed arithmetic skills and conceptual abilities.

• Pull from their current class all failing students after the first marking period, and provide them with a different approach to learning algebra that starts all over but is taught in a more hands-on way and is led by a pair of teachers who team to do more intensive coaching work. (There would be only one or two "extra" teachers who would rotate across all sections, to keep costs down.)

• Have an already-built online course and extra workshop sections each day for 8th graders and 9th graders, to bridge the gap between the performance level of weaker students and the demands of regular algebra classes. Ensure that those courses are not just more low-level drill but are based on case studies and interesting applications of the content.

As it stands now, we act like Charlie Brown, hoping that, this time, Lucy will hold the football still and let him kick it. We keep thinking and hoping, against all odds, that *this* year it will be different in algebra: that the same algebra course, taught the same way, will somehow cause the success that has always been elusive. The "failure" is then falsely attributed to the students.

This is a revealing problem, with its correlate in individual classrooms: we keep thinking that "coverage" will work, that what the teacher does is far more important than what learners try to do and whether they succeed or not at trying to do it. Curriculum design and lesson planning still reflect a passive blank-slate and teaching-as-telling view of learning, as if nothing learners do should influence how instruction unfolds. Yet if there are no explicit learning goals and priorities outside the content, as we noted earlier, there is no basis for adjusting the curriculum; on it must go, then, in spite of results crying out for institutional and teacher adjustments.

Alas, we have often been startled to hear some teachers say, "But there is no time for that. I can't take time to do more formative assessing and use the feedback, because then I'll fall behind!" This is a sadly ironic statement, because what the teacher is saying, without realizing it, is that "there is no time to maximize learning because there are so many more things to teach." Although we should have empathy for the teachers who make this claim, it reflects a profound misunderstanding of their job of causing learning and achieving worthy results.

In fact, the opposite is needed. The curriculum needs to explicitly give teachers permission and advice about how to effectively and appropriately deviate from the plan when the plan isn't working to achieve the goals. At its most basic, this approach demands built-in adjustment time for students to get feedback against desired transfer goals and receive coaching on how to improve their performance without this seeming like "lost" time. (A teacher we met told us that he has learned to build "speed bumps" into his curriculum plan to accommodate regular checkpoints and the frequently needed reteaching.) In short, the lack of troubleshooting guides and feedback systems is as important a problem as the absence of cornerstone tasks. Both are essential for achieving goals and for making those goals more transparent.

Here is a larger-scale example of building in such feedback and adjustment. In South Brunswick, New Jersey, students in the 3rd through 5th grades participate in a district writing assessment. Nothing seems novel there. But here's the catch: it is the same test, the same writing prompt given to all, and the papers are all scored against the same rubric and performance standard. In other words, 3rd graders get three (or more) opportunities to meet the 5th grade standard, based on feedback and opportunities to use it.

So let's get more practical. What would a better framework for curriculum look like? How should we write curriculum to achieve long-term mission-related results (mindful of content standards), focus instruction toward transfer goals and tasks, and avoid the aforementioned problems? We turn to these questions in Chapter 3.

Ideas for Action

- Develop and use appropriate diagnostic assessment in all courses (pre-tests and ongoing feedback against desired results).
- Have subject-area committees produce valid and peer-reviewed lists of "cornerstone assessment tasks" that will guide the writing of curriculum and shape the teaching of content.
- Design and implement recurring tasks and rubrics related to key performance tasks that are, in turn, related to mission and long-term program goals.
- Regularly check the gap between the intended, implemented, and attained curriculum in terms of student learning results on tasks and tests.
- Have departmental and grade-level teams meet to analyze student performance and achievement deficits in light of cornerstone assessment tasks, and collaboratively plan activities to improve results.

3

How Should Curriculum Be Re-Formed?

> Acquisition of a modicum of information in each branch of learning, or at least in a selected group, [unfortunately] remains the principle by which the curriculum is formed. . . . The complaints of educators that learning does not enter into character, the protests against . . . gradgrind preoccupation with "facts" . . . and ill-understood rules and principles, all follow from this state of affairs.
>
> —John Dewey

In Chapter 2 we identified inadequacies in existing curricula and described general features of a curriculum designed to develop students' understanding and capacity for transfer. In this chapter we describe the redesign of a curriculum framework around 10 components that will make it far more likely that mission-related goals are achieved and far less likely that understanding-related goals and vital habits of mind will fall through the cracks of short-term lesson planning, instruction, and local assessments.

A key feature of this re-formed curriculum is graphically displayed in Figure 3.1. Notice that content does *not* supply the "headers" for this new approach to curriculum writing. Rather, mission-related learning goals are the categories that serve as filters for selecting and shaping particular subject area content so these encompassing institutional goals do not get lost in the processes of curriculum design and implementation. Figure 3.1 is a graphic representation of how mission-related goals should suffuse programs, courses, and units.

This approach to curriculum development helps to ensure that K–12 programs and courses are written *after* a careful analysis of both the relevant program goals (including content standards) *and* mission-related goals. For example, in developing a 9th grade English course, curriculum writers would constantly consider the following questions:

Figure 3.1

A Mission-Based Curriculum Framework

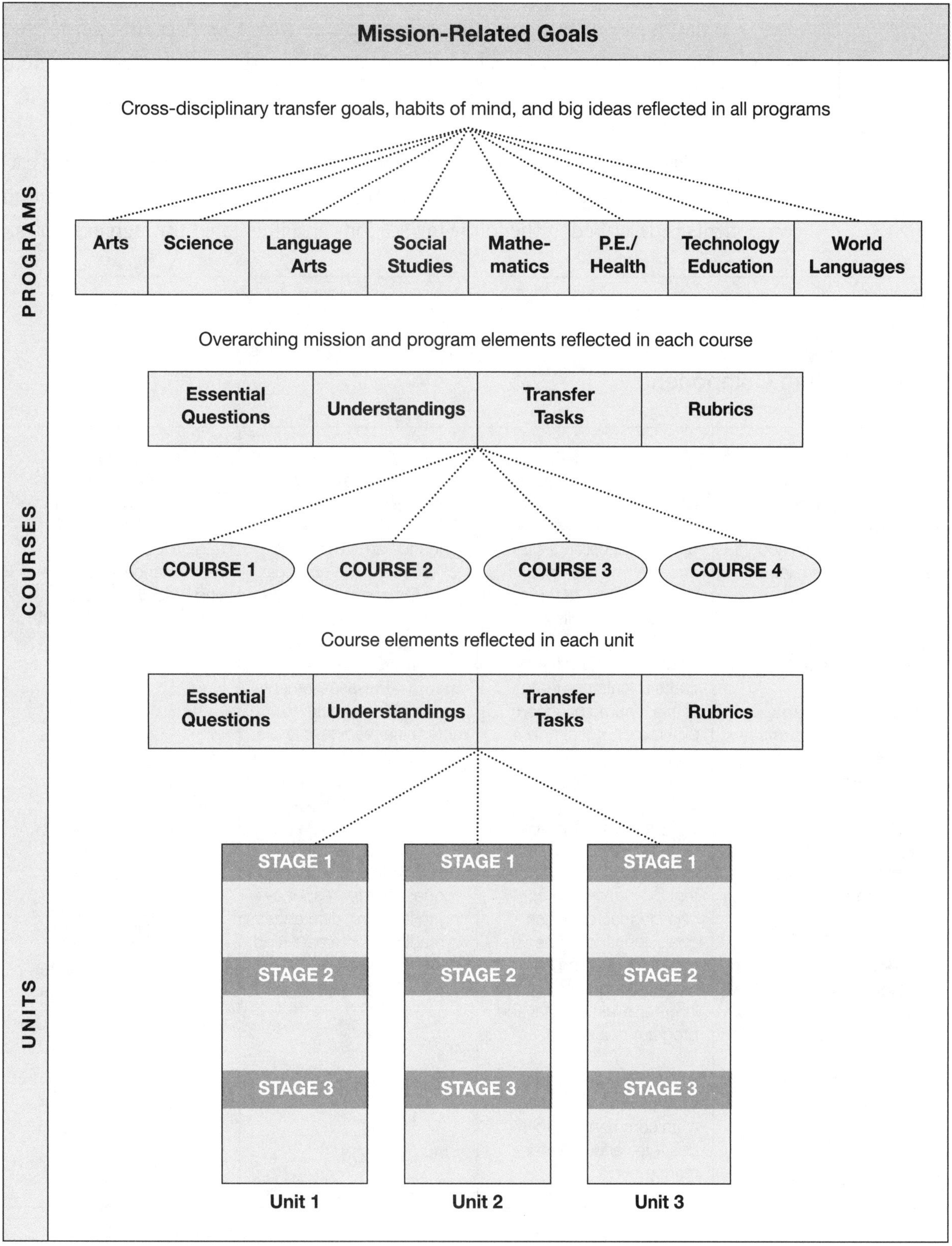

• What must our English/language arts program address throughout its courses and cornerstone assessments to reflect mission-related transfer goals, habits of mind, and big ideas?

• What must our 9th grade English course address to reflect mission-related and program-related transfer goals, habits of mind, big ideas, and relevant content standards?

Curriculum is then constructed around 10 components, organized into four broad categories reflecting backward design, as shown in Figure 3.2. Each of these curriculum components is described in the following sections and illustrated through examples.

Figure 3.2

Ten Curriculum Components

1. Mission-Related Accomplishments and Curricular Philosophy—Specifying the integrated accomplishments sought, indicative of transfer and habits of mind; the underlying beliefs about learning that the curriculum must embody. **2. Understandings and Essential Questions Derived from Mission and Content Standards**—Specifying the big ideas and recurring questions that should anchor the curriculum and shape how content is framed. **3. K–12 Curriculum Mapping**—Showing how habits of mind, big ideas, essential questions, and cornerstone assessment tasks spiral through the curriculum, bringing intellectual coherence.	**4. Cornerstone Assessments and Collections of Evidence**—Specific authentic tasks reflective of the key challenges and accomplishments in the disciplines, requiring transfer and habits of mind; collections of evidence in portfolios, so that students graduate with a résumé of accomplishments, not simply a transcript. **5. Analytic and Longitudinal Rubrics**—Common analytic rubrics for providing more consistent evaluation and specific feedback against goals; longitudinal benchmarks for gauging and reporting progress against long-term institutional and program goals. **6. Anchors**—Tangible examples of student work (with commentary) to illustrate various performance levels.	**7. Suggested Learning Activities, Teaching Strategies, and Resources**—Including guidance and resources for teachers and strategic tools for learners. **8. Diagnostic and Formative Assessments**—Pre-assessments and ongoing checks to determine readiness levels, to reveal potential misconceptions, and to gauge progress along the way. **9. Suggestions for Differentiation**—Specific suggestions for responding to learners' differences in readiness, interests, and learning profile.	**10. Troubleshooting Guide**—Advice and tips for addressing predictable learning-related problems (e.g., misconceptions, performance weaknesses) and teaching predicaments (e.g., running out of time).

Component 1. Mission-Related Accomplishments and Curricular Philosophy

We have argued that a primary mission of school is the development and deepening of understanding and its corresponding habits of mind so that students are able to transfer their learning to new and important situations, leading to genuine accomplishments. With these ends in mind, we are then obliged to construct curricula and assessments to help us realize them. For example, if "critical thinking" and "effective real-world transfer" are key aspects of any mission, then the development of curriculum within and across subjects must ensure that critical thinking and transfer are the focus of learning and at the heart of what is assessed; if "write engagingly and creatively" is a goal of the English/language arts program, then we must ensure that this goal is addressed within each course in that program at all levels.

In other words, all program-area and course goals are framed to embody broader institutional aims and transfer accomplishments within the subject; they are not framed in terms of discrete content objectives. The more specific content objectives are addressed *as a part of* broader understanding and transfer goals in subject areas and the overall mission. So in history, mathematics, or art, we select and shape "core content" to serve as the *means* for developing critical thinking and transfer performances.

We begin this process by identifying the kinds of understandings, abilities, and habits of mind we would see *if* our subject-based instruction successfully incorporated our mission-related goals (Stage 1). Then we consider the kinds of accomplishments that school graduates would ideally be able to achieve on their own, given appropriate curricular preparation. The following prompts can help us envision such autonomous accomplishments:

If we were successful, students would have

- Accomplished . . .
- Developed autonomy in . . .
- Used their learning to . . .
- Faced and overcome such key challenges as . . .
- Created . . .
- Overcome such misconceptions and habits of thinking as . . .

What would such a curriculum look like in action? Let's trace a mission-related goal, critical thinking, to see how a new curriculum framework in history could be built around long-term accomplishments reflective of mission and important program goals, not just content coverage.

Mission-Related Goal: Critical Thinking

Related habits of mind: Open-mindedness, suspension of disbelief and belief, persistence, care about precision, not jumping to conclusions or sweeping generalizations.

Overarching essential questions: What is the evidence and the argument? How valid are they?

Mission and Program Link

Critical thinking in history: By graduation, the students should have successfully accomplished such critical-thinking tasks as

- Crafting many histories to explain the past, understand the present, and predict the future—while confronting gaps and disagreements in the evidence.
- Using and critically evaluating primary and secondary sources.
- Critiquing peers' historical arguments and narratives.
- Analyzing various purported "histories" for bias/propaganda (including "official" and professional histories).

Related historical habits of mind:

- Avoiding present-centeredness and ethnocentrism.

Key historical transfer goals, related to the mission goal:

- Careful and substantiated causal reasoning.
- Analysis and criticism of historical texts and artifacts.

Related program-level essential questions to be addressed in all courses:

- How reliable is this source? Who is speaking and what might be their bias or point of view?
- How valid is this interpretation? What is assumed? How well supported is the argument?
- Whose "story" is this? Are there other "stories" to consider?

Related program-level assessments:

- Tasks that require students to consider varied sources for potential bias.
- Tasks that require students to identify faulty assumptions, conclusions, and evidence in primary and secondary sources.
- Tasks that demand careful causal reasoning.
- Common rubrics for critical thinking in history.

Related program-level learning activities:

- Activities that provide students with the skills needed to question and analyze sources.
- Activities that provide students with the experiences of discovering that a seemingly authoritative text is biased or distorted in its presentation.
- Activities that require students on their own to consider varied sources for potential bias.
- Activities that require students to construct their own "story" based on primary and secondary sources.

Therefore, designing a course and writing a public syllabus for each history course would *require* explicit reference to the framework elements, to show where and how the goals at the next-higher level are being addressed in the curriculum component at the next-lower level. And, of course, other program areas would be expected to use the same mission-related goal categories and analysis in their documents (see Figure 3.3). A key implication is that the textbook is no longer the de facto syllabus (as it is in most classes now). The curriculum can be thought of as the document designed to ensure that the textbook serves only as a resource to support mission-based goals, with guidance on when to use the textbook, and when not to use the textbook, in support of local goals.

Here are two more examples of this kind of framing of accomplishments at the program level (in English and mathematics) from higher education. The English example is from Towson University in Maryland, and the math example is from San Jose State University in California.

> At graduation, English majors demonstrate instrumental knowledge of reading and writing in the discipline. They can
>
> - Conduct purposeful analysis of literary discourse, including discussion of the history, forms, and conventions of the different periods and genres.
> - Read literary works with understanding of their background, structure, meanings, implications, and relevance.
> - Read scholarly works with understanding of their contexts, concerns, and terminology.
> - Interpret written materials flexibly, understanding how multiple meanings are possible and, conversely, how individual interpretations sometimes can be wrong.
> - Understand and use evidence to support interpretations.
> - Write in a variety of forms (expository, argumentative, imaginative, academic, business/technical, literary, etc.) as appropriate to audience, purpose, and occasion.

> Goal 4. The Ability to Use Mathematical Models to Solve Practical Problems
>
> Specific learning objectives to be assessed:
>
> - Ability to extract relevant information from a practical problem and give a mathematical formulation of the problem.
> - Ability to use numerical results to validate (or modify) a model and to understand the limitation of a model.
> - Ability to clearly describe models, including an analysis of the strengths and weaknesses of models and their relationship to the underlying problem.

Figure 3.4 summarizes the kinds of program-level accomplishments we are referring to in the core subject areas.

Figure 3.3
A Mission-Based Curriculum Framework for U.S. History

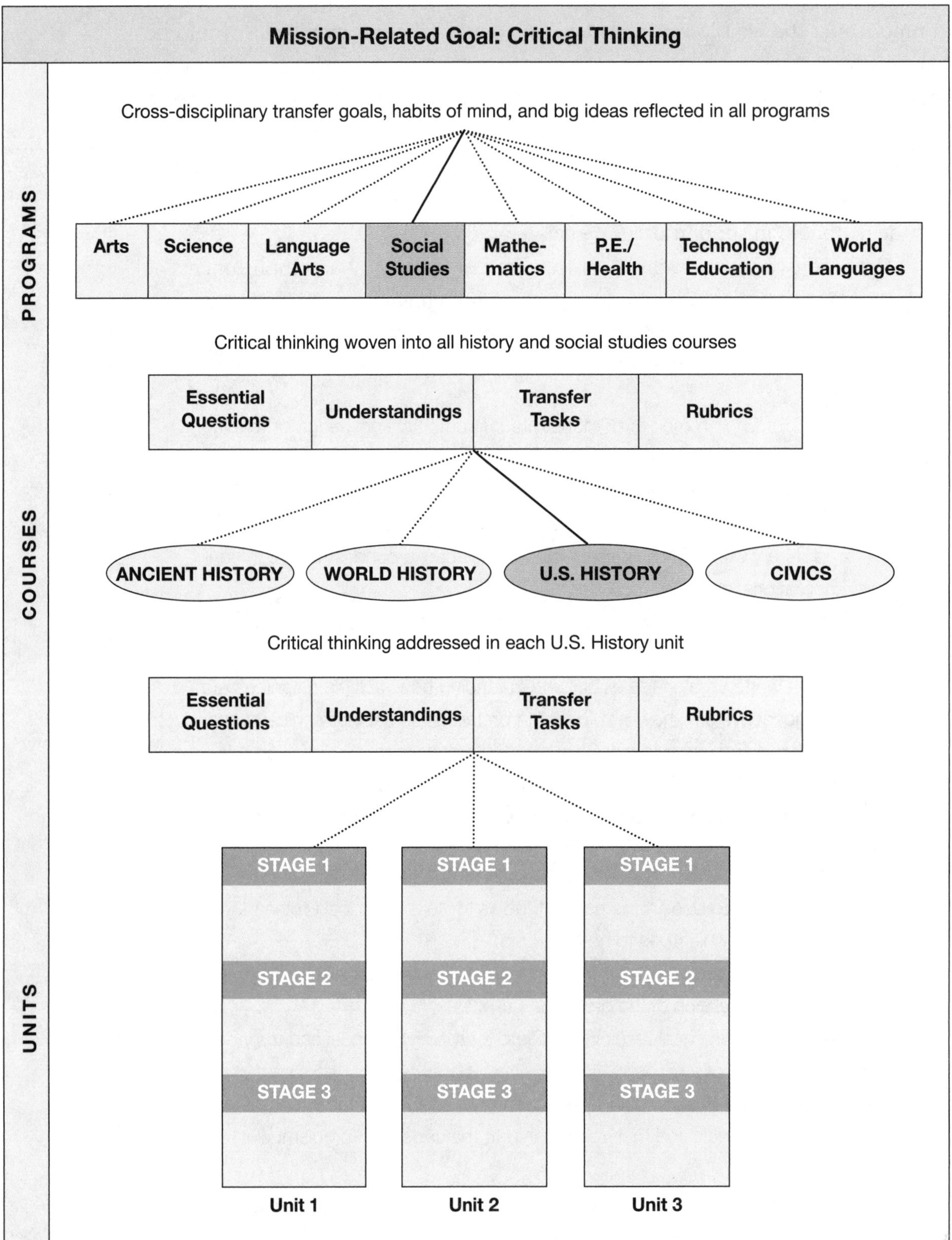

Figure 3.4

Program-Level Accomplishments for Core Subject Areas

English/Language Arts

- **Read and respond to sophisticated and challenging texts in various genres** (literature, nonfiction, technical) through
  - Global understanding (the "gist").
  - Interpretation (between the lines).
  - Critical stance.
  - Personal connections.
- **Create oral or written pieces in various genres for various audiences** in order to
  - Explain (narrative).
  - Entertain (creative).
  - Persuade (persuasive).
  - Help perform a task (technical).
  - Challenge or change things (satirical).
- **Listen to various sources** (e.g., lecture, radio commercial) **for various purposes**, including for
  - Learning.
  - Enjoyment.
  - Performing a task.
  - Reaching a decision.

Mathematics

- **Create a mathematical model** of complex physical phenomena (e.g., quantity, size, rate, change).
- **Perform data analysis**
  - Observe.
  - Collect.
  - Measure.
  - Record.
  - Display.
  - Analyze data.
- **Make and justify predictions** based on pattern analysis.
- **Design a physical structure in response to a need or problem** (e.g., a three-dimensional shipping container to maximize volume and safety).
- **Evaluate mathematical/statistical claims.**

Science

- **Design and conduct an experiment** to answer a key question or explain phenomena.
- Effectively **use scientific tools** to
  - Observe.
  - Collect data.
  - Measure.
  - Record data.
  - Classify.
  - Draw conclusions.
- **Evaluate confusing scientific claims.**
- **Critique experimental designs or conclusions.**
- **Analyze current issues** involving science or technology.

History/Social Studies

- **Carefully evaluate historical claims or interpretations** based on
  - Primary source evidence.
  - Secondary source evidence.
  - Personal opinion.
- **Critically analyze current events/issues.**
  - Summarize/compare key points.
  - Analyze causes and effects.
  - Identify points of view and potential bias.
  - Debate possible courses of action.
- **Make predictions for current or future events or issues** based on understanding of historical patterns.
- **Make informed decisions** using critical thinking and understanding of historical patterns.
- **Act as a responsible citizen** in a democracy (e.g., stay informed, study issues, participate in community events, vote).

Visual and Performing Arts

- **Create engaging and purposeful artistic expressions** in forms that vary in terms of
  - Media (e.g., pastel, photography).
  - Genre (e.g., jazz music, modern dance).
  - Styles (e.g., impressionism, cubism).
- **Create artistic expressions for various audiences and purposes**, including to effectively
  - Entertain (e.g., tell a story).
  - Evoke emotion.
  - Commemorate.
  - Persuade.
  - Challenge (e.g., the status quo).
- **Respond to artistic expressions** through
  - Global understanding.
  - Interpretation.
  - Critical stance.
  - Personal connections.

Source: Designed by Grand Island Public Schools, K–12 Social Studies Curriculum and Assessment Team, Nebraska. Used with permission.

In short, long-term program goals would be written in terms of performance accomplishment—successful "doing" of the subject to high standards with minimal teacher prompting and scaffolding, the result that would follow from the ultimate integration of a repertoire of knowledge and skill with understanding. This is the only way to ensure that long-term habits of mind and transfer goals are achieved: by ensuring that major assignments and assessments require them for success and are seen as the building blocks of curriculum instead of content.

With these culminating accomplishments in mind, more specific assessments relating these tasks to content are then designed backward to identify key recurring performance tasks (and big ideas—see Component 2 in the following section) around which content would be coherently grouped—the spiral curriculum. Students, like athletes and artists, are thereby alerted to—and always being prepared for—the ultimate accomplishments expected of them from the start and throughout their school career. In art and athletics, we don't postpone playing the game until later years, and we should not do so in academic disciplines either. Otherwise we arbitrarily and unhelpfully parcel content and skill out in isolated grade-level bits, thus impeding or even preventing effective long-term preparation for meeting long-term transfer and habit-of-mind goals.

Curricular Philosophy

We recommend that district curricula (and by extension academic departments) include a statement of philosophy based on beliefs about teaching and learning and the role that curriculum should play in schooling. (This is a natural place to include a set of Principles of Learning, described in Chapter 4.)

Statements of philosophy can be included for the curriculum as a whole, as well as for individual disciplines. Consider Figure 3.5, an example from the social studies curriculum in Grand Island Public Schools, Nebraska. Notice how mission and subject area goals are integrated with beliefs about learning and implications for teaching.

Component 2. Understandings and Essential Questions (Big Ideas) Derived from Mission and Content Standards

A second way in which the curriculum needs to be re-formed to ensure that the focus is on long-term and in-depth meaning making, transfer abilities, and the relevant habits of mind involves the identification of the few key or big ideas in each subject area. We must identify these big ideas as elements that recur in all instruction and assessment. These big ideas are framed around provocative essential questions that focus teaching and learning and help uncover the content; these big ideas

Figure 3.5

K–12 Social Studies Program Philosophy

The goal of social studies education is to prepare students to be responsible and productive citizens in a democratic society and a globally interdependent world. Through an integrated study of social studies disciplines, students will acquire necessary knowledge, skills, and attitudes as they become lifelong learners.

Social studies provides content that students will use to understand political, social, and economic issues and apply their knowledge and skills to make effective personal and public decisions. A standards based social studies curriculum builds knowledge of specific discipline content, thinking skills, commitment to democratic values, and citizen participation, all essential to maintaining a democratic way of life.

GIPS K–12 Social Studies Program BELIEFS

- **All students learn through a variety of relevant experiences.**
  Therefore, we will provide interactions that activate and build on prior knowledge and promote higher level thinking skills.
- **Research shows active learning is essential.**
  Therefore, we will provide students with a variety of active, student centered, multisensory learning opportunities.
- **Instruction should be relevant, meaningful, and based on student needs.**
  Therefore, we will provide opportunities for students to make connections to their own lives using a variety of instructional strategies.
- **The world is constantly changing.**
  Therefore, we will provide the opportunities for students to understand that the present connects to the past and affects the future.
- **We live in a culturally diverse society.**
  Therefore, we will develop student understanding of diverse cultures that honors equality and human dignity.
- **Assessment should be ongoing, diagnostic, and aligned with instruction.**
  Therefore, we will provide multiple authentic assessment tools.
- **The use of community resources is essential for effective instruction.**
  Therefore, we will use the rich history and ethnic diversity of our community to enhance learning.
- **Active and informed citizen participation is essential to democracy.**
  Therefore, we will provide instruction and curriculum designed to develop students who will be informed, active problem solvers, and willing participants in the democratic process.

Source: Designed by Grand Island Public Schools, K–12 Social Studies Curriculum and Assessment Team, Nebraska. Used with permission.

are framed in understandings that students are helped to realize as a result of different lessons, units, and courses over time. We then teach the more specific facts, concepts, and skills (that are typically assessed on standardized tests and taught in isolation) in the context of exploring and applying the larger ideas and processes. This approach is consistent with the recommendations of other experts in curriculum and assessment, such as Lynn Erickson (2002) who calls for "concept-based curriculum," and Douglas Reeves (2003) who advocates identifying the "power standards" as a means of prioritizing content by focusing on transferable concepts and processes. Figure 3.6 presents a few examples of understandings and essential questions related to various topics.

Notice that we can use all these ideas repeatedly, across grade levels and courses, and that the essential questions suggest the long-term desired accomplishments

Figure 3.6
Examples of Understandings and Essential Questions

Content Topic	Understanding	Essential Questions
Statistics	Statistical analysis and display often reveal patterns in data, enabling us to make predictions with degrees of confidence.	How well can you predict the future? What will likely happen next? How sure are you?
World Literature	Great literature from various cultures explores enduring themes and reveals recurrent aspects of the human condition.	What makes a "great" story? How can stories from other places and times be about me?
Adaptation	Living organisms have developed adaptive mechanisms to enable them to survive in harsh or changing environments.	Will they survive? What is required for organisms to survive in harsh or changing environments?
Friendship (literary theme)	True friendship is revealed during hard times, not happy times.	Who is a "true friend," and how will you know?

mentioned earlier. That's what should frame curricula: recurring and interesting ideas that we can use to promote purposeful learning, generalization, and connections—the engines of transfer and habit development.

This approach is actually part of the standards clarification materials developed for the state of Delaware in history (a project in which one of us was involved as chief consultant). Here is an example of the K–12 strand of chronological thinking from the document (see www.doe.k12.de.us/ProfDev/History.pdf):

> **History Standard One K–3a: Students will use clocks, calendars, schedules, and written records to record or locate events in time.**
>
> Essential Question:
> - Why does *when* matter?
>
> The best way to approach any standard is to read the standard benchmarks by grade levels. The standards spiral upward toward a deeper understanding of how to use that particular concept. What is the goal of this standard? Ultimately, what are students expected to know and understand at the 9–12 level? We live our lives chronologically.
>
> At the K–3 level, History Standard One asks a student to be able to do more than just tell time or read a calendar. They must be able to use a clock or calendar or schedule. They master time as a concept in order to be able to do the reverse at the higher grades, to apply time as a conceptual tool in the study of history.

History Standard One 4–5a: Students will study historical events and persons within a given time frame in order to create a chronology and identify related cause-and-effect factors.

Essential Question:

- To what extent does one event *always* lead to another event?

In the 4–5 cluster, students add two new features: students learn how to create a chronology based on information given to them, using time frame devices. Secondly, the student uses the chronology to begin to apply the concept of cause and effect.

For example: Create a chronology of events leading up to the American Revolution and identify logical cause and effect, using time lines and time frames. Did the Boston Massacre cause the Revolutionary War? It happened five years before the war began, but anger over the massacre could have contributed to the ill feeling that eventually did lead to the war. Just because an event precedes another event does not mean that there has to be a relationship between them. Events in history can be like a TV schedule: there may be no connection between a program and the preceding program.

History Standard One 6–8a: Students will examine historical materials relating to a particular region, society, or theme; analyze change over time; and make logical inferences concerning cause and effect.

Essential Questions:

- Is change inevitable?
- To what extent does the past predict the future?
- What's the evidence for my conclusion?

In the 6–8 cluster, students learn how to analyze long-term change and to draw logical inferences concerning cause and effect over time. Students should study trends and themes. After gathering, examining and analyzing data, students will develop inferences and cause-and-effect relationships.

For example: Using a chronology of events leading up to the American Revolution, students will explain why and how one specific event led to subsequent events, logically drawing inferences based on historical understanding. Would it have been likely that war with Great Britain could have been avoided after the initial battles of Lexington and Concord? A teacher might give the students facts from the time period and let them brainstorm through the facts, arranging them in their order of importance. This requires that a student studying the American Revolution knows some events or trends that can be used to analyze what was happening in this period and can draw conclusions that explain cause and effect with factual support.

History Standard One 9–12a: Students will analyze historical materials to trace the development of an idea or trend across space or over a prolonged period of time in order to explain patterns of historical continuity and change.

Essential Questions:

• Were contemporary issues also problematic for past societies? Why are those issues difficult? Is there a pattern of continuity or change?

• To what extent can we learn from studying historical responses to societal problems?

In the 9–12 cluster, students continue deeper into the understanding of the results and consequences of chronologies by analyzing how some things change in history, and how some don't. They also are ready to apply it to daily adult life as a citizen by analyzing contemporary issues.

This standard provides teachers and students with a great opportunity to research their local communities. Both schools and local communities have a wealth of unmined documents available for research. Look at old yearbooks with a purpose in mind. What clothing styles were fashionable? What hair styles? How do the advertisements reflect the community at that time? How many of these businesses are still in existence? What happened to the others, particularly in the context of historical events? Does the local newspaper have a file of old newspaper clippings? When was a particular neighborhood built? Can you interview the older residents about that experience? Tracing an idea or trend over a time span or over a space is easier than explaining the resulting pattern of continuity and change. Students should take any topic selected for teaching this standard to the conclusion of the explanation of the pattern. And, try the reverse: show the pattern and have the students explain how it sheds light on the evolution of that trend or idea.

Here is a similar example from Delaware in English/language arts, illustrating how a state content committee revised the presentation of state standards to reflect program-level essential questions and understandings to guide K–12 curriculum development. The committee developed the following list of "enduring understandings" for the process of writing:

1. Audience and purpose (e.g., to inform, persuade, entertain) influence the use of literary techniques (e.g., style, tone, word choice).
2. Writers do not always say what they mean. Indirect forms of expression (e.g., satire, irony) require readers to read between the lines to find the intended meaning.
3. Punctuation marks and grammar rules are like highway signs and traffic signals. They guide readers through the text to help avoid confusion.

4. A writer selects a form based on his purpose.
5. A writer's point of view is influenced by his experience.
6. Conventions of language help readers understand what is being communicated.
7. The purposeful use and nonuse of language conventions help readers understand.
8. A writer's word choice and syntax are characteristics of voice which help to personalize text.

The committee developed the following list of essential questions for the process of writing:

1. Why write? What if writing didn't exist? Why share personal experiences in writing? To what extent is the pen mightier than the sword?
2. How is written language different from spoken language? What makes writing worth reading?
3. How do writers express their thoughts and feelings? Where do ideas for writing come from? What makes writing flow?
4. How do effective writers hook and hold their readers? What makes writing easy to follow? What is the best beginning? What is the best ending? What is the best order (sequence)? What is a complete thought?
5. Why am I writing? For whom? What am I trying to achieve through my writing? Who will read my writing? What will work best for my audience?
6. Why does a writer choose the form of writing he/she does?
7. What is the relationship between reader and writer?
8. How do writers communicate clearly?
9. To what extent do conventions of language impact communication?
10. What is the voice thing, anyway?
11. Why do we need grammar?

As we discuss later in this chapter, once understandings and essential questions have been established, it becomes vital to have longitudinal rubrics to chart progress over time in the learners' ability to consider and use such ideas with increasing sophistication and power.

Content Standards

In recent years, national subject-area associations, states, and provinces in North America have established content standards to specify what students should know and be able to do in the various disciplines during the K–12 school years. These standards are intended to focus teaching and learning, guide curriculum development, and provide a basis for accountability systems. Despite all good intentions and many positive effects, the standards as typically written can pose practical challenges to curriculum planners and teachers alike. In some states and provinces, the standards present an unreasonably ambitious volume of content knowledge and skills. In these cases, the content greatly exceeds the available time to teach all of the established standards. To complicate the matter, many content standards documents present an unclear mixture of content standards and performance standards.

A related problem centers on the fact that some standards are stated in ways that make them difficult to address. We liken this problem to the nursery tale of Goldilocks; that is, some standards are *too big*. Consider this one: Students will "recognize how technical, organizational, and aesthetic elements contribute to the ideas, emotions, and overall impact communicated by works of art." Such a statement, by itself, is simply too global to provide goal clarity and guidance to instruction and assessment. Different teachers in the arts could, in good faith, emphasize very different aspects of the content and believe that their actions honor the standard.

Conversely, some standards are *too small*. For example, consider this 7th grade state history standard, which declares that students will "compare the early civilizations of the Indus River Valley in Pakistan with the Huang-He of China." Although this statement provides a much narrower target than the previous example, the focus is too specific and seems somewhat arbitrary. This problem is exacerbated by high-stakes tests that rely on selected-response items to assess the discrete grade-level benchmarks. When content is reduced to a series of factlets and assessments are built upon decontextualized items, teachers are faced with a laundry list to cover without any sense of priority. Moreover, they may fail to grasp the more important performance goals and big ideas that should be framing their instruction and assessments. The larger, transferable concepts and processes can get lost in a sea of details.

Some states and provinces have attempted to address one or more of these problems by publishing companion "clarification" documents to explain the intent of the standards, identify more specific grade-level benchmarks, and specify performance indicators. While such guides can be helpful, we propose that it makes far more sense to see the standards as subsumed under the more general and complex performance goals and big ideas to which they relate.

Practically speaking, identifying performance goals and big ideas helps us address the Goldilocks problems. To play this out, let's consider our two previous examples. The standard in the arts ("recognize how technical, organizational, and aesthetic elements contribute to the ideas, emotions, and overall impact communicated by works of art") is too vague to be useful and needs a conceptual focus. Consider the following examples of possible *understandings, essential questions,* and *assessment tasks* for clarifying the standards and focusing instruction and assessment around big ideas and transfer performances:

• Great artists often break with established traditions, conventions, and techniques to express what they see and feel. What makes art "great"? Present your ideas (using any medium) on how a museum should set criteria for distinguishing "great art" from the rest; then propose works of art that meet the criteria and works that are not quite great enough.

• An artist's culture and personal experiences inspire the ideas and emotions they express. Where do artists get their ideas? In what ways do culture and experience inspire artistic expression?

• Available tools and technologies influence the ways in which artists express their ideas. How does the medium influence the message? Develop a multimedia exhibit to illustrate how the ideas of artists reflect their culture and experiences. Also, explain how their choices of medium and artistic techniques influence their message.

In the second example ("compare the early civilizations of the Indus River Valley in Pakistan with the Huang-He of China"), students would benefit from examining larger ideas and associated questions that lead to transfer tasks reflective of more general performance standards:

• The geography, climate, and natural resources of a region influence how its inhabitants live and work. How does where people live influence how they live? Give students a map of a region not yet studied and pose this task: You are leading a group of Asian pilgrims to a new land. Where should you settle and why?

• Cultures share common features while retaining unique qualities. What makes a culture? Are some cultures more "cultured" or "civilized" than others? Transfer your learning about culture by comparing other cultures with your own: For example, you have been hired to produce a tourist Web site for ancient China in which its various traditions and cultures are highlighted to help people from other river civilizations recognize similarities and differences between your culture and theirs.

• The past offers insights into historical patterns, universal themes, and recurring aspects of the human condition. What can we learn from studying other places and times? How (and how much) does the past affect the present? Present the history of a present situation by tracing it back to its historical roots. For example, you are a reporter for *Time* magazine and have been asked to write an essay on the history of Chinese–American relations by tracing the history that led to the current relationship so as to help Americans better understand the Chinese perspective.

Notice that in both examples the standards are reframed in a way that unites the content and transferable big ideas into a coherent and clear set of intellectual priorities. Facts and skills that are more specific are taught in the context of the larger ideas and transfer performances. This approach provides a means of managing large quantities of content knowledge while supporting meaningful learning. Concurrently, clarity is provided about the nature of the assessments demanded by the standards. Such an approach is the only antidote to what far too many schools and districts are now doing: focusing exclusively on the list of (out-of-context) content standards—and the improvement of scores on accompanying accountability tests—as *the* goals. In such cases, the curriculum becomes skewed toward "covering" the isolated content in the standards, especially in the tested subject areas, and local assessments (at both the district and classroom levels) tend to mimic the format of the external tests.

Rather, the content standards should be seen as more of a set of criteria for *auditing* the local integrated curriculum—the building code—and not the shape of what a finished curriculum should look like. As we have noted, a list of content standards is not a true goal; it is an analytical breakdown of elements that need to be considered in framing goals and in determining desired performances. Ironically, this important point is highlighted in many standards documents, such as in the following examples from the Mississippi and New Jersey curriculum frameworks:

> Many of the objectives/benchmarks are interrelated rather than sequential, which means that *objectives/benchmarks are not intended to be taught in the specific order in which they are presented. Multiple objectives/benchmarks can and should be taught at the same time.* (Bounds et al., 2006, p. 8) (emphasis in original)

> NOTE: Although each content standard is discussed in a separate chapter, it is not the intention that each be treated separately in the classroom. Indeed, as noted in the Introduction to this Framework, *an effective curriculum is one that successfully integrates these areas to present students with rich and meaningful cross-strand experiences.* (Rosenstein, Caldwell, & Crown, 1996, p. 175) (emphasis added)

The "goal" in building a house is not to meet the many individual standards in the building code. It's the other way around. An attractive building that satisfies the clients' needs has to be built. The construction must also meet the local building standards, but no beautiful and functional house will ever emerge merely by considering the building code. Unfortunately, that is the equivalent of what many educators are doing in order to discharge what they think is their responsibility to the standards. That's why the overarching performance goals (with their related understandings and questions) are critical for shaping how the content standards are organized and used to guide teaching and assessment.

The concomitant accountability tests should be seen as analogous to a visit by the building inspector to the building site, not as the test of whether all the goals have been embodied and achieved in the design. Or, to shift analogies, the state tests are more like a once-a-year annual physical exam—a brief sampling of indicators to see if we are "healthy." Just as we don't "practice" for our annual physical (because this confuses the *goal* of healthful living with the measures of health), our curriculum should focus on a healthful learning regimen—meaningful and engaging use of content in authentic situations, *not* on decontextualized test preparation.

When curriculum, instruction, and assessment focus on such big ideas and essential questions, they signal to students and parents that the underlying goal of all school efforts is to improve students' understanding of important content so that they can *use* it—not to merely traverse a textbook or practice for standardized tests.

Component 3. K–12 Curriculum Mapping

Curriculum mapping is now a well-established process for orchestrating the scope and sequence of a curriculum to insure a coherent flow across grade levels, avoid unnecessary redundancies, and make sure that important knowledge and skills are not "falling through the cracks." Although we endorse the intent of the process, we have observed that many current curriculum maps unwittingly undermine reform when they simply highlight the content currently being taught without including the long-term performance goals and how to assess them. In other words, the map categories used—knowledge/skill/assessment/activity—ensure that the problems highlighted in this book are not addressed, no matter how much is gained in coherence by mapping.

The most telling failure of most maps is that instead of describing what the teacher is looking for in the learning, they simply summarize in a phrase the *method* of assessment used—for example, "quiz" or "essay." In other words, curriculum maps replicate the inadequacies of state standards when they merely offer an analytic breakdown of instruction in terms of the *inputs* without revealing the desired accomplishments and how to assess them (the *outputs*) related to mission and program goals.

When curriculum mapping builds upon our recommended elements in Stage 1 (long-term transfer goals, understandings, and essential questions), a more coherent and results-focused curriculum follows. The best maps provide a structure for identifying the key understandings and essential questions, and for ensuring that they spiral vertically across grade levels—by design—as a means of developing and deepening students' understanding of important ideas and processes. By also being built around the key (what we call "cornerstone") assessment tasks that have been designed backward from the ultimate transfer goals, the curriculum provides the scaffolding needed to help teachers understand how to avoid coverage and help learners achieve the long-term goals.

In the following pages, we present several segments of more effective curriculum maps at the program, course, and unit levels to highlight what should be included as part of a mission-focused, performance-based curriculum. Although the formats vary somewhat, you'll recognize that each map contains one or more of the key Stage 1 elements we have highlighted thus far—understandings and essential questions, and key performances linked to content standards.

Program-Level Maps Focused on Transfer Goals

The example in Figure 3.7 shows a map of districtwide performance goals for writing at the secondary level. This map illustrates the use of recurring performances, embodied in quarterly writing assessments judged by common rubrics. (An example of one of the district's accompanying rubrics appears in a later section.) This coordinated focus on common assessments related to a common performance goal has brought greater coherence to the instructional program for writing, resulting in improved student performance.

Figure 3.8 presents an example of a program-level curriculum map for world languages framed around big ideas. Note that a more complete version of this map would

Figure 3.7

Map of Districtwide Performance Goals for Writing

Grade	Expository	Persuasive	Literary Analysis	Creative/Expressive
6	Research report	Position paper	Literary essay on setting or conflict	Original myth
7	Autobiography	Policy evaluation	Literary essay on character	Personal writing
8	Research report	Problem/solution essay	Literary essay on symbolism	Narrative fiction
9	Cause/effect essay	Editorial	Analysis of multiple literary elements	Poetry
10	Research report	Social issue essay	Critical lens essay	Historical persona
11	Definition essay	Argumentative essay	Comparative genre essay	Parody/satire
12	Research paper	Position paper	Response to literary criticism	Irony

Source: Greece Central School District, North Greece, New York. Adapted with permission.

Figure 3.8

Program-Level Curriculum Map for World Languages

Enduring Understandings	Essential Questions	New York State Standards
• Each culture has unique characteristics and values. • Geography influences who we are and how we respond to others.	• What impact do geography, culture, and language have on who I am? How I live? My view of the community? My view of the world?	CulA1a CulB1a, CulB1b, CulB1c, CulB1d
• Language requires you to solve problems. • You can't identify and correct your mistakes unless you have the courage to make them. • There are multiple ways to express the same idea.	• What do I do when I'm stuck? How am I working to get myself out of it?	A1a, A1b, A1c, A1d B1a, B1c, B1d, B1e, B1f, B2a, B2b, B2c, B2e
• Each culture has unique characteristics and values. • Language connects people. • Some gestures are culture specific.	• What can I learn about my own language and culture from the study of others?	CulA1a CulB1a, CulB1b, CulB1c, CulB1d
• The interplay between language and culture enriches and accelerates learning.	• Where do I go to experience this language? Where can I go?	A1a, A1b, A1d B1a, B1b, B1c CulA1a, CulB1a, CulB1b, CulB1c, CulB1d
• There are multiple ways to express the same idea. • Language acquisition requires much more than word-for-word translation. • You can't identify and correct your mistakes unless you have the courage to make them. • The language(s) that you already know can help you learn a new one. • What I say (and what I think I'm saying) may be different than what is received.	• What adjustments do I have to make to acquire this language?	A1b, A1c B1d, B1f, B2b CulA1a CulB1c, CulB1d
• Body language, gestures, and tone can add to or detract from the message. • Listening is an active part of language acquisition.	• What is the speaker trying to communicate? How does the delivery influence my response?	A1a, A1b, A1c, A2a B1a, B1b, B2a, B2b, B2c CulA1a CulB1c, CulB1d
• Body language, gestures, and tone can add to or detract from the message. • What I say (and what I think I'm saying) may be different than what is received.	• What am I trying to communicate? How does my delivery influence audience response?	A1d, A2b B1c, B1d, B1e, B1f, B2d, B2e, B2f CulA1a CulB1c, CulB1d A2a

(Figure continued next page)

Figure 3.8

Program-Level Curriculum Map for World Languages *(continued)*

Enduring Understandings	Essential Questions	New York State Standards
• Some words are more important than others. • There are clues in the text to help you figure out the meaning. • Language acquisition requires much more than word-for-word translation.	• What is the text trying to communicate? How does the delivery influence the interpretation?	B2a, B2b, B2c
• Some words are more important than others. • There are clues in the text to help you figure out the meaning. • Listening is an active part of language acquisition. • The clarity of the question you ask determines the usefulness of the response.	• How do I get the information I want?	A1a, A1c, A1d, A2a B1a, B1b, B1d, B1f, B2a, B2b, B2c, B2d
• There are clues in the text to help you figure out the meaning. • Some words are more important than others. • Language acquisition requires much more than word-for-word translation.	• How do I figure out meaning when I don't understand all of the words?	A1a, A1b, A1c, A2a B1a, B1b, B2a, B2b, B2c
• Conversations are more than just questions and answers.	• How can I keep the conversation going?	A1c, A1d B1c, B1e, B1f
• Language connects people. • There are multiple ways to express the same idea. • You are judged by what you say and how you say it.	• How do the words I choose show consideration for my audience?	A1d, A2b B1c, B1d, B1e, B1f, B2d, B2e, B2f CulA1a CulB1c, CulB1d
• Language connects people. • Geography influences who we are and how we respond to others. • The interplay between language and culture enriches and accelerates learning.	• How are language and culture linked?	B2f CulA1a, CulB1a, CulB1b, CulB1c, CulB1d
• Language connects people. • People appreciate your effort to learn and use their language. • Being multilingual makes you more qualified to work in an increasingly global society.	• How does learning a language open up doors of opportunity?	A1a, A2b B1b, B1c, B2a, B2d, B2f CulA1a CulB1a, CulB1b, CulB1c, CulB1d

Source: Nanuet Public Schools, Nanuet, New York. Reprinted with permission.

include cornerstone performance tasks and developmental rubrics, such as those developed by the American Council on the Teaching of Foreign Languages (1998).

Course-Level Maps

Figure 3.9 is an example of a framework for building a course syllabus in U.S. history. Notice that the column headings contain the state standards for "process," and the rows turn the key content into recurring essential questions. Notice also that the course design features conceptual and performance threads to connect the otherwise discrete unit topics, helping learners come to understand the big ideas and key tasks at the heart of "doing" history.

Unit-Level Maps

Some school districts develop curriculum maps down to the unit level. Figure 3.10 is an example of a unit-level map for 3rd grade mathematics from Montgomery County, Maryland. Again, you'll note that the more specific performance indicators are clustered under larger ideas (enduring understandings) and essential questions.

Component 4. Cornerstone Assessments and Collections of Evidence

In education, *what* we choose to assess and *how* we assess it makes concrete what we value and what our goals really mean in practice. For example, if we *say* that we value critical thinking in history, how will we assess for it? What does critical thinking look like as a *specific* task in 10th grade U.S. history or 5th grade geography? The curriculum must answer these questions. To signal that content should be viewed as a resource, we must ensure that curriculum is designed backward from key assessment tasks reflective of key performance goals. In other words, the evidence that we collect signals to students what is most important for them to learn and how to learn. If we do not assess it, it's seen as unimportant. A school or district that values understanding and transfer signals that these goals are important through the assessments it embeds within the curriculum.

Currently, few schools or districts have a robust assessment system that is designed from the start to align closely with standards, program goals, or long-term mission. In part, this is because few educators have been adequately trained to design valid assessments of broader, long-term goals. Moreover, the great majority of classroom- and district-level assessments tend to focus on content mastery and the lower-order cognitive processes of Bloom's Taxonomy, not on understanding and performance on complex tasks that demand transfer.

Yet it is just these latter kinds of assessments that are needed to provide evidence that students truly understand and can apply their learning. Accordingly, we

Figure 3.9

Course-Level Framework for U.S. History

	Key Challenges in Doing History						
Essential Questions of U.S. History	1. Identify and evaluate the validity and usefulness of sources, primary and secondary.	2. Apply an understanding of the past to an analysis of the present and a prediction of the future.	3. Analyze and synthesize conflicting historical accounts and interpretations.	4. Demonstrate perspective in considering other narratives, interpretations, arguments.	5. Critique the work of other historians; identify slant, bias, distortion, oversight, and misinterpretation.	6. Develop an independent thesis, and support it to construct a sound historical argument.	7. Construct and defend a historical narrative—your story.
A. Who is an American? Says who? How has the answer changed, and why?							
B. Who has the power and who doesn't, in theory and in fact? How and why have the location and balance of power changed over time?							
C. What is the ideal role of our government? When is it too much, too little, just right?							
D. *E pluribus unum*—what should it mean? What has it meant?							
E. How democratic is the United States? How has democracy been advanced and been undermined in our history, and why?							

F. How and why has America changed? When has it been evolution and when revolution? Which debates are timeless and which new? Healthy or unhealthy?							
G. In terms of key policy decisions and new law: What *really* happens? How important is the "almighty dollar"? The "people"? The elite? Religion? Politics? Rights? "Factions"? Media?							
H. What is the American Dream? Is it real or a hoax? What has been its impact, regardless?							
I. What is the pioneer spirit and how has it influenced national politics and international relations? When has it helped us and when has it hurt us?							
J. Why have we fought? When have those fights been just or needed and when wrong or foolish? How did we get in and how did we get out, and why?							
K. Life, liberty, and the pursuit of happiness: what does it mean? Are we more or less free than our founders envisioned?							

Figure 3.10
Unit-Level Map for 3rd Grade Mathematics

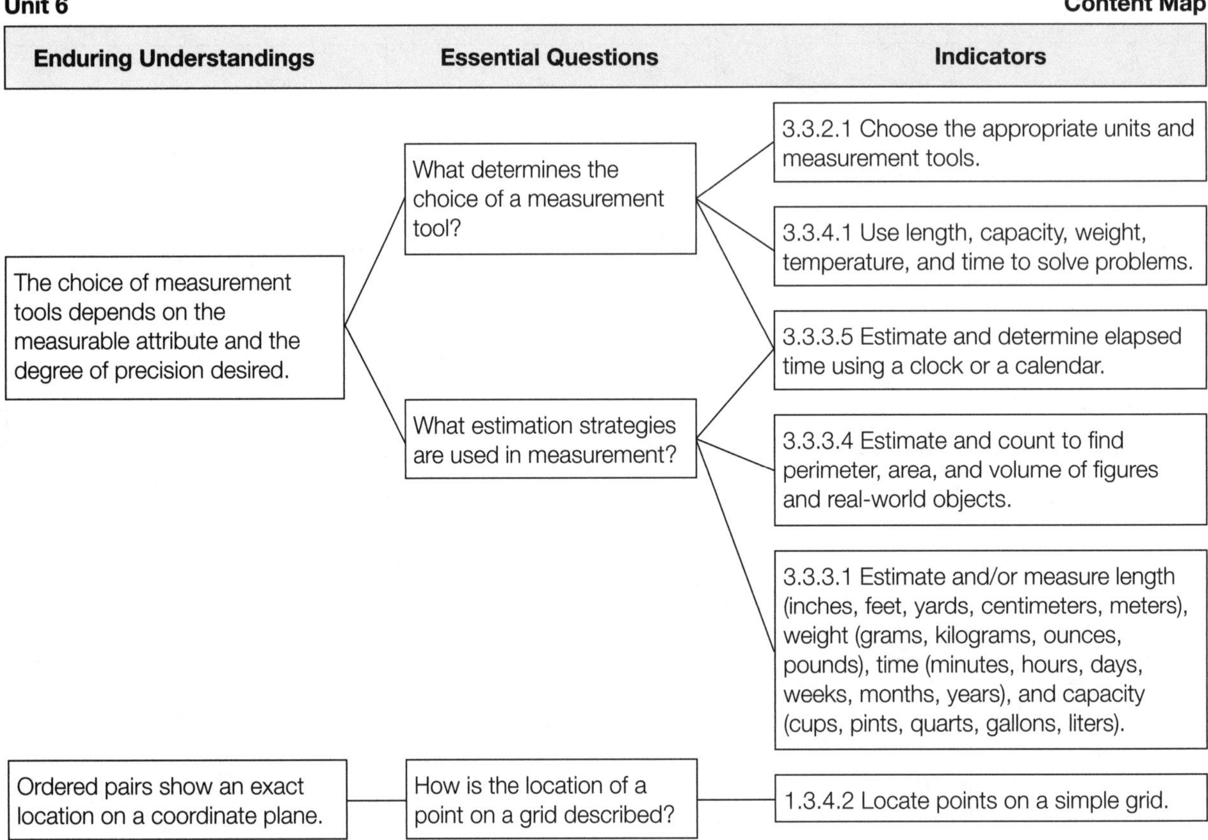

DRAFT—Grade 3
Unit 6
Content Map
Enduring Understandings
Essential Questions
Indicators
What determines the choice of a measurement tool?
3.3.2.1 Choose the appropriate units and measurement tools.
3.3.4.1 Use length, capacity, weight, temperature, and time to solve problems.
The choice of measurement tools depends on the measurable attribute and the degree of precision desired.
3.3.3.5 Estimate and determine elapsed time using a clock or a calendar.
What estimation strategies are used in measurement?
3.3.3.4 Estimate and count to find perimeter, area, and volume of figures and real-world objects.
3.3.3.1 Estimate and/or measure length (inches, feet, yards, centimeters, meters), weight (grams, kilograms, ounces, pounds), time (minutes, hours, days, weeks, months, years), and capacity (cups, pints, quarts, gallons, liters).
Ordered pairs show an exact location on a coordinate plane.
How is the location of a point on a grid described?
1.3.4.2 Locate points on a simple grid.

Source: Montgomery County Public Schools, © 2003 Montgomery County, Maryland. Adapted with permission.

recommend that educators identify *cornerstone* performance assessments, of increasing complexity and reflecting authentic contexts, to anchor the curriculum. Just as an anchor prevents boats from aimless drift, these assessments are designed to prevent "curriculum drift" by focusing content instruction around important *recurring* performances. It is only when students are able to apply their learning thoughtfully and flexibly to a new situation that they are able to demonstrate true understanding of the content. When we call for authentic application, we do not mean recall of basic facts or mechanical plug-in of a memorized formula. Rather, we call for students to transfer—to use what they know in a new and realistic situation.

Some of the cornerstone assessments will reflect recurring performances, such as those seen in the secondary writing examples from Greece, New York. Certain program areas, such as athletics, writing, and world languages, are familiar with recurring performances, where the same genres or performance situations keep occurring over time. What changes are the complexity and open-endedness of the performance demands, and expectations for the learners. Other cornerstone tasks are more specific to the content goals for a course or unit.

Here are three examples of more specific performance assessment tasks for secondary students (Figures 3.11–3.13). Notice that each example is authentic in nature; in other words, students are asked to apply what they have learned in ways that reflect real-world uses of knowledge and skills. The tasks require thoughtful application and transfer—and are thus markedly different from the decontextualized, selected-response items featured on most standardized accountability tests. Also, notice that these particular tasks are connected to recurring performances, which are shown at the bottom of each figure.

These tasks are substantive in nature and require students to apply factual knowledge, concepts, and skills along with higher-order thinking (e.g., evaluation)

Figure 3.11

Tour Director, Secondary World Languages

Level I—You are required to take a "trip" around the school (or town or mall). Incorporate the following vocabulary: *directions* (left, right, near, far, next to, etc.), *places* (classrooms, cafeteria, gym, library, labs, churches, police and fire stations, schools, restaurants, stores) and *transportation* (bus, taxi, train, car, bike, stairs, escalators, elevators). Keep sentences simple and narrate—in the target language—your "trip" to five *places* using a variety of *directions* and *transportation*.

Level II—You are to plan a trip to the capital of [fill in country]. You will be in that city for only two days. Keep a diary—in the target language—and tell which places you have visited and what you have seen. Be sure that these places are close enough to each other to be visited in a two-day period and are open on the days you will be there.

Level III—You have been selected by the members of the World Languages Club to plan their annual trip to two of the countries whose languages are studied in your school. You must plan an itinerary that will include at least five places of cultural and historic importance. You must include at lease one site/activity that might be of particular interest to teenagers (e.g., Euro Disney, a bullfight, or a soccer game). Use public transportation wherever possible. Create a brochure to advertise the trip and be prepared to give a presentation to those students who may be interested in traveling with you.

Level IV—You are traveling in the foreign country of your choice on business. Be prepared to role play, with a partner(s), making reservations with the airline and the hotel; narrate: arriving and checking in at the airport in the United States; going through customs upon landing; and getting to the hotel by taxi. Since you will have some limited time when you are not involved in your business dealings, you will want to make some brief cultural excursions and will need to get information from and make arrangements with the concierge in your hotel.

Source: World Languages Department, Woodbury High School, Woodbury, New Jersey.

Recurring Performance: Successfully communicate in the target language in realistically complicated and "messy" situations.

Figure 3.12

Analyzing a Mixture ("Sludge") in Science

In pairs, 8th grade students must analyze a complex "sludge" into its constituent parts (solids and liquids), drawing upon over a dozen individual techniques that they learned and used in individual labs throughout the year. Each pair has a different mixture. They draw from their portfolio of prior lab work to recall how to do the techniques, sometimes having to redo individual labs as they find flaws in their original work. Finally, having identified the elements of their "sludge," they present their findings to the class, where their results and methods are critiqued. The entire year of science is naturally designed backward from the demands of the "sludge" investigations.

Source: South-Orange Maplewood, New Jersey.

Recurring Performance: Successfully identify and control for variables in the design, debugging, and execution of scientific experiments.

Figure 3.13

Public Policy Letter for Social Studies/History/Civics, Grade 12

After investigating a current political issue, write a letter to a public policy maker regarding the official's position on that issue. Assume that this public policy maker is opposed to the student's position. You will be given documentation of the public policy maker's position and background information. You will be given a choice of several situations if the materials do not propose an issue.

Your letter should present your opinion and attempt to persuade the public policy maker to vote accordingly.

Source: Adapted from Littleton High School, Colorado.

Recurring Performance: Successfully identify purpose and audience and tailor communication and content to that context.

and habits of mind (e.g., persistence) in order to achieve successful results. Although these particular tasks are targeted for secondary-level students, earlier grades would help prepare students to perform well. Cornerstone assessment tasks need not be showcase events or special projects. Instead, they should be viewed by students as *typical* assessments, constantly recurring in different guises—the equivalent of a decathlon in each subject area.

Authentic transfer tasks such as these serve as more than just a means of gathering assessment evidence. These tasks are, by design, "worth teaching to" because they embody worthy learning goals and accomplishments by design. Additionally, they provide meaningful and concrete learning targets for students when presented at the beginning of a course or a unit. Greater transparency in assessment is needed if important performance standards are going to be met. Students must know the tasks to be mastered well in advance, and those tasks must repeatedly recur if they are to master them—just as happens in the wider world, where test secrecy would be foolish if not downright immoral.

Consider the athletic analogy once again. Coaches routinely conduct drills to develop and refine basic skills, and these drills are purposefully pointed toward performance in the game. Too often, however, classroom instruction and assessment overemphasize decontextualized drills and provide too few opportunities for students to actually "play the game." Just as in sports, both are necessary in the classroom. Students need to learn key facts and master the basics, and skill drills support that need. But learners also need a chance to use their knowledge and skills—to play an actual game. Authentic performance tasks provide a worthy goal and help students see a reason for learning the basics.

Collections of Evidence

It is useful to think of cornerstone assessments and the tasks derived from them as providing *evidence* of learning, understanding, and transfer. As such, cornerstone assessments can contribute to *collections* of student work, embodied in singular tasks and supplemented by other evidence. The use of portfolios as a means of collecting evidence is well established in the arts, writing, and technical subjects, and we encourage that they be considered for use in all program areas.

A portfolio is a purposeful collection of student work that exhibits the student's effort, progress, and achievements in one or more areas over a significant period of time. Unlike the information from a "snapshot" assessment taken at a point in time, a portfolio functions more like a photo album containing a variety of photos taken at different times and in a variety of contexts. It is this "over time" quality that makes portfolios so well suited to documenting development, growth, and improvement.

Prior to establishing a portfolio system, educators must carefully consider the intended purposes. Most often, portfolios are used to document achievement and progress, showcase "best" work, evaluate performance, or communicate with parents, higher-education prospects, or employers. Once the purpose for keeping a portfolio is established, other portfolio decisions follow—what kind of student work to include ("best" work, representative work, work related to a specific subject), who should decide what work is included (student, teacher, student and teacher), and who should own and manage the portfolio (student, teacher, school district). Figures 3.14 and 3.15 present examples of possible portfolio entries for fine arts, language arts, and mathematics.

Recognizing the communications value of actual samples of student work, many schools and teachers are using a student's portfolio as the centerpiece of parent

Figure 3.14

A Portfolio Assessment Framework for Fine Arts

Course	Elements of the Portfolio	Portfolio Expectations
Fundamentals of Art (Fulfills Fine Arts Graduation Requirement)	• Pre-instruction diagnostic evaluation • Three artworks representing "benchmarks of progress" • Sketchbook/journal • Midterm examination • Final examination	Process Portfolio and three "benchmark works" emphasizing evidence of artistic growth in— ◦ using sketches and notes to generate ideas and experiment with media ◦ solving visual problems that reflect quality in concept/idea development, planning, and execution ◦ developing technical proficiency with media ◦ reflecting on progress and process
Fine Arts	• Fundamentals of Art Portfolio • Six benchmark artworks ◦ two quality drawings ◦ four other media to demonstrate breadth • Sketchbook/journal • Midterm examination or performance task (locally designed) • Final examination or performance task (locally designed)	Best Works Portfolio (6+ best works and process samples) showing evidence of artistic growth in— ◦ using sketches and notes to generate ideas and experiment with media ◦ solving visual problems that reflect quality in planning and execution ◦ creating artworks showing technical proficiency with media ◦ creating artworks representing breadth in ideas and use of media ◦ reflecting on progress and process
Studio I GT/AP	• Fine Arts Portfolio • Minimum of 12 artworks • Sketchbook/journal • Midterm examination or performance task (locally designed) • Final examination or performance task (locally designed)	Best Works Portfolio (12+ best works and process samples) showing evidence of continued artistic growth in— ◦ using sketches and notes to generate and refine ideas ◦ solving visual problems in an area of concentration showing quality in planning and execution ◦ creating artworks showing technical proficiency with media ◦ creating artworks showing breadth in use of media ◦ reflecting on progress and process
Studio II GT/AP	Similar expectations as above plus Studio I GT/AP portfolio	Similar to above

Source: Baltimore County Public Schools, Maryland. Adapted with permission.

conferences. Increasingly, students are being involved as active conference participants, describing and explaining the work in their portfolio as barometers of their growth toward desired accomplishments. The portfolios should provide evidence of not merely content mastery or fun projects but the ability to transfer learning in a variety of media and situations that are valid and authentic. Coupled with developmental rubrics, portfolios offer concrete evidence of learning and growth, providing

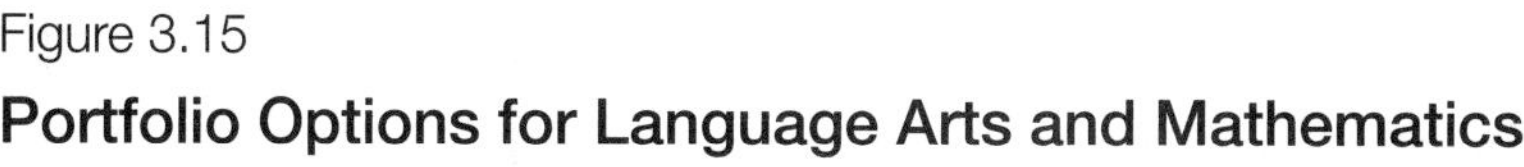

Figure 3.15

Portfolio Options for Language Arts and Mathematics

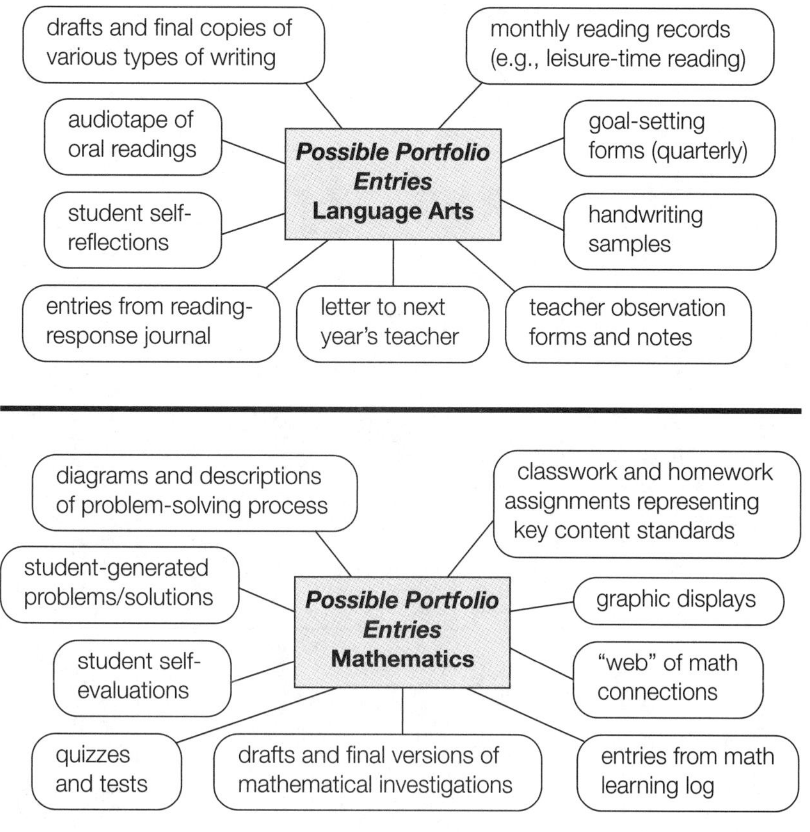

the equivalent of a learner's résumé of accomplishments instead of simply a transcript of letter grades and Carnegie units.

Component 5. Analytic and Longitudinal Rubrics

A rubric is a criterion-based evaluation tool, consisting of a fixed measurement scale (such as four "score points") and descriptions of the characteristics for each score point. Holistic and analytic rubrics are used to judge the degree of understanding or proficiency revealed through student products and performances. A holistic rubric provides an overall impression of a student's work. Holistic rubrics yield a *single* score or rating for a product or performance. An analytic rubric divides a product or performance into distinct traits or dimensions and judges each separately, with a separate score for each. Analytic rubrics provide the kind of specific and useful feedback necessary for grasping the elements of quality performance at each level and making improvements. Figure 3.16 is an example of an analytic rubric for persuasive writing from the Greece Central School District in New York.

Figure 3.16

Rubric for Persuasive Writing at the Secondary Level

Skill Area	6 Responses at this level:	5 Responses at this level:	4 Responses at this level:	3 Responses at this level:	2 Responses at this level:	1 Responses at this level:
Meaning: The extent to which the writing exhibits sound understanding, analysis, and explanation of the writing task and text(s).	• Convey an accurate and in-depth understanding of the topic, audience, and purpose for the writing task. • Offer insightful and thorough analysis and explanation in support of the argument or position.	• Convey an accurate and complete understanding of the topic, audience, and purpose for the writing task. • Offer clear and explicit analysis and explanation in support of the argument or position.	• Convey an accurate although somewhat basic understanding of the topic, audience, and purpose for the writing task. • Offer partial analysis and explanation in support of the argument or position.	• Convey a partly accurate understanding of the topic, audience, and purpose of the writing task. • Offer limited analysis or superficial explanation that only partially supports the argument or position.	• Convey a confused or largely inaccurate understanding of the topic, audience, and purpose for the writing task. • Offer unclear analysis or unwarranted explanations that fail to support the argument or position.	• Provide no evidence of understanding the writing task or topic. • Make incoherent explanations that do not support the argument or position.
Development: The extent to which ideas are elaborated using specific and relevant details and/or evidence to support the thesis.	• Support the position clearly and fully with arguments that effectively integrate and elaborate on specific ideas and textual evidence from a variety of sources. • Effectively anticipate and convincingly refute opposing viewpoints.	• Support the position clearly and consistently with arguments that incorporate and explain ideas and specific textual evidence from a variety of sources. • Anticipate and somewhat convincingly refute opposing viewpoints.	• Support the position with arguments that use ideas and relevant textual evidence from a variety of sources. • Anticipate and attempt to refute opposing viewpoints at a basic level.	• Support the position partially, using some ideas and textual evidence but without much elaboration or from limited sources. • Partially anticipate and with a limited or confused attempt to refute opposing viewpoints.	• Attempt to support the position, but textual ideas and evidence are vague, repetitive, or unjustified. • Allude to opposing viewpoints but make no attempt to refute them.	• Completely lack development and do not include textual evidence. • Make no attempt to anticipate or refute opposing viewpoints.
Organization: The extent to which the writing establishes a clear thesis and maintains direction, focus, and coherence.	• Skillfully establish and maintain consistent focus on a clear and compelling thesis. • Exhibit logical and coherent structure with claims,	• Effectively establish and maintain consistent focus on a clear thesis. • Exhibit a logical sequence of claims, evidence, and interpretations	• Establish and maintain focus on a clear thesis. • Exhibit a logical sequence of claims, evidence, and interpretations, but ideas within paragraphs	• Establish but fail to consistently maintain focus on a basic thesis. • Exhibit a basic structure but lack the coherence of consis-	• Establish a confused or irrelevant thesis and fail to maintain focus. • Exhibit an attempt to organize ideas into a beginning,	• Fail to include a thesis or maintain focus. • Completely lack organization and coherence.

	evidence, and interpretations that convincingly support the thesis. • Make skillful use of transition words and phrases.	to support the thesis. • Make effective use of transition words and phrases.	may be inconsistently organized. • Make some attempt to use basic transition words and phrases.	tent claims, evidence, and interpretations. • Make an inconsistent attempt to use some basic transition words or phrases.	middle, and end, but lack coherence. • Make little attempt to use transition words and phrases.	• Make no attempt to use transition words or phrases.
Language: The extent to which the writing reveals an awareness of audience and purpose through word choice and sentence variety.	• Are stylistically sophisticated, using language that is precise and engaging, with a notable sense of voice and awareness of audience and purpose. • Effectively incorporate a range of varied sentence patterns to reveal syntactic fluency.	• Use language that is fluent and original, with evident awareness of audience and purpose. • Incorporate varied sentence patterns that reveal an awareness of different syntactic structures.	• Use appropriate language, with some awareness of audience and purpose. • Make some attempt to include different sentence patterns but with awkward or uneven success.	• Rely on basic vocabulary, with little awareness of audience or purpose. • Reveal a limited awareness of how to vary sentence patterns and rely on a limited range of syntactic structures.	• Use language that is imprecise or unsuitable for the audience or purpose. • Reveal a confused understanding of how to write in complete sentences and little or no ability to vary sentence patterns.	• Use language that is incoherent or inappropriate. • Include a preponderance of sentence fragments and run-ons that significantly hinder comprehension.
Conventions: The extent to which the writing exhibits conventional spelling, punctuation, paragraphing, capitalization, and grammar.	• Demonstrate control of the conventions with essentially no errors, even with sophisticated language.	• Demonstrate control of the conventions, exhibiting occasional errors only when using sophisticated language (e.g., punctuation of complex sentences).	• Demonstrate partial control, exhibiting occasional errors that do not hinder comprehension (e.g., incorrect use of homonyms).	• Demonstrate emerging control, exhibiting frequent errors that somewhat hinder comprehension (e.g., agreement of pronouns and antecedents; spelling of basic words).	• Demonstrate lack of control, exhibiting frequent errors that make comprehension difficult (e.g., subject-verb agreement, use of slang).	• Are illegible or unrecognizable as literate English.

Source: Greece Central School District, North Greece, New York. Adapted with permission.

Teachers and curriculum developers have struggled to understand what is expected of them in states and provinces where the standards and benchmarks consist of nothing more than lists of broad, declarative statements of what students should know and be able to do. The job of curriculum and assessment design becomes easier when the standards and benchmarks are framed by performance indicators or performance standards, because these signal what types of performances and what level of performance are expected as an outgrowth of learning the facts, concepts, and skills listed in the standards. The performance indicators suggest the kinds of assessments that are needed, and the performance standards provide the basis for evaluating and reporting how well the expected performance was achieved. Figure 3.17 illustrates how a standard and a set of corresponding benchmarks in language arts are reflected through performance standards, described within a four-point rubric.

Figure 3.17

Rubric for a State Performance Standard in Speaking and Listening

Content Standard 3—Speaking and Listening Students use listening and speaking skills for a variety of purposes and audiences.	
Benchmarks for Grade 4	**Performance Standards Level Descriptors Grade 4**
1. Students speak on a focused topic with organization, volume, posture, pace, eye contact, and relevant gestures. 2. Students use speaking strategies appropriate to different types of presentations. 3. Students understand techniques used in various media such as basic propaganda techniques. 4. Students read aloud their own and others' texts fluently and expressively. 5. Students speak and listen in small groups cooperatively.	*Advanced Performance* 4th grade students performing at the advanced level speak with a clearly intended purpose and audience. Ideas are presented clearly and supported by specific and precise details with strong oral delivery skills and clear, relevant feedback. *Proficient Performance* 4th graders performing at the proficient level speak with an intended purpose and audience. Ideas are supported with sufficient, relevant details. They exhibit appropriate organizational and delivery skills when speaking and provide relevant feedback while actively listening. *Basic Performance* 4th graders performing at the basic level need support to show evidence of intended purpose and audience when speaking. Ideas are evident, but supporting details may be minimal or irrelevant. Organization and delivery skills are sufficient with support. Students provide minimal feedback during active listening. *Below Basic Performance* 4th grade speakers/listeners performing at the below basic level require extensive support or provide little or no evidence in meeting the standard.

Source: Wyoming Department of Education, 2003.

Longitudinal Rubrics

Given a school mission and set of program goals, how should we measure progress toward those goals? We do not think that this question has ever been adequately considered in mainstream U.S. education. Why? Because most curricula are built in terms of short-term content exposures, rather than around long-term performance goals and recurring big ideas. As it stands now, the primary measures of progress are test scores and course grades. These can be thought of as snapshots, or discrete data points on separate scales that cannot add up to a coherent measure of progress toward end goals. What we believe is needed is akin to a motion picture—a continuous stream of images that can provide teachers, students, and parents with a more detailed and accurate picture of learning and growth. Analogies include the degree of difficulty schemes in diving and figure skating, the colored belts in the martial arts, and the graded licenses in the technical trades, such as plumbing and carpentry.

A third type of rubric—longitudinal—describes mission-related growth along a fixed, novice-to-expert continuum, in which each level represents a key benchmark on the road to exit-level performance. These longitudinal rubrics provide a basis for designing backward from mastery performance so that teachers and learners at all levels know where they stand along a developmental continuum against exit-level performance goals. Longitudinal rubrics are not tied to any particular performance or assessment task. Rather, the rubrics enable teachers, parents, and learners to chart *progress* toward desired accomplishments.

We propose that longitudinal rubrics should provide the "performance backbone" for every subject area in the curriculum. A hint of such an approach was provided in the Delaware history example that charts the sophistication of thinking about chronology and causality over the course of a student's career. Indeed, such systems already exist. In Great Britain, longitudinal rubrics have been in place nationally since the mid-1990s in all subject areas, even as developmental rubrics in literacy have been used for decades in Australia and New Zealand. Figure 3.18 presents an example of longitudinal rubrics in science from England's national curriculum. Similar longitudinal rubrics exist for every subject area. The entire curriculum and rubrics (called "attainment targets" in the national curriculum) can be found at www.nc.uk.net/.

In the United States, Samuel Meisels developed the Omnibus system for literacy development. Other groups such as the American Council on the Teaching of Foreign Languages (2003) have created developmental rubrics for listening, speaking, reading, and writing for use in gauging performance in world languages (see www.actfl.org). Similarly, the National Assessment of Educational Progess, often termed "The Nation's Report Card," uses longitudinal scales for describing performance levels and equating scores in its tests (see www.nagb.org/).

Figure 3.18

Longitudinal Rubric for Scientific Inquiry

Level 1
Pupils describe or respond appropriately to simple features of objects, living things and events they observe, communicating their findings in simple ways, *for example, talking about their work, through drawings, simple charts*.

Level 2
Pupils respond to suggestions about how to find things out and, with help, make their own suggestions about how to collect data to answer questions. They use simple texts, with help, to find information. They use simple equipment provided and make observations related to their task. They observe and compare objects, living things and events. They describe their observations using scientific vocabulary and record them, using simple tables when appropriate. They say whether what happened was what they expected.

Level 3
Pupils respond to suggestions and put forward their own ideas about how to find the answer to a question. They recognize why it is important to collect data to answer questions. They use simple texts to find information. They make relevant observations and measure quantities, such as length or mass, using a range of simple equipment. Where appropriate, they carry out a fair test with some help, recognizing and explaining why it is fair. They record their observations in a variety of ways. They provide explanations for observations and for simple patterns in recorded measurements. They communicate in a scientific way what they have found out and suggest improvements in their work.

Level 4
Pupils recognize that scientific ideas are based on evidence. In their own investigative work, they decide on an appropriate approach, *for example, using a fair test* to answer a question. Where appropriate, they describe, or show in the way they perform their task, how to vary one factor while keeping others the same. Where appropriate, they make predictions. They select information from sources provided for them. They select suitable equipment and make a series of observations and measurements that are adequate for the task. They record their observations, comparisons and measurements using tables and bar charts. They begin to plot points to form simple graphs, and use these graphs to point out and interpret patterns in their data. They begin to relate their conclusions to these patterns and to scientific knowledge and understanding, and to communicate them with appropriate scientific language. They suggest improvements in their work, giving reasons.

Level 5
Pupils describe how experimental evidence and creative thinking have been combined to provide a scientific explanation, *for example, Jenner's work on vaccination at key stage 2, Lavoisier's work on burning at key stage 3*. When they try to answer a scientific question, they identify an appropriate approach. They select from a range of sources of information. When the investigation involves a fair test, they identify key factors to be considered. Where appropriate, they make predictions based on their scientific knowledge and understanding. They select apparatus for a range of tasks and plan to use it effectively. They make a series of observations, comparisons or measurements with precision appropriate to the task. They begin to repeat observations and measurements and to offer simple explanations for any differences they encounter. They record observations and measurements systematically and, where appropriate, present data as line graphs. They draw conclusions that are consistent with the evidence and begin to relate these to scientific knowledge and understanding. They make practical suggestions about how their working methods could be improved. They use appropriate scientific language and conventions to communicate quantitative and qualitative data.

Level 6
Pupils describe evidence for some accepted scientific ideas and explain how the interpretation of evidence by scientists leads to the development and acceptance of new ideas. In their own

investigative work, they use scientific knowledge and understanding to identify an appropriate approach. They select and use sources of information effectively. They make enough measurements, comparisons and observations for the task. They measure a variety of quantities with precision, using instruments with fine-scale divisions. They choose scales for graphs and diagrams that enable them to show data and features effectively. They identify measurements and observations that do not fit the main pattern shown. They draw conclusions that are consistent with the evidence and use scientific knowledge and understanding to explain them. They make reasoned suggestions about how their working methods could be improved. They select and use appropriate methods for communicating qualitative and quantitative data using scientific language and conventions.

Level 7
Pupils describe some predictions based on scientific theories and give examples of the evidence collected to test these predictions. In their own work, they use scientific knowledge and understanding to decide on appropriate approaches to questions. They identify the key factors in complex contexts and in contexts in which variables cannot readily be controlled, and plan appropriate procedures. They synthesize information from a range of sources, and identify possible limitations in secondary data. They make systematic observations and measurements with precision, using a wide range of apparatus. They identify when they need to repeat measurements, comparisons and observations in order to obtain reliable data. Where appropriate, they represent data in graphs, using lines of best fit. They draw conclusions that are consistent with the evidence and explain these using scientific knowledge and understanding. They begin to consider whether the data they have collected are sufficient for the conclusions they have drawn. They communicate what they have done using a wide range of scientific and technical language and conventions, including symbols and flow diagrams.

Level 8
Pupils give examples of scientific explanations or models that have had to be changed in the light of additional scientific evidence. They evaluate and synthesize data from a range of sources. They recognize that investigating different kinds of scientific questions requires different strategies, and use scientific knowledge and understanding to select an appropriate strategy in their own work. They decide which observations are relevant in qualitative work and include suitable detail in their records. They decide the level of precision needed in comparisons or measurements, and collect data enabling them to test relationships between variables. They identify and begin to explain anomalous observations and measurements and allow for these when they draw graphs. They use scientific knowledge and understanding to draw conclusions from their evidence. They consider graphs and tables of results critically. They communicate findings and arguments using appropriate scientific language and conventions, showing awareness of a range of views.

Exceptional performance
Pupils give examples of scientific explanations and models that have been challenged by subsequent experiments and explain the significance of the evidence in modifying scientific theories. They evaluate and synthesize data from a range of sources. They recognize that investigating different kinds of scientific questions requires different strategies, and use scientific knowledge and understanding to select an appropriate strategy in their own work. They make records of relevant observations and comparisons, clearly identifying points of particular significance. They decide the level of precision needed in measurements and collect data that satisfy these requirements. They use their data to test relationships between variables. They identify and explain anomalous observations and measurements, allowing for these when they draw graphs. They use scientific knowledge and understanding to interpret trends and patterns and to draw conclusions from their evidence. They consider graphs and tables of results critically and give reasoned accounts of how they could collect additional evidence. They communicate findings and arguments using appropriate scientific language and conventions, showing their awareness of the degree of uncertainty and a range of alternative views.

Source: National curriculum materials for England. © 1999 Department for Education and Skills and the Qualifications and Curriculum Authority. Reprinted by permission.

The attention to grade-level objectives, called for by No Child Left Behind (NCLB) and other standards-based initiatives, is necessary but insufficient and potentially counterproductive. NCLB provides no guidance for how to ensure that the curriculum progresses toward exit-level standards. The attainment of long-term performance goals will be more likely if we have a systematic capacity for assessing current performance, tracking progress, and targeting needed instruction. Longitudinal rubrics provide the tools for such benchmarking.

Common sense tells us that we need feedback against our long-term goals, not just scores on individual quizzes and tests, if we are to know how to properly move forward. Districts need to ensure that everyone at every level of the system is getting the feedback against long-term goals that they need, or the key long-term goals will never penetrate day-to-day thinking or schoolwork.

Needed: Common Rubrics

Well-designed rubrics, based on clearly defined criteria, communicate the important dimensions in a product or performance. When common rubrics are used throughout a department or grade-level team, school, or district, the result is more consistent evaluation because the performance criteria do not vary from teacher to teacher. Common rubrics also support standards-based grading and reporting, and help to reduce the apples-and-oranges problem of teachers emphasizing different factors in their grading.

Common rubrics provide more than just evaluation tools to use at the end of instruction; they help clarify instructional goals and serve as teaching and learning targets. Educators who have worked in teams to score student work often observe that the very process of evaluating student work against a common rubric teaches them a great deal about what makes the products and performances successful. As teachers internalize the qualities of solid performance, they become more attentive to those qualities in their teaching.

Common rubrics benefit students as well. When students know the criteria *in advance* of their performance, they are provided with clear goals for their work. There is no mystery as to the desired qualities or the basis for evaluating and grading products and performances. Learners don't have to guess about what is most important or how their work will be judged—both within and *across* classrooms. When they understand a rubric, students can self-assess their work. In this way, common rubrics serve to *enhance* the quality of student learning and support the long-term growth needed to achieve the ultimate transfer goals.

Component 6. Anchor Work Samples

Anchor work samples are examples of student performance that characterize each of the levels (or score points) on a performance scale (or rubric). These anchors provide tangible and specific illustrations of various levels of quality or degrees of proficiency based upon established criteria. The anchor for the top performance level is known as an exemplar.

Anchors help teachers understand and consistently apply the criteria and standards when judging student products or performances. They provide teachers and students with clear targets to motivate and guide their efforts, and they help students to better understand and apply the criteria when engaged in self-assessment and peer assessment.

As noted, the secondary English/language arts curriculum for Greece Central School District in New York includes a foundation of quarterly writing assessments and a set of common rubrics for each writing genre—expository, persuasive, literary analysis, and creative/expressive. Having the cornerstone writing assessments and common rubrics enables the selection of districtwide anchors. Secondary English staff members periodically meet to evaluate students' quarterly writing assessments using common rubrics for each genre. As part of their evaluation, they select and annotate exemplars. An example, a 9th grade persuasive essay, appears in Figure 3.19. Notice that this exemplary paper includes annotations in the margins. The annotated comments, derived from the rubric, identify the specific qualities that qualify this work as exemplary.

Here's a particularly noteworthy aspect of the Greece writing assessment system: the assessment map, writing rubrics, and exemplar papers are all posted on the school district's Web site (see http://web001.greece.k12.ny.us/academics.cfm). All staff, parents, and students have access to the same information. The transparency and accessibility of the district's writing assessment system fosters clarity of expectations, promotes greater consistency of evaluation, and provides models of excellence. In other words, there is no mystery about what is expected, how student work will be judged, and what excellent work looks like.

A growing number of states and provinces have posted similar anchors on their Web sites for their writing assessments. For example, the New York Department of Education provides anchor examples for document-based questions in history. Also, the Advanced Placement (AP) program provides booklets to AP teachers with student samples, scoring rubrics, and scorer commentary. The use of existing systems permits a much closer alignment between local grading and state performance standards, a highly desirable reform to ensure that students as well as teachers get the feedback they need.

Figure 3.19

Exemplar (Anchor) Paper with Annotations

GRADE 9

ANNOTATED EXEMPLAR

Persuasive

School is meant to be a place of learning, an opportunity to acquire knowledge and insight, and it was at Greece Olympia High School that I learned this lesson. It was one of those rainy day mornings when little could be heard above the squeak of wet rubber soles against the tile floor of the freshman hallway. I was heading into homeroom early; I thought I'd be the first to arrive. However, just as I was about to enter the room, I saw that a girl with vibrant brown hair, jeans, and a pink sweater had already gone into the room. Seemingly because her shoes had no texture, with a bottom as smooth as the complexion of her youth, she slipped, hung in the air for a moment, then crashed to the ground. I took a step backward to laugh out in the hall. When I peered back in the room, I expected that after such a fall she would be unable to move. However, she had already leapt to her feet. That's when I noticed her fervent glances. Left and right. Left then right. Her head quickly turned. Satisfied in her anonymity, she slowly, and I believe painfully, walked to her seat.

The writer engages the reader by establishing a context and using an appropriate tone.

The writer's use of imagery helps to create a context for the reader.

The writer utilizes vivid and precise language.

The writer varies sentence patterns for effect.

At that moment, I became consciously aware that people, including myself, seem to concern themselves more with the opinions and wants of others than with what they themselves think or desire. This girl had been so worried about what someone else might think that she didn't even stop to catch her breath. It's no wonder that a phrase like, "What will the neighbors think?" sounds cliché. For years people have been interested in owning a better house, buying a faster car and having a more attractive mate. Yet, are these things going to bring self-fulfillment? Is somehow having these items going to impress people, and, if so, why do we care what these people think? We are raised to do just that. From a young age, we are taught to please mostly our parents, then our teachers, coaches, and friends. From the moment we are born, others expect us to behave, think, and value in a certain way, and being the impressionable youths that we are, we usually unwittingly comply.

The writer chooses and employs specific rhetorical devices to support assertions and strengthen persuasiveness of the argument (anecdote) based on the topic, audience, and purpose.

The writer uses effective interpretation that offers insights.

In subject areas such as music, world languages, and visual arts, some schools and districts are assembling audiotaped and videotaped anchors. For example, in Fairfax County, Virginia, the world languages department has developed districtwide cornerstone assessments for listening, speaking, reading, and writing, along with accompanying rubrics (in both analytic and holistic formats) for Levels 1, 2, 3, and

Advanced (see www.fcps.k12.va.us/DIS/OHSICS/forlang/PALS/rubrics/index.htm). Over the years, teachers in the district have collected audiotaped and videotaped samples of speaking performances in the various languages taught in the district. Committees then select examples to anchor the rubrics for each level. In addition to anchoring the assessment system, the anchors can be used to instruct students and inform parents. At the national level, the AP assessment in art provides similar resources.

Component 7. Enabling Learning Activities and Resources

Curriculum guides typically provide instructional suggestions and helpful resources, but these are often divorced from specific transfer goals, worthy tasks, and performance standards. The learning activities should therefore be those that are most likely to enable learners to achieve success on the cornerstone assessment tasks and meet performance standards related to transfer.

Along with such guidance, we recommend that an understanding-based curriculum guide include specific learning strategies and tools for *students*. After all, *it is the student who must meet the standards*. The degree to which students can perform, self-assess, and self-adjust with the least amount of teacher direction is a crucial element in success. We further suggest that the curriculum provide teachers with instructional protocols to support the kind of constructivist, iterative learning that lies at the heart of coming to understand and learning to effectively transfer. The following sections provide further information and examples of such resources.

Learning Strategies

In every field of endeavor, effective performers use specific techniques and strategies to boost their performance. Olympic athletes visualize flawless performances; writers seek feedback from "critical friends"; law students form study groups; coaches share tips at coaching clinics; busy executives practice time-management techniques. Students also benefit from specific strategies that can improve their learning and performance on academic tasks. For example, webbing and other graphic organizers help students see connections, cognitive reading strategies boost comprehension, brainstorming techniques enhance idea generation, and mnemonics assist retention and recall. Unfortunately, few students spontaneously generate and use such thinking and learning strategies on their own, so the strategies need to be explicitly taught and reinforced using a direct instruction model, such as the following:

1. Introduce and explain the purpose of the strategy.
2. Demonstrate and model its use.

3. Provide guided practice for students to apply the strategy with feedback.
4. Allow students to apply the strategy independently and in teams.
5. Regularly reflect on the appropriate uses of the strategy and its effectiveness.
6. Assess the student's ability to transfer the repertoire of strategies, with less and less teacher prompting over time.

With an increased emphasis on complex performance in the curriculum and assessments, students and teachers will need to understand that increasing student control of a repertoire of key strategies has priority over any particular topical content.

Strategy-Embedded Tools

Many teachers have found it helpful to incorporate thinking and learning strategies into tangible products, such as posters, bookmarks, visual symbols, or cue cards. Figure 3.20 provides an example of a process poster used to reinforce the skill of comparing, one of Marzano's top research-based, "high-yield" instructional techniques (Marzano, 2003). In another example, students in a middle school mathematics class have constructed desktop spinners depicting six problem-solving strategies they've been taught (Figure 3.21). The spinners provide students with a tangible reminder of the value of using strategies during problem solving.

Teaching Protocols

Teaching for understanding and transfer requires an instructional shift from simply covering content to helping learners *construct meaning* about important ideas. Fortunately, a variety of research-validated teaching methods and techniques have proven effective at helping students develop and deepen their content understanding and transfer their learning:

- Concept attainment
- Cooperative learning
- Experimental inquiry
- Feedback and coaching
- Graphic representation
- Guided inquiry
- Problem-based learning
- Questions (open-ended)
- Reciprocal teaching
- Simulation (e.g., mock trial)
- Socratic seminar
- Writing process

Figure 3.20
Comparison Process Poster

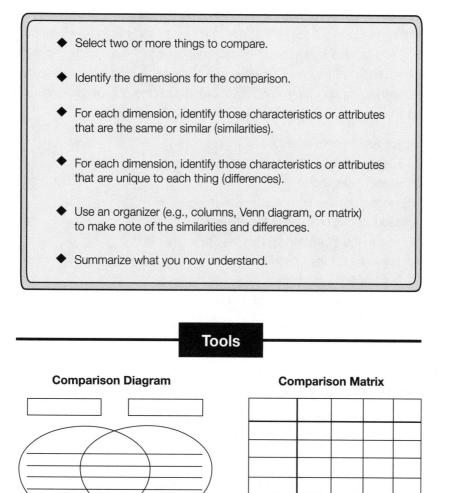

A Process for Comparing

- Select two or more things to compare.
- Identify the dimensions for the comparison.
- For each dimension, identify those characteristics or attributes that are the same or similar (similarities).
- For each dimension, identify those characteristics or attributes that are unique to each thing (differences).
- Use an organizer (e.g., columns, Venn diagram, or matrix) to make note of the similarities and differences.
- Summarize what you now understand.

Tools

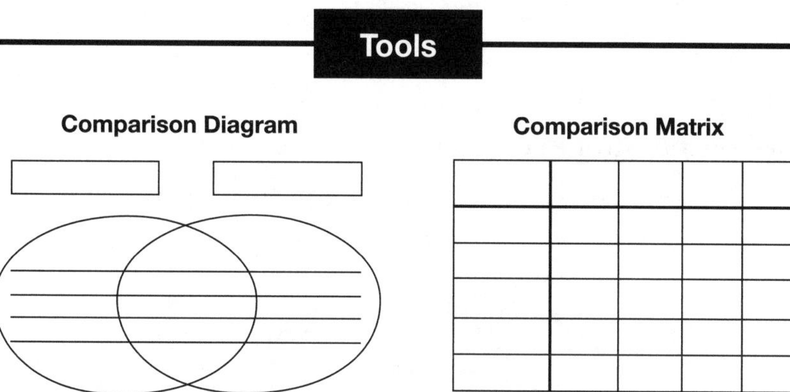

We recommend that curriculum documents provide explicit procedural directions and recommendations for those methods and techniques most appropriate for the particular content and transfer goals. Put bluntly, these approaches cannot be optional because they are vital for achieving understanding-related goals. Therefore, the curriculum must contain as much direction as possible in how and when to use these core facilitative techniques. Of course, some teachers will need additional professional development to fully master a technique, but the protocols should be included in the curriculum.

Let's take one example of such a protocol for the technique known as "concept attainment." Here is what a curriculum guide might include:

Introduction to Concept Attainment

Concept attainment is an inductive teaching technique that uses a structured inquiry process to distinguish examples of a given group or category from non-examples. In concept attainment, the teacher presents examples that contain the attributes of a concept and examples that do not contain those attributes. Students try to figure out the distinguishing characteristics of the concept by comparing and contrasting the "yes" examples with the "no" examples—those that do not contain the attributes. The technique engages all students in active thinking and meaning making. With carefully chosen examples, it is possible to use concept attainment to teach almost any concept in any subject.

Concept Attainment Protocol:

1. Select and define a concept.
2. Select the attributes.
3. Develop positive and negative examples.
4. Introduce the process to the students.
5. Present the examples and list the attributes.
6. Develop a concept definition.
7. Give additional examples.
8. Discuss the process with the class.
9. Evaluate.

Figure 3.21

Problem-Solving Strategies Wheel

Effective problem solvers use the following strategies when they're stuck.

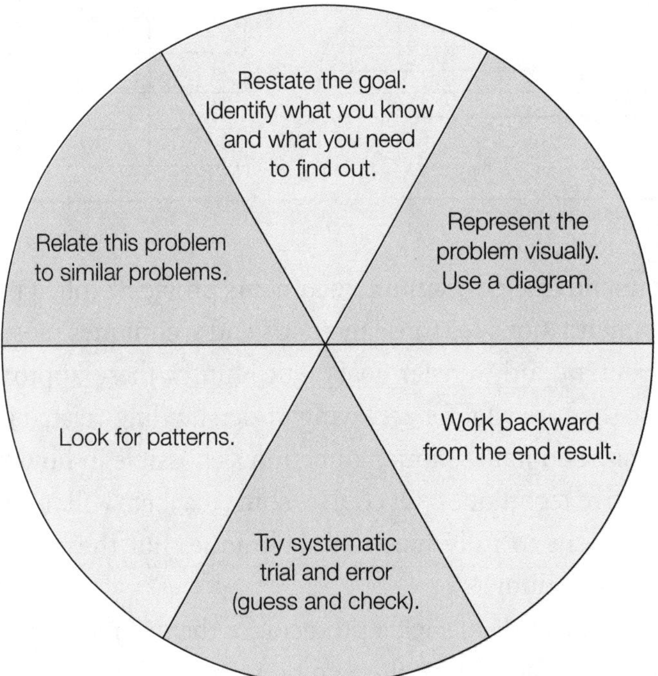
Restate the goal. Identify what you know and what you need to find out.
Represent the problem visually. Use a diagram.
Work backward from the end result.
Try systematic trial and error (guess and check).
Look for patterns.
Relate this problem to similar problems.

Listed below is a set of "yes" and "no" examples for use in a concept attainment lesson in science for the concept of *vectors* (i.e., a quantity possessing both magnitude and direction).

YES Person swimming across river
NO Car moving at 55 m.p.h.
NO A 6:30 p.m. date
NO Object weighing 100 grams
YES The force acting on potted plant hanging from ceiling
YES Train moving at 30 km per hour east
NO Child drinks one bottle milk daily
YES Motion of water leaving hose nozzle
NO The potential energy of butterflies' four wings is 113 erg
YES Paper route of girl delivering newspapers

Imagine if all curriculum documents contained such helpful teaching resources linked to specific learning goals!

A related resource in a curriculum is a complete set of *recurring graphic organizers* and other such tools for students that support the strategies and protocols in question. School districts are including such resources on their Web sites, but the curriculum needs to make clear the link between core learning strategy and possible graphic organizers, or the tools will be used too haphazardly.

Component 8. Diagnostic and Formative Assessments

Just as any successful coach or sponsor of extracurricular activities (such as yearbook, orchestra, debate, theater) recognizes the importance of ongoing assessments and continuous adjustments as the means to achieve maximum performance, so do the best teachers. Indeed, recent research has confirmed the instincts of effective teachers by documenting the benefits of regular use of diagnostic and formative assessments as feedback for learning (Black, Harrison, Lee, Marshall, & Wiliam, 2004).

Diagnostic Assessments

Diagnostic assessments, or pre-assessments, provide information to aid teacher planning and guide differentiated instruction. Examples of diagnostic assessments include checks of prior knowledge and skill levels, and surveys of interests or learning-style preferences. Because pre-assessments serve diagnostic purposes, their results should *not* be graded.

One kind of efficient, yet powerful, diagnostic assessment addresses a worrisome phenomenon reported in a growing body of literature (e.g., Gardner, 1991) that a sizeable number of students come to school with misconceptions about subject matter (for example, *a heavier object will drop faster than a lighter one*) and about themselves as learners (for example, *"I can't draw well and never will"*). If these misconceptions are not identified and confronted, they will persist, even in the face of "good" teaching. To reveal existing misconceptions, teachers can use a short (20 or fewer items), nongraded, true-false diagnostic quiz or learner self-assessment. Included among the quiz items are several potential misconceptions related to the targeted learning. By indicating whether they think a statement is true or false, students inform the teacher of any prevailing misconceptions that must be addressed through instruction. (Identifying the likely misconceptions in the curriculum occurs in the Troubleshooting component, discussed later.)

Here is an example of a short misconception check adapted from a task developed for the Kentucky Department of Education. It was presented to middle school science students at the beginning of the year. The results gave the teacher invaluable feedback about the students' understanding of isolating variables, an important aspect of scientific inquiry:

> Chris wants to decide which of two spot removers is best. First, he tried Spot Remover A on a T-shirt that had fruit stains and chocolate stains. Next, he tried Spot Remover B on jeans that had grass stains and rust stains. Then he compared the results.
>
> Explain what Chris did wrong that will make it hard for him to know which spot remover is best.

An understanding-based curriculum will include such content-specific misconception checks so that teachers can incorporate them routinely in their teaching.

A practical way to think about pre-instruction and post-instruction assessment is to imagine using the same essential question or questions at the start and at the end of a unit or course of study. Similarly, using an open-ended transfer task or writing prompt provides an important measure of progress (or lack of progress) at achieving key long-term goals.

Formative Assessments

Formative assessments occur concurrently with instruction. These ongoing assessments provide specific feedback to teachers and students for the purpose of guiding teaching to improve learning. Formative assessments are both formal and informal and include such things as ungraded quizzes, oral questioning, observations, draft work, think-alouds, student-constructed concept maps, dress rehearsals, peer-response groups, learning logs, and portfolio reviews, as well as many others. Although the results of formative assessments may be recorded, we recommend that these results *not* be factored into summative evaluation and grading (compare the need for risk-free practice in our learning principles).

We cannot stress enough the importance of such formative assessment as a central aspect of better curriculum design and instruction. To optimize student achievement, we have to "design in" space in the curriculum for formative assessment and opportunities to use the feedback to meet performance goals. The failure to do so, in the name of content coverage, paradoxically leads to less learning in the end, hence lower achievement on tests (although few teachers truly believe this). But the research on learning is quite clear: some of the greatest gains in achievement require opportunities to get feedback and use it as part of the syllabus (Black & Wiliam, 1998; Bransford, Brown, & Cocking, 2000). This just makes sense when you think about it: the more you teach without finding out who is getting it and who isn't, the greater the likelihood that only students who are already able will succeed. Similarly, Richard Light's (2001) research under the heading of the Harvard Assessment Seminar, a multiyear examination of Harvard undergraduate education, noted that the adequacy of feedback and opportunities to use it were hallmarks of the most effective courses:

> I expected students to prefer courses in which they could work at their own pace, courses with relatively few quizzes and exams and papers until the end of the term. Wrong again. A large majority of students say they learn significantly more in courses that are highly structured, with relatively many quizzes and short assignments. Crucial to this preference is getting quick feedback from the professor. (p. 8)

In the original report from which he summarizes, Light (1990) went on to say:

> The big point—it comes up over and over again as crucial—is the importance of quick and detailed feedback. Students overwhelmingly report that the single most important ingredient for making a course effective is getting rapid response on assignments and quizzes. Students suggest that it should be possible in certain courses to get immediate feedback. They suggest that the professor should hand out an example of an excellent answer. Secondly . . . an overwhelming majority are convinced that their best learning takes place when they have a chance to submit an early version of their work, get detailed feedback and criticism, and then hand in a final revised version. . . . Many students observe that their most memorable learning experiences have come from courses where such opportunities are routine policy. (p. 24)

By including diagnostic and formative assessments within curriculum documents, and advice on how to use their results to adjust curriculum, a school or district signals that such practices support effective teaching and must be used.

Component 9. Differentiation

We teach people, not just content—and people differ in their prior knowledge, interests, talents, and preferred ways of learning. The more we understand the natures and needs of our learners, the better we are able to tailor instruction to maximize learning for all. Thus, diagnostic assessment is as important to teaching as a physical exam is to prescribing an appropriate medical regimen.

As discussed in the previous section, effective curricula include pre-assessments to help teachers find out students' readiness, interests, and learning preferences, *and* ongoing assessments to inform necessary instructional adjustments. For teachers to gather and use this information on a timely basis, the curriculum must specify how to collect, diagnose, and apply what is learned (and the school calendar must ensure that teachers have time to meet in teams to discuss the implications of what is found out at the start of a course of study). With this information at hand, responsive teachers can use a variety of instructional strategies and tactics to meet various learners' needs. Here are a few examples:

- *Flexible grouping*—based on knowledge and skill levels, interests, and learning preferences.
- *Tiered activities*—having students focus on essential understandings and skills, but at different levels of complexity, abstractness, and open-endedness.
- *Compacting*—multilevel assignments based upon pre-assessment data results, including documentation of what students already know and what they do not know, with a meaningful plan that emphasizes both student needs and interests.
- *Student choice*—allowing for appropriate student choice regarding *content* (e.g., exploring a particular interest around a topic), *process* (e.g., working with a group), and *product* (e.g., visual).
- *Personalized agendas*—lists of tasks a particular student must complete within a specified time.
- *Learning contracts*—a negotiated agreement between teacher and student that gives the learner some freedom in acquiring skills and understanding.
- *Small-group activities*—activities that draw upon the strengths and needs of students to maximize group achievement while minimizing impediments extending from skills or knowledge deficiencies.
- *Independent studies*—investigations aligned with core standards.

We recommend that *specific* suggestions for differentiated instruction, *connected directly to the desired results,* be provided within the curriculum (including examples of surveys and pre-tests, and how to use that information to plan upcoming work or modifications of work, based on results). Of course, teachers are encouraged to use professional judgment based on their learners and the unique classroom context

Figure 3.22

Ideas for Supporting Inclusion Students in Math and Science Classrooms

- Use concrete objects and manipulatives to teach abstract concepts (e.g., weight, width, energy, shape, dimension, force).
- Provide students with a list of steps necessary to complete an activity or the entire task.
- Teach and model problem-solving strategies (e.g., using pictorial representation, tallying, charting, simplifying the problem).
- Post a basic problem-solving strategies chart in the room.
- Check students' understandings of key vocabulary and skills.
- Have students restate the problem/task in their own words.
- Assist students in breaking complex problems/tasks into specific steps or sub-parts.
- Use color coding to help students distinguish math/science symbols and operations/processes.
- Allow students to use calculators to perform calculations for drill problems as a means of demonstrating that they know the appropriate operation.
- Have students verbalize steps as they work in order to help them monitor their progress and identify errors.

Source: Maryland Assessment Consortium.

in which they work. Nonetheless, the curriculum should provide a wellspring of proven ideas so that teachers aren't left to grapple with the challenges of student variability on their own. Ongoing action research, made a required part of the teacher, team, and leader job descriptions, would gather this information over time. We discuss this and other changes in job descriptions in the next few chapters.

When special education (SPED) and English language learners (ELLs) are included in regular classrooms, the curriculum should provide concrete suggestions for accommodating these students. Accordingly, it is recommended that SPED and ELL specialists work in conjunction with content teams on curriculum development. Figure 3.22 is an example from such a partnership, with specific ideas for inclusion in mathematics and science.

Component 10. Troubleshooting Guide

What's the first thing you do when you run into difficulties with your Web browser or word processor? You probably look for the frequently asked questions (FAQs) or the help section of the software manual or supporting Web site. It is inevitable that even the best software doesn't quite do what you want it to do; sometimes you need to troubleshoot a problem. That's true in education, too. The best unit designs and lesson plans still may not be perfect. Invariably, in even the best classes, things don't work quite as envisioned. Even when the majority of students get it, some learners don't. Then what? Despite diligent attention to pacing, we have run out of time for students to complete all major assignments. What to do? That's when the curriculum needs to provide help by capturing the accumulated wisdom of veteran teachers and experienced curriculum users. Alas, in education we still do not build in the equivalent of FAQs, help desks, or hardware troubleshooting guides. In a results-based curriculum, such a guide is vital.

What would a troubleshooting guide for the curriculum contain? Figure 3.23 presents a generic matrix for developing a troubleshooting guide. We suggest that the matrix be completed based on the experiences of veteran teachers who will be able to identify possible causes and solutions for predictable problems encountered when teaching particular concepts and skills. There would also be advice about which future units of study and lessons to shorten or perhaps skip if key learning goals are to be achieved despite unexpected slowdowns and tangents.

Figure 3.23

Matrix for a Troubleshooting Guide for Academic Problems

Problem	Possible Causes	Possible Solutions
Difficult concepts for students to grasp (e.g., dividing fractions)		
Predictable student misunderstandings (e.g., the heavier object falls faster)		
Common errors in skill performance (e.g., no follow-through after throw)		
Parts of the curriculum where students become confused or bored (e.g., rules of grammar)		
Running out of instructional time before the unit/course is completed		
Resource materials (e.g., textbooks) that do not align well with the goals		
Some students finishing early while others rarely finish		
ELL students' inability to read the text		

In this chapter, we have described 10 components of a long-term, results-based curriculum designed to lead to worthy accomplishments within and across the disciplines. By designing backward from such desired results, we ensure that important ideas, questions, and recurring tasks coherently spiral throughout the curriculum.

The ideas presented in this chapter reflect our conception of the requisite components of an accomplishment-based curriculum with a focus on understanding and transfer. Some components (such as mapping the curriculum against standards) are familiar and exist in many districts. Some (such as framing the standards around big ideas and essential questions) are becoming more common. Others (such as developing cornerstone assessments, common rubrics, and anchors) call for significant efforts. And some components (such as troubleshooting guides) are largely absent from current curriculum documents.

A Postscript: Standards for the Curriculum

No matter how intrigued readers are by these ideas, the type of curriculum we describe will never achieve its full promise until we treat curriculum development the way we teach the writing process. There have to be explicit processes and criteria by which the emerging curriculum document is produced, self-assessed, evaluated via peer reviews, pilot tested, and revised based on feedback and results. As it stands now, the curriculum writing is done when the writers are done writing—not exactly practicing what we preach. We maintain that the curriculum is only truly finished when it meets explicit design standards *and* has proven effective with learners.

Figure 3.24 shows the full cycle of the curriculum design process. It is important to note that this curriculum process includes multiple opportunities for review and revision, just as in the writing process. So, just as with any essay or narrative, academic leaders must establish three critical components for the curriculum development process: (1) rubrics (design standards) and models (exemplary curricula); (2) protocols and schedules for self-assessment, reviews, and field testing; and (3) built-in opportunities for revision based on feedback and results. Such a process will result in greater understanding and ownership of the curriculum by teachers while equipping students to better understand and transfer their learning.

Ideas for Action

We recognize that such an ambitious agenda can seem daunting. So take heart: think big; act small; work smarter, not harder. Here are related recommendations, based on forthcoming tactical suggestions, for starting to take on the challenge of constructing a mission-based and results-focused curriculum over time.

• Think big and plan backward. Major curriculum reforms of the type described in this chapter will take 5 to 10 years to fully implement. Although the

Figure 3.24
Curriculum Design Cycles

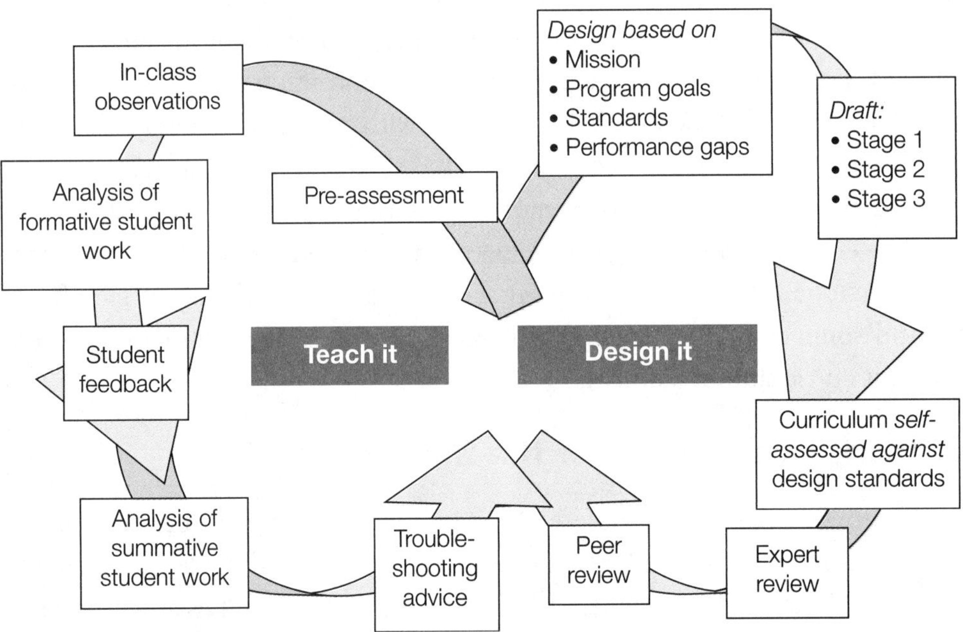

Source: From *Understanding by Design* (p. 273), by G. Wiggins and J. McTighe, 2005, Alexandria, VA: ASCD. Copyright © 2005 by ASCD. Adapted with permission.

workload can seem overwhelming, it's critical for educational leaders to develop a vision and take the long view. Then, plan backward from that vision.

• Start small and go for an early win. Don't bite off too much too soon. Begin with a feasible target (such as mapping *one* subject area or developing common rubrics for general performance areas such as writing or problem solving). Some school districts have an existing curriculum-revision cycle (for example, each subject's curriculum is revised at least once every seven years), and it makes sense to follow it.

An early win suggests starting with those subjects and curriculum committees that are ready, willing, and able to take on the reforms outlined. Once again, don't feel compelled to implement all 10 components at once. Begin with the ones that you believe can be successfully achieved. Success breeds success, whereas an early failure can be difficult to recover from. Use the chart in Figure 3.25 to monitor curriculum progress, celebrate successes, and target your next steps.

• Work smarter through collaboration and technology. Developing these 10 curriculum components requires a robust skill set in several areas: in-depth disciplinary knowledge, familiarity with real-life applications of content, extensive teaching experience, and effective writing and editing abilities. It is a rare educator who possesses them all. Thus, most districts establish curriculum-writing *teams* to develop and refine their curricula.

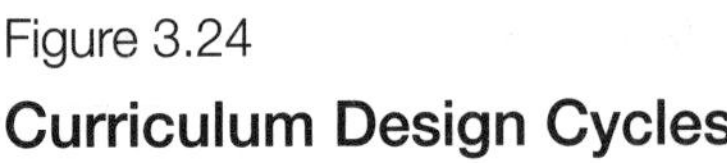

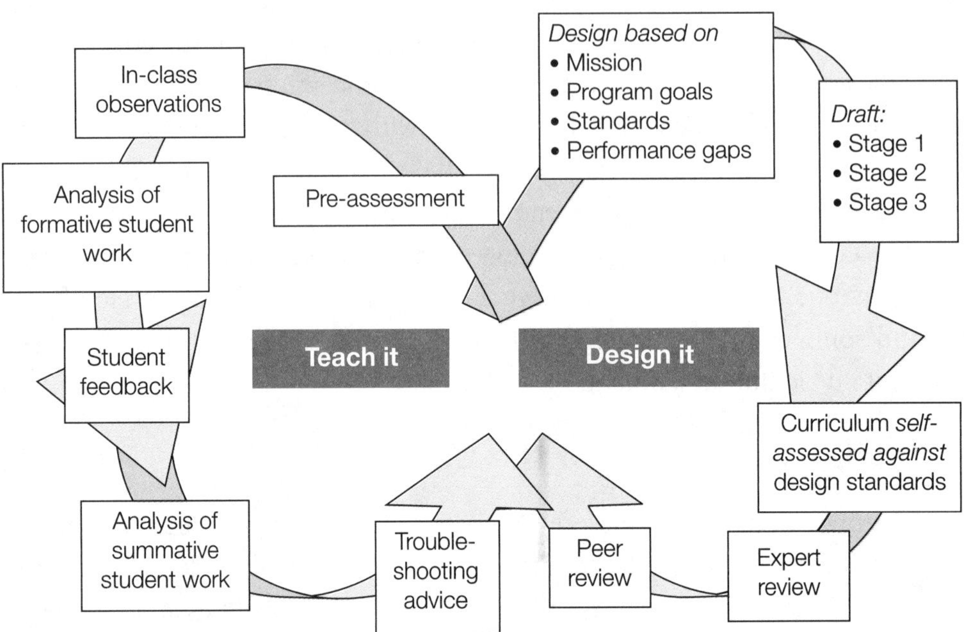

Figure 3.25

Monitoring Curriculum Progress

To what extent does the curriculum . . .	Validated	Complete	Partially	Not yet
1. Incorporate established content standards, benchmarks, performance indicators?				
2. Frame the "big ideas" of content in terms of understandings and essential questions?				
3. Include program- and course-level maps to show conceptual throughlines?				
4. Include cornerstone performance assessments (i.e., authentic transfer tasks)?				
5. Include common rubrics for cornerstone assessment tasks?				
6. Include "anchors" (examples of work) for the cornerstone assessment tasks?				
7. Include diagnostic and formative assessments specific to the targeted content?				
8. Provide suggested teaching protocols (e.g., concept attainment), learner resources (e.g., theory-embedded tools), and recommended support materials (e.g., Web sites)?				
9. Provide specific ideas for differentiation to address special populations (SPED, ELL, gifted) and learner variables (readiness, interests, learning profile)?				
10. Include course-specific (or unit-specific) troubleshooting guides?				

Key: Validated = completed and validated by internal and external reviews; Complete = finished but not yet validated by internal and external reviews; Partially = incomplete, not reviewed; Not yet = not completed

This process can seem particularly challenging for small schools and districts that may not have sufficient resources, expertise, or staff to successfully undertake this work. In such cases, we have seen the benefits of establishing regional curriculum-design consortia to collaboratively develop and share curriculum products. Often smaller districts and schools are served by educational service agencies, and these organizations are well positioned to facilitate such a regional consortium. After all, we're obliged to work toward the same state or provincial standards, so it makes no sense to work in isolation on the same work that others are doing.

Thankfully, there is no need to reinvent the (curriculum) wheel now that we have access to the Internet and powerful search engines. Today's educators can work smarter by accessing the numerous Web sites that provide excellent resources in many of the curriculum component areas, including understandings and essential questions, curriculum maps, performance assessment tasks and rubrics, and teaching and learning resources.

Having described the specific components of a performance-based curriculum, we now turn, in Chapter 4, to the requisite roles and job descriptions needed to bring our vision to life.

4

How Should Teaching Be Appropriately Depersonalized?

> Rules are not necessarily sacred; principles are.
>
> —Franklin D. Roosevelt

If understanding and transfer performances are the goals of the teaching of content, and if curriculum is reframed to better focus on the accomplishments envisioned in the mission, what must be true of the instructional pathway that will lead to the desired results? As previously noted, the answers to questions about instruction derive from the goals themselves and not primarily our personal views, preferences, and beliefs about teaching. In other words, schooling ultimately succeeds "by design" only if teaching policy is derived from two sources: (1) an analysis of the learning goals of school and (2) sound principles about learning for understanding. Unfortunately, in most schools, staff have not reached professional consensus about what goals demand of teaching or what constitutes "best practices" for learning—nor have they ever been expected to. And so, many timeless and unexamined bad teaching habits persist, generation after generation.

Indeed, schooling and reform have been hindered by the view that it is most "professional" if individual teachers decide for themselves how to teach. The result is not merely an inconsistent array of unexamined approaches to instruction (as if medicine were still what any country doctor 200 years ago thought it should be); a more harmful effect is that any critique of teach*ing* inevitably is seen as an attack on teach*ers*. We believe teaching is currently far too personalized. Without long-term results and shared analysis of goals to study together or shared standards of best practice to which we refer, teachers have little choice but to (over)emphasize personal beliefs, habits, and style. Naturally, then, any criticism of our teaching makes most of us defensive and resistant to the message. (After all, the critics are merely relying on *their* personal beliefs to critique ours.)

Our response is that the terms of the discussion are thoroughly confused. Though teaching is, of course, "personal" in the sense that we are all personally invested in our work in the unique context of our classroom, teaching effectiveness is as impersonal as the final score on the soccer field when we coach. Nothing personal, but we lost 4–0, and we didn't look good doing it. Nothing personal, but all the drill work we did on corner kicks seems to have been for naught. "Nothing personal, but . . ." can thus be thought of as a mantra of schooling by design. Why? Because when the goals are clear and we are committed to them, we can judge instructional methods and plans impersonally as either effective or ineffective—just as in soccer, medicine, band, or cooking. As we used to tell our Little Leaguers: it's not that the umpire doesn't like you or is favoring the other team. He saw your foot touch the base after the tag.

The professional perspective is "What were the results?" not "What was I personally trying hard to do?" The general question is "What works?" not "What is your personal philosophy of teaching?" Professionals deal with results; they do not have license to violate principles and best practices. Their freedom involves the ability to innovate tactfully and creatively, *given* the desired results that obligate them and the principles and a body of best practice that the profession endorses as the general path to cause those results.

Why is such depersonalization a *good* thing? Because if basic disagreements about what counts as good teaching, learning, assessment, grading, and other matters cannot be referred to a set of commonly held beliefs about learning (related to an objective mission), then there is no rational basis for school decision making. Change cannot occur when students and staff feel personally criticized or insulted for their practices. Consensual change can occur only when we grasp the hard fact of the disconnect between what we stand for, what we are trying to cause, and the effects of our actions.

Thus, schooling has to be informed by a set of shared local standards for teaching. In addition to a mission statement, related program goals, and a curriculum more carefully focused on those goals, schooling can be coherent and effective only if staffs craft and honor principles of learning that derive from mission, research, and best practice. Such principles would make clear both where we *must* agree to agree and where we can responsibly agree to disagree. In the absence of common and objective principles, it becomes far too easy for every teacher to rationalize all methods and results. With explicit guidelines as to what constitutes our pedagogical obligations and freedoms as teachers, we finally have a counterweight to the habit of coverage and a fair basis for the resolution of disputes about teaching and learning.

Again, the basic logic of reform for schooling by design—vision/reality/close the gap—is at work. Here we use it to heighten the intrinsic motivation to change teaching approaches that do not work. Principles reflect the desired accomplishment (and indicators for each principle); ongoing action research helps us identify the current reality, mindful of the principles. Each teacher then has a perpetual agenda for professional improvement, based on the analysis.

A Set of Learning Principles

The dictionary defines the word *learn* as follows: "to gain knowledge, comprehension, or mastery." Notice that to learn is an achievement, not just an activity or a process. It does not make sense to say that a student or staff member "learned" but did not "understand." Nor will it do, then, for teachers to say, "I taught them, but they didn't learn." Nor is it right for a teacher to say, "They did *A* work for me!" as a defense if students fail to meet program and school goals. Learning principles are needed because far too much of conventional school teaching and learning does not yield the accomplishments we seek, and too many of the most common approaches to teaching cannot yield understanding and the desired habits of mind. In other words, precisely because "coverage" and "cute but aimless activities" are so common, we need to make a formal and deliberate attempt to overcome them by principles (and supportive structures and policies) that remind us of our true obligation—regardless of our good intentions and years of experience.

The learning principles we propose derive from a close reading of the current literature on learning, our own work in designing curriculum and teaching for understanding, and our analysis of the mission-critical tasks and deficits related to current schooling (American Psychological Association, 1995; Brandt, 1998; Resnick, Hall, & Fellows of the Institute for Learning, 2001). They are cast in such a way to remind us that "coverage" and aimless activities are not the aim of teaching, no matter how common in schools.

Learning Principles

1. A key goal of school learning is fluent and flexible transfer—successful *use* of one's knowledge and skill, on worthy tasks, in situations of importance.
2. Engaged and sustained learning, a prerequisite for understanding, requires that learners constantly see the value of their work and feel a growing sense of efficacy when facing worthy challenges.
3. Success at transfer depends on understanding the big ideas that connect otherwise isolated or inert facts, skills, and experiences so that new challenges can be met and new experiences understood.
4. An understanding is a learner realization about the power of an idea. Understandings cannot be given; they have to be engineered so that learners see for themselves the power of an idea for making sense of things.

5. Learners need clear, completely transparent priorities and a practical understanding of how learning goals are to be met in terms of work products and standards of excellence.

6. Learners require regular, timely, and user-friendly feedback in order to understand goals, to produce quality work, and to meet high standards.

7. Understanding can be attained only by regular reflection, self-assessment, and self-adjustment in trying to apply prior learning to new situations and tasks via activities and assessments that demand such reflection and transfer.

8. The capacity to deeply understand depends greatly on the capacity to think things anew (and other related habits of mind), because any insight typically requires the refining of earlier ideas. Becoming willing and able to rethink requires a safe and supportive environment for questioning assumptions and habits.

9. Because achieving understanding and transfer require a willingness to think, rethink, and push beyond one's normal comfort level, learners need a safe and supportive environment for intellectual risk taking and questioning assumptions and habits.

10. Learning is enhanced when it is personalized—when the learners' interests, preferences, strengths, contributions, and prior knowledge are sufficiently honored.

The principles clarify what "learning for understanding" means and requires. Successful learning means that each learner is helped to see new meaning and to become more accomplished; successful instruction translates content into tools and experiences needed to achieve this. Any experience in learning is successful if it permits learners to see and to use the experience to become more competent at worthy and challenging tasks. (That's also where persistence and a sense of efficacy come from.) Learners will need lots of feedback and opportunities to use it in order to gain such understanding and overcome misunderstandings. Class time is poorly spent if the majority of time is devoted to "teaching" instead of opportunities in which learners try to understand and test their understanding. And any learning, to be effective, requires personalization so that students are coached in a way that is mindful of their particular strengths, weaknesses, interests, and needs.

Our learning principles are neither arbitrary nor without an underlying point of view. We think that at some level, they reflect common sense as well as best practice. But because we also believe that certain educationally vital ideas have been obscured by how school typically operates, these principles have been cast to illuminate our sense of the critical gaps between mission and common practice, between what we *say* we value and what we actually *do* in schools.

Unfortunately, school is not typically organized to close this gap. So the learning principles and accompanying policies for ensuring that they are constantly addressed need to serve as an explicit ongoing source for self-assessment and peer review of teaching practices, and for resolving disputes about pedagogy (we discuss job descriptions for teachers and leaders in later chapters).

We think that these learning principles oblige everyone. They are suggestive without being prescriptive. They provide guiding standards without standardization. In the words of an old folk song, "A river needs banks to flow." Think of the learning principles as providing the banks within which professional prerogative, academic freedom, and teacher creativity can flow.

What our principles suggest is that schooling succeeds only to the extent that practice and proposed reform reflect common sense and best practice. The ideal response to what we have proposed should be, "Well, this just makes sense; this is what good teachers have always done and tried to do." Yes, reform is not so much about "new" ideas, but learning how to better understand and honor our timeless obligations and proven practices. Like the "Nothing personal, but . . ." mantra mentioned earlier, the principles reflect *common*—not "personal"—sense. Again, professional work requires a depersonalization of the challenges and disagreements we perpetually face, the unending gap between vision and reality.

So a key reform goal is to develop a culture and a set of governance structures and policies in which "Nothing personal, but . . ." becomes common language or attitude. For example, "Nothing personal, Joe, but if you're lecturing 80 percent of the time, that seems inconsistent with the departmental goal of students learning how to transfer their knowledge and skill of history" or "Nothing personal, Ann, but your success with first period suggests that your second-period class could more likely meet the content standards in math if you used some of the same differentiation tactics."

Think of learning principles, then, like the Bill of Rights of the U.S. Constitution—intended to serve as objective criteria for teasing out the implications of the mission of school for planning and instruction. They safeguard the mission by providing a self-assessment mechanism for ensuring that our practices are valid in terms of what is known about how people learn, just as the Bill of Rights safeguards Americans' rights when powerful forces or bad habits threaten them. Otherwise, all we have is goodwill and personal beliefs, a poor recipe for a *common* sense. If all we have is a mission statement, we have no way to address the endless practical problems and disagreements about teaching that will crop up. Principles take root and are protected when schools (like the judiciary) regularly assess, in a disinterested way, whether or not a practice supports the mission of understanding and the principles of good pedagogy. (To establish such "legislation" and "judicial review" requires new structures and policies, which we discuss in later chapters.)

What the Learning Principles Imply

A principle is an idea, and as with all abstract notions, common understanding has to be achieved, not just assumed; misunderstandings and confusions are inevitable. With the learning principles, like mission, we also need a vision: what would we see (and no longer see) in our school if the principles were honored? The stage is then set for valid and lasting school reform when staff come to understand the need for and the value of hard work to achieve consensus about what such principles imply for practice. "Common sense" (literally and figuratively) is possible only if everyone is constantly working to understand the ideas—to "own" and "envision" them—regardless of who first proposed them and how abstract or problematic they seem at first. A major reform challenge for everyone—be it the individual teacher who wants to change her teaching or the district supervisor who wants to mobilize a large district staff—is to grasp what key ideas about learning for understanding imply and what we would see if the principles were realized.

So we offer here a few implications of each principle to better clarify the vision of what school would look and be like if the principles were honored.

> Principle 1: A key goal of school learning is fluent and flexible transfer—successful *use* of one's knowledge and skill, on worthy tasks, in situations of importance.

What would we find if this principle were honored? We would see the following:

- Local curriculum built upon the twin elements of understanding: big ideas and transfer tasks. The curriculum would include clear guidelines for assessment so that everyone would understand the transfer performances expected as a result of all teaching and learning. The curriculum would no longer be based on lists of content knowledge but would be developed from desired performances—the thoughtful and effective *use* of content.
- Every syllabus focusing on equipping students to achieve transfer. The textbook would thus be a resource, not the syllabus. Didactic teaching would never take up a majority of class time, any more than it does on the playing field in practice. Because the goal is transfer, significant amounts of class time would be devoted to students learning how and practicing to *use* content to accomplish meaningful tasks.
- Professional development clearly focused on transfer goals, so that significant amounts of time would be spent in helping teachers try out and transfer best practices to their own situation.
- Supervision focused on the extent to which teachers are designing, teaching, and assessing for transferability as opposed to merely covering content and assessing discrete knowledge and skill.

• Indicators that students are increasingly experiencing the joy of engaged learning, the growth in confidence from effective performance on challenging tasks, and the desire to keep learning that come from such success.

> Principle 2: Engaged and sustained learning, a prerequisite for understanding, requires that learners see the value of their work and feel a growing sense of efficacy when facing worthy challenges.

What would we find if this principle were honored? We would see the following:

• Grading and assessment systems that make clear the progress we are making toward exit goals and the value outside school of such assessments.

• Assignments, lessons, and assessment tasks that show clearly the answer to the questions, "Why do we need to learn this? What does this help us do?"

• Assessments that reflect real-world tasks.

• Ongoing assessments that provide helpful, user-friendly feedback and opportunities to use it. Teachers function as coaches, helping learners use feedback to deepen understanding and successfully transfer their learning.

• A supervision and professional development system that provides staff with training and ongoing, useful feedback and advice for improving practice.

• Regular surveys of students and parents about how interested, engaged, and competent students feel in school.

> Principle 3: Success at transfer depends on understanding the big ideas that connect otherwise isolated or inert facts, skills, and experiences so that new challenges can be met and new experiences understood.

What would we find if this principle were honored? We would see the following:

• Recurring essential questions framing units, courses, and the entire curriculum, and everyone understanding that the job is, in large part, to connect lessons to those larger ideas.

• Students able to confidently tackle unfamiliar-looking tasks or problems; that is, not going into shock and paralysis, or simply "plugging in" prior learning blindly and unthinkingly.

• Students showing their work, explaining their reasoning, and reflecting on the effectiveness of their work as an expected part of their assessment requirements.

• Lessons, units, and courses designed to constantly provide students with "the big picture," the "why?" and the "so what?" No student would ask of individual lessons, "What does this relate to? Why are we doing this? What's the value of learning this?"

• All staff understanding how particular reform initiatives relate to one another and add up to a coherent effort related to mission.

> Principle 4: An understanding is a learner realization about the power of an idea. Understandings cannot be given; they have to be engineered so that learners see for themselves the power of an idea for making sense of things.

What would we find if this principle were honored? We would see the following:

- Regular use of "hooks," essential questions, and probes (for example, What is the evidence? Do you agree?).
- Constructivist learning experiences (for example, inquiry lessons, problem-based learning, interactive notebooks, authentic tasks) to help students make meaning of content.
- Unit designs that reflect more "uncoverage" than "coverage," with teachers acting more like facilitators of an "Aha!" experience than "tellers" of what the idea is, as if it were just another fact to learn.
- Assessments designed to reveal the extent to which students can use ideas on their own, with minimal cueing and prompting to connect seemingly unrelated information.
- Greater engagement by learners as their schoolwork is seen as interesting and purposeful.

> Principle 5: Learners need clear, completely transparent priorities and a practical understanding of how learning goals are to be met in terms of work products and standards of excellence.

What would we find if this principle were honored? We would see the following:

- Every syllabus and unit framed in terms of the key transfer goals that the content and lessons address.
- Students who can explain where the work or course is headed because the ultimate performance goals, tasks, rubrics, and models would be clear from the start.
- Agreed-upon rubrics, consistently used by teachers across classrooms and grade levels.
- Teachers helping students understand the standards of excellence by looking at anchors and examples of work of varying quality, and discussion of the differences between those examples that meet the standards and those that don't meet the standards.
- Leaders ensuring that all teachers have access to and study print and video examples of best practice.
- Teachers regularly meeting in teams to review results (achievement data and student work) and to plan for needed improvements.
- Teachers and teams having clear personal improvement plans, based on standards and models for such plans, related to transfer goals and areas of current weakness against the goals.

• Hiring and supervision ensuring that staff have a clear sense of what the job requires in terms of *accomplishments*, not just credentials, role, and the content of the work.

> Principle 6: Learners require regular, timely, and user-friendly feedback in order to understand goals, to produce quality work, and to meet high standards.

What would we find if this principle were honored? We would see the following:

• Every syllabus providing for built-in time for giving students opportunities to learn from feedback.

• Teachers and teams routinely making major adjustments to the syllabus for the rest of the year, based on formative results related to year-end goals.

• Students at all levels of performance making gains over time in response to effective feedback and opportunities to use it.

• Pre-assessments, ongoing monitoring, and post-tests to ensure that feedback is given against the ultimate and recurring big ideas and transfer goals, not just feedback related to specific tests of content.

• Supervisors ensuring that every teacher gets feedback on a timely basis and opportunities to use the feedback to improve a key practice.

• Teacher teams routinely looking at both student work and feedback from students and parents in order to make effective and timely adjustments.

> Principle 7: Understanding can be attained only by regular reflection, self-assessment, and self-adjustment in trying to apply prior learning to new situations and tasks via activities and assessments that demand such reflection and transfer.

What would we find if this principle were honored? We would see the following:

• Most assessments requiring students to self-assess their work as part of the assessment, and making adjustments once the work was returned.

• Students regularly expected to reflect on their learning—what they understand, what they don't, what strategies worked well, what they would try next time.

• Teachers coaching students in various metacognitive strategies and making a great effort to understand what students do and do not do when confronting a learning assignment.

• Teachers helping students develop a better understanding of their own profile as a learner, an inventory of their strengths and weaknesses, and a plan for working on their areas of weakness.

• Evaluation of staff that would require staff, as both individuals and teams, to be effective at self-assessment and self-adjustment.

> Principle 8: The capacity to deeply understand depends greatly on the capacity to think things anew (and other related habits of mind), because any insight typically requires the refining of earlier ideas. Becoming willing and able to rethink requires a safe and supportive environment for questioning assumptions and habits.

What would we find if this principle were honored? We would see the following:

• Syllabi designed to provide regular opportunities to revisit (and rethink) big ideas and transfer tasks to introduce new perspectives, approaches, or shades of gray. We would no longer see syllabi as a march through the content, with topics addressed only once.

• Teachers continually returning to the essential questions as new content is introduced.

• Students provided with many opportunities to try out ideas and performance without fear of penalty. Grades would never be given for first tries.

• Essential recurring questions framing the year of staff, department, and team meetings. The culture of the team would be such that no one would fear raising a problem or feeling a need to rethink an earlier policy or practice.

• Leaders modeling openness to rethinking habits and assumptions in their conduct as well as in their goals and practices for running meetings.

• Supervision and professional development making people feel eager to learn, not stupid or ignorant.

> Principle 9: Because achieving understanding and capacity for transfer require a willingness to think, rethink, and push beyond one's comfort level, learners need a safe and supportive environment for intellectual risk taking and questioning assumptions and habits.

What would we find if this principle were honored? We would see the following:

• Teachers would model and encourage intellectual risk taking, rethinking, and respect for diverse opinions.

• Leaders would model and encourage the openness to rethinking our habits and assumptions in their conduct as well as in their goals and practices (such as running meetings and reaching decisions).

• Supervision and professional development making people feel eager to learn, not inadequate or ignorant.

• Learning from mistakes would be valued as a necessary element of continuous improvement.

> Principle 10: Learning is enhanced when it is personalized—when the learners' interests, preferences, strengths, contributions, and prior knowledge are sufficiently honored.

What would we find if this principle were honored? We would see the following:

- Syllabi designed to provide a differentiated experience based on who the students are in this class, this year.
- Teachers routinely doing an initial survey of learner styles, interests, talents, and readiness levels prior to launching into teaching and adjusting the syllabus in light of the results from the pre-assessment.
- Differentiation through flexible groupings, appropriate choices of learning process and products, multimodal instruction, and other options.
- Professional development differentiated in response to teacher subject, style, and interest.
- Clear guidelines for staff to know when they must differentiate, when they might differentiate, and when they must not differentiate, given standards that must be met.
- Supervision based on a clinical model in which teachers ask supervisors to look at an area of their practice related to personal goals.

An Ironic Consequence of the Particularity of Principles

A mission-critical challenge, then, is for schools to construct a way for *all* staff members to come to deeply understand and make such learning principles their own. Until and unless there is a common understanding of such principles, a shared vision of what learning is, there cannot be a coherent and mission-focused school. Once teachers are behind closed doors, we have to be confident that everyone not only understands the mission but also knows the kind of learning that is required to honor it (not just general views about how people learn).

Thus, the movement toward a common understanding of a *particular* mission in a *particular* school community has an ironic consequence for our own learning principles. It would hardly do for us to recommend that you unthinkingly accept our learning principles if the message is, "Constantly work together to aim for understanding." So, do *not* accept our learning principles as gospel and do not demand that others bow down before them. On the contrary: the goal is a lifelong commitment to mission analysis and learning for understanding as a school community. That's why earlier in the chapter we qualified what we said by talking about "principles such as these." Our learning principles should thus be thought of as provocations, a rough draft for getting started in developing your own set of understandings about learning that faculty *willingly* endorse and commit to as representing the local "common sense" about what the profession says about how people best learn.

Powerful and lasting change depends upon this inquiry and subsequent agreement. The dual meaning of "common sense" reminds us of this point: we reach a shared set of ideas and we come to a shared agreement about how we should hold ourselves accountable. Merely establishing study groups or a professional learning community is insufficient, therefore, because there will never be fundamental change and a stable framework for decision making without *credible* common principles. Credible to whom? To staff, first and foremost. Because staff are going to hold themselves accountable against these principles, they must own them at a deep level if significant reform is to occur and if schools are to truly become learning organizations. So consider our principles as a working draft for a team or staff to work from, a jump start on a challenging but invigorating task at the heart of learning about learning (American Psychological Association, 1995; Brandt, 1998; Resnick et al., 2001).

"Yes, but . . . What About Standardized Testing?"

"That's all well and good," some educators will say, "but we're being held accountable for results on standardized tests that do *not* assess for deep understanding or care about principles of learning. And we have too much content to cover to go into depth on anything. So what you are proposing is nice but totally unrealistic." This widely held view reflects a fundamental misconception (no matter how strongly believed). It is not true that teaching for understanding is somehow incompatible with content standards and high-stakes accountability tests. Indeed, all that we know about learning from cognitive psychology, supported by studies of student achievement, validates the centrality of teaching for understanding. Consider information from several sources.

A readable synthesis of research findings from cognitive psychology is compiled in the book *How People Learn: Brain, Mind, Experience, and School* (Bransford et al., 2000), a recent publication of the National Research Council that summarizes the past 30 years' worth of research in learning and cognition. The book offers new conceptions of the learning process and explains how skill and understanding in key subjects are most effectively acquired. Here are just three insights reported:

> We turn now to the questions of how experts' knowledge is organized. . . . Their knowledge is not simply a list of facts and formulas that are relevant to the domain; instead, their knowledge is organized around core concepts or "big ideas" that guide their thinking about the domain. (p. 24)

> Research on expertise suggests that a superficial coverage of many topics in the domain may be a poor way to help students develop the competencies that will prepare them for future learning and work. (p. 30)

> Learning with understanding is more likely to promote transfer than simply memorizing information from a text or a lecture. (p. 224)

A second source of information comes from a study that examined the relationship between the nature of classroom assignments and performance on standardized tests. Researchers systematically collected and analyzed classroom assignments in writing and mathematics in grades 3, 6, and 8 from randomly selected and control schools over the course of three years. In addition, they evaluated student work generated by the various assignments. Finally, the researchers examined correlations among the nature of classroom assignments, the quality of student work, and scores on standardized tests:

> Students who received assignments requiring more challenging intellectual work also achieved greater than average gains on the Iowa Tests of Basic Skills in reading and mathematics, and demonstrated higher performance in reading, mathematics, and writing on the Illinois Goals Assessment Program. Contrary to some expectations, we found high-quality assignments in some very disadvantaged Chicago classrooms and [found] that all students in these classes benefited from exposure to such instruction. We conclude, therefore, [that] assignments calling for more authentic intellectual work actually improve student scores on conventional tests. (Newmann, Bryk, & Nagaoka, 2001, p. 29)

Related studies in Chicago confirm these findings. (The complete research reports are available online at ccsr.uchicago.edu/content.)

Similar results emerged from the Trends in International Mathematics and Science Study (Martin, Mullis, Gregory, Hoyle, & Shen, 2000). These findings are reassuring: even if we want students simply to learn factual information and master basic skills, we will enhance such learning as measured on tests by emphasizing understanding. In other words, teaching for understanding is both a *means* (to induce more effective learning) and an *end* (to enable transfer).

Look at it the other way around. Most standards documents and local curricular frameworks stress the importance of helping learners make connections and engaging in real-world applications, yet the history of research is grim about how rare it is for conventional schooling to cause transfer:

> Research shows that very often students do not carry over facts and principles they acquire in one context into other contexts. They fail to use in science class or at the supermarket the math they learned in math class. They fail to apply the

> writing skills that they mastered in English on a history essay. Knowledge tends to get glued to the narrow circumstances of initial acquisition. (Perkins, 1993, p. 32)

When you teach via the big ideas and core processes contained within established content standards, students recall more and do a better job of transferring earlier lessons.

What may surprise many readers is the fact that most secure, standardized tests include items that require transfer, not simply recall and recognition. Because the student will be seeing questions or problems not seen before, the test is really asking: *Can you adapt your learning to our questions? If you are stymied by our version of the question, then you were not taught for transfer.* Indeed, the brutal fact is that our students perform very poorly on those higher-level items found in current state, national, and international tests that demand understanding.

Consider a case in point. The Pythagorean theorem is a topic included in *all* content standards in mathematics, taught in every geometry course, and routinely tested. Now look at two state test items, both from 2003, in which questions on the Pythagorean theorem were presented in unfamiliar circumstances. The item in Figure 4.1 turned out to be the most difficult question on the 10th grade math test in the state of New York, correctly answered by less than 30 percent of all students! Massachusetts had similar results. Only 33 percent selected the right answer to a Pythagorean theorem problem with an unfamiliar look (see Figure 4.2).

In the two examples, students were presented with questions framed without the most obvious and customary cues. That's what turns a recall question into a

Figure 4.1

New York State Mathematics Test Item

A straw is placed into a rectangular box that is 3 inches by 4 inches by 8 inches, as shown in the accompanying diagram. If the straw fits exactly into the box diagonally from the bottom left front corner to the top right back corner, how long is the straw, *to the nearest tenth of an inch?*

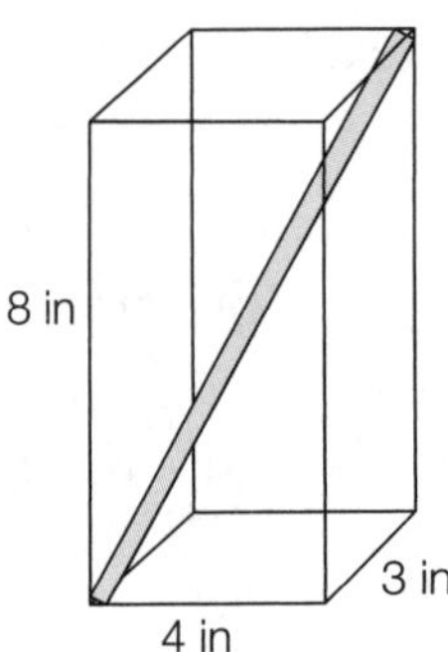

Source: New York State Department of Education.

Figure 4.2

Massachusetts State Mathematics Test Item

You may want to use the grid below to answer question 7.

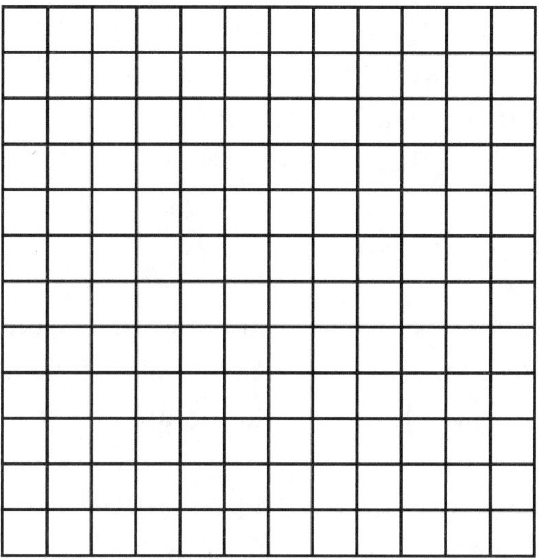

7. On the coordinate plane, what is the distance between the points (3, 4) and (11, 10)?

A. 10
B. 7
C. 5
D. 14

Source: Massachusetts Department of Education.

transfer question: Can you recognize which knowledge to tap? Can you *adapt* what you know to a problem that looks unfamiliar? In these two examples, the questions were *perceived as novel* because the typical features of triangle problems are missing. Because conventional curriculum and instruction do not equip students to *understand* content in this way, students end up doing quite poorly on test questions that require such adaptive transfer of knowledge and skill. The data are clear and have been for decades, not only on state tests but on NAEP and the results of international assessments such as TIMSS and PISA (Programme for International Student Assessment): U.S. students do poorly on questions that go beyond simple recall or comprehension. Our analysis helps explain why.

Unfortunately, instead of seeking to enhance student understanding, many educators, in their understandable fear of test results, believe that the route to improved scores lies in practicing for the test using recall items and mimicry of the test format. This is a flawed conclusion based on a misunderstanding about how testing works, how validity is established, and how learners are best prepared for transfer. (We elaborate on this misunderstanding in Chapter 5.)

Toward Understanding-Based Schooling

So what must schooling be to signal a constant focus on understanding and transfer? Success at this mission will depend upon a professional life in which staff are *required* to formally and constantly face a host of important interconnected issues about the gap between the reality of school and the point of school:

• If understanding is our goal, how do we better plan for it? Teach for it? Achieve it?

• What is solid evidence of understanding (or not understanding)? Are we truly assessing understanding and transfer, or simply assessing what is easiest to test and grade? Given the mission, how credible and useful is the evidence we currently collect?

• How well do students understand what they have learned? How deep is their learning? What does the evidence show about their ability to wisely use what they have learned? To what extent do students believe that their job is to strive to understand, not just recall what was taught? To what extent do staff believe their job is to teach, coach, and assess for understanding, not simply cover content?

• What feedback do we need about the learners' attempts to understand in order to better help them understand? What adjustments based on feedback must we make to achieve successful learning by the end?

• What must *staff* better understand and keep trying to understand in order to achieve more *student* engagement and understanding? To what extent are we doing what the learner needs in order to understand, and to what extent are we doing only what is familiar or comfortable? What school practices unwittingly impede learning for understanding?

In Chapter 5 we turn to these questions and discuss how to continually and effectively address them in school as part of the curriculum and as part of the job of being an educator.

Ideas for Action

• Engage staff in an exercise on "What We Believe About Learning." This can occur by presenting them with existing principles such as those offered in this chapter and having them discuss their reaction. Alternatively, start with a blank slate and have groups generate a list of their beliefs; then share and discuss the group lists with the entire staff. Seek general agreement on a list of key learning principles.

- Using a list of agreed-upon learning principles, lead staff discussions based on questions such as the following:
    - To what extent do our actions and structures support each principle?
    - What changes in our school practices do the principles suggest?
- Excerpt select passages from *How People Learn* that summarize key research findings and present these for discussion, using questions such as those in the preceding bullet item. (The entire text of the 1999 edition of *How People Learn* is available online at http://newton.nap.edu/html/howpeople1/.)
- Have subject and grade-level teams examine frequently missed questions from your state test (assuming that this information is available). Analyze the items to identify the understandings and the transfer demands in the questions.
- Ask subject and grade-level teams to respond to the following question: To what extent are we having our students "do" the subject? Ask for specific examples from each group, and generalize from the responses.

5

What Is the Teacher's Job When Teaching?

> A key goal of Coach Wooden was the development of players who were creative, confident problem-solvers. . . . He wanted us to be so automatic in our fundamentals and so versed in the concepts that we were ready to quickly devise our own solutions from the constantly changing problems our opponents posed. . . . Coach Wooden wanted, as he said, "to be as surprised as our opponent at what my team came up with when confronted with an unexpected challenge."
>
> —Sven Nater, a former player for Coach Wooden (Nater & Gallimore, 2005)

Any school or district committed to the educational mission described in Chapter 1 would expect certain instructional and assessment practices from its teaching staff. Similarly, the type of curriculum and instructional activity described in Chapters 2 through 4 calls for particular roles from the people charged with its implementation. Accordingly, in this and the following chapter, we propose six key job functions for teachers working in understanding-based, performance-oriented schools.

The need to define a teacher's job may strike readers as unnecessary. After all, aren't teachers hired to teach subjects and grade levels, mindful of the established standards for their state or province? Don't teachers sign a contract and undergo an annual performance evaluation? Yes, but . . . we contend that the lack of a more precise job description for teachers, along with concomitant expectations and appropriate appraisals, unwittingly interferes with desired school reforms. To state the problem more dramatically, we contend that many hardworking teachers actually harbor misunderstandings about what their job requires, and that many educational leaders unintentionally abet these misunderstandings by not confronting them or providing clearer expectations. In sum, there needs to be far greater clarity about a *teacher's* mission.

Over the years, we have observed countless examples of teachers who, though industrious and well meaning, act in ways that suggest that they misunderstand their jobs. It may seem odd or even outrageous to say that many teachers misconceive their obligations. But we believe this is the case. Nor do we think this is surprising or an aspersion on the character or insight of teachers. We believe that teachers, in good faith, act on an inaccurate understanding of the role of "teacher" because they imitate what they experienced, and their supervisors rarely make clear that the job is to *cause* understanding, not merely to march through the curriculum and *hope* that some content will stick. So what *is* the job of a teacher? How are the job expectations made clear, and how are job requirements reflected in school life, supervision, and evaluation?

In this chapter, we describe various roles for a teacher's work with students within a school or district committed to the mission of schooling we have proposed. (In the next two chapters we describe additional nonteaching job requirements and supervision.) We conclude by examining three potential job misunderstandings that can undermine the reforms we advocate.

The Job of a Teacher

The word *teach* is unhelpfully ambiguous. It can refer to our all-encompassing job as educator in the broadest sense (we are all teachers). It can refer to different kinds of approaches (teach by questioning, teach by telling). And it can imply a range of purposes (inform, expand awareness, develop performance ability). It can even refer to isolated teacher behavior, irrespective of the results, as in the old joke, "I taught them, but they didn't learn." So how should we best clarify the job of the teacher?

Backward design suggests one answer. The teacher's role, behavior, and strategies must stem deliberately from established mission and goals, the curriculum, and agreed-upon learning principles. In other words, the particular approaches, methods, and resources employed are not *primarily* subjective "choices" or mere matters of style. They logically derive from the desired student accomplishments and our profession's understanding of the learning process. We teach to cause a result. Teaching is successful only if we cause learning related to purpose.

More specifically, we can distinguish mandatory from optional teacher roles and approaches by recalling the categorization of intellectual goals mentioned in Chapter 1 (academic excellence, understandings, key competence, habits of mind, mature conduct). Mortimer Adler, in *The Paideia Proposal* (1982), presents us with three broad categories of instructional roles for teachers related to these intellectual goals: (1) didactic (or direct) instruction, (2) facilitation of understanding and related habits of mind, and (3) coaching of performance (skill and transfer). (See Adler's *The Paideia Program* [1984] and follow-up volumes for further insight into the rationale for the three categories and how to decide what kind of teaching best suits what kind of objective.)

Didactic/direct instruction. In this role, the teacher's primary goal is to *inform* the learners through explicit instruction—that is, telling and lecturing, supplemented by textbooks and demonstrations.

Facilitation of understanding. Facilitative teaching seeks to help students "construct" meaning and *come to an understanding* of important ideas and processes. Teachers in this role guide student inquiries into complex problems, texts, cases, projects, or situations. Their principal methods are questioning, probing, and process-related commentary, with little or no direct instruction.

Coaching performance. Coaching seeks to support the learners' ability to *transfer* their learning to succeed in complex and autonomous performances. The teacher/coach establishes clear performance goals and then supervises the development of skills and habits through ongoing opportunities to perform, accompanied by specific feedback and modeling.

In Figure 5.1, we show how the three roles relate to examples of specific instructional methods and the concomitant learner actions for each.

The implication should be clear from these categories: there is no one *best* teaching approach. Rather, the choice of a pedagogical method or a particular instructional move should be determined by what the desired results imply and thus what kind of help and experience the learners need. When the learning goal requires

Figure 5.1

Teacher Roles and Related Learner Actions

Teacher Role (Method the Teacher Uses)	Learner Actions (What Students Need to Do)
Didactic/Direct Instruction	**Receive, Take In, Respond**
• Demonstration, modeling	• Observe, attempt, practice, refine
• Lecture	• Listen, watch, take notes, question
• Questions (convergent)	• Answer, give responses
Facilitation of Understanding	**Construct, Examine, Extend Meaning**
• Concept attainment	• Compare, induce, define, generalize
• Cooperative learning	• Collaborate, support others, teach
• Discussion	• Listen, question, consider, explain
• Experimental inquiry	• Hypothesize, gather data, analyze
• Graphic representation	• Visualize, connect, map relationships
• Guided inquiry	• Question, research, conclude, support
• Problem-based learning	• Pose/define problems, solve, evaluate
• Questions (open-ended)	• Answer and explain, reflect, rethink
• Reciprocal teaching	• Clarify, question, predict, teach
• Simulation (e.g., mock trial)	• Examine, consider, challenge, debate
• Socratic seminar	• Consider, explain, challenge, justify
• Writing process	• Brainstorm, organize, draft, revise
Coaching	**Refine Skills, Deepen Understanding**
• Feedback/conferencing	• Listen, consider, practice, retry, refine
• Guided practice	• Revise, reflect, refine, recycle through

information cast in a helpful way, use didactic teaching approaches. When the goal is to ensure that ideas are understood and misconceptions overcome, facilitate student discussions and inquiries so that students come to see for themselves. When the aim is for the learners to transfer their knowledge and skills to new situations, then coach for the desired performances.

Clearly, then, an effective teacher not only demonstrates skill in all three roles but also understands *when* they should be used, in what combinations, and for how long. That's the *teacher's* transfer task! The decision flows from mission and learning priorities. Yes, there are times when direct telling can be efficient and effective. However, when the learning goals highlight *understanding* and *transfer performances* (as we have stressed in this book), we would logically expect to see an emphasis in the classroom on facilitation of student inquiry and coaching toward transfer performance. So the endless quarrels about "which teaching method is best" miss the point entirely. There is no unqualified answer; there is no "politically correct" response. The question about how to teach always demands an "if, then" answer; it's completely dependent on desired results.

So we must begin our thinking about any upcoming teaching with an essential question: Given the learning goals that have priority, what is the best use of *inherently limited* class time, in terms of "teacher" and "learner" roles? What should teachers and learners be doing inside class (and outside class) to best accomplish those aims? What form of interaction between learners, materials, and teacher—in what balance of time—offers the greatest likelihood of achieving the various explicit results related to mission? What are the highest-leverage actions we as educators can take to cause important changes in learners? These questions typically go begging in classrooms as habits take over.

Let's look more closely at teaching as facilitation and as coaching to better understand these two roles and why they are so vital in teaching for understanding and transfer.

Teacher as Facilitator

In the Paideia framework, Adler proposes that, in addition to being a teller and a coach, a teacher can facilitate understanding through a (Socratic) seminar format in which great books and ideas are discussed collaboratively. During a seminar, the teacher plays the role of questioner, prober, devil's advocate, and includer. In this role, teachers rarely give their opinions but strive to evoke the thinking of the student participants. In addition to Socratic seminars, many other kinds of inductive, facilitated experiences have been used for years. Indeed, the case method in law, problem-based learning in the sciences and medicine, and the seminar in the humanities are time-honored approaches to facilitating learning for understanding.

More generally, understanding requires proactive development and testing of ideas by the learner. Whether in responding to a text, an experience, a problem, or a case study, the students are charged with making meaning of deliberately ambiguous content and the open-ended questions involved.

But there is no meaning for students to make if the design does not clearly establish opportunities and incentives to try to make sense of things. The facilitator has two jobs, then: the first is to artfully set up the proper situations for students to try out and test ideas collaboratively and individually—through questions or problems, for example; the second is to moderate the inquiry and resist the urge to "teach" (a very hard habit to break!). To describe the case study method, a Harvard business professor wrote:

> Teachers . . . are particularly beset by the temptation to tell what they know. . . . Yet no amount of information, whether of theory or fact, in itself improves insight and judgment or increases ability to act wisely. (Gragg, 1954, p. 8)

Practically speaking, students and teachers must all learn to recognize that when facilitation of understanding is taking place, *conventional* "teaching" and "learning" will be suspended. The teacher will continually have to make clear—via the design of inquiry and reference to appropriate rules and norms—that new and perhaps unfamiliar practices and roles will be governing the classroom experience.

Here is a simple example of the kind of small but profound change in classroom dynamics that reflect facilitative teaching. All facilitators of seminars know that students have to be made conscious of their tendency to be passive, to constantly wait for the next "move" to come from the teacher. The most obvious indicator of this problem is what happens when a student contributes to a teacher-led discussion in a typical class: all eyes immediately and unconsciously go back to the teacher following a student's response. (Look for this in class visitations.) It is a deeply engrained habit: teachers and students fall into the trap of thinking that the teacher's job is to respond as a "teacher" to each student's comment. But this pattern is upended in a seminar, because the teacher's job is to encourage learners *not* to wait for teacher responses and to actively respond to the comments of fellow students.

In other words, a facilitator's job is to bring people in and keep everyone questioning and responding. Over the long term, the teacher/facilitator is needed less and less because students become better at managing the process of collaborative inquiry on their own—what we like to call "intellectual Outward Bound." But it takes discipline and explicit training to break the many common habits and familiar routines associated with "sit and get" learning.

Small-group seminars are not the only place for such facilitation. Here is an example from a large lecture course at the college level:

> [In psychologist Donald Dansereau's classes at Texas Christian University] after fifteen to twenty minutes of lecture, students are paired by the teacher so that teammates vary from one class session to the next. Students review class notes, taking turns as recaller-summarizer and checker. The recaller summarizes the content of the prior lecture segment and the checker assesses the summarizer's accuracy and detail. After determining the accuracy of the notes, students jointly work on developing strategies that will help them remember the content, such as constructing examples and developing mnemonic or memory devices to assist in long-term retention. (Cooper & Robinson, 2000, p. 20)

Although it is among the oldest of methods (think Socrates!), facilitative teaching is being enhanced by technology. Here is an account from the *Boston Globe* newspaper of the ever-growing use of a computerized student-response system using handheld "clickers":

> Hoping to make large classes more interactive, a growing number of professors on large campuses are requiring students to buy wireless, handheld transmitters that give teachers instant feedback on whether they understand the lesson—or whether they're even there.
>
> Use of the $36 device has exploded this fall at the University of Massachusetts, where faculty say class sizes are creeping up following $80 million in system-wide budget cuts. Close to 6,000 of the 17,500 undergraduates on the Amherst campus are required to have transmitters in classes this fall, compared with fewer than 500 two years ago, said Richard Rogers, an economics professor and adviser to the provost on the classroom experience.
>
> To connect with students in vast auditoriums, professors sprinkle multiple-choice questions through their lectures. Students point and click their transmitters to answer, pushing blue buttons numbered 1 through 9 on their keypads. A bar graph appears on the professor's laptop, showing the number of right and wrong answers; teachers can slow down or backtrack when there are too many wrong answers. Each device is registered and assigned a number, so professors can check who is present, and reach out after class to those who give wrong answers frequently. (Russell, 2003)

Consider the implication about learning in these examples. Whether in small seminars or large lectures, students are guided to actively process information and test their understanding rather than simply listening and taking notes. Facilitative teaching rests on the common belief that learners can develop understanding (even in large lecture courses) only by being asked to continually question and rethink their answers in light of feedback in order to make sense of ideas. This is not time "lost" from "teaching" but time well spent in causing learner understanding.

Let's generalize. Regardless of the setting, what do the best facilitators do? They

1. Set up issues, problems, and investigations for inquiry and discussion.
2. Guide the learners in "making meaning."
3. Refrain from excessive instruction.
4. Model and encourage the use of strategies and habits of mind.
5. Work to make themselves unneeded.

Let's briefly examine each of these characteristics of facilitators.

1. Set up issues, problems, and investigations for inquiry and discussion. A major goal of facilitation involves the development and deepening of student understanding. To this end, skillful facilitators select provocative issues to explore and debate, worthy texts to interpret, significant investigations to conduct, and challenging problems to tackle. With these intellectual challenges as the grist for understanding, the facilitator's job is to ensure that students generate, test, probe, and adjust ideas via peer feedback and salient results.

2. Guide the learners in "making meaning." The understandings of an expert simply cannot be passed on verbally. Thus, the learner's job is to actively try to construct meaning and make sense of things, and the facilitator's job is to assist this construction process.

"But isn't content being sacrificed?" No. This is a basic misconception about facilitative instruction. Just because all related content isn't being didactically "taught" doesn't mean that the content isn't being learned—namely, through student attempts to use what they have thus far encountered in and out of class. Here is what Harvard physics professor Eric Mazur (1997) has to say about his long-term research on how best to structure his use of time in a large class by doing "less" teaching and more facilitation of understanding through diagnostic assessment and discussion:

> The basic goals . . . are to exploit student interaction during the lectures and focus student attention on key concepts. Instead of presenting the level of detail covered in the textbook or lecture notes, lectures consist of a number of short presentations on key points, each followed by a ConcepTest—short conceptual questions on the subject. The students are first given time to formulate answers and then asked to discuss their answers with each other. (pp. 10–11)

Answers are tallied, and Mazur continues with the lecture if the results indicate understanding and shifts gears if the results are weak. In this approach, these instant-feedback tests and discussion "take one third of each lecture period" (p. 14). In so doing, "it is possible to greatly improve student performance on [concept tests] and conventional examinations," a claim backed by years of formal research by Mazur and his colleagues. As Mazur (1997) says elsewhere, "No lecturer, however engaging and lucid, can achieve this level of improvement and participation simply by speaking."

3. Refrain from excessive instruction. Thus, a facilitative role relocates the teacher from being only a "sage on the stage" to being a "guide on the side," from mostly telling to eliciting the making of meaning and the testing of ideas. A facilitator moderates discussions and guides inquiry without being an intrusive or directive participant. Instead of giving talks and answers, facilitators question, clarify, and comment on process and the state of the inquiry.

4. Model and encourage the use of strategies and habits of mind. The open-ended nature of inquiry-based learning can be unsettling, especially to dutiful students who have come to expect clear directions from the teacher. The facilitator also models and encourages the use of strategies and habits of mind when learners encounter difficulties in the course of their inquiry, answering questions such as these: What do you do when you don't understand the text? What strategies can help when you've hit the wall during problem solving? How do you respond when your best ideas are challenged?

5. Work to make themselves unneeded. Unlike traditional instruction in which the teacher takes center stage, facilitators seek to progressively develop student autonomy over time (the intellectual Outward Bound we referred to earlier). In other words, they work at making themselves increasingly unneeded. This outcome typically comes about through a systematic "weaning" process during which teacher directions and support are gradually reduced. Here are specific ways in which teachers promote growing independence:

• Encourage students to set personal learning/performance goals related to the overall desired results.

• Give students appropriate choices over the processes of learning (for example, working in groups versus working alone) and their products (for example, visual, verbal, written).

• Expect students to regularly self-assess their work and their progress toward explicit goals.

• Teach facilitation skills and allot time for students to apply them (for example, via student-led seminars or problem-solving groups).

Teacher as Coach

Coaches are in business to maximize performance and develop discipline. The coach focuses all efforts on getting the learner to reach a performance standard by designing backward from desired transfer proficiency and the self-discipline (skill and habits of mind) needed. Mortimer Adler (1982) describes this goal and the implications for "teaching":

> Since what is learned [in acquiring core intellectual competence] is skill in performance, not knowledge of facts and formulas, the mode of teaching cannot be didactic. It cannot consist in the teacher telling, demonstrating, or lecturing. Instead it must be akin to the coaching that is done to impart athletic skills. A coach does not teach simply by telling or giving the learner a rulebook to follow. A coach trains by helping the learner to do, to go through the right motions, and to organize a sequence of acts in correct fashion. He corrects faulty performance again and again and insists on repetition of the performance until it achieves a measure of perfection. . . . Only in this way can skill in reading, writing . . . be acquired. . . . Only in this way can the ability to think critically—to judge and discriminate—be developed. (p. 27)

Adler's quote could not put the matter more starkly: the overly didactic "teacher" or designer of activities merely offers information and experience, but takes little self-conscious responsibility for *ensuring* that learners learn to be disciplined from the talk or activity, as reflected in learned action and accomplishment.

In contrast, think about highly effective coaches you know or have known. (Note: Do not limit your thinking to athletic coaches. Consider other performance-based instructors such as band directors, drama coaches, and art teachers.) Now consider what they *do* and what they *strive to accomplish,* not what they are like as people—their "coaching" as opposed to their personal traits or style. How do they begin with their charges? How does the coaching unfold over time? What distinguishes their use of time and their work with learners in each session? How do they work effectively with large numbers of learners (such as an orchestra)? What do they do to focus everyone on quality work, regardless of ability level? What strategies do they use to guide and improve performance?

Here are 11 characteristics that we have observed in the best coaching in various fields. How does this list match your observations? The most effective coaches

1. Establish explicit performance targets clearly related to long-term transfer goals.
2. Show models and exemplars for all goals.
3. Design practice and assess progress backward from the ultimate transfer demands.
4. Assess from the start to see where learners are and what the learning needs to focus on to accomplish goals
5. Devote most time to having learners perform so the coach is freed up to coach.
6. Personalize their coaching, mindful of individual profiles (ability and personality).

7. Provide ongoing feedback and immediate opportunities to use it.
8. Provide "just-in-time" instruction in small, focused doses.
9. Adjust plans in light of unexpected or inappropriate results.
10. Strive to make learners autonomous, thus making self-assessment and self-adjustment a key goal of teaching.
11. Set high standards, but design the work so that learners come to believe "I can do this!"

Let's explore each of these coaching roles in more a bit more detail.

1. Establish explicit performance targets clearly related to long-term transfer goals. Effective coaches ensure that everyone has clarity about the desired performance results. There is no mystery about what learners are trying to achieve or what "success" looks like. Thus, you rarely hear athletes or band members ask, "Why are we doing this?" or "What should my work look like?" Contrast this clarity with the experience of many students, who do not know the learning goals they are expected to attain, the ways in which their learning will be assessed, the instructional methods by which their learning will be supported, or their role as a learner in the process. Lack of clarity on any of these points can diminish student motivation and achievement.

2. Show models and exemplars for all goals. If we seek exemplary performance, the learner must know what exemplary performance looks like. Recognizing this, effective coaches make the "invisible visible" through countless models and examples. The basketball coach shows videotapes of the games of championship teams so that players can see excellence in action. The yearbook sponsor has the staff review award-winning yearbooks from previous years and challenges them to produce a better one for their graduating class. Yet how many history teachers do you know who show students examples of experts' critical examinations of historical artifacts? How many teachers of science do you know who routinely distribute and discuss excellent laboratory reports *before* students begin their lab work?

3. Design practice and assess progress backward from the ultimate transfer demands while providing multiple opportunities to learn and apply the same skill in context. The nature of "practice" distinguishes effective coaches of performance from teachers who ask students to merely complete drills. The coaches have their charges place emphasis on authentic performance in context, rather than focusing on discrete skills practiced in isolation. Coaches always focus the "sideline drills" on improving performance in the game.

Consider the U.S. Soccer Federation (USSF) guidelines for coaching youth soccer. In each practice in which a specific skill is to be learned, a progression (derived backward from game performances) is used: (1) practice the technique; (2) practice the technique in *game-related* conditions (with token opposition in pairs, for example); (3) practice the skill in *gamelike* conditions (with more realistic complexity and opposition); and then (4) practice the skill under *game conditions* in a scrimmage in which the focus is on the skill being used. The mantra in soccer coaching is "The game is the best teacher. . . . Our coaching school instructors often talk about 'specificity of training.' They want to make certain that training accomplishes the objective of highlighting a skill or tactical factor in a way that is demanded by a real match" (Howe, 1999, p. 111). The federation's materials underscore the point: "The game will tell you what the team needs to practice. We say that the game and training have a reciprocal effect. The game indicates what we need to train for, and in training we prepare for the game" (Howe, 1999, p. 24). We contend that the same logic applies to academic areas in which transfer performances are also desired.

4. Assess from the start to see where learners are and what the learning needs to focus on to accomplish goals. Athletic coaches, sponsors of extracurricular activities, and performance-based teachers (for example, in art and technology) recognize that before you begin teaching, you need to find out the knowledge and skill levels of the learners in light of goals. Indeed, coaches of all stripes routinely begin their "season" with diagnostic assessments, because it is crucial to get to know the strengths, desires, and needs of each player.

5. Devote most time to having learners perform so the coach is freed up to coach. A coach doesn't merely teach learners how to perform. The essence of coaching is to set up conditions whereby learners must constantly try and display what they have (or have not) learned for a period of time, through self-sustaining activities, so that they can be coached.

An illustration of this approach was documented in a yearlong study of John Wooden, the legendary UCLA basketball coach whose approach we've cited previously. When researchers carefully observed Wooden's coaching methods in order to tease out the "secrets" of his success, they noted an extraordinary pattern that they took to calling a "Wooden":

> There were no lectures and no extended harangues. None. Not one in all the months they observed. . . . He seldom praised or scolded. Ten percent of his instruction was a "Wooden"—show the model, identify the player's non-example, re-show the model. (Nater & Gallimore, 2005, p. 93)

Ted Sizer (1984) suggests the same approach applied to academics: "The material of coaching is the *student's work,* in which skill is displayed for a teacher to assess, give feedback to, and give advice for improvement" (p. 41; emphasis added). This is a crucial distinction. The "teller" thinks the best use of class time is to share knowledge, cover content, inform the student. The "coach" thinks the best use of limited time is for the learner to try to learn and apply that learning in front of the coach, so that feedback and guidance can be given to improve performance. Too few teachers spend considerable time watching students try to perform and trying to "get into their heads as they work" (for example, by having learners think aloud while engaged in a task). In designing backward from transfer, we use class time *primarily* to better understand what happens when learners *try* to transfer, and we take effective steps to improve the methods and the transfer. Otherwise, any "teaching"—no matter how sound and clearly presented—remains abstract and unlikely to transfer into action.

6. Personalize their coaching, mindful of individual profiles (ability and personality). The best coaches know their players inside and out as learners and as people. They know who needs a kick in the butt and who needs TLC to perform their best. How do they do it? By freeing themselves up to study learners trying to learn, to figure out their strengths, to watch how they react to adversity, and to observe how well they adjust based on feedback. (How many teachers keep a record in their gradebook of student behavior and attitude related to tackling their work in class, to capture their intellectual profile as a learner? If a big chunk of time every day is given over to students trying to use their learning, this is not only feasible but effective.)

Effective coaches identify the positions and roles that play to the strengths of various team members without sacrificing common standards. The slow and heavyset boy has a place on the football team, as does the short and swift boy. We need flutes and tubas to round out the sound range in the orchestra. Prima donnas and shy stagehands work together to pull off a successful play. Not everyone has to learn the same skills in the same way to become competent on the field.

Similarly, a key to personalization in the classroom is to ensure that we design complex "work" involving different roles for learners. In this regard, Carol Ann Tomlinson (1999), an expert in differentiated instruction, advises that learners need "respectful tasks" (p. 12) that both challenge them and allow them to work in ways that reflect their readiness levels, interests, and styles of learning. Given individual differences, a one-size-fits-all approach is unlikely to maximize performance for all—on the field or in the classroom.

7. Provide ongoing feedback and immediate opportunities to use it. The mantra here is "less teaching, more formative assessing." One of the authors was profoundly struck by an experience with his son that illustrates the power of ongoing feedback. We paid for a "pitching clinic" for Little Leaguers at a local college, hosted by its highly successful varsity baseball coach. We were there for five hours, but only about one hour was spent in formal teaching. The bulk of the clinic involved the young pitchers pitching and receiving feedback and advice as they did so from the coaching staff. The last activity involved looking at videotape of each youngster, quickly edited down during lunch by the staff to highlight strengths and weaknesses in each learner's performance, followed by a single personalized piece of advice by the coach. The boys were absolutely riveted, even when the focus was not on them. On the drive home, I asked, "So, what did you think of the clinic?" My son answered, "It was fantastic! That's the longest I have ever listened to adults without getting bored!" In addition to their attentiveness, it was clear that each boy improved, on the spot, and left charged up. How often can we say that about our students in school?

8. Provide "just-in-time" instruction in small, focused doses. In a coaching context, the timing of direct instruction and focused practice is based on results. As soccer coaches say, "The game is the teacher." Just-in-time teaching means we do not frontload lots of content out of context—what might be called "just-in-case" teaching, which leads to the amnesia that plagues so much of conventional education. If your goal is to learn how to cook, you would undoubtedly be frustrated if you were obliged to sit through 30 lectures about every aspect of cooking without ever setting foot in a kitchen and "doing" some cooking with guidance from an expert chef. Yet many courses make this mistake—to the detriment of engagement, as well as results.

Just-in-time teaching means, rather, that we judiciously parcel out direct teaching when it is needed and when learners are ready for it. At the extreme end it means completely reversing traditional sequence, as is done in problem-based learning: no direct instruction is imposed until the problem that opens each unit of study is fully explored. Nonetheless, there are times when direct instruction serves the goal of understanding. Research from cognitive psychology affirms this point:

> A common misconception regarding "constructivist" theories of knowing is that teachers should never tell students anything directly, but instead should always allow them to construct knowledge for themselves. This perspective confuses a theory of pedagogy (teaching) with a theory of knowing. . . . There are times, *usually after people have first grappled with issues on their own,* that "teaching by telling" can work extremely well. (Bransford et al., 2000, p. 11) (emphasis added)

9. Adjust plans in light of unexpected or inappropriate results. A teacher's job is not to *assume* that learning is occurring, based on the teaching. The job is to *ensure* that learning occurs, and when it doesn't, to intervene decisively, quickly, and often. In other words, a key part of a teacher's job is to regularly assess and learn from the results as quickly as possible so as to make the necessary adjustments to improve learning.

How many members of the secondary mathematics department say to one another in November, "Gee, we're 2 out of 6 in problem solving. What should we be doing differently?" How many primary-grade teachers say, "Gee, whatever our beliefs about reading, 14 of our kids cannot read, based on our current approach. What do their struggles tell us we should do differently? Are we on track to realize successful performance by May, and do we have sufficient evidence against end-of-year measures to know?" These are the kinds of questions that coaches regularly ask—and so should every teacher.

Consider one direct implication of thinking like a coach: we would build flex-time into each unit and the syllabus as a whole for the *inevitable* reteaching and relearning needed. In our experience, this is uncommon. In fact, many teachers overplan their lessons, leaving minimal built-in time for the unavoidable adjustments that will be needed to improve results.

10. Strive to make learners autonomous, thus making self-assessment and self-adjustment a key goal of teaching. The best artists, writers, actors, and athletes are capable not only of being coached but also of internalizing the coaching. The ability to accurately self-assess and self-adjust is critical to maximizing performance, and the same principle applies to school learning. Research in cognitive psychology underscores this point: "Metacognition also includes self regulation—the ability to orchestrate one's learning: to plan, monitor success, and correct errors when appropriate—all necessary for effective learning" (Bransford et al., 1999, p. 85).

Accordingly, effective coaches of performance deliberately engage students in reflecting on their performance. For example, regularly asking learners reflection questions—What worked well? Where are problem areas? How will you apply this feedback? What do you need to work on?—can help cultivate these reflective, metacognitive capacities.

11. Set high standards, but design the work so that learners come to believe "I can do this!" Research on learning reveals important variables that have an impact on students' willingness to put forth effort and persist in demanding learning situations. Those variables include the following: the learner (1) clearly sees the learning goals and understands what is expected, (2) sees the content as relevant and useful to learn, (3) perceives that she is capable of succeeding at the learning tasks, and (4) feels accepted and supported by the teacher.

Effective coaches address each of these variables. Indeed, developing intrinsically motivating work in the face of relevant and authentic challenges is the essence of "coaching" for understanding and engagement. John Goodlad (1984) noted this more than 20 years ago in the landmark study *A Place Called School*:

> What do students perceive themselves to be learning? We asked [them] to write down the most important thing learned in school subjects. . . . Most commonly students listed a fact or topic. . . . Noticeably absent were responses implying the realization of having acquired some intellectual power. . . .
>
> A somewhat different emphasis pervaded the arts, physical education, vocational education and several courses outside the mainstream such as journalism. There was a noticeable shift away from the identification of subjects and topics toward the acquisition of some kind of ability or competence. (p. 234)

This commonsense finding is central to our thesis: work that is more authentic and performance based is inherently more engaging than typical seatwork.

An Example: Coaching Critical Thinking About Content

Given these various "moves" in effective coaching, let us conclude this section by considering a brief example. What would be a wise use of time in a class if we thought of ourselves as *coaches of critical thinking in the transfer of content* as opposed to just transmitters of content? Here is an example from the content-laden sphere of history.

Have students read, discuss, and summarize the textbook account of the Revolutionary War period using a traditional textbook and companion references. Then ask them to consider two excerpts from *other* countries' textbooks:

> As a result of the ceaseless struggle of the colonial people for their political rights, the 13 colonies practiced bourgeois representative government by setting up their own local legislatures. As electoral rights were restricted in many ways in every colony, those elected to the colonial legislatures were mostly landlords, gentry, and agents of the bourgeoisie, without any representation whatsoever from the working people. There were struggles between the Governors and the legislatures. These struggles reflected the contradictions between the colonies and their suzerain state. . . .
>
> The British administration of the colonies was completely in the interests of the bourgeoisie in Britain. . . . The British colonial rule impeded development of the national economy in North America. It forced certain businesses into bankruptcy. As a consequence, contradictions became increasingly acute between the ruling clique in Britain and the rising bourgeoisie and broad masses of the people in the colonies. . . .
>
> The Declaration of Independence was a declaration of the bourgeois revolution. The political principles enunciated in it were aimed at protecting the system of capitalist exploitation, legitimizing the interests of the bourgeoisie. In practice, the "people" referred to in the Declaration only meant the bourgeoisie, and the "right of the pursuit of happiness" was deduced from the "right of property" and intended to stamp the mark of legitimacy on the system of bourgeois exploitation. The Declaration was signed by 56 persons, of whom 28 were bourgeois lawyers, 13 were big merchants, 8 were plantation slave owners and 7 were members of the free professions, but there was not one representative of the working people.
>
> During the time of the war, America began its westward expansion on a large scale. From the first, the colonies had been founded on the corpses of the Indians. . . . In 1779 George Washington sent John Sullivan with a force of soldiers to "annihilate" the Iroquois tribe settled in northern New York. In his instructions he wrote: "The present aim is to completely smash and flatten their settlement, take as many prisoners as possible, the more the better, whether they are men or women. . . .

> You must not only mop up their settlement but destroy it." Thus at the time of its founding, America had already nakedly exposed its aggressive character.
>
> After the outbreak of the war, America not only failed to organize the enslaved Negroes but guarded them even more closely, thus intensifying their oppression. This seriously impeded their participation in the war and was one reason why the war for Independence was slow in achieving victory. (Barendsen et al., 1976, p. 9)

> What, then, were the causes of the American Revolution? It used to be argued that the revolution was caused by the tyranny of the British government. This simple explanation is no longer acceptable. Historians now recognize that the British colonies were the freest in the world, and that their people had rights and liberties which were enjoyed in no other empire . . . the British government was guilty of a failure of understand the American situation.
>
> The great majority of colonists were loyal, even after the Stamp Act. They were proud of the Empire and its liberties. . . . In the years following the Stamp Act a small minority of radicals began to work for independence. They watched for every opportunity to stir up trouble. (Barendsen et al., 1976, p. 16)

Now ask the following question: Given these two "stories" of the same events (the first is from a Chinese textbook; the second, from a Canadian textbook), how should the American Revolution be interpreted from a historical point of view? Where is each textbook account fair and justified, and where might it be biased? How should we best resolve the discrepancies? The skills of considering sources, analyzing arguments, and detecting bias would thus need to be taught and assessed. Indeed, such activities would be used throughout the course, given the express goal of cultivating critical thinking in history. Ultimately, students would be expected, on their own, to use the skills of critical analysis when reading documents as part of their final assessments. In the beginning, we would not assume that students could perform such a task. We would know that our key role is to coach them on how to do such tasks, through skill development and feedback.

In sum, what distinguishes the "teacher as coach" from the "teacher as teller" and "teacher as activity provider" is the overarching commitment to assist with and study the student's attempt to learn and perform with understanding, to enable the student to perform autonomously "with" content, and to be continually confronted with challenges that require critical thinking.

Matching the Approach to the Situation

We agree with Adler that all three categories of teaching—didactic instruction, facilitation, and coaching—come into play in a robust instructional program. Given the mission and goals advocated in this book, we offer these suggestions:

• Emphasize facilitation when you seek conceptual understanding, the overcoming of misunderstandings, and student construction and testing of key ideas.

• Use coaching when you desire skilled, fluent, and self-disciplined transfer in performance, in response to feedback and advice.

• Offer direct instruction more on a "need to know" basis in light of clear performance goals and feedback from students' attempts to perform with their knowledge.

As a rough rule of thumb, each approach gets about a third of the time in class.

Teacher Misunderstandings

We opened the chapter with the proposition that despite good intentions and diligent efforts, some teachers harbor a fundamental misunderstanding of their job. We now examine three such misunderstandings that, if left unchecked, are likely to undermine the mission of schooling by design.

Misunderstanding 1: "My Job Is to Cover the Content"

Teachers from kindergarten to graduate school wrestle with a common problem—too much content to teach and not enough time to teach it all. In theory, the standards movement promised a solution to the problem of "content overload" by identifying curricular priorities. Content standards were intended to specify what is most important for students to "know and be able to do," thus providing a much-needed focus and prioritization for curriculum, instruction, and assessment. In practice, content standards committees at the national, state, and district levels often worked in isolation to produce overly ambitious lists of "essentials" for their disciplines. Rather than streamlining the curriculum, the plethora of standards and benchmarks contributed to the overload problem, especially at the elementary level, where teachers are charged with teaching standards and benchmarks in multiple subjects.

The matter is further complicated by the propensity of teachers to focus on textbooks as the primary resource for addressing their obligations to the content. Here's a particularly sobering case in point that illustrates the belief that one's job is to cover a textbook. A high school principal asked each department chair to work with members of their departments to develop curriculum maps for each listed course. The intent was to encourage greater uniformity and coherence between and among course offerings. The staff was given the better part of the year to work on the maps. Toward the end of the year, the principal collected and reviewed the maps and was shocked when one department chair turned in photocopies of the tables of contents from the various course textbooks! The sobering part of the story lies in the fact that the department chair was not being rebellious. On the contrary, he and his colleagues actually believed that they were doing what the district expected. After all, they had met to carefully review prospective texts, and the district had invested considerable funds in the purchase of the recommended ones. Surely, they should be using them.

The problem with textbooks lies in part with the propensity of educational publishers to try to "cover the waterfront" in order to appease state textbook adoption committees, national subject-area organizations, and various special interest groups. The result is often a superficial, "mile wide, inch deep" treatment of subject-matter knowledge.

Nonetheless, the de facto job requirement of teaching to content standards raises an important question regarding the fit between state content standards and a nationally marketed textbook or commercial resource. Consider the exercise that asks teachers to review their textbook against state or district content standards to determine the degree of correlation and then to select the illustration in Figure 5.2 that best represents that relationship. The point of the exercise is straightforward: in the absence of a perfect correlation (illustration 4), the textbook, at best, should serve as one resource to support learning the standards. Illustrations 2 and 3 suggest that a portion of the textbook's content does not contribute to learning the standards (and thus will not need to be covered), but that other resources will be needed.

Interestingly, when teachers maintain that they are required to march through texts and syllabi (*irrespective* of the degree of student understanding or the learning results), they often cite external pressures from supervisors. Yet we have never been able to trace such reports to the administrative source, nor have we found a supervisor who claimed to have issued such an edict. Moreover, we have never seen a teacher's contract in North America that specifies that a teacher's job is to "cover a textbook." But don't we all know teachers who act as if that is their job, and who resist any suggestions to the contrary?

Simply put, it is a misunderstanding to claim that one's job is to teach the textbook. The textbook is a reference book. Its purpose—like that of an encyclopedia—is to summarize knowledge. Treating the textbook as the syllabus is akin to marching through the encyclopedia from *A* to *Z*. Logical and efficient? Yes. Purposeful, coherent, and effective? Questionable.

Regardless of whether a teacher relies on textbooks, the perceived need to "cover" content is problematic, as a closer examination of the term reveals. The two most common meanings of the term *cover*—to "conceal" (as in cover up) or to "skim the surface" (like a bedspread)—seem at odds with teaching for understanding and transfer. Indeed, if our intent is to cover more content, we can accomplish this by talking faster in class! But "teaching by mentioning" is unlikely to ensure that students

Figure 5.2

Correlation Between Textbooks and Standards

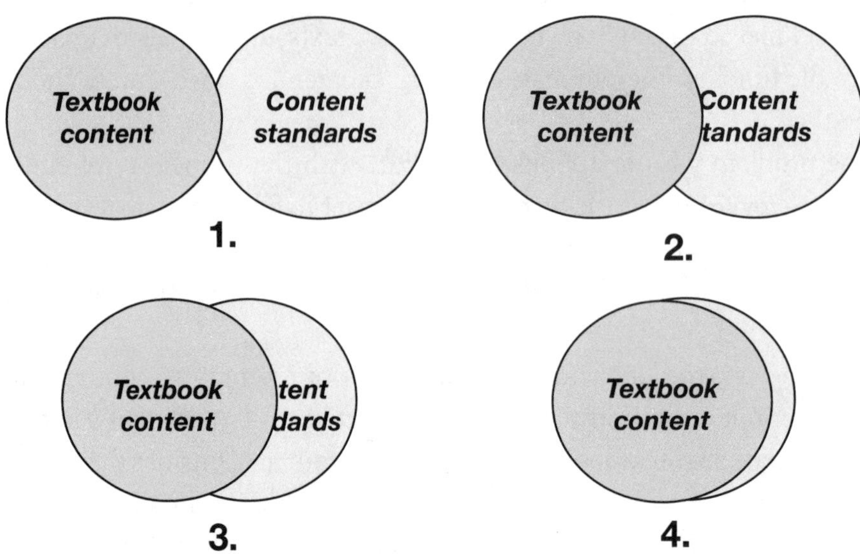

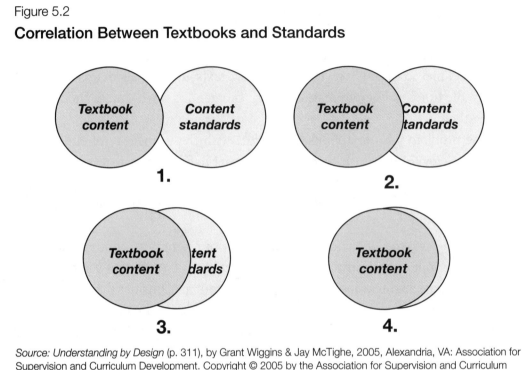

Source: Understanding by Design (p. 311), by Grant Wiggins & Jay McTighe, 2005, Alexandria, VA: Association for Supervision and Curriculum Development. Copyright © 2005 by the Association for Supervision and Curriculum Development. Adapted with permission.

know, much less understand, the key ideas and core processes of the subject. A superficial and disconnected teaching of information simply cannot yield optimal results.

We know of no research that supports the merits of a coverage mode of instruction. On the contrary, a synthesis of 30 years of research on learning and cognition points out the following:

> Research on expertise suggests that a superficial coverage of many topics in the domain may be a poor way to help students develop the competencies that will prepare them for future learning and work. (Bransford et al., 1999, p. 30)
>
> Curricula that emphasize breadth of knowledge may prevent effective organization of knowledge because there is not enough time to learn anything in depth. Instruction that enables students to see models of how experts organize and solve problems may be helpful. (Bransford et al., 1999, p. 37)

What, then, is the job of a teacher, if not to cover content? Our contention is straightforward: a teacher's job is to cause understanding, as reflected in worthy accomplishments. That requires facilitating the learners' insights and coaching them to transfer their knowledge and skill, as reflected in significant performances involving such transfer. Toward these ends, the content and "professing" serve as means and the textbook serves as a resource, *but not the syllabus!*

Misunderstanding 2: "My Job Is to Engage Learners with Interesting Activities"

Teachers who harbor this belief do not feel bound to the textbook. Indeed, many of them disdain the coverage mentality and pride themselves on getting away from the book to make learning more interesting. To this end, they develop (or find) interesting activities and projects for learners. Although we applaud the aim, we have observed numerous cases of well-intentioned teachers who get lost in the activities and lose sight of purpose as well as results.

Consider the following classic case of an activity-oriented unit at the middle school level. The 8th grade teachers at this particular middle school have developed an elaborate interdisciplinary unit, "The Victorian Tea." Here is a description of the unit prepared by the participating teachers:

> A study of Victorian England, Charles Dickens, and *A Christmas Carol* takes place annually in our 8th grade. This interdisciplinary unit allows for tremendous infusion and promotion of the visual and performing arts. A few of the objectives include allowing students the opportunity to view and produce works of art in the style of the period; to role-play, write skits, and produce videos; to learn and perform at least one period dance; to appreciate the human experience of the 1800s; and to enhance observation skills, artistic and literary analysis, and oral interpretation. The objective of involving parents in our school is also met. After exposure to the basics about the period, including fashion and etiquette, students assemble a Victorian outfit and arrive at the annual Victorian Tea prepared to simulate a social gathering of the 1800s. Students and the invited staff are greeted by parents in servant attire and are escorted into the tea room (school library), which is adorned with period antiques and tables set with fine china and decorations. Students, making light and proper conversation, are careful to remember etiquette instructions. If a serious breach of manners should occur, young ladies must feign convincing swoons. While parents serve the authentic courses, community members perform a humorous skit on Victorian customs while interacting with the students. Background music is typically provided by a parent/student duo. Next students still dressed in Victorian attire use dancing skills that they learned in physical education class to perform a waltz or other period dance. Students then often listen to a community member read Victorian poetry or prose. In the days preceding or following the tea, students perform skits/news broadcasts in social studies and/or science classes, reporting on such topics as child labor, the life of the poor, and water conditions during Victorian times. In English class they learn about Dickens' contributions to the literary world, listen to and participate in candlelight readings of *A Christmas Carol*, and critique artists' book jackets and illustrations of the work. The band director even infused Victorian music into the concert band last year. The teaching duty now really shifts to the students, who, individually or in small groups, investigate in depth a segment of Victorian times. After extensive research

> and much work with the art and English teachers, they create an oral presentation (The Victorian Project), which could be in the form of an original play, videotape, formal speech, or monologue. Students also conduct demonstrations of artwork/crafts produced or antiques acquired. Some presentations have included a full-course student-made Victorian dinner; designing and producing Victorian jewelry and greeting cards; teaching the art of setting a proper table; reciting Victorian poetry while students play period pieces on flute, piano, and violin; reporting on visits to Victorian Cape May; sketching Dickens' characters and settings; and designing or reproducing models of Victorian homes, furniture, and parks. Students formally critique each other's works through teacher-made sheets. Extra credit can be earned by viewing and critiquing a play or movie about the time period. Students seem to love this unit. Being an active participant promotes high student achievement, which can be proven by the wonderful products made, the actual grades earned, and more importantly by the general enthusiasm. Invariably, we are greeted on the first day of school with, "When do we get to do the TEA!?"

Certainly, this unit has many positive aspects, including its interdisciplinary connections, active student engagement, and parental involvement. The students had access to a variety of resources, including relevant literature, historical artifacts, and guest speakers. They had the opportunity to conduct research from primary and secondary sources and to develop tangible products and performances. Unquestionably, the teachers worked collaboratively, putting in many hours to orchestrate the various activities. Clearly, the students learned things, including information about the Victorian period, social skills, flower arranging, and how to waltz. They will likely remember the Victorian Tea experience with fondness.

Nonetheless, despite some worthwhile learning and positive feelings, one must step back and question whether the "juice is worth the squeeze." Here are critical questions to consider for this or any "activity-oriented" experience: Are the learning outcomes clearly identified and embodied in the work? Do they reflect important enduring outcomes (big ideas in the disciplines) or simply things that are "nice to know"? Do the students know the intended learning results and spend time processing the activities in terms of those goals? Can the students explain the purpose behind the various activities? Do we have appropriate evidence of learning important ideas and skills? Have students shown that they understand and can transfer what they have learned in meaningful ways? Were the time and energy devoted to the activities commensurate with the resultant learning and a wise use of time given all the other obligations?

If the answer to such questions is no, then one has a professional obligation to question the purpose behind the activities and to eliminate or adjust those that are lacking. To be clear, we are certainly *not* opposed to trying to engage students. Rather, our critique centers on lack of purposefulness.

Here's another interesting staff exercise that can be used at a faculty meeting or workshop to expose the problem of "activity-oriented" curriculum. First we pose two general questions:

- When are students most engaged and effective, in and out of school?
- What factors make these activities so engaging and effective?

Then we ask half of the group to break into subgroups of three to six people to consider the first category (engaging activities), while the other half divides into subgroups to explore the second category (effective activities). Each subgroup lists activities and situations first, and then generalizes from them, recording their comments on a flip chart. Lists from each subgroup are then shared and synthesized by category. Here are typical responses from each respective group:

Students are most *engaged* when the activities

- Are active ("hands-on").
- Involve mysteries or problems.
- Provide variety.
- Allow student choice of product and/or process.
- Offer opportunity to personalize the task/challenge.
- Offer opportunities to work in collaboration with others.
- Are built upon real-world situations or meaningful challenges.
- Use interactive approaches such as case studies, mock trial, group investigation.
- Involve real or simulated audiences.

Activities are most *effective* when

- They are focused on clear and worthy goals.
- The students understand the purpose of, and rationale for, the work.
- Clear, public criteria and models allow the students to accurately monitor their progress.
- There is limited fear and maximal incentive to try hard, take risks, and learn from mistakes without unfair penalty.
- Ideas and skills are made concrete and real through activities linking students' experiences to the world beyond the classroom.
- There are many opportunities to self-assess and self-adjust based on feedback.
- The teacher serves as a coach and facilitator to help the learner succeed.

Finally, the two groups share their respective lists, and the entire group is asked to identify the common elements found on both lists. In other words, when are learning activities both highly engaging *and* effective? The mixture is revealing: many of the traits that are at the heart of engagement enhance effectiveness, and vice versa (for example, genuine, hands-on, real-world problems; opportunities to "do" early and often; getting feedback along the way).

The resulting synthesis list becomes a set of criteria by which teachers can evaluate existing activities (such as the Victorian Tea). Because the list has been locally constructed, derived from people's own learning and teaching experiences, teachers are more likely to see it as credible. Such a list then serves as a common touchstone by which they can examine and, when necessary, improve all learning activities.

Once again, this second misunderstanding should be obvious. Despite teachers' good intentions and hard work, activities must always be seen as a means to important learning ends, not ends in themselves. In sum, a teacher's job is to engage students in purposeful activities that are both engaging *and* effective.

Misunderstanding 3: "My Job Is to Teach to the Test"

State and provincial content standards and concomitant testing programs have emerged during the past decade with the intention of focusing local curriculum and instruction and boosting student achievement by holding schools accountable for results. Ironically, the key lever in this standards-based reform strategy—the use of high-stakes accountability tests—has unwittingly led to a misconception on the part of some teachers—namely, that their job is to teach to the test. This view is understandable given the unrelenting pressures to "get the scores up" and meet the Annual Yearly Progress (AYP) requirements.

Although seeking improved performance on standardized achievement measures is not inherently wrong, the misunderstanding lies with *how* to best achieve that aim. We have observed many teachers (often at the behest of administrators) who have redirected their instruction toward the format of their state or provincial test. In the worst cases, the curriculum has morphed into a test-prep regimen of practicing testlike items and learning test-taking strategies.

Although it is certainly true that teachers are obligated to teach to established standards, it does not follow that the best way to meet those standards is to mimic the format of the state or provincial test and to cover prescribed content via superficial, multiple-choice teaching. Must we sacrifice more effective and engaging forms of instruction to raise test scores? Is more passive and fragmented teaching more or less likely to maximize student interest and performance? Do we have to teach *worse* to get higher test scores? We think that the problem reflects an underlying misunderstanding about how testing works, how validity is established, and how learning is maximized.

To expose the flaw in this reasoning, consider an analogy. Once a year, we go to the doctor for a physical exam. No one particularly relishes the thought of such an exam, but we go with the understanding that it is in our long-term interest to get an objective (yet superficial) measure of our health. The doctor performs a few tests in a short span of time (blood pressure, pulse, temperature, blood work to measure cholesterol). The "physical" is a small sample of tests, yielding a few useful indicators of one's health status. Its validity and value stem from the fact that the results *suggest* our state of health, not because the physical *defines* healthfulness. We take a relatively quick and nonintrusive physical exam so that various "indicators" can be examined for signs of any deeper trouble demanding further scrutiny.

Now suppose we are terribly concerned about the final numbers (weight, blood pressure, and other measures) and that these results ultimately link to the costs of our health insurance. What we might do, in our panicky state before each annual physical, is "practice" for the test—focus all our energy on the physical exam (as opposed to what its indicators suggest). If our doctor knew of our actions, the response would surely be, "Whoa! You're confused. You have mixed up causality and correlation here. The best way to 'pass' your physical is to live a healthful life—exercise, watch your weight, lower your intake of fats, eat more fiber, and get sufficient sleep."

Note that *none* of the elements of true healthfulness—diet, fitness regimen, or stress management—is *directly* tested in the physical. Doctors use *indirect* indicators, such as blood pressure, weight, skin tone and color, and cholesterol levels, to gauge our health status. The indicators are correlational, not causal. In other words, the effects of our healthful regimen will be reflected in the test indicators. In fact, the more we concentrate only on what is on the physical exam, the less likely it is in the long run that we will be healthy.

Like the doctor, state education agencies give schools an annual checkup via such indirect testing of student performance. A state test, like the physical exam, consists of indicators of local "health"—a set of "items" that sample indirectly from the broader domain of the content supposedly addressed through a local educational regimen. The test yields valid inferences to the extent that test results correlate with more complex and meaningful learnings—in the same way that the physical exam relies on tried-and-true indicators like blood pressure and cholesterol level. Simple items are used to test indirectly for a "healthy regimen" in the same way that the physical is a proxy for the daily "tests" of genuine fitness and wellness. That is the nature of test validity: establishing a link between one set of easy-to-obtain indicators and a related set of more complex and desired results. (Although it may surprise many readers to hear us argue this way, given our longstanding, documented opposition to overreliance on indirect tests, the issue here is more narrowly focused on test validity. Numerous arguments can be made on behalf of more performance assessment in educational testing, but the issue here is the reverse: indirect—"inauthentic"—tests can yield valid inferences, just as "authentic" tasks can yield invalid inferences.)

People would think it silly to practice a physical exam as a way to be healthy. But this confusion is precisely what we see in schools all over North America. Local educators, fearful of the consequences of poor results or failure to show gains, focus on the indicators, not their causes. The format of the test misleads us, in other words.

Please understand that this explanation does not constitute an endorsement of current standardized-testing practices that rely too heavily on one-shot external testing. In fact, we feel strongly that state agencies and policymakers bear a responsibility for allowing this confusion to persist by not making local assessments a part of a comprehensive state accountability system. What matters most in educational reform is that we take to heart the point of the analogy: we—not the state—are responsible for wellness. The state's job is to audit. Just as the physical exam is not the regimen we should engage in at home, but rather is a set of superficial indicators to see if our regimen is adequate, the state test does not try to duplicate all the "healthful" activities and assessments that should be taking place day in and day out at the local level in classrooms, schools, and districts. Indeed, the state could not possibly assess everything of value in an authentic way, even if we all wanted that to occur, because of excessive costs and the desire to limit the intrusions of external testing. This is true for doctors, too: to require all patients to come in for several days of comprehensive tests at a medical lab would be excessively time-consuming and costly (never mind expecting our insurers to foot the bill).

"Are you then saying that a more concerted effort to 'teach to the test' *lowers* scores?" No. Teaching to the test clearly has *some* effect, particularly if before such practice there was little attention to common standards and a focus on results. Scores do increase in the short run when a school or district focuses more carefully on a common goal. No surprise here: greater attention to an outcome will improve performance on *any* measure. But once the test particulars are figured out and students have become familiar with the test format and test-taking skills, long-term progress rarely occurs, and the scores typically drop when the test is altered or renormed.

It appears to us that educators are confused by the lack of "face validity" of the tests into assuming that teachers must mimic the test format. Worse, they wrongly infer that their own instruction should focus on a superficial survey of content and decontextualized treatment of facts and skills, as suggested by the test's construction.

A related misunderstanding lies in the view that external test scores determine educational success. Without debating the merits and demerits of particular tests, we are saying what should be more obvious than it is: the test score is not the end; good test scores do not signal "mission accomplished." Test scores are indicators in relation to *some* of our goals. Few state standards and tests even attempt to address all worthy educational goals, such as those related to character, study skills, the arts, employability, and lifelong learning. It is perhaps leadership's greatest challenge in the new world of standards and accountability to help staff understand that their job is to focus on *mission-critical results* and not fixate on the once-a-year audit of indicators.

In sum, we are not saying "do not concern yourself with tests." Rather, we propose that the best way to raise test scores over the long haul is to (1) teach the key ideas and processes contained in content standards (the content that is purportedly tested) in rich and engaging ways, (2) collect evidence of student understanding and transferability of that content via robust local assessments, and (3) raise the standards and quality control for local assignments and assessments to gather evidence of all that we value, not just what is easiest to measure.

Designing Backward to Determine the Teacher's Role

So what is the job of a teacher when teaching? As Mursell (1954) succinctly put it more than 50 years ago:

> Successful teaching is teaching that brings about effective learning. The decisive question is not what methods or procedures are employed, and whether they are old-fashioned or modern, time-tested or experimental, conventional or progressive. . . . The ultimate criterion for success in teaching is—results! (p. 1)

Thus, a teacher's job description needs to be derived by working backward from the stated mission and goals. As a teacher, we must ask, in a backward-design way, what kinds of learning accomplishments are sought? What should be our role as a teacher in that learning situation, given the desired results? If the mission calls for developing student understanding leading to genuine transfer performances, not simply knowledge acquisition, then our job as teachers is dictated by those aims.

In this chapter, we examined the job of teachers when they are teaching—when they are *with* students. In Chapter 6 we turn our attention to the important noninstructional roles that are part of a teacher's job.

Ideas for Action

• Ask teachers to write a summary of their job description as they perceive it. Collect, review, and discuss these at a team or faculty meeting. What patterns are evident? What staff misunderstandings are revealed? What important job functions are missing?

• Review an existing job description for teachers. Does it include specific job responsibilities and performance indicators? Does it explicitly call for the kinds of functions described in the second part of this chapter? What changes or clarifications are needed?

• Review the current teacher evaluation process. To what extent is the current appraisal system in sync with expected job functions? What does the current process signal to staff about what really matters? What changes or clarifications are needed?

• Conduct the textbook/standards analysis exercise shown in Figure 5.2. What patterns were found? Discuss the implications of the results.

• Review the current hiring process. How are teacher applicants evaluated? What do prospective teachers believe the job to be? What does the current hiring protocol signal about expected job functions? What changes or clarifications are needed?

• Review the current teacher induction program. What do beginning teachers believe their jobs to be? To what extent is the content of the induction program in line with expected job functions? What changes or clarifications are needed?

• Use the "Effective/Engaging" exercise described on pages 149 to 150 at a faculty meeting or inservice session. Discuss the resulting list and its implications. Ask teachers to plan specific actions to revise or eliminate activities that are not *both* effective and engaging.

• Show the chart of the three teaching roles (Figure 5.1) and facilitate a staff discussion of how current instructional practices fit into these categories. What patterns are noted within and across subjects and grades? Review the school's mission and goals. Do the teaching methods align with the mission and goals?

• Create a Job Responsibilities chart with two columns. Label one column "Individual Autonomy"; the other, "Collective Responsibility." Have staff complete the chart to gauge how they see the two categories. Then share and discuss as a faculty or team in order to clarify the distinctions.

6

What Is the Teacher's Job When Not Teaching?

No man is an island.

—John Donne

In Chapter 5 we examined three categories of classroom teaching and discussed their place in understanding-focused and performance-based schooling. In addition to the primary instructional roles, a teacher's job typically involves a number of other duties, such as advisor, disciplinarian, confidant, mentor, extracurricular sponsor, and hall monitor. While acknowledging the importance of these varied functions, we propose that in the kind of schooling we envision, three particular noninstructional roles of a teacher are critical to the success of the proposed educational mission. These aspects of a teacher's job are reflected in three essential questions: (1) How can we make our curriculum more coherent, engaging, and effective? (2) How well are our students achieving, and how might we enhance their performance? (3) How can we become more effective as professionals? In sum, learning about learning must become more overtly part of the job of being a teacher, not an option for only the most curious. In this chapter, we examine these three noninstructional roles and describe the specific job functions of each.

Saying that schools should be more focused on "research" may cause readers to miss a crucial point. The job of causing results related to mission, we believe, can occur only if teachers look carefully at the effects of their intentions as a key and regular component of the job, for which time and other resources are regularly allocated.

Role 1: Contributor to the Curriculum

As discussed in Chapters 2 and 3, a robust curriculum designed backward from mission and established goals functions as the centerpiece of schooling. Such a curriculum frames the content around big ideas, transfer goals, and habits of mind to guide classroom assessment and instruction. The centrality of the curriculum as a framework for learning demands a commitment from teachers, not only as users, but also as contributors because, as we noted earlier, endless adjustments based on troubleshooting will need to be part of the curriculum. Teachers can actively contribute to a curriculum's effectiveness in several ways, and there are good reasons for making this activity part of the job, not an option.

Curriculum Designer

Teachers can and should play a prominent role in curriculum development—not because their participation makes the process more efficient (it doesn't), but because having a hand in crafting and continually shaping the curriculum ensures greater buy-in and understanding of the curriculum and its purpose. Expressed the other way around, when teachers merely "receive" and "implement" the curriculum, the result tends to be rigid and aimless instruction that loses sight of mission and long-term program goals.

In colleges, independent schools, and smaller school districts, professors and teachers tend to assume a greater responsibility for curriculum and assessment design and ongoing adjustments to the framework. In larger districts, curriculum work is often centralized, undertaken by curriculum committees composed of representative teachers. Although we understand the need to have work done in manageable committees, the process of approving the curriculum should require that all faculty have a say in sign-off, ongoing feedback, and proposed adjustments as part of the job via academic departments and grade-level teams. Only when everyone "owns" the document will schools have the authority and mechanisms to examine practice in a principled way.

When teachers are engaged in any level of curriculum planning or adjusting (whether a unit, a course design, or a preK–12 program framework), we strongly suggest that they use the three-stage backward-design process described in *Understanding by Design* (Wiggins & McTighe, 2005). We also recommend that curriculum/assessment design be conducted in teams. It is unlikely that even the most capable teacher working alone will be able to generate the amount and quality of work that an effective, competent team can produce. Senge (2006) agrees on the centrality of the team in a learning organization: "Unless teams can learn the organization cannot learn" (p. 10). The team approach is particularly important if the curriculum is intended to develop understanding and equip students for transfer performances. Creating such curricula demands that the developers have solid content expertise, including an understanding of how adults use the relevant content and skills in real-world applications. Whereas any individual teacher is unlikely to have in-depth content knowledge in all areas of a discipline, a team of teachers working together benefits from distributed expertise, making it more likely that various topics are properly addressed in deep and rich ways. Additionally, a teacher may have content expertise but be less skilled at documenting and communicating that knowledge to guide others. Thus, including curriculum team members with strong writing skills is beneficial.

Part of the charge to each team must also be to run their ideas about transfer goals and tasks past experts in the field. Just as teachers in vocational programs must typically have their ideas vetted by veteran practitioners, academic programs should be routinely expected to have their assessments and curricular approach evaluated for appropriateness by professionals and veteran practitioners. History teachers, for example, should be expected to run their program goals and transfer tasks by historians, journalists, curators, and archivists. Math teachers should have their assessments critiqued by statisticians, accountants, engineers, demographers, and mathematicians.

In addition to the curriculum *products* that are generated, participation in such a design *process* over time strengthens teachers' content knowledge, assessment skills, and pedagogical effectiveness. Indeed, districts and schools that actively involve teachers in curriculum and assessment design have come to realize that the process of curriculum development provides substantive professional development, enriching all participating staff members. Accordingly, we encourage leaders to consider commingling funds for curriculum and staff development so as to include a greater number of teachers in curriculum design activities (including peer reviews, discussed in the next section).

Collaborative curriculum design may be difficult to undertake in very small schools and districts, in which one teacher is the only person responsible for a course or a grade level. In such cases, we propose that curriculum be developed through a regional consortium model, facilitated through regional service agencies or established consortia. As an example, a one-week summer curriculum workshop in chemistry could involve four chemistry teachers from different high schools in a region, working in conjunction with local scientists and professors.

Given that most states and provinces already have an established framework of standards to guide local curriculum design, it makes sense to "work smarter, not harder" by pooling expertise and resources rather than reinventing the same wheel. Moreover, our experience has shown us that most "singleton" teachers treasure the opportunity for professional exchange with others who teach the same topics. Such collaboration reduces feelings of isolation and helps establish regional networks of supportive colleagues.

Critical Friend Reviews

Regardless of the extent to which a teacher is directly involved in curriculum design, we propose that *all* teachers should actively contribute to the curriculum's effectiveness by playing the role of a critical friend through peer reviews, field testing, and troubleshooting.

As educators working on curriculum design, we can sometimes get too close to our work and have a difficult time seeing any weaknesses. Too often the curriculum document is never critically reviewed by users as part of the process—with the consequence that many such documents gather dust. Curricular peer review is a structured process through which teachers examine the draft curriculum designs developed by others. The reviewers play the role of critical friends, offering "user eyes" to enhance the clarity, alignment, completeness, and ultimate effectiveness of curriculum products (such as curriculum maps, course designs, and unit plans).

We recommend that peer reviews be guided by a set of curriculum design standards so that the feedback is always "standards based" and depersonalized, as discussed earlier. In Chapter 3, we listed such standards for program and course design, and a companion set of unit design standards is presented in the *Understanding by Design: Professional Development Workbook* (McTighe & Wiggins, 2004). The workbook also includes a detailed description of a tried-and-true protocol for conducting peer reviews, along with suggestions for getting started with the process.

Although the primary purpose of peer review is to provide feedback to improve curriculum designs, residual benefits accrue as well. Participants in peer review sessions regularly comment on the value of the process as an opportunity to share and discuss curriculum, assessment, and instruction with colleagues. Such sessions focus attention on essential questions of teaching and learning: What are the key ideas in targeted standards? What counts as evidence that students really understand and can transfer their learning? What and how should we teach to enable students to achieve expected results?

Participating in structured peer reviews underscores the *P* in *professionalism*. When peer reviews occur as a part of the job, teachers will be "walking the talk" of standards-based education by using design standards to guide, evaluate, and improve the quality and effectiveness of their own curricula.

Field Tester

Just as writers rarely produce a polished manuscript in the first draft, few written curricula are perfect right out of the gate. In addition to undergoing peer reviews, it is essential that a newly developed curriculum be tested in the classroom as a means of validation. Although the adults may agree that X essential questions, Y assessment tasks, and Z activities are fine, the rubber meets the road when the curriculum meets the learners. Indeed, the ultimate validation of a curriculum lies in its results; that is, did it help students achieve the desired outcomes?

Software development provides an apt analogy for curriculum design. When a new software program is developed, it typically undergoes beta testing by a wide range of users. Software designers aggressively seek feedback from the testers because the designers realize that it is impossible for them to anticipate all variables related to usage and users. Feedback from these initial trials guides the necessary debugging before release of version 1.0. But as all computer users have come to understand, software development does not end there. Ongoing use and concomitant feedback from users informs the *continuous* process of refinement, the results of which appear in versions 1.01, 1.02, 1.03, and so on. At some future point, a "next generation" version of the software containing more or better features is released as version 2.0, with subsequent refinements expected to follow.

We contend that curriculum development should be thought of similarly. Teachers can, therefore, play a critical role in the overall curriculum process by serving as "beta" field testers to try out draft curricula (just as there must be "alpha" testing of the unit as a design, against design standards). Once version 1.0 is released, their continuous feedback as users is needed to fine-tune the curriculum for maximum effect.

The virtue of developing, storing, and transmitting curricula electronically should be obvious. Electronically framed curricula can be incrementally adjusted and improved on the basis of classroom feedback. It is no longer necessary to wait three to seven years according to a curriculum renewal schedule before reprinting a massive guide with changes. Immediate adjustments are not only possible but necessary, so that teachers can use the curriculum most effectively to maximize learning.

Troubleshooter

Even when reviews and successful classroom field testing have validated curricula, teachers should be expected, *as a part of their job,* to identify problem areas in student learning and to work with colleagues to find solutions. In this regard, we recommend that schools and districts periodically use scheduled faculty or team meetings for collegial problem solving, during which teachers identify persistent difficulties in student learning and performance, and brainstorm possible remedies. The resulting ideas can then be tried and evaluated, with the most successful solutions recorded in the troubleshooting guides that we recommend be included for each curriculum area. In other words, it becomes part of the job (and part of supervision and evaluation, therefore) to contribute to the living document of curriculum. Staff, team, and department meetings would be devoted to such troubleshooting, and the teams would be required at year's end to issue a formal report on what worked, what didn't, and what needs changing in the curriculum.

Systematically involving all teachers in troubleshooting the curriculum has at least three tangible benefits: (1) it fosters purposeful collegiality and collective responsibility for results ("we are all in this together"), while reducing teacher isolation; (2) it harnesses the experience of the veterans and provides guidance to the less experienced teachers (although sometimes the "newbies" offer fresh solutions to seemingly intractable problems); and (3) it captures the wisdom of practice in a permanent record for the benefit of current and future teachers.

Role 2: Analyzer of Results

Increasingly, educators are being encouraged to use data as a basis for instructional decision making and school improvement planning. But this call to become data driven requires more than simply establishing mechanisms for quantifying, collecting, and distributing results. As noted organizational-change consultant Jim Collins (2001) writes, organizations need to turn "information" into "information that cannot be ignored" (p. 79) and then confront the "brutal facts of reality" (p. 71) in the data. In other words, given our mission and desired results, what data are *needed* and what do those data tell us, especially about what is *not* working well? We have observed that the most effective schools and districts do not shy away from confronting the "brutal facts" of core results. In fact, educators in such educational institutions recognize that the pathway from "good to great" requires them to actively seek information about learning.

How, then, does a school or a district become data driven in this sense of "nothing personal, but we have work to do"? In some cases, this call has been translated into action by a small group of district- and school-level administrators who dissect the annual test score report and summarize the results for the teaching staff. We think that such a plan is inadequate, though it is surely better than nothing. Alternatively, we propose that all teachers be actively involved at some level in the analysis of achievement data and the formulation of improvement plans, so that they will come to better understand and "own" student performance data.

Such analysis does not have to be excessively time-consuming. It is simply a matter of designing staff meetings "backward" from the need for data analysis, however many meetings are scheduled for staff as a whole and in teams for the year. Consider the following example reflected in the minutes from a regularly scheduled, 45-minute meeting of a high school department. Notice how the meeting was sharply focused on analyzing the results from a recent state assessment in order to understand how to better prepare students.

Minutes of the Meeting

The meeting began at 2:15. Margaret explained what she hopes departments will accomplish by meeting on a grade 7–12 basis. We have to make sure all students have similar learning experiences as they go through the grades and through the state exams. Although our results on the state exams at the end of grades 8, 10, and 11 have been good, they could be even better, particularly in terms of having even more students perform at the mastery level.

The three state exams (global history and geography, economics, government and U.S. history) for June 2001 were distributed, along with an item analysis for the multiple-choice (MC) questions.

The data on the grade 8 exam had been broken down so we could see how many students selected each of the four choices for the 45 MC questions. Margaret asked us to look at the questions that were most frequently missed, focusing not just on the content of the question, but also on the most popular wrong answer for each of those questions. She feels we can get a better idea of where our students have gaps in their understanding if we examine their incorrect answers.

We looked at question #23 on the grade 8 exam, dealing with the free-enterprise system. Why did nearly as many students pick the wrong answer of stockholders being guaranteed a profit as picked the right answer of businesses competing for consumer dollars? Was it the wording of the question, or are they lacking some understanding of the free-enterprise system?

The item analyses for the two high school exams were less revealing, since they only provided the percentages of students who answered each question correctly, without the number of students selecting the four choices for each of the 50 questions.

We spent some time examining question #25 on the global history exam, dealing with the main cause of the mass starvation in Ireland during the 19th century. The correct answer was the failure of the potato crop. We suspect many students blamed it on the war between Protestants and Catholics in Northern Ireland, since they had studied that topic not long before they took the exam. They probably learn more about the potato famine in 11th grade, but is there a reason why they didn't know it prior to that? The state expects social studies teachers to be teaching that topic, and our library media centers should soon receive a State Ed. guide to teaching about the potato famine.

In terms of what to do with this in future meetings, we agreed that everyone would focus on one of the three exams, preferably not an exam at that teacher's grade level. Margaret asked us to look not so much at the specific content or the wording of the problem questions, but rather to look at the concepts or larger understandings that the students might be missing. Also, are there particular types of questions that our students tend to miss, e.g., cartoons, speaker questions, tables and graphs? Each person selected one exam to study.

> We agreed to hold future meetings on the third Tuesday of the month, so the next meeting will be on Tuesday, October 16, in room C120 at the high school. When we meet on the 16th, we'll break down into three groups, according to the three exams, so people can discuss what they noticed on the exam they reviewed.
>
> Meeting adjourned at 3:00 p.m.

Although undeniably important and public, the results of high-stakes accountability tests are *not*, in our judgment, the most robust or even the most appropriate evidence of success, given an understanding- and performance-based educational mission. Such analysis is necessary, but not sufficient. At best, an annual standardized score report offers a narrow snapshot of student achievement on easily testable content knowledge and skills. And rarely do external standardized tests provide adequate evidence of understanding and transfer capacity. Moreover, such reports are not sufficiently detailed or timely enough to inform and guide continuous improvement actions at the classroom and school levels.

In addition to analysis of external test results, it is important that staff engage in *ongoing analysis* of student performance data from *multiple sources,* including—especially—locally developed cornerstone assessments and collections of student work such as the kind described in Chapter 3. Such ongoing analysis of local work offers more comprehensive and far more credible measures of student accomplishment, thus providing the needed fuel for continuous improvement. Schmoker (2003) echoes this sentiment in his description of a straightforward approach:

> Using the goals that they have established, teachers can meet regularly to improve their lessons and assess their progress using another important source: formative assessment data. Gathered every few weeks or at each grading period, formative data enable the team to gauge levels of success and to adjust their instructional efforts accordingly. Formative, collectively administered assessments allow teams to capture and celebrate short-term results, which are essential to success in any sphere. (p. 22)

We recommend that teachers work in grade-level or department teams of two to six members and use agreed-upon rubrics for evaluating student responses, products, and performances. The sets of questions in Figure 6.1 move the examination of student work beyond scores or grades to help teachers better understand the meaning of the work and to plan adjustments that are likely to improve the results.

In addition to such questions, we have found it beneficial to provide organizers for teacher teams to use when analyzing student work. Figure 6.2 provides an example of a completed organizer for middle school mathematics. Notice how the

Figure 6.1
Questions to Ask When Examining Student Work

Describe
- What knowledge and skills are assessed?
- What kinds of thinking are required (for example, recall, interpretation, evaluation)?
- Are these the results I (we) expected? Why or why not?
- In what areas did the student(s) perform best?
- What weaknesses are evident?
- What misconceptions are revealed?
- Are there any surprises?
- What anomalies exist?
- Is there evidence of improvement or decline? If so, what caused the changes?

Evaluate
- By what criteria am I (are we) evaluating student work?
- Are these the most important criteria?
- How good is "good enough" (the performance standard)?

Interpret
- What does this work reveal about student learning and performance?
- What patterns are evident?
- What questions does this work raise?
- Is this work consistent with other achievement data?
- Are there different possible explanations for these results?

Identify Improvement Actions
- What teacher actions are needed to improve learning and performance?
- What student actions are needed to improve learning and performance?
- What systemic actions at the school/district level are needed to improve learning and performance (such as changes in curriculum, schedule, grouping)?

careful analysis resulted in clearly identified weaknesses followed by highly specific instructional adjustments tied directly to the performance deficits.

By regularly using such questions and planning organizers to examine student work, teachers properly focus on the broader goals and mission-related aims (understanding, transfer, habits of mind) and avoid fixating on standardized test scores alone. Several structured protocols have been developed to guide teachers when examining student work (see, for example, the Tuning Protocol; Arter & McTighe, 2001; Blythe, Allen, & Powell, 1999; McTighe & Thomas, 2003). We believe that regular use of such processes provides the antidote to the aforementioned "teach, test, and hope for the best" attitude.

Figure 6.2
Sample of a Data-Driven Improvement Planning Worksheet for Math

Based on an analysis of achievement data and student work

- What *patterns* of weakness are noted?
- What *specific* areas are most in need of improvement?

- Problem solving and mathematical reasoning are generally weak.
- Students do not effectively explain their reasoning and their use of strategies.
- Appropriate mathematical language is not always used.

What *specific* improvement actions will we take?

- ☐ Increase our use of "nonroutine" problems that require mathematical reasoning.
- ☐ Explicitly teach (and regularly review) specific problem-solving strategies.
- ☐ Develop a poster of problem-solving strategies and post in each math classroom.
- ☐ Increase use of "think-alouds" (by teacher and students) to model mathematical reasoning.
- ☐ Develop a "word wall" of key mathematical terms and use the terms regularly.
- ☐ Revise our problem-solving rubric to emphasize explanation and use of mathematical language.

Anchoring Curriculum and Assessment

As discussed in Chapter 3, "anchoring" refers to the process of selecting examples of work to represent each of the score points on a rubric scale. These examples, known as "anchors," provide tangible and specific illustrations of various levels of quality or degrees of proficiency based upon established criteria. Anchors are an important component of a performance-based curriculum, and their selection is a natural by-product of the collaborative evaluation of student work. We think it imperative that, as part of their job, faculty regularly establish anchor performances and review those anchors for appropriateness. We also believe that each teacher should routinely publish anchors for students, parents, and colleagues to ensure that everyone is on the same page about what quality work looks like. The top-level anchors are often referred to as "exemplars." (Recall the writing exemplars identified in Greece, New York, and presented in Chapter 3.) Specific processes for anchoring are presented in *Scoring Rubrics in the Classroom* by Arter and McTighe (2001).

We have seen the following tangible benefits of involving teachers in identifying anchors for the curriculum:

- Anchors help teachers understand and consistently apply the criteria and standards when judging student products or performances.
- Anchoring provides a basis for setting performance standards. By selecting examples of student work correlated with various levels (score points) in a rubric, educators and other stakeholders are better equipped to answer the question "How good is good enough?"
- By providing tangible illustrations of the rubric descriptors, the potentially ambiguous language in a rubric (such as the terms *well organized* or *persuasive*) is exemplified, helping both teachers and students develop a better understanding of the qualities of effective performance.
- When anchor examples are collected and published at the grade, school, or district level, we see greater consistency in evaluation among teachers and schools. Moreover, the "public" anchors help teachers explain scores and grades to parents and students. In fact, many teachers report that grading quibbles virtually disappear when clear rubrics and anchors are available.
- The availability of anchors is especially beneficial to new teachers, because it provides them with immediate access to the expected levels of performance for the students in their grade/subject area.
- Anchors can be used instructionally to provide students with clear targets to motivate and guide their efforts and help them better understand and apply the criteria when engaged in self- and peer evaluation.

McTighe and Emberger (2006) summarize the benefits of such teacher collaborations:

> Collaborative designs and peer reviews honor and enhance teachers' professionalism, expertise, and collegial learning. Working in teams to evaluate student work against established criteria, identify models of excellence (anchoring), and plan needed improvements promotes a results-oriented culture of quality.
>
> By designing performance assessments, educators enhance their understanding of content standards and of the evidence needed to show that students really understand the important ideas and processes contained in those standards. Teachers discover that the connection between curriculum and assessment becomes clearer, teaching is more sharply focused and the evaluation is more consistent. (p. 44)

Role 3: Continuous Learner

One important aspect of a school's mission is to develop the capabilities and dispositions for lifelong learning, and we contend that this mission applies to staff as well as to students. Indeed, continuous learning is a hallmark of professionalism in any field and especially relevant to a profession devoted to learning.

So what should teachers keep learning about? Well, clearly they should continue to learn about their subjects, their students, and the mission—learning about the learning they must cause, whether they have caused it, and what they might do better to cause more of it. Although this may seem obvious, we caution readers about dismissing this statement as merely a bland truism. To put the matter more pointedly, people who *really* are lifelong learners *keep* learning in the face of psychological and social pressures to stop learning and keep from changing. Alas, many adults, including too many teachers, end up coasting on comfortable habits and routines. To paraphrase Dewey's caustic line, sometimes a 20-year veteran teacher is merely someone who has taught the same year, 20 times.

As an antidote to professional *stasis* (where it may exist), we propose that an explicit and expected part of a teacher's job involve continuous learning—about subject matter, about teaching effectiveness, and about ways of doing a better job of causing learning. More specifically, we propose that ongoing teacher learning occur through three interrelated actions, which would be considered in supervision and evaluation: (1) keeping abreast of current research on teaching and learning, (2) enhancing professional skills, and (3) engaging in action research.

Keeping Abreast of Current Research on Teaching and Learning

Professionalism requires that professionals stay in touch with new information in their fields, and today's educators have many resources to help them keep current with relevant research and best practices on teaching. For example, teachers enrolled in university coursework are typically exposed to the contemporary research literature. However, a majority of educators are not involved in formal university programs and thus need other sources for keeping up-to-date. Some teachers accomplish this through membership in professional organizations, such as the Association for Supervision and Curriculum Development and subject-area associations, and we endorse these affiliations. Unfortunately, such memberships are generally voluntary, undertaken by only a percentage of the teaching force. A few teachers attend state, regional, or national conferences in which "state-of-the-art" information is presented, but these opportunities are not regularly or widely available to the mainstream.

What is needed, we think, is *on-the-job* learning for *all* teachers—*by design*. In other words, continuous learning about relevant research and best practices would be job embedded as a regular and expected part of a teacher's role. Staff would be expected to routinely report on a summary of findings from study groups, action research, and personal reading. Consider the following example (a true story) of what this could look like in practice.

A middle school principal told his staff that for the next two years he would evaluate half their performance on their ability to learn about and experiment with innovative "best practices." He asked the faculty to come up with a list of the most promising-sounding innovations in the field appropriate for their school. The eventual list was whittled down to six (including such things as differentiated instruction and authentic assessment). He then asked each staff member to "buddy up" with two or three others to form a working research and development group on any one of the six topics. Their job for two years was to learn about, try out, and report to the faculty on their learning. Many of the staff at the school reported that this single action dramatically changed the culture of the school.

To act on this idea of "expected continuous learning," school-based and especially district-level administrators might initially assume primary responsibility for locating and distributing relevant articles and research summaries if they felt staff were not ready to do so. Then, school administrators and teacher leaders (such as department chairs and grade-level team leaders) would lead discussions and propose experiments as part of regularly scheduled meetings. Eventually, though, it would be understood that part of the job, for individuals and teams, would be to initiate and manage such job-embedded learning.

Enhancing Professional Skills

Knowledge is insufficient. Reading an article or attending an introductory presentation on a research-based teaching technique will not equip teachers to successfully implement a new practice. Just hearing a keynote address on the qualities and benefits of "essential questions" will not prepare teachers to "unpack" content accordingly and use essential questions to frame their instruction and their assessments. Understanding and the ability to apply new skills require practice, coaching, and ongoing support—for adults as well as younger learners.

All teachers should be expected to engage in ongoing professional development to expand their knowledge and skills. "Well, of course," you might be thinking. "Who would argue with that?" However, not everything that now passes for professional development qualifies. All too frequently, staff development translates into large-group sit-and-get presentations on a topic. Such an event-based approach to professional development is akin to superficial coverage of a topic by a teacher. In neither case is the learner (student or teacher) sufficiently prepared to transfer knowledge.

Clearly, a more comprehensive and ongoing approach to staff learning is needed to develop the competencies outlined in this book. The National Staff Development Council underscores this point when characterizing its Standards for Professional Development: "Staff development must be results-driven, standards-based, and job-embedded." The authors of *Supervision for Learning* elaborate on this point:

> Data from various sources can serve a number of important staff development purposes. First, data on student learning gathered from standardized tests, district-made tests, student work samples, portfolios, and other sources provide important input to the selection of school or district improvement goals and provide focus for staff development efforts. This process of data analysis and goal development typically determines the content of teachers' professional learning in the areas of instruction, curriculum, and assessment. (Aseltine, Faryniarz, & Rigazio-DiGilio, 2006)

Although the orchestration of formal professional development programs typically falls to administrators, teachers have a professional responsibility to engage in continuous learning. In addition to traditional professional growth activities such as taking graduate coursework and participating in school/district staff development experiences, teachers have an array of ongoing methods for enhancing their learning, including professional reading, peer-to-peer coaching and mentoring arrangements, and personalized growth plans.

Engaging in Action Research as Part of the Job

Readers might interpret the preceding ideas as dependent on the leaders to organize staff development and individual teachers to pursue personal areas of interest as they see fit. Our intent, however, is to argue that action research and professional improvement must become an expected part of everyone's ongoing work, part of each team's obligation, and a cornerstone of each personal improvement plan. In other words, learning about learning is not optional; it is required by the job—and by contract.

Consider the academic departments in the high school and the grade-level teams in middle school. We are proposing that departmental action research and intervention reports become a job requirement. Twice a year, each department would issue a written report to all staff describing performance strengths and weaknesses measured by local assessments against program goals, actions taken to improve areas of weakness, and areas of concern to be targeted via future action research, as prioritized by the department in meetings. Similarly, each member of the department or team would write up a personal report describing her own research agenda and results. Reports would have to include feedback from students and parents on what is working and what isn't working.

In addition to research conducted by individuals and teams, we propose that action research be undertaken at the school and district levels. Research would target larger mission goals and curriculum-related goals, and include feedback from alumni and employers on their experiences with "our" students. Former students would also be surveyed or interviewed regarding the effectiveness of their K–12 preparation for their current schooling or work.

Because models are key to improvement, departments would also be expected to share and learn from examples of best practices in meeting the mission and program goals. These model units would be housed in a local database, available to all teachers over the Internet. We know that the Japanese practice of lesson study (whereby a team of teachers works on a model unit of study and shares results with staff and colleagues) is a key to improved teacher effectiveness over time. Indeed, the researchers in the international comparison of teaching viewed lesson study as the answer to the question of why the average teacher in Japan is so much better than the average teacher in the United States. It just makes sense: if every teacher were engaged in action research every year, the quality of teaching would improve significantly in the United States, and the dysfunctional school culture of "every man for himself" would be undermined.

We disagree, therefore, with current hand-wringing in policy circles about the lack of quality teachers in U.S. schools and their inadequate preparation by schools of education. Our view, supported by research and common sense, is that teacher education *in their place of employment,* through ongoing professional action research and study groups, is a far more likely source of significant long-term improvement in teaching than looking to reforms in preservice education. If nothing else, we are comparing a professional lifetime with four part-time years in college by a novice learning out of context. As a manager at IBM once said to us, "You in education just stick a rookie in the job, close the door and say goodbye. We give them eight weeks of summer training before we even let them touch equipment, and they must work in teams because we know even with their fancy engineering degrees that they are not ready for excellent performance by themselves in a complicated workplace."

Speaking practically, every teacher (especially new ones) should be expected to work on a 10-month schedule. It makes no sense to make the teacher's calendar the same as the student's when there is so much work to be done outside class. Three noncontact days might be added each year to the yearly calendar over a six-year period to make the change smooth and cost-effective.

Our idea about in-school research as part of the job is not new. Robert Schaefer (1967) proposed it 40 years ago in *The School as a Center of Inquiry:*

> We can no longer afford to conceive of schools simply as distribution centers for dispensing cultural orientations, information, and knowledge developed by other social units. The complexities of teaching and learning have become so formidable that the school must . . . be a center of inquiry—a producer as well as a transmitter of knowledge. (p. 1)

What *is* new is that 40 years later we now have a far better understanding of the complexity of learning and organizational development, as well as accountability demands that combine to make the recommendation less "utopian in spirit" (p. 77) and more realistic and pressing than when Schaefer proposed it.

In the previous chapter, we examined three teaching roles—presenter of knowledge, facilitator of meaning making, and coach of transfer performance. In this chapter, we discussed three critical nonteaching roles—contributor to the curriculum, analyzer of learning results, and continuous learner. Now, we turn our attention to academic leaders and their role in achieving schooling by design.

Ideas for Action

- Form a book study group, using *Understanding by Design* (expanded second edition) and the companion *UbD Study Guide, The Teaching Gap,* or *How Students Learn* as core texts. Have the group read and report its findings and recommendations to the faculty.
- Identify one or more essential questions to explore for the year (by grade level, academic department, school, program, and/or district). Encourage each teacher to design some activities and assessments related to the questions. Provide time during faculty meetings to discuss the questions and the outcomes of your actions (for example, "How are we doing?").
- Develop subject-area rubrics on key processes, understandings, and performance tasks, linked to state standards, for use across teacher and grade level to provide students with a clear and consistent framework of assessment.
- Schedule a peer review session for teachers to exchange their work (such as unit plans, assessments, rubrics, course maps) and provide feedback and guidance based on agreed-upon design standards.
- Investigate the question "What's falling through the cracks of current student assessments (both external testing and local assessments)?" Present findings by department and grade level; then devise action research to target priority areas.
- Investigate the questions "When are students most engaged in their work? In what areas are we most in need of acting on the findings?" (Get feedback from students regularly on what worked, what didn't, and why.)

- Develop research lessons (lesson study) on key misunderstandings and/or performance weaknesses. Ensure that staff in each subject area provide a written summary of the work, findings, and recommendations. Collect student feedback on what works, what doesn't, and why.
- Work in grade-level or department groups to analyze results from external assessments (such as the state test) and student work (from cornerstone assessments and common assignments). Use the Data-Driven Improvement Planning Worksheet (Figure 6.2) to identify areas of weakness and plan specific actions to address them.

7

What Is the Job of an Academic Leader?

> Leadership [of nonprofit organizations] is not about being "soft" or "nice" or purely "inclusive" or "consensus-building." The whole point is to make sure the right decisions happen—no matter how difficult or painful—for the long-term greatness of the institution and the achievement of its mission.
>
> —Jim Collins, *Good to Great and the Social Sectors*

The words *leader* and *to lead* have many connotations, reflective of the different views about what leadership ought to be. And hundreds of books have been published on the topic of leadership, each with its own spin on the recommended traits, values, and actions of good leaders. But in our view, much of the current writing about academic leadership focuses far too much on style, process, and inputs, and not on the leader's reason for being—guiding the educational institution to achieve specific goals related to its mission. Instead of writing on what a leader needs to *accomplish,* far too many books and articles focus on what a leader needs to *be.* Drucker (1990) puts it sharply:

> The most common question asked me by non-profit executives is: What are the qualities of a leader? The question seems to assume that leadership is something you can learn in a charm school. . . . What matters is not the leader's charisma. What matters is the leader's mission. Therefore the first job of the leaders is to think through and define the mission of the institution. (p. 3)

Drucker opens his book, in fact, by defining the job of the leader in terms of the function: "The task of the non-profit manager is to try to convert the organization's mission statement into specifics" (p. 1). As in our discussion of why curriculum cannot be divorced from assessment and why teachers' job descriptions need to be clarified in terms of outcomes, prescriptions for leadership similarly need to be inferred from the desired educational results. After all, if you are going to "lead" people anywhere, you must have a specific and worthy destination in mind from which to derive direction and approach.

This is especially true in the realm of academic leadership, the focus of this chapter, for, although superintendents and principals have arguably become more adept in managing the complex resource, personnel, and infrastructure "output" demands of schooling, we think that few academic deans, assistant superintendents of curriculum and instruction, department heads, instructional team leaders, or subject-area coordinators are fully prepared to effectively execute their critical roles as effective leaders and managers of needed curricular reforms. Put more bluntly, we need far more "leadership" and less "management" of the status quo from our academic leaders if schools are to honor their obligations and close the huge gap between vision and reality.

We don't mean to imply that leadership style and philosophy are not important, that results matter more than people, or that vision counts more than effective nuts-and-bolts management. We merely propose that any useful conception of academic leadership must be based primarily on clarity about the goals of school, analysis of current results, and purposeful actions to close existing gaps between desired results and present reality. In short, regardless of one's leadership style or the particular school or district context, academic leaders face really only one essential question: What does "mission accomplished" require of *me* as a leader and *us* as a school?

So regardless of the particular job title and position description, we want to consider in this chapter what an academic leader must work to accomplish in order to realize the kind of mission set forth in *Schooling by Design*. More specifically, we recommend that academic leaders assume five primary job functions, related to the key ideas presented in this book. Although these professional responsibilities clearly interact, we discuss each one separately to highlight its salient requirements. Acting on them together will create a mission-driven, results-oriented culture of schooling.

Job Function 1: Responsibilities Related to Mission and Learning Principles

Academic leaders must assume the critical role of helping craft a clear, inspiring, and actionable mission to guide the educational institution, be it an individual school or an entire school district. Not only should leaders have an appropriate and compelling vision of schooling, but they must also engage board members, staff, and community in helping shape, and come to "own," the mission. As an example, the head of a newly chartered school facilitated a planning retreat for trustees and key faculty members. He led the participants in an opening exercise, "Picture the Graduate," in which they envisioned the kind of learner that they hoped and believed would emerge as a result of an education in their school. The retreat participants met in small groups and generated lists of desired knowledge, skill sets, character traits, and habits of mind. The individual group lists were then posted on chart paper and discussed by the total group. After rich conversations, a consensus list emerged that led to the drafting of a school mission statement and framed much of the ensuing discussions about how to organize the school to better realize their "picture" of the ideal graduate.

When a school or district has an existing mission, academic leaders have a primary obligation to reinvigorate it, to make it central to decision making, and to ensure that staff and others continually explore its meaning *and* implications for the work in school. In one case, a private school more than 200 years old rededicated itself to exploring the meaning of its mission, a set of worthy goals about student character and thoughtfulness that had gotten lost over the years as a result of staff turnover and the pressures of test scores and college admissions. The effort led to passionate and practical conversations about how to make sure that syllabi reflected those traits and assessment demanded them.

Effective academic leaders have primary responsibility for keeping mission-related questions in the foreground with staff to prevent the most vital outcomes from falling through the cracks as a result of excessive attention to content coverage, test preparation, and the various diversions of conventional schooling. For example, if a school district claims to develop "critical thinkers" and "responsible citizens," then several questions logically follow about such desired results: How will these envisioned competencies and accomplishments be explicitly addressed within the curriculum? How will they be assessed throughout the grades? What observable indicators in classrooms will show that these desired outcomes are receiving proper attention? Leaders must engage staff and the wider educational community in exploring and answering in actionable terms such mission-related questions.

In addition to the importance of an articulated and understood mission, we have made the case earlier in the book for the adoption of learning principles to guide instruction and depersonalize educational decision making. More generally, a long-term obligation of academic leaders is to ensure that staff members operate as professionals—namely, basing decisions on defensible criteria and principles closely tied to best practice in their respective curricular areas. Because most schools do not have an explicit or mutually agreed-upon set of such pedagogical principles, it falls to leaders to work with staff to craft or adopt them. Such actions provide the foundation upon which a true learning organization or professional learning community must stand. (See Chapter 4 for suggestions for leadership actions related to specific learning principles.)

Job Function 2: Responsibilities Related to Curriculum

As described in Chapters 3 and 4, a coordinated curriculum/assessment system plays a central role in schooling by design and must therefore assume a high priority for academic leaders. To ensure that an understanding-based and mission-focused curriculum/assessment system is developed and refined over time, we recommend the following leadership actions to involve and support staff in vital curricular work.

Directing the Analysis and "Unpacking" of Standards

Many schools and districts in North America lack a process for analyzing the state and provincial standards to which they are obligated. Indeed, countless numbers of schools have inexplicably never set aside meeting and workshop time for teachers to carefully analyze what their standards imply for curriculum and, especially, for assessment. Without a clear expectation of the importance of this work and a designated time to do it, many teachers are likely to give the standards a cursory look when planning and simply "check off" any standard or benchmark that is in any way remotely related to their habitual lesson or unit, even though the standard is hardly addressed during instruction or ever appropriately assessed.

As discussed in Chapter 3, an understanding-based curriculum calls for an unpacking of the standards to identify the big ideas worth understanding and the essential questions needed for student inquiry into those ideas. These ideas and questions are then mapped within and across the grade levels within disciplines to ensure that the curriculum rests upon a conceptually rich armature. Additionally, the standards are scrutinized as a basis for identifying the key transfer tasks needed to provide evidence of students' understanding and their ability to apply the learning identified by the standards. Cornerstone assessment tasks and concomitant rubrics are then selected or developed. Here is a simple example from our workshops of how this might be done (we've added italics to highlight the verbs in the standards):

> Below is a state standard. In small groups, analyze the standard for what it requires of local assessment. In other words, what would count as a valid local assessment of this standard? What evidence in student work would we have to see to conclude with confidence that a student can (or cannot) meet the standard? Then, identify very common current assessments of that standard and critique them in light of your analysis.
>
> **Standards:**
>
> *Analyzes* patterns, trends, or distributions in data in a variety of contexts by determining or using measures of central tendency (mean, median, or mode), dispersion (range or variation), outliers, quartile values, or estimated line of best fit to

analyze situations or to solve problems; *evaluates* the sample from which the statistics were developed (bias, random, or nonrandom).

Students show understanding of human interaction with the environment over time by

- *Describing* how human activity and technology have changed the environment in the United States and world for specific purposes (e.g., development of urban environments, genetic modification of crops, flood control, reforestation).
- *Generating* information related to the impact of human activities on the physical environment (e.g., through field studies, mapping, interviewing, and using scientific instruments) in order to *draw conclusions and recommend* actions (e.g., damming the Yangtze River).
- *Evaluating* different viewpoints regarding resource use in the United States and the world (e.g., debating drilling for oil in a national wildlife refuge).
- *Examining* multiple factors in the interaction of humans and the environment (e.g., population size, farmland, and food production).

Teachers involved in this exercise quickly see that the assessments need to involve more higher-order thinking and explanation, not simple recall questions of the sort typically seen in local assessments. Such analysis and unpacking of standards require collaboration among teachers working in department or grade-level teams in schools or as members of district-level curriculum committees. Some of this work is well suited to regularly scheduled meetings and professional days, whereas the more labor-intensive curriculum and assessment design work may be best scheduled during the summer. Academic leaders assume responsibility for organizing, budgeting for, and monitoring this critical work.

Facilitating Curriculum Reviews and Troubleshooting

In Chapter 6, we described various noninstructional roles for teachers. These included providing "critical friend" peer reviews of curriculum units, course maps, cornerstone assessments, and companion rubrics. Few schools and districts currently have a formal process for reviewing local curricula or vetting local assessments against design standards. In our experience, such a process invariably enhances the quality of curriculum and assessments, with resulting improvement in student performance.

The orchestration of such reviews falls to leaders. Here's one example. A curriculum director recently incorporated structured peer reviews into the district's curriculum development process. She scheduled three separate curriculum design teams to review drafts of each other's course plans against the UbD design standards. During the process, she overheard rich professional conversations, and much helpful feedback and guidance were shared across teams. Following the process, she asked for feedback from the participants. To a person, the teachers extolled the value of the peer review, and every team asserted that their curriculum products would be stronger as a result. Interestingly, several midcareer folks who had never been involved in this process before wondered aloud why peer review had not been a regular part of their professional work, because they found it so beneficial. These comments dovetail with our experience—countless faculty we have trained in peer review have told us that what they initially resisted or feared has become a professionally satisfying and helpful process.

Sharing teacher-developed lessons, units, and assessments for others to critically review is counter to the culture of most schools, and the process may be uncomfortable for some. Thus, when initiating peer review, we recommend modeling the process to help people better understand the design standards and become comfortable with giving and receiving feedback. A detailed description of the peer review protocol and suggestions for facilitating the process are available in *Understanding by Design: Professional Development Workbook* (McTighe & Wiggins, 2004, pp. 242–244).

Reviews occur as curricula are drafted, and troubleshooting takes place once the curriculum is enacted. Leaders need to establish a process for systematically recording teachers' observations of student difficulties in learning and their suggestions for addressing those problems. In many cases, this troubleshooting work can be delegated to curriculum committee chairs and team leaders. But the leader must ensure that the work is done well and done regularly.

Job Function 3: Responsibilities Related to Results (Gap Analysis)

The natural follow-up to the curriculum and assessment work previously described lies in attention to results. In other words, if curriculum represents the important "inputs" of schooling, what are the "outputs" in terms of learning? First and foremost, academic leaders need to ensure that every educator understands that his or her job is to work toward the mission and goals by *identifying and working to close the inevitable gaps* between mission and reality, between learning principles and teacher practice, between desired learning results and actual performance by students on measures that matter. Thus, a priority in reform is for leaders to create and model practices, policies, and structures that institutionalize *honesty* and proactive problem solving in looking at these gaps, and to ensure that staff "own" the problem of closing the gaps.

Being honest with ourselves about how we are doing at accomplishing our mission is the key to continually focused and ultimately effective reform. The adjustments ultimately matter more than the original blueprint. Again, we highlight the finding of Collins (2001):

> We found no evidence that good-to-great companies had more or better information than the comparison companies. None. Both sets of companies had virtually identical access to good information. The key, then, lies not in better information, but in turning *information into information that cannot be ignored*. (p. 79) (emphasis in original)

In previous chapters, we have discussed the critical importance of regularly examining results from a variety of sources, including external tests, local cornerstone assessments, and samples of student work. We have offered examples and protocols for such analysis. Now we need to broach another fruitful (yet underused) arena for gap analysis—feedback from students, parents, alumni, and related institutional clients about what is working and what isn't.

Making Feedback Central to Reform

Academic leaders must accomplish reforms by design. Reform "by design" means that the actions taken are deliberate and focused on a clear and defensible end result. Merely exhorting, demanding, and hoping won't accomplish reform. Nor will success derive from rigid implementation of a plan made long ago. Reform therefore requires the coexistence of two paradoxical elements: (1) unwavering commitment to core principles and (2) constant willingness to change direction, approach, and personnel based on feedback.

Certainly the only way to stay focused and be deliberate amid the chaos of change is to keep focused on core principles. That's why clarity about the mission, clarity about the nature of understanding, and the existence of explicit learning standards are so important. Otherwise, decisions may be made impulsively or without foundation. Then reform is not "by design" but "by the seat of the pants" or "by the blind leading the blind" or "by fiat."

But no plan can ever anticipate all that will be needed in the future. We agree with Fullan (2001) that "change cannot be managed. It can be understood, but . . . it cannot be controlled" (p. 33). So leaders must ensure that any academic reform plan includes a plan to adjust. In other words, new structures and policies must be in place that demand and encourage constant review of educational decisions by getting and using feedback. Educators have for too long labored in isolation from feedback related to goals. Academic work must be structured to ensure that more deliberate, unflinching, and effective self-assessment and self-adjustment occur via a built-in plan for such adjustment. As Jim Collins (2001) puts it in *Good to Great:*

> There is nothing wrong with pursuing a vision for greatness. After all, the good-to-great companies also set out to create greatness. But unlike the comparison

> companies, the good-to-great companies continually refined the path to greatness with the brutal facts of reality. (p. 71)

One failure of conventional schooling and of school reform in general relates to the deeply held belief that if we just get good people trying hard to do good things, it will all work out. The truth is otherwise: excellence in leadership as in teaching is a function of constant and deliberate self-correction, mindful of clear and agreed-upon goals while unflinchingly seeking out feedback and thus dealing with "the brutal facts of reality," as we noted in Chapter 6.

Speaking of the school as a "learning organization" would be unnecessary if today's schools were focused clearly and coherently on a commonly understood mission and the key results related to that mission. In fact, the school reforms of the past 25 years continue—and continue to be needed—because many schools are far from facing the *information that cannot be ignored*. That information is of two kinds: feedback about how deeply and effectively students are learning and are engaged, and feedback suggesting that many time-honored actions and policies in school are dysfunctional—counter to the mission.

Many students are bored, frustrated, and made to feel stupid by school. But school cannot achieve its purpose if that is the case. The best schools do not ignore these facts, therefore. A mission-focused school wants to understand *why* students are bored or made to feel stupid, and it takes action to correct conduct at odds with the mission. Does this seem far-fetched? Indian Hill Schools outside Cincinnati already do this—and they publish both a range of performance data and client and teacher feedback on their district Web site! (See www.ih.k12.oh.us/Improvement%20Week/Improvement%20Week%202005_files/frame.htm.)

Collecting student and parent feedback can be extremely useful in informing needed school improvement. So why don't we routinely seek it? Fear is a major reason—but good artists, actors, and athletes thrive on feedback and don't necessarily fear it. So why do teachers? Academic leaders need to figure out and solve this problem: how can schools be learning organizations if faculties resist learning (which is what they are doing when they balk at collecting or acting on feedback)? Let's start, in fact, by learning why faculties do not seek and use student and parent feedback more often. Is it fear of the results? Ignorance of how to collect useful data? Concern that power will be lost and too much power will be given to the client? We need to know, and we need to solve this embarrassing problem.

Why embarrassing? Because all of us want to be heard when we are unhappy with or have pressing questions about service in hotels, airplanes, or doctors' offices. It is thus hypocritical and a poor model of learning to signal to the world that somehow teachers should be exempt from client feedback. "But sometimes the client has a grudge or doesn't understand or . . ." We didn't say the client was right. We didn't say the feedback is true. It is feedback, to be analyzed and evaluated like any other set of data. As Drucker (1990) says,

> To achieve results requires marketing to one's customer's. [Drucker defines a customer as "someone who can say No!"] It needs what I call marketing responsibility, which is to take one's customers seriously. Not saying, We know what's good for them. But, What are their values? How do I reach them? (pp. 55–56)

The Internet has brought about some significant changes in this regard, and leaders had better prepare faculty to deal with the matter. Sites such as RateMy Teachers.com have millions of student posts. One of the authors noted that almost all the teachers he once taught with were rated online, publicly. Without endorsing the site or the public feedback, he agreed with almost every posted remark made, based on his experience in working with those teachers and in hearing a decade's worth of comments from students about their experience. The nasty exceptions stood out as just that—outliers. There are *always* data outliers; the trend is what matters. And we inspire greater student respect if we seek and act on the unambiguous aspects of feedback. So leaders must gently but firmly ensure that policies are put in place whereby teachers seek and act on credible feedback from clients and report on their findings to other staff in team/department meetings.

More generally, it is the job of the leader to make it mandatory, not optional, for staff to collect data and feedback on the vision-reality gap, propose action research on closing the gap, and report on the attempt to do so. More specifically, every academic department at the high school and every middle/elementary school team would be expected to answer questions such as the following: What is working in mathematics, writing, foreign language, and other subjects? What isn't working? What do you propose to do about it? What resulted from your action research? Consequently, a main responsibility of department heads and team leaders would be to manage this regular review of results, followed by research, development, and planning for improvement. In other words, teacher leaders would be hired, supervised, and evaluated *primarily* on their ability to conduct this action research process with their staff and use the results to improve student performance.

Job Function 4: Responsibilities Related to Personnel

As this example of the role of the department head and team leader suggests, in schooling by design, a fundamental aspect of educational leaders' jobs involves clarifying the job expectations of personnel under their direction and providing the necessary training, supervision, and evaluation guided by mission-related and results-focused criteria. In Chapters 5 and 6 we described the proposed job functions of teachers in both instructional and noninstructional roles, respectively. Now we examine the implications of those functions for school leaders.

Hiring and Placement

Arguably one of the most significant influences a leader has on an organization involves hiring and firing decisions. Indeed, most educators can point to specific cases in which a careless selection of a teacher applicant (or a desperate need to quickly fill a vacant teaching position) has resulted in years of ineffective performance with the ensuing casualties of student motivation and lost learning. Organizational reformers such as Buckingham and Coffman, the authors of *First, Break All the Rules* (1999); Collins (2001); and Fullan (2001) agree that it is critical to "get the right people on the bus, and in the right seats" (in the words of Collins, 2001, p. 41). Unfortunately, in many public schools the problems related to poor hiring are exacerbated by tenure provisions and union protectionism, whereby ineffective teachers are allowed to remain in place or are transferred every few years, enabling the same weaknesses to resurface in a different school.

Form follows function in hiring. We have observed that a lack of clarity and specificity regarding the elements outlined in *Schooling by Design* make it less likely that mission-focused hiring will occur. Let us reverse the contention: when an unambiguous school mission, agreed-upon learning principles, crystal clear job descriptions, and a robust curriculum/assessment system are in place, the evaluation of candidates for teaching and administrative positions can be much more sharply focused, resulting in the hiring of teachers with skills, philosophy, and expectations that are better matched to mission.

Evidence of the efficacy of this approach comes from a large school district in New Jersey. After a comprehensive overhaul of their supervision and evaluation process and the institution of a new results-based system derived from Danielson's *Framework for Teaching* (see Danielson, 1996, 2007), a dozen faculty members resigned—most of whom were teachers that administrators had been trying to move along for years.

Similarly, in terms of hiring, leaders have to wait for the right person to fill a key job and must look beyond paper credentials. Andy Greene, principal of Candlewood Middle School on Long Island in New York, has developed a highly revealing interview protocol for finding out if would-be teachers understand the concept of backward design from goals.

He and his colleagues ask teacher-candidates to pick a topic that they would teach in a course they would be teaching—say, industrialization in 7th grade history, or fractions and decimals in math—and do a "think-aloud" about the big ideas they would want students to leave with. Andy reports that this often stymies less experienced teachers because they fall back on saying what they would like students to leave being "able to do," and they just list discrete skills. No, says Andy, in addition, what insight or big idea about the content should students be leaving with? As Andy remarks, "We're quite sure [the teacher-candidates] won't have a perfect answer. That's OK, because what we are really listening for is how well they think on their feet and how well they seem to know their subject."

This discussion of a big idea is followed by a question about assessment: "So, tell me, if you were going to teach such a unit, what would you be looking for in your assessment?" Andy reports what the authors well know: teachers first think the question is about what format they would use. "We ask them, 'OK, you might ask students to write an essay, but what would you be looking for in that essay?'" Then Andy asks them to talk about the difference between a sophisticated answer in the essay versus a naive answer—"not one that's wrong, but just naive or simplistic. What does that look like?" Then they are asked, "What would you do to move kids beyond a naive response? What would you do instructionally to move the less sophisticated answers along?"

Finally, the candidate is asked to think through necessary differentiation: "We give them a class profile: 'You have 25 kids; 3 or 4 are resource room kids, 1 is a mainstreamed self-contained student, 15 are regular students, 5 are very gifted. What would you do to make this more fair, more differentiated, more successful for more kids?'"

Andy has another interesting strategy to reveal the candidate's big-picture thinking: "Sometimes I'll ask them, 'What do you teach first and why?' I get a set of topics for their course, each one on an index card, provided for me by the subject supervisor. So I ask them, 'Put these in order for me. What's a good sequence for learning this? Where would you start and why?'" As Andy comments, "Again, you want to see their thinking, have them justify their response: 'Why did you choose that sequence?'" Andy then laughs and says what we were thinking: "We have a reputation for having really hard interviews! But in the end, it's good for them as well as for us, and they tell us that."

We encourage all educational leaders with hiring in their purview to carefully examine existing selection protocols and make any changes necessary to choose candidates better matched to the identified mission and program needs.

In reality, most readers work in settings where the majority of staff members are already employed. Thus the need for placing the right people in the right places becomes a key leadership prerogative. Typically, such placement decisions apply less to traditional teaching roles than to assignment of nonteaching duties. For example, who should serve on the curriculum review committee? Who is best suited to "pilot test" a new textbook series? Who would relish the chance to develop a survey of student satisfaction? Selecting the right people for such roles can mean the difference between reform actions flourishing or foundering.

In cases in which habit or bureaucratic inertia conspire to thwart needed changes, clever leaders have invented new roles, job descriptions, and ad hoc groups. As an example, a district curriculum coordinator established pairings of department teams (at the secondary level) and grade-level teams (at the elementary level) for peer reviews of emerging curriculum work. For instance, a 3rd grade team reviewed 4th grade curriculum maps (and vice versa); the secondary music teachers reviewed unit plans developed by the visual arts department (and vice versa). Such structured collaborations can enhance the quality of curriculum products while promoting staff collegiality and professional connections.

Professional Development

Hiring the right people and placing them in appropriate roles is a necessary, but insufficient, responsibility of leaders in a learning organization. Ongoing professional learning and continued staff development enable teachers and administrators to keep abreast of emerging research and best practices. To that end, effective academic leaders communicate to staff that continuous learning is an expected part of their jobs, and they orchestrate varied opportunities for ongoing, job-embedded, and results-oriented professional development. Of course, we are *not* referring to the familiar one-size-fits-all, sit-and-get workshop sessions that most educators have encountered. Schooling *by design* implies that the topics and structures for staff development are determined by what is needed to close the gap between goals and results. For example, *if* achievement data from external tests and samples of student writing reveal that students produce more effective creative writing than persuasive writing, and *if* teachers of writing reveal that they need help in doing a better job teaching the persuasive genre, *then* targeted training and support for those needs would follow.

Beginning teachers require special attention, especially because these novices often find themselves assigned to the most challenging classes and schools. Savvy educational leaders recognize the need to support new teachers during their formative early years through carefully sequenced induction programs and mentorship arrangements. One example of a well-conceived and comprehensive approach to developing new teachers appears in Figure 7.1.

In addition to formalized professional development and induction programs, efficient academic leaders use available time proactively to help teachers keep abreast of current information about teaching and learning. Consider the following example, again from Principal Andy Greene, who periodically selects a set of journal articles describing relevant research-based instructional practices. He distributes these to each

Figure 7.1

Example of a Teacher Induction Program

Induction Curriculum

Hinsdale Township High School District 86—Hinsdale, Illinois

Teachers are non-tenured for the first four years of their employment in a school district in the state of Illinois. During that period of time, teachers in Hinsdale Township High School District 86 participate in a four-year "induction" workshop sequence. The goal of this induction process is to equip all teachers with the fundamental skills they will need to be effective facilitators of student learning. (Tenured teachers are able to elect participation in these workshops as part of their personal Professional Growth Plan.)

Years 1–4

Instructional Improvement Process: Each non-tenured teacher will participate in at least twelve observation cycles prior to receiving tenure status. The pre-observation, observation, post-observation process is guided by a set of characteristics of professional practice developed by the faculty. In their third and fourth year, non-tenured teachers develop with their department chair a personal Professional Growth Plan that corresponds with the Induction curriculum.

Year 1

Mentoring: Each teacher new to the district is assigned a mentor from their department, and, if possible, from their instructional team within the department. Each mentor receives training; the mentor-protégé relationship is guided by a curriculum.

Workshops: The focus of professional development for teachers in their first year in District 86 is orientation to the **Research-Based Instructional Practices** identified by **Robert Marzano.**[1] This cohort of teachers spends five and one half days (38 hours) in workshops developing understanding of what we know to be true about effective instructional strategies and classroom management strategies based on thirty years of research. Teachers share lessons in which they incorporate these strategies.

Year 2

Workshops: The focus of professional development for teachers in their second year in District 86 is to understand and apply the **backward design** curriculum development framework designed by **Jay McTighe and Grant Wiggins** (*Understanding by Design (ASCD)*). This cohort of teachers spend four days (28 hours) in workshops developing understanding of this unit design framework and designing a unit that they will teach during the year. Whenever possible the teachers work in development teams.

Year 3

Workshops: The focus of professional development for teachers in their third year in District 86 is to understand and apply the **Cooperative Learning** structures articulated by **Spencer Kagan.**[2] This cohort of teachers spend three days (21 hours) in workshops developing understanding of this learning management system. Teachers use the techniques and provide feedback.

Year 4

Workshops: The focus of professional development for teachers in their fourth year in District 86 is to understand and apply the professional growth structures of **Action Research** or **Lesson Study.** Teachers receive initial orientation from an expert facilitator, then form teams within their academic content area and complete either an Action Research or Lesson Study project during the year under the supervision of a faculty facilitator.

[1] Marzano, R., Pickering, D., and Pollock, J. (2004). *Classroom Instruction That Works: Research-Based Strategies for Increasing Student Achievement*. Alexandria, VA: Association for Supervision and Curriculum Development.

[2] Kagan, S. *Cooperative Learning*.

Source: Hinsdale Township High School District 86, Hinsdale, Illinois. Reprinted with permission.

staff member with the request that they read one designated article and prepare to discuss it at a forthcoming faculty meeting. The articles are then summarized and discussed via a "jigsaw" process during the meeting. (The principal's memo appears in Figure 7.2.) As a result, Greene's teachers have the opportunity to explore new ideas and discuss their practical implications as part of *a regularly scheduled staff meeting*.

The regular structure of schools could easily accommodate such an activity without extra resources. Imagine a school or a district in which all teachers participated in such focused faculty meetings three or four times during the school year. In addition, the increasing use of professional learning communities further promotes continuous "learning about learning," as does action research and lesson study protocols.

Figure 7.2

Memo for a Faculty Meeting

MEMORANDUM

To: Faculty
From: Andrew Greene, Principal
Date: February 1, 2005

Our next faculty meeting will take place on Monday, February 28, in the 500 Wing. For this meeting, I would like to do something a bit different. Each staff member will receive one article to read prior to the meeting (your assigned article is attached to this cover note). Indicated below are some essential questions that accompany the articles. Teachers should be prepared to discuss their thoughts on these questions as a result of the reading.

The "why" behind the activity is twofold: first, our mission/vision calls for us to be "continuous learners" and embrace "shared values." Secondly, with the grades 3–8 testing requirements in place for next school year, it is essential that we find our "voice" with regard to how we view our job, i.e., how can we continue to teach "well" and still prepare students for state assessments (I believe these are not mutually exclusive goals).

At the meeting, teachers will be placed in groups of six or seven, with each person reporting out on their individual article. Please appoint someone in your group to report out on the common themes that were discussed.

PLEASE DO NOT FORGET TO BRING THE ARTICLE TO THE MEETING

- What words/phrases stand out?
- What was the article primarily about?
- What insights did you gain?
- What ideas did you take away?
- How does the information contained in the article affect your work?
- What questions/concerns do you have about the ideas that were present?
- How does the information "match" the reality of giving state assessments?

In your group discuss any common themes that arose.

I look forward to sharing our collective thoughts.

Source: Andrew Greene, Principal, Candlewood Middle School, Dix Hills, New York. Reprinted with permission.

Feedback and Appraisal

Hiring the right people, clarifying job descriptions, and providing ongoing professional development is one thing; ensuring that the job is done well is something else entirely. This is especially true in the early stages of reform, when ingrained attitudes and comfortable habits may cause staff to lose sight of their obligation to facilitate student understanding and coach for transfer performance. Irrespective of the particulars of school reform, effective academic leaders regularly appraise teacher performance, through both formal and informal means, and provide helpful feedback to enhance staff effectiveness.

In terms of formal job appraisal, we wholeheartedly support the trend toward "supervision of *learning*." Instead of fixating on the actions and behaviors of the teacher, learning-focused supervision concentrates on the *desired results* of teaching—purposeful engagement of learners along with evidence of their understanding and transfer. Such an orientation emphasizes attention to outcomes—including student performance on external measures and local cornerstone assessments—while reducing the time spent on perfunctory classroom observations of teachers. In fact, given the enormous responsibilities of reform-minded leaders and the precious time available to support their efforts, we question the benefits of requiring principals, assistant principals, and central office supervisors to make formal evaluation visits to every teacher's classroom once or twice a year. Alternatively, we believe that considerably more can be gained by "managing results" in ways that we have suggested in this book. Of course, if learning results and other evidence signal problems, then administrators have an obligation to take a closer look at a teacher's actions. However, if learning results are positive or show sustained improvement, we think that a leader's time and energy are more productively spent on the other duties described herein. (Of course, we see merit in more frequent observations of beginning teachers who typically need greater guidance and support until their competence is proven through results.)

When contracts require formal observations, we recommend that such visits be guided by a set of criteria based on the mission, agreed-upon learning principles, curriculum goals, and data-based needs. As an example, a committee of teachers and administrators in the New Hope–Solebury School District in Pennsylvania agreed on a set of indicators, related to their districtwide adoption of Understanding by Design, to guide classroom observations and coaching (see Figure 7.3).

Beyond formal appraisals, many leaders have found that they can monitor learning in their schools by simply "wandering around" with eyes and ears open. In this regard, Kim Marshall (2005), a veteran elementary principal in an urban school, developed a highly effective system that he called his "5 by 5" commitment. Each day, he vowed to visit five different classrooms for five minutes each. The purpose of these drop-in visits was clearly established with the staff—to help him watch the

Figure 7.3
Example of Indicators to Guide Classroom Observations and Coaching

Observable Indicators of an Understanding-Based Classroom

Big ideas and essential questions are central to the work of students.

- Teachers can explain the connection between big ideas, essential questions, and state standards.
- Big ideas and/or essential questions are posted in classrooms and referred to on a regular basis.
- Students continually return to the examination and understanding of big ideas and essential questions throughout the program.

Classroom instruction and assessment practices reflect the WHERETO elements.

- Students are informed of big ideas, essential questions, performance requirements, and evaluative criteria.
- "Hooks" are used to motivate and interest students in learning the big ideas and pursuing essential questions.
- Students explore knowledge and skills in connection to big ideas and essential questions.
- Students work toward success on performance tasks and other assessments.
- Multiple assessments (including self-assessments) are used regularly to provide feedback on student understanding, improve student work, and measure achievement.
- Significant classroom time is spent on inquiry and reflection.
- Differentiated instruction is evident in various ways (e.g., flexible grouping, attention to learning styles, student selection of assessments, etc.).

Students explore and reveal understanding through the six facets.

- Assessments (not necessarily all) require students to explain, interpret, apply, give perspective, empathize, or examine something about themselves.
- Instructional strategies (not all) require students to explain, interpret, apply, give perspective, empathize, or examine something about themselves.
- Students explain and justify their work on a regular basis.

Authentic performance is used regularly to apply knowledge and explore and reveal understanding.

- Performance tasks and other assessments that apply knowledge are an integral part of the learning/assessment process.
- Rubrics and models/exemplars are used regularly and shared with students.
- Teacher regularly monitors authentic student work and provides feedback to help students improve their work.

Teachers use a range of teaching techniques, with an emphasis on interactive instructional strategies.

- Teacher acts as coach and facilitator of learning.
- Teacher creates situations in which students ask questions, develop strategies for solving problems, and communicate with one another.
- Students are expected to explain their answers and show how they arrived at their conclusions.

Teachers can explain alignment connections.

- Evidence of alignment exists through an analysis of big ideas and essential questions, assessments, and instructional practices.
- Evidence of alignment can be seen in curriculum maps that support instructional practice.

Source: New Hope–Solebury School District, New Hope, Pennsylvania. Reprinted with permission.

curriculum and learners in action, *not* to evaluate the teachers. He followed the drop-in visits with a personal contact or a note to indicate something positive that he observed. When he witnessed problems, he gently brought up what he had observed and offered to provide helpful feedback and guidance. As a learning-focused school leader, he credits this "5 by 5" system as being a much more effective use of his time than the perfunctory annual evaluation visits required by the district.

Appraising results (not process) through formal and informal means helps leaders identify the various strengths of their staff members and informs needed professional development and other supports. Regular appraisals also signal, when necessary, the need to get the "wrong" people out of their comfortable seats or, in the worst-case situations, off the bus entirely for the greater good of learning.

Job Function 5: Responsibilities Related to Structures, Policies, and Resources

If the ideas in this book come to fruition and remain in place over time, it will be because leaders put the needed structures in place to ensure the viability and sustainability of those ideas. What exactly do we mean by "structures"? We mean the policies, decision-making and governance mechanisms, organizational routines, schedules, incentives, and resources that make the school function well, no matter who is in a leadership or staff position. To put it bluntly, when the appropriate structures are in place, the school's success or direction no longer depends upon personalities: an important person could leave, yet the school would still be effective in achieving its mission. In other words, good structures are the embodiment of our "Nothing personal, but . . ." philosophy articulated in earlier chapters.

Readers who have come with us this far will not be surprised when we argue that a *vital* job of academic leaders is establishing new (and revitalizing old) structures and policies to undergird the curriculum/assessment/gap analysis system previously described, and to provide the necessary incentives and resources to support these tasks being done continuously and well. Although we could write much about the many varied structures and policies needed to support schooling by design, we will concentrate on two issues: (1) wise use of arguably the most precious commodity in schools—time—and how its wise use can support mission and understanding-based goals, and (2) the establishment and support of *results-based* teams and departments.

The primary resource of school reform is not money, but time. We hear everywhere the same lament: teachers complain that they lack the time to work together to design lessons and assessments, look at student work, discuss results, and plan better ways of causing learning. We agree that the job requires that sufficient time be built in *by design* to accomplish these tasks. Academic leaders can effect no greater change in substance as well as perception than by ensuring that use of time better parallels school priorities related to mission and goals.

Finding new chunks of time to permit work groups to meet is, of course, a challenge. It requires creative thinking and political skill (because finding "new" time means stealing "old" time, in most cases). We offer some suggestions here, based on what some of our clients have done. Note how many of these ideas involve not only new uses of time, but new uses of people:

- Half the faculty covers for the whole faculty once per month on pre-assigned days; classes double up and teachers of "specials" plan large-group activities.
- Teachers spend one hour per month on "results-oriented" actions, taken as needed from current faculty/department/team meetings and inservice days.
- Schools introduce late start/early release one day per month.
- Each grade-level/departmental team is allocated two hours per week, with coverage provided by other teams, administrators, resource specialists, student teachers, or substitutes.
- Five days of summer work become part of the contract, with one day per year added for five years.
- Two hours of noncontract staff time are added to each Monday, then traded for three days added to vacation.
- One permanent substitute per grade level is hired for each department.
- The school year is reorganized—half-days, twice a month, are scheduled with no students; five minutes are added to other instructional days for the minutes lost.
- Teachers meet for an extended lunch and during resource periods or scheduled assemblies.
- Providers of special group-learning programs (such as Project Adventure) give assemblies to release teachers for three half-days per year.
- Roving substitutes, hired for a day, provide release time for grade-level/departmental teams.

When thinking about time in a results-focused, backward-design way, earlier questions should be considered: Given our mission and goals, what is the best use of our time together? Do current uses of time get the job done most effectively and efficiently? How much "new" time do we need to accomplish identified tasks? It is interesting to note that most schools have approximately 24 hours per year of scheduled staff and team meetings, and that doesn't count the two to four days that most districts have allotted for professional development events. Realistically, most schools have more than 40 hours a year that could be devoted to curriculum and assessment design and collaborative inquiry into student achievement.

In sum, the issue is not so much how to find massive amounts of "more" time or other resources. Rather, we need to make *wiser use* of the time we already have. Wise use of time suggests that merely developing a new schedule of freed-up time for curriculum work and gap analysis is insufficient. We have personally witnessed a number of teams with up to one hour of team-planning time per day end the year having done precious little planning. This is not to say that the team's work was pointless or that the time was wasted. It is merely to say that "planning" of the kind discussed in this book does not typically happen just because more time is afforded. Rather, what leaders must accomplish is a performance-based and product-focused use of time—a clarification of *the results sought* from the use of "planning" or "staff meeting" time.

As Covey (1989) puts it in *The Seven Habits of Highly Effective People,* many people (in both their professional and personal lives) get confused about the difference between the "urgent" and the "important," and they neglect the important. (Note that Covey identifies the following activities as being at the heart of the "Important but Not Urgent" quadrant of his matrix: prevention, planning, relationship building.) In our view, a significant way for educators to keep better focused on the important is through clearly defined performance and product goals that obligate their use of available time. In other words, in exchange for "more" time, staff must also agree to performance and product goals related to the use of the time.

Consider one example. Given the need to ensure that ongoing reviews of learning results (gap analysis) and action research become central to staff life, each academic department and grade-level team would be charged as follows:

> Your primary job as a group is to analyze, research, and improve student performance in your area each year. During the school year, you will continually monitor student achievement and progress against mission and standards, propose research and interventions, and report your findings to one another. What's working? What's not? What should we do to achieve more success? Twice per year, you will issue a written report to the rest of the faculty stating your recent findings about current patterns of achievement, what works and what doesn't, and your action plan, based on your findings. In addition, you will propose any schoolwide changes (for example, in curriculum, assessment, instruction, use of resources, scheduling) you think are needed to better achieve your team's goals.

Such a directive would not only require time but might necessitate the invention of new structures (such as ad hoc committees, each one focusing on a priority academic weakness) or the retooling of familiar ones (making department and grade-level meetings focus on analyzing achievement results and student work, and recommending needed changes in the curriculum/assessment system and instruction). It could be as simple as devoting monthly faculty meetings to analyzing results and sharing ideas for improvement, with the announcements and related "administrivia" previously dominating such meetings communicated primarily through e-mail. The general principle is clear enough: to paraphrase Marshall McLuhan, the "meeting is the message." When meetings become more results focused instead of based largely on "covering" topics, leaders have begun to institutionalize the use of resources and structures (meeting time) to support the mission more effectively.

Here are other examples of *product-oriented* expectations for using available time:

- By October, each teacher will have established a personal learning plan and action research project with one or more colleagues, based on mission-related performance issues.
- By spring, each grade-level team will have designed a survey of parents and students, administered it, acted on the findings, and reported to the faculty at the March staff meeting.
- By year's end, each department at the high school will have issued a written report on student performance, highlighting strengths and weaknesses and proposing action plans for improving in areas of weakness.
- By the end of the semester, each grade-level team will have scored student work together, explored disagreements about quality of work, and put in place a system for ensuring better cross-teacher consistency in grading.

Such product goals make it far more likely that the gap between desired results and current performance will be narrowed.

What other structures need to be developed to ensure that analysis of the vision-reality gap is a front-burner issue at the heart of jobs and roles? Here are a few ideas.

For secondary schools, in addition to departments organized by traditional subjects, another set of departments or committees can be organized around key cross-disciplinary goals related to mission and state standards—for example, effective communication, critical thinking, problem solving, lifelong learning. The job of these committees would be to study local assessments and curricula for ways to embed these goals more effectively and to analyze results on assessments of these goals, with suggestions on how to improve performance. (This is parallel to the model of Alverno College, discussed in Chapter 1, in which each faculty member serves on two standing committees—one departmental and one related to competency.)

Many folks have remarked to us that the work done in self-study before school accreditation visits is a perfect example of what we are advocating—yet that work occurs only once every five or six years and is usually done merely to please the visiting committee. Why not institutionalize the ad hoc committees developed for the reaccreditation?

As mentioned previously, few faculties have thoroughly analyzed what state standards demand of local curriculum and assessment. That analysis should be a required product of grade-level teams and academic departments each year.

Each staff team should be required to survey graduates of the program/grade level/school as to how well prepared they were for the next level. In addition, faculty should be required to know and report on the assessment demands placed upon their former students and the degree to which they succeeded at those demands.

Please note the underlying principle suggested by these examples: such committee work would require active staff participation and the production of actionable reports as part of everyone's job. Unlike the current system, where such "results-oriented" work is an option, we would make it a job requirement.

Job Function 6: Responsibilities Related to Culture

One of the most lasting influences of academic leaders results from their efforts to establish and maintain a culture and climate of collaborative and open inquiry; that is, to make the school a *model* learning organization. Although much has been written about school *culture* and its importance, we offer a more results-based view of that term, reflective of the book so far.

For example, Deal and Peterson (1999, p. 116) have identified the following general criteria of a positive school culture:

- A mission focused on student and teacher learning.
- A rich sense of history and purpose.
- Core values of collegiality, performance, and improvement that engender quality, achievement, and learning for everyone.
- Positive beliefs and assumptions about the potential of students and staff to learn and grow.
- A strong professional community that uses knowledge, experience, and research to improve practice.
- An informal network that fosters positive communication flow.
- Shared leadership that balances continuity and improvement.
- Rituals and ceremonies that reinforce core cultural values.
- Stories that celebrate successes and recognize heroines and heroes.
- A physical environment that symbolizes joy and pride.
- A widely shared sense of respect and caring for everyone.

Although this is a fine list, beware of confusing cause and effect. Many of these elements are *correlates,* not *causes,* of effective cultures. In other words, healthy cultures reflect these traits; it doesn't follow that trying to institutionalize these elements in an unhealthy culture will cause a healthy and effective results-based culture. For example, without a mission-driven focus, "a physical environment that symbolizes joy and pride" and "a widely shared sense of respect and caring for everyone" mean little. In other words, a school may be a nice place to work if these traits exist, but they may not necessarily lead to more effective learning. There are currently many *conventionally* successful schools that meet the Deal and Peterson criteria but fail to honor the vision we have laid out in *Schooling by Design*.

Thus, we contend that the academic leader's job is to ensure that the culture of the school is mission focused. This requires that the following cultural norms be eventually reflected not only in the structures of the school but also in the social and relational conduct of day-to-day organizational life:

- A focus on long-term, mission-related goals (as opposed to "I just need to cover my content").
- Results-based approach (as opposed to merely good intentions and hard work).
- Feedback regularly sought from multiple sources (as opposed to avoiding feedback from varied assessments and from clients).
- "Backward" planning from desired results (as opposed to jumping to solutions and actions).
- Long-term-goal orientation (as opposed to quick fixes).
- Transparency of work, products, and results (as opposed to being uncomfortable with visitors or with revealing teacher/student work).
- Focus on inquiry and openness to new approaches (as opposed to "This is the way we have always done it").
- Collaborative style (as opposed to teachers as "lone rangers").
- Adjustment as a way of life (as opposed to "We developed a plan and now we must follow it to completion").

The challenge is to place staff in a world that works this way so they can see its benefits. In other words, the goal should not be to change people's values, beliefs, and attitudes. The goal should be to change their job-related behavior, from which a better attitude will follow more readily and freely.

Becoming a Learning Organization

Getting staff to come to think and feel this way requires a long-term strategy for making school a true learning organization, or "professional learning community," as recent literature has come to call the culture of a healthy and accountable institution. Schaefer (1967) made the point well 40 years ago:

> It is not only our need for new knowledge but also our responsibility for the intellectual health of teachers which suggest that schools should be conceived as centers of inquiry. . . . By concentrating upon the distributive function alone, the school effectively imprisons rather than liberates the full power of the teacher's mind. (p. 2)

Many of the tasks we propose can be accomplished only if academic leaders model, invite, and ultimately demand learning about learning on a regular and formal basis—not only as a formal part of job expectations but also informally through the establishment of rituals, routines, and experiences that are constantly inviting (and expecting) people to learn. A key job of the academic leader is to make clear that the school must be a model learning organization—and to make it one. See additional, related information in Senge and others (2000), DuFour and Eaker (1998), Lewis (2002), and Darling-Hammond (1997).

But here, as in most important areas of life, modeling the behavior we seek is a prerequisite. The academic leader must model thoughtful inquiry and learning in the reform process. Rather than jumping to conclusions and quick actions, academic leaders must demonstrate that a careful diagnosis and openness to multiple possible solutions are always preludes to action. Translated: the leader's job is not to pose solutions but to raise questions and demand thoughtful analysis of problems, leading to solutions "owned" by all parties affected.

Too many academic leaders jump to prescriptions for problems the staff didn't even know existed. As a result, we perpetually hear teachers ask, "So why are we doing curriculum mapping, and how does that relate to Understanding by Design?" It doesn't matter if *we* see the connections as long as teachers do not. And the staff will never understand why we chose the prescription (such as mapping and UbD) if they weren't made privy to deliberations about the weakness of student performance and curriculum framing (the diagnosis). This is a parallel to the problem of student misconception in teaching: rather than aiming for staff understanding, leaders in their impatience or naïveté too often settle for merely "informing" staff or "covering" the details of reform.

The most effective academic leaders, like the best teachers, resist the impatience to "cover" because they understand that it is crucial for the staff to truly understand the need for reform and thus the wisdom of any particular proposed solution. They ensure that staff members reach a *common diagnosis based on understanding*. The leader's challenge, then, is to put staff in a position to "own" any diagnosis, so that any later prescription will seem natural and just common sense. In other words, leaders must ensure that they themselves, as well as staff, really *learn:*

> We must, in other words, become adept at learning. We must become able not only to transform our institutions, in response to changing situations and requirements;

> we must invent and develop institutions which are "learning systems," that is to say, systems capable of bringing about their own continuing transformation. (Schön, 1983, p. 28)

Exhortation and information will not accomplish this understanding, any more than exhorting students and giving them lots of content enables them to grasp the meaning of their lessons and apply them wisely. So new structures and supportive policies are required to ensure that the new job roles and functions become familiar and habitual.

Reforms rarely last beyond the reformer, a fact noted in countless writings on schooling and school change. Thus, "sustainability" may best sum up the long-term "transfer" goal of any leader aiming to implement schooling by design.

All of the elements of leadership discussed in this chapter speak to sustainability. The long-term viability of a school organized in the ways we have outlined in the book requires clarity about mission; a curriculum and assessment system derived from mission; a results focus with emphasis on gap analysis; hiring, supervising, and training to support mission; structures and policies that put mission into operation; and a culture that reinforces all mission-driven actions.

The academic leader's job is not to personally perform all of these tasks (or even know how to), but to ensure that they are accomplished. We do not seek superhuman leaders or autocratic managers. Long gone are the days when the headmaster or principal teacher commanded or single-handedly transformed the school. What we seek are academic leaders who understand what jobs need to get done and who figure out ways of involving the staff in helping complete them.

Part II

A Plan for Schooling by Design

8

How Should Backward Design Apply to School Reform?

> Give me six hours to chop down a tree and I will spend the first four sharpening the axe.
>
> —Abraham Lincoln

In earlier chapters, we outlined the key ideas related to school mission and learning principles and described what a results-focused curriculum would look like. The implications for key roles and job descriptions were next considered. Beginning with this chapter, we explore a planning process for closing the gap between current reality and the desired accomplishments embodying the mission. How should we approach the process of school change to achieve our long-term goals? What strategies should guide our actions to make success more likely?

Effective people in all walks of life (including education) not only have a clear vision of what they want to accomplish, they think *strategically* about the means to reach their goals. Unfortunately, because most educators are extraordinarily busy and because conventional planning focuses so often on short-term actions, strategy often gets neglected. Given a full plate of multiple initiatives; staff, student, and parent demands; and the inevitable crisis *du jour,* it is not surprising that thoughtful strategizing frequently gives way to reactive, knee-jerk responses or to impulsive calls for action. Even without immediate pressures, action-oriented educators tend to identify a goal and quickly propose actions, often with no mechanism for critiquing the validity of the action or adjusting it when necessary. Although we doubt that the pace of schooling will lessen, we do believe in the power of strategic thinking to focus our energies and actions. To have a strategy is to go from some sort of aim to planned and committed action. "The statement 'This is what we are here for,' must eventually become the statement 'This is how we do it. This is the time span in which we do it. This is who is accountable. This is, in other words, the work for which we are responsible'" (Drucker, 1990, p. 142).

When we are working directly with staff or colleagues based on our strategy, we employ various tactics to honor strategy and achieve our long-term goals, such as the tactic of organizing a study group around *Understanding by Design* to increase staff understanding of high-quality unit planning. An individual action in a study group might be to appoint Sue as the leader of the study group, based on our sense of her talents and the respect others have for her. The individual action may fail, but the study group may eventually succeed; the study group may not change a majority of staff methods, yet the strategy may be sound. The strategy, of course, is to make people dissatisfied with their current habits and aware of better ones tied to mission and accountability.

So, just as it is useful in the military, sports, or contract negotiations to differentiate between a strategy, a tactic, and an individual action, these distinctions are important in school reform. This is especially the case because educational leaders have an unfortunate temptation to grab at short-term tactics and prescriptions—professional learning communities, authentic assessment, curriculum mapping—without having an overall strategy that justifies the choice or permits leadership to judge whether the tactic is working to achieve longer-term goals of reform. We believe it helpful to see school reform as failing in recent decades not because the tactics were inherently flawed but because there has been no local, coherent, long-term strategy to plan effectively, validly select and coordinate tactics, and react quickly and decisively, mindful of strategy and goals.

Strategies and Tactics for Reform

The word *strategy* has military roots (it derives from the Greek word for general), though it is now more broadly applied in athletics, politics, and corporate planning—the latter all being more civilized versions of warfare. If the military connotation is distasteful, focus on the broader definition, found in the *Oxford English Dictionary:* the "art of developing the larger movements and operations of a campaign." Strategy is distinct from *tactics,* the "art of handling forces in battle." Drucker's (1990) change of heart in adopting these terms when talking about change in nonprofit organizations is instructive:

> I was once opposed to the term 'strategy.' I thought it smacked too much of the military. But I have slowly become a convert. That's because in many . . . non-profit organizations, planning is an intellectual exercise. You put it in a nicely-bound volume on your shelf and leave it there. Everybody feels virtuous: we have done the planning. But until it becomes actual work you have done nothing. Strategies, on the other hand, are action-focused. . . . [S]trategies are not something you hope for; strategies are something you work for. (p. 59)

Strategy tells us how to organize staff, use resources, and act in the face of all the specific decision points and obstacles ahead. From a broad strategy comes a "game plan," involving *tactics* to move us toward our desired long-term goal (e.g., training staff to become competent in *Understanding by Design,* making the grading and reporting system reflect mission-related goals). Finally, we take specific actions that flow from the strategy and tactics.

So then, what is strategy as it relates to school reform? It answers this question: What are the best principles for determining short-term reform decision-making in order to engineer the long-term result of mission accomplished? A strategy is an overarching imperative to avoid getting lost in the details or the inevitable setbacks. For example, in this book we are arguing that a key strategy for honoring mission in schooling is to write curriculum differently so as to focus everyone on understanding and transfer. That strategy, if followed, will permit everyone in school to better understand their job and how their daily work and obligations fit with long-term aims. The strategy can be simply and broadly defined as *root out inconsistency and illogical habit, given mission and what it implies.*

A strategy is thus not an abstract idea; it is a proactive and sustained way to keep mission in view and make it happen. As Drucker (1990) put it, "There is an old saying that good intentions don't move mountains; bulldozers do. In non-profit management, the mission and the plan—if that's all there is—are the good intentions. Strategies are the bulldozers. They convert what you want to do into accomplishments . . . they tell you what you need to have by way of resources and people to get results" (p. 59). A strategy is a specific and public commitment to marshal political, material, and human capital in a coordinated way to achieve an end to which we have obligated ourselves.

Here is a simple illustration of these distinctions related to coaching soccer. Soccer at the middle school level and beyond is typically a low-scoring affair, and of the few goals that are scored, many are scored as a result of crucial errors in coverage or misplays by the defense. So my strategy as a youth soccer coach was to *concentrate on defense*. From the kids' perspective, the strategy was summarized as: *minimize mistakes on defense by forcing the offense outside and always covering for one another*. With this strategy in mind, our practices concentrated more time on defense than offense and we worked hard to ensure that each of our defenders always had back-up on the field, understood positioning to minimize penetration by the other team, knew how to fake a move to get the opposing player to commit first, and could quickly and decisively clear the ball from the most dangerous areas. The strategy demanded that some of my best and fastest players were used on defense, not offense. Tactically, the strategy calls for putting at least four players in the back, always closing off space in the center of the field, and willingly giving up space on the sidelines. This set of ideas, plus a few other tactics and moves related to slowing down the offense, was the gist of our approach, because the game is too fluid to be scripted. During practices, drills and feedback during controlled scrimmaging reinforced the tactics and overall strategy in gamelike situations; we rarely did isolated sideline drills that were unrealistic. Game plans were never set in stone, though strategy was; instead, they flexed to accommodate what was working and what wasn't. The team was successful—we won the league once and came in second another year, while giving up the fewest goals. These achievements were notable because our team did not have the most talented players in the league.

Consider four transferable points from this example: (1) always have a priority strategy from which all individual decisions and specific actions flow—a strategy that is powerful yet clear and transparent enough to guide everyone's thinking; (2) always play to your strengths by putting your best people in the most vital positions and marginalize your weakest in light of your goals and strategies; (3) make clear that executive control rests with the players (e.g., the staff, workers, learners) who must be encouraged to and educated in how to "plan to adjust" based on feedback and a few strategic principles; and (4) minimize unhelpful drills (simplistic activities, divorced from mission) and maximize gamelike situations (e.g., constant challenges and problem solving related to mission) so that players learn to apply their skills and strategic thinking in authentic contexts. In sum, you *cannot* win without a strategy that is sound and fully understandable, and capable of being enacted by the players, not the coach. Personnel must be prepared to adjust, not just thoughtlessly execute, based on understanding how strategy makes long-term aims practical, because surprises, impediments, dilemmas, and inadequate resources on the way to the goal are inevitable.

Strategic Principles for Accomplishing Mission

We noted in earlier chapters that schooling needs to be conceived like architecture. A vision is needed, but it isn't sufficient. A blueprint is a necessary document for turning vision into possibilities and strategic (i.e., focused, effective, and coordinated) action. So, too, with the process of reform. Instead of jumping headlong into arbitrary moves and tactics, we propose a strategy for systematic planning and implementation of coherent reform. We propose that *any* school reform, no matter what the particulars, has to be founded on three principles: (1) plan backward from mission and program goals by carefully analyzing what mission demands, (2) confront and close the gap between the vision and reality, and (3) set in place *from the start* a plan to adjust the plan (i.e., plan to adjust). Let's consider each idea briefly, then follow up in more detail.

Plan backward from "mission accomplished." This is just common sense and in harmony with the definition of strategy. A strategy is devised by thinking backward from victory (mission accomplished), from successful reform—while mindful of our current situation and resources (both human and material). If backward design works well for curriculum design, then it should work for the design of schooling. It is, after all, a general approach to good planning and acting, irrespective of the content. Indeed, this book follows the backward design logic. Recall that we began by examining the nature of school mission and then described the curriculum and assessment system, because our aim is unachievable without a set of coherently planned actions for getting there. Next, we considered job descriptions, because effective teaching and effective leadership are meaningless phrases prone to endless disagreements without a clear mission and curriculum for attaining it.

Similarly, educational reform succeeds to the extent that we have a clear vision of what we are aiming for and a mechanism for assessing progress against our long-term goals. Great care has to be taken to develop a clear vision *and* indicators of what "mission accomplished" looks like to guide the development of a coherent and effective reform action plan.

Confront and continually work to close the gap between the vision and the reality. The engine of reform is the intrinsic incentive that comes from seeing where you are versus where you desire to end up. It is imperative that the change process focus on giving staff the challenge to develop models and indicators of mission accomplished while collecting credible and helpful information about where we stand against the desired results. Then, the reform charge is always to close the gap. Yet many educators actually resist facing up to an accurate and honest account of where we stand against what we are in business to accomplish. Any change strategy must also ensure that mechanisms and incentives for willingly—even enthusiastically—finding and exploring the gap are developed and acted upon as part of everyone's experience in school. Given that changing habits is difficult, we have to get the incentives right for adults as well as students.

Plan to adjust and have systems in place for proactively getting and using feedback to make timely and effective adjustments, early and often. No educator can predict the future and what obstacles will be encountered along the reform journey. Hence, establishing committees to adjust the plan based on timely feedback must be seen as a vital action, not a sign of weakness. We refer to this as the humility axiom: our initial plans are *likely* to be inadequate; we are *likely* to run into unanticipated troubles. What we need more than a great initial plan is a plan to adjust on a timely and effective basis.

That plan to adjust starts right at the beginning. We need a great deal of data even before we develop a strategic plan to check our hunches against reality about who is ready, willing, and able, and what the real needs and possibilities are in student achievement.

Let's now look more closely at each of these three principles for developing a feasible and successful reform strategy for schooling by design.

Applying Backward Design to School Reform

As we noted in describing the curriculum framework, backward design asks teachers and curriculum committees to consider the following three stages when planning.

Stage 1—Identify desired results. What should students know, understand, and be able to do? What content is worthy of understanding? What "enduring" understandings are desired? In short, what does mission require us to accomplish in student learning? In Stage 1 we consider our transfer and other learning goals. We frame a few priorities in the form of "understandings sought" and "essential questions" that should become learner habits of mind. We frame the knowledge and skill goals mindful of our obligations and prerequisites for achieving transfer related to mission. This first stage in the design process calls for clarity about priorities, expressed as achievements.

Stage 2—Determine acceptable evidence. How will we know if students have achieved the desired results? What will we accept as evidence of student understanding and proficiency? Backward design encourages planners to "think like an assessor" *before* designing specific lessons and activities. Thus we consider *in advance* the assessment evidence needed to document and validate that the desired learning (identified in Stage 1) has been achieved.

Stage 3—Plan learning experiences and instruction. What enabling knowledge and skills will students need in order to perform effectively and achieve desired results? What activities, sequence, and resources are best suited to accomplishing our goals? With clearly identified results and appropriate evidence of understanding in mind, we now think through the most appropriate instructional activities. The goal is to make our teaching engaging *and* effective, while always keeping the end in mind.

In matters of schooling and reform, the logic of backward design suggests the same three-stage process, with only minor variations for reform planning.

Stage 1—Identify desired results. In Stage 1, change agents establish the aim of a particular reform, in terms of long-term mission and program goals. They identify more specific short-term goals and objectives related to the long-term aims. They ask the following questions: What do we want staff to understand, to really "own"? What essential questions do staff members have to confront, and work through, if the goal is to be achieved? What new knowledge and skills are required to effectively enact the desired reforms?

Stage 2—Determine acceptable evidence. In Stage 2, reformers are reminded to first "think like assessors" *before* designing specific action plans. The backward-design orientation suggests that we think carefully about the evidence we need to show that we have achieved the desired results.

This approach departs from the common practice of thinking about assessment and evaluation as something we do at the end, once our action planning is completed. Rather than creating an evaluation plan near the conclusion, backward design calls for us to develop a feedback plan right from the start based around the evidence and indicators related to our goals. This is vital because we need to *plan* to make intelligent adjustments all along the way to achieve our goals. Only with clear and appropriate evidence in mind can we gauge our progress and know when we need to modify our actions. Waiting until the end to "see how (or *if*) it worked" is simply too late, as any effective coach or sponsor of extracurricular activities will attest.

Thus reformers need to ask the assessor's questions: How will we know if we have achieved the desired results? What will we see if we are successful? What will we accept as evidence of staff understanding and proficiency? What data do we need from the start to set a baseline in relationship to our goals—to measure the gap between goal and reality? How will we track our progress along the way? By what feedback system will we make timely adjustments to our plans to achieve our goals? These questions and their answers are key not only for making wise plans, but also for clarifying our understanding of the goals and learning principles.

Stage 3—Plan actions to achieve goals. With clearly identified results and appropriate evidence of our aims in mind, it is *now* the time to plan for action. Several key questions must be considered at this stage of backward design: What professional development activities and support will equip staff with the needed knowledge and skills to perform effectively and achieve desired results? Who is responsible for the various actions? What time schedule will we follow? What resources are needed to accomplish the goals? Is the overall plan coherent? It is important to note that the specifics of planning—choices about tactics and actions, sequence of activities, resources, and so on—should be decided only *after* we have identified desired results and specific evidence and after we have collected baseline data from which a sensible plan can be derived.

To help leaders apply backward design to school and district planning, we have developed a template for school reform, a variation of the backward-design curriculum-planning template (see Figure 8.1). The template contains questions to consider for each of the backward-design elements.

What Makes Backward Design "Backward"?

Although backward design makes sense for planning, its logic is not always followed within the hectic operation of schools and districts. Yet failure by reformers to follow the precepts of backward design can result in variations on the "twin sins" of teacher planning we noted in *Understanding by Design* (Wiggins & McTighe, 2005). One sin may be labeled "activity orientation"—professional activities that fail to lead to goal-related results. We see this problem manifest on professional development

Figure 8.1

Backward-Design Template for School Reform

<table>
<tr><th colspan="2">Stage 1—Desired Results</th></tr>
<tr><td colspan="2">Goal(s):
What is our vision for this reform? What do we want to accomplish as a result of this initiative?</td></tr>
<tr><td>Understanding(s):
What understandings and attitudes do teachers, administrators, parents, policymakers, and others need for these goals to be met?</td><td>Essential Question(s):
What essential questions about teaching, learning, results, and change should guide our improvement actions?</td></tr>
<tr><td colspan="2">Knowledge: Skills:
What knowledge and skills will teachers, administrators, policymakers, parents, and students need for this vision to become a reality?</td></tr>
<tr><th colspan="2">Stage 2—Assessment Evidence</th></tr>
<tr><td>Direct Evidence:
What will count as evidence of success?
What are the key observable indicators of short- and long-term progress?</td><td>Indirect Evidence:
What other data (e.g., achievement gaps; staff understandings, attitudes, and practices; organizational capacity) should be collected?</td></tr>
<tr><th colspan="2">Stage 3—Action Plan</th></tr>
<tr><td colspan="2">What short- and long-term actions will we take to achieve our goals (in curriculum, assessment, instruction, professional development, policy, resource allocation, and job appraisal)?
What strategies will help us achieve the desired results?
Who will be responsible? What resources will be needed?</td></tr>
</table>

days and at meetings, where staff dutifully participate but without a clear long-term purpose or targeted follow-up. (Is it any wonder that we often hear veteran staff lament, "This too shall pass," because it often does?)

The second sin parallels the teaching sin of "coverage," whereby staff members are "informed" about new policies, initiatives, or programs without ever having to act or be held accountable for implementation. They are merely told, "Here's what we're doing," without being helped to understand the need, rationale, or long-term implications of an initiative or a program. (Is it surprising that staff often respond to mandated initiatives they do not fully understand with minimum-compliance behavior or passive-aggressive resistance?)

A related problem in school reform boils down to confusion between results and process. It is not uncommon to observe hardworking committees investing many hours in determining how decisions will be made, how inquiries will be conducted, how all constituencies will be heard, *before* first asking, "Toward what end?" What is the desired result, and how does that answer affect the process? If anything, it is "backward" to concentrate on the process before the end goal is agreed upon. That's like asking the contractor for a work plan before the blueprint.

Here's a large-scale example of this problem. In the late 1980s and early 1990s, several states mandated a site-based decision-making process for all schools—without advising schools on the *kinds of decisions* they should make! More recently, Douglas Reeves (2006) conducted research on school improvement planning and discovered an *inverse relationship* between the complexity of the required format for the plan and student achievement! Reeves's comment on this finding echoes our own caution: "Planning can be effective and necessary, but when the plan supplants the purpose, the entire enterprise is misguided" (p. ix). The backward-design approach we advocate is meant to avoid these potential problems.

A Case in Point

Region 9 of the New York City Board of Education consists of more than 100 schools serving more than 100,000 students in the boroughs of Manhattan and the Bronx. Regional leaders recognize the value of planning backward and encourage their teachers to use the UbD process for instructional planning. In addition to classroom use, the process has proven valuable for leadership planning. The region has adopted the schooling-by-design template as the framework for school administrators to use in developing their annual school goals. After the first year of using backward design for developing school goals, Region 9 Local Assistant Superintendent Dr. Alan Dichter observed,

> The [backward-design] approach helps us develop the habits we wish we had around planning and assessment, especially ensuring there is a connection between what we want and what we do. While this seems simplistic, experience tells us it's a bit elusive.

In addition to using backward design at the school level, regional office staff members use a version of the template to plan coordinated professional development within the region. This multileveled use of backward design reinforces its effectiveness across an entire system. Teachers will observe their school administrators walking the talk, and school administrators will see the same planning process being used by their regional leaders.

Closing the Gap Between Vision and Reality

As we have argued throughout the book, a fundamental reform strategy depends upon continually assessing and acting on the gap between vision and reality. If there is no vision, why think of changing? If there is no gap, why change? If the gap in question is not of interest or credible to me personally, why change? We presume that change, especially change of habits, is demanding and quite difficult. So the reasons to persist must be compelling, and support systems must be in place to keep us motivated and positive.

But as we have also previously argued, few educators willingly confront the discrepancy between action and belief of their own accord. Many resist or deny that a discrepancy exists. So it is naive to presume that merely knowing we can do better by kids will be sufficient motivation to change the habits of schooling. The research on human motivation suggests that the opposite is true: because changing our habits will be painful and difficult, with backsliding and resistance likely, we must ensure that we tap every intrinsic and extrinsic motive possible through a well-thought-out incentive system. At the very least, we have to ponder the myriad *disincentives* that exist in the current approach to school.

Planning to Adjust

In addition to using backward design, strategic reformers are encouraged to regularly assess progress toward closing the vision-reality gap and to adjust the plan when necessary. These related principles call for us to develop a feedback plan right from the start about the evidence and indicators related to our goals. This is vital because we need to *plan* to make intelligent adjustments all along the way to achieve our goals. Only with ongoing assessment evidence can we gauge our progress and know when we need to modify our actions.

This idea of ongoing assessment and adjustment is certainly not original to this book. Indeed, Walter Shewhart (1934) introduced the PDSA cycle of Plan, Do, Study, Act in the 1930s. Today, the Shewhart Cycle is cited as a harbinger for most contemporary approaches to quality control and continuous improvement popularized by Deming and others. The PDSA cycle is a simple but powerful (and somewhat counterintuitive) idea that suggests the logic of backward design. In Stage 3, we *study* the impact of our *actions* (Stage 2) to verify that they are having the desired effects and that we remain on course. If not, we amend our planned actions—we make midcourse corrections.

Athletic coaches naturally apply this cycle in every game and throughout the season. In addition to a carefully thought-out playbook in the preseason, they have a specific game plan for each opponent, based on results as the season unfolds.

Despite the most carefully crafted game plans, adjustments are inevitable throughout the game itself. The coach plans but plans to adjust to respond to the inherently unpredictable. Success depends upon both thoughtful planning *and* timely and effective adjustments.

Thus, reform leaders need to help staff continually assess against the desired results. *Feedback against goals—early and often—has to be the motto.* Not because we "have to," but because that is the best way to avoid self-deception, stagnancy, and a lack of success at achieving the mission.

How, then, can we use these principles to guide reform plans? To this question we now turn as we explore specific tactics and actions framed by the three stages of backward design.

What Are the Desired Results of School Reform?

> To begin with the end in mind means to start with a clear understanding of your destination. It means to know where you're going so that you better understand where you are now so that the steps you take are always in the right direction.
>
> —Stephen Covey, *The Seven Habits of Highly Effective People*

In Stage 1 of school reform, we analyze and clarify the implications of *mission,* with an emphasis on our *vision* of what the mission implies, *goal* setting, and a rationale for any goals. We consider what staff and others (such as policymakers, parents, students) will need to *understand* in order to embrace the rationale and actions associated with the initiative. We also generate *essential questions* to use in stimulating thinking and reflection about the proposed reforms (and to keep us looking at some key "brutal facts"), questions that we keep considering as the initiative moves forward. Finally, we identify the specific *knowledge and skills* that staff will need for successful implementation of our action plan. Let us explore each of these elements in more detail.

Mission-Related Reform Goals

The point of Stage 1 is to identify reform goals that are valid, feasible, and have high leverage related to achieving the mission of school. Such identification requires three different kinds of analysis to inform and guide goal setting for the reform process—analysis that can be framed around three questions:

- What does mission imply?
- What do intermediate goals and obligations such as state standards imply?
- What are the most pressing needs, deficits, and opportunities related to mission?

Strangely enough, we have seen few reform efforts in which staff spend concentrated time up front and during reform clarifying these questions. For example, we find it inexplicable that most schools have no system in place for doing a close reading of the standards to which they are obligated (especially in terms of what the standards imply for local assessment) and for closing the gaps in performance on key standards. We find it even odder that few schools and districts have a reporting system, for themselves as well as for parents and students, on how students are doing *in terms of* the standards. The failure to adapt internal and external reporting systems to give feedback on the standards to which we are obligated is another indicator of how habit-bound schooling is.

Consider the following two state standards in history and mathematics:

> Educational experiences in Grades 9–12 will assure that students
>
> • Apply an understanding of historical and contemporary conflicts over constitutional principles.
>
> • Analyze historical and contemporary conflicts through the respective roles of local, state, and national governments.
>
> • Explain how the design of the U.S. Constitution is intended to balance and check the powers of the branches of government.

> All students will connect mathematics to other learning by understanding the interrelationships of mathematical ideas and the roles that mathematics and mathematical modeling play in other disciplines and in life.

What exactly do these standards demand of local assessment, hence local curriculum writing and instruction? And how should these standards be properly addressed within the curriculum framework and departmental mission statement? What intermediate goals should be set in reference to standards? How will those goals fit within our larger strategic plan? Few schools have adequate answers to such vital questions.

More generally, determining a particular direction for school reform requires an initial inquiry by leaders into the *highest-leverage and mission-critical* changes. The following questions can help identify the most fruitful areas of reform:

• Where is the greatest potential for improved student achievement?

• Where is the gap between our vision and the reality most obvious and correctable?

• In what areas of student performance weakness do we have local examples of exemplary instruction and some consensus about what constitutes best practice?

• Where do we have data that is so credible to staff about a performance weakness that they will quickly embrace the challenge?

The initial goal of reform, of course, is to establish consensus that the vision is shared, the gap is real, and the problem has priority and is worth solving. A lack of good answers to any of these questions suggests that a public announcement of a major reform effort is premature.

Vision

As mentioned in earlier chapters, we need to identify what we would see *if* the mission were accomplished and our reform goals were achieved—in other words, a vision. Any reformer, be it an individual teacher working in a classroom or the assistant superintendent for instruction in a large district working with all staff, must develop a powerful vision of what the learning would look like if the mission were accomplished and what schooling would look like if the proposed reform were accomplished. The vision provides detail and inspiration for what the mission, the learning principles, and the curriculum framework really mean. It provides a strong incentive for moving us out of the status quo. It also permits us to identify the most appropriate evidence to collect and the feedback to give ourselves in Stage 2.

Again, we are not saying that a vision is an utterly fantastic and impossible dream. Rather, the vision represents what we would see if the reform were successful. Our vision (and any goal derived from it) is neither wishful thinking nor arbitrary. The vision helps all members of the school community realize that the goal is both worthy and doable and that a gap exists between vision and reality, no matter how good the school or district seems at present; it also helps them be more likely to commit to closing the gap. Until staff members have a vision of what *could* be and what *ought* to be, they have *no need to change* and hence no deep-seated obligation to really extend their learning and refine their practices. The vision-reality gap supplies an important intrinsic incentive for the hard work of institutional renewal and personal change.

A vital leadership challenge, then, is to ensure that even the most habit-bound members of the school community come to understand that there is *always* more to be done to add value to learning and schooling—that there is, indeed, a moral imperative to do so. As we've noted in previous chapters, until and unless staff truly own both the vision and the reality of the current deficiencies of local schooling in light of results, they have no incentive to make significant changes.

Thus, in Stage 1 we need to establish a clear, specific, and compelling vision intellectually and morally justified by a mission and a stated or implied depersonalized account of the inadequacies of current student performance. This vision and "gap analysis" then direct the development of more specific goals and targeted actions for achieving them. That's the key strategy.

As an example, consider a vision related to the learning principle, discussed in Chapter 4, that identifies transfer of learning as a key goal. If a focus on transfer were truly honored, we would see

• A clear majority of local assessments grounded in authentic performance through which students demonstrate understanding—that is, an ability to transfer knowledge and skills.

• Staff meetings and professional days devoted to the analysis of assessment results and student work, followed by plans to improve those results.

• Academic departments and grade-level teams conducting action research (such as lesson study) around key transfer deficits.

• Differentiated professional development targeted to support staff in addressing areas of student weaknesses.

• A grading and reporting system that documents standards-based *achievement,* rewards *progress* toward high standards, and describes learners' *work habits* or habits of mind.

The particulars of this vision matter less than its intent and effect: this is a concrete (though imagined) picture of a learning principle being honored. These elements are specific and credible enough to provide not only a clearer target for would-be reform and assessment of current status, but also a better incentive for making changes.

Let's now look more closely at the backward design strategy by considering stage one (desired results) and associated tactics for achieving them.

Goals

Goals are feasible and appropriate intermediate aims that derive from the analysis of where we stand now, in reality, against the mission and our particular vision of where we are headed.

Content standards and assessments against them serve an important function in shaping a gap analysis between vision and reality—hence, in framing goals. Many important goals for school improvement may well be found by looking carefully at what the standards demand, in combination with learning principles, as compared with current achievement results and practices. Indeed, it may be politically wise to build the initial vision and gap analysis in a way that highlights better learning of the standards.

However, we reiterate that the vision and concomitant goals *need to extend beyond* the standards because the standards are means for achieving the mission, not the essence of the mission. For example, a district's mission may call for the development of lifelong learners, physically fit individuals, and responsible citizens, whereas the health and physical education standards might concentrate more narrowly on subject-specific knowledge and skills (such as facts about nutrition, exercise skills), and the accompanying standardized tests might focus even more narrowly on what is easily assessed in a large-scale format.

Recommendations and Tips

We recommend that the goals for any school or district initiative be framed in ways that meet five basic criteria. The goals should

- Clearly contribute to improving student learning achievements (directly or indirectly).
- Reflect established principles of learning.
- Respond to needs based on *credible* achievement data (such as test results, quality of student work, classroom observations).
- Be assessable—that is, be able to provide staff with useful, rich, "actionable" feedback.
- Call for the highest-leverage actions we can imagine, given the reform vision.

The chart in Figure 9.1 presents examples of goals that meet these criteria contrasted with examples of goals that do not, along with explanatory comments. Note

Figure 9.1

Effectively Framed Goals Versus Problematic Goals

Goals	Effective	Problematic	Commentary
Improve staff morale.		✓	*Too broad; not directly linked to improving student learning; not clear what to assess.*
All staff will have participated in "lesson study" teams; teams will identify and implement specific instructional refinements to improve learning, based on their analysis of where performance most needs improving and what approaches to design and instruction will most likely do so.	✓		*Specific; clearly focused on improving learning; assessable.*
Increase participation in extracurricular activities. Implement a "walk through" checklist and procedure.		✓	*Specific and assessable, but not based on achievement data or closely linked to student learning.*
Increase the use of differentiated instruction and assessment strategies to *satisfactory* levels in all subject areas, to address the gender gap in reading (which implicitly addresses the mission of success for all learners).	✓		*Specific and focused on improving learning; assessable via surveys of teacher designs and from student feedback.*

that the better goal statements explicitly summarize the rationale for the goal. In fact, any action plan should be based on a rationale related to mission and key gaps between mission and reality. This explicitness is important, because often in education, reformers jump to solutions without providing either a careful diagnosis or a rationale for the chosen solution among other plausible possibilities.

In addition to our general recommendations, here are three more tips on goal setting:

- **Beware of the "Goldilocks" problem in relation to state standards.** As we discussed earlier, some reform goals are simply too global (for example, "Raise achievement") or focus too narrowly on subskills far from mission-related goals (for example, "Third graders will achieve 85 percent or better on weekly spelling tests"). Goals that are "just right" fall in between, addressing significant achievement needs in ways that are assessable.
- **Be careful to distinguish between ends (desired learning achievements) and means (actions to get there).** For example, "We will establish a four-by-four block schedule in our high school" may be an important structural *action,* but there is no rationale to support it—no explicit connection to a learning-related goal. Indeed, a change in schedule without changes in instruction and assessment practices is *unlikely* to yield significant achievement gains. In other words, this so-called goal isn't really a goal, though it sounds like one, because no justification for it as a goal has been provided. The statement is purposeless. Any worthy goal statement addresses the "Why?" question as well as mission-related outcomes.
- **Beware of arbitrary quotas in goal setting.** To say that our goal is to achieve an 80 percent passing rate on local exams is to state a goal based on an arbitrary measure of success. On the one hand, why isn't the goal 100 percent? On the other hand, would we really be pleased if the actual result were 80 percent, thrilled if it were 81 percent, and crushed if it were 79 percent? Realistically, the margin of error in the measurement is greater than the differences in the scores! This groundless use of quotas is also like saying in a history essay that an excellent paper has four or more footnotes and a poorly supported paper has only two or fewer footnotes. No, the issue is the *quality* of the support. Yes, goals should be cast in "measurable" terms—but without reference to arbitrary quantities. (This is why Deming, the father of modern quality control, offered this as a key principle: eliminate quotas.)

One way of revising the earlier goal statement ("We will establish a four-by-four block schedule in our high school") is to consider its underlying questions. For example, "How might we most effectively structure existing time to help more students achieve important learning goals? How do various scheduling options support student achievement based on agreed-upon principles of learning?" So our revised goal might end up looking like this:

> Goal: A schedule, in place by next year, designed to help students learn more deeply so that they are better able to transfer their learning.

Although less concrete than the original formulation (because specific actions are not yet recommended; that happens in Stage 3), the restated goal speaks more directly to the *purpose* of proposed reforms and avoids the rush to action without a clear end result in mind. From the goal, we can frame a more specific objective (a subgoal):

> By May 12, have two different schedules (based on research) ready for consideration, discussion, and vote by staff.

Focusing on the Goals Closest to Mission and Need

Just as it is easier to target mechanical errors in students' writing than the quality of their rhetoric, it is easier to focus on concrete but relatively less important goals in reform. As we said about strategy, the key to success is to spend your precious time wisely on the highest-leverage actions related to your long-term goals, needs, and resources. To do so requires that you not commit to goals until you have analyzed the needs and opportunities related to mission. Alas, school leaders often fail to do this.

Consider this common scenario related to curriculum mapping. A school principal is convinced that the curriculum needs to be improved and that to do so will improve student performance. Because she goes into everyone's classroom, she sees that not everyone appears focused on the same curricular priorities. So she establishes a goal, a desired result: all staff will map the curriculum this year. The goal statement says this: "By year's end, the entire curriculum will be mapped, we will have identified any gaps and misalignments, and we will have developed a plan for addressing these problems." The staff members spend a year ensuring that lessons, units, and courses align horizontally and vertically, within and across subject areas and grade levels. The teachers work hard to complete their maps (though sometimes privately grumbling about whether all the work is worth it). At the end of the year, the principal and staff assess the coherence of the mapped curriculum. They agree on a plan for shifting some topics to ensure greater integration across content. Many teachers feel that the mapping was useful in that it made them more aware of what others in the building are doing. Success!

Hold on a minute. What, exactly, was the desired result of that effort related to mission? And to answer that question, we need to have an answer to another question: Why use mapping as the key *means*? So let's state the reform goal more carefully, with a rationale related to long-term student performance aims: "By the end of the year the curriculum will be sufficiently aligned *so that* the students' experience is more coherent and focused, *so that* their performance on assessments related to key performance goals improves significantly." Hmm. Not once in the planning process did the principal's hunch get tested to justify a priority commitment to mapping. No evidence was initially collected to justify curricular incoherence as the *key* impediment to significant improvement in student performance. The principal jumped to the solution before understanding the problem. In addition, she did not measure the effectiveness of the tactic.

Perhaps a higher-leverage goal would have been to improve the quality of local assessment. Ouch! The maps reveal that, as in most maps around the country, the assessments were not given much thought during the mapping process; teachers simply listed "quiz" or "project" in the assessment column for their units and courses, telling us nothing about what evidence they would collect or how they would evaluate student work. Finally, not once were current and resultant student performance considered during the process, even though the mapping work crowded out all other professional development for the year. The teachers neither examined baseline student performance data when mapping started nor examined whether the quality of student work had improved as a result of mapping.

Alas, it is thus *likely* that student performance would not appreciably improve simply because the staff designed more thorough and aligned maps. Mapping, by itself and in the absence of a more careful diagnosis, is *not* a high-leverage action related to the mission *unless* the curriculum is significantly fragmented, incoherent, and redundant. Even if the curriculum is incoherent, it isn't clear that adults working together (apart from kids and student work) will produce greater effects than they will when working directly on analyzing student performance results and identifying needed interventions.

The problem is a depressingly common one in school reform. Educators often jump to programmatic solutions with a tenuous link to improvement in student performance. Why tenuous? Because the goal is improved student performance—the output—related to mission and standards. When reform efforts are being directed entirely at the adults, we can predict that results will likely not justify the time and other resources invested. This is why we recommend conducting a preliminary analysis of goals against current achievement results, and *then* considering the highest-leverage actions for narrowing the gap. In sum, a careful diagnosis is needed *before* the prescription.

Never forget the principle that the *student* is the key worker, the person who has to achieve the mission, not the teacher. The student's work and its quality are thus likely to be the key output to analyze and the area of highest leverage in many cases. Reformers need to spend their limited time on reforms that most directly target improved student learning and performance quality, related to key aims and deficits. What kinds of goals, then, should have been set in our scenario? Here are a few:

• The curriculum could be coherent but teacher grading very incoherent; that's a big problem. So *when formulating grades, all teachers will consistently apply agreed-upon criteria based on state standards as well as school mission.*

• Because it is the student's perceptions about work quality that matter, *we will train students to score student work reliably against state standards and district goals, in the same way teachers are trained in Advanced Placement training and statewide writing assessment.*

• Incoherence and lack of validity in the assessment are arguably worse than incoherence in a curriculum where sound assessment exists. So *we will monitor and improve the quality of assessment to ensure that local assessments are valid measures of state standards and school mission.*

Such goals are more likely to have higher leverage than curriculum mapping in the case mentioned because they target the quality of student performance more directly.

Understandings

In this section of Stage 1, leaders consider what understandings the staff and other constituents (such as policymakers, parents, students) will need in order to implement an improvement plan thoughtfully and with commitment. As with teaching for understanding in the classroom, the key is to help staff realize the need for change and the value of the new directions proposed—by design.

Leaders at the school, district, and state/provincial levels typically understand the need for educational reform and have anticipated its implications for current practice. However, staff may not have examined the data or may not see the need to change. Failure of staff and constituents to understand the *reasons* for a particular school reform and the *implications* for their work has sabotaged many well-intentioned and needed initiatives. Haven't we all witnessed cases in which faculty display minimum-compliance behavior or passive-aggressive resistance to reforms that they do not understand or have had no hand in shaping? Thus, effective leaders recognize the need to cultivate an understanding *before* expecting staff to adjust practices (to use rubrics, for example) or making a structural change (changing the schedule, for example). Indeed, as shown in our scenario, too often in education the reformers' impatience leads them to skip the diagnosis and goal-clarifying actions and jump straight to a solution—a new textbook series, a revised schedule, a "hot" inservice topic, a new lesson plan format.

Now we see better why the UbD template as a basis for the planning tool in Figure 9.1 and an emphasis on understanding is so appropriate. The vision can be realized only to the extent that staff are helped "by design" to *understand for themselves* the need for change, the appropriateness of any vision, and the significance of the hard work of reform. In other words, a clearer vision is an understanding we help staff "see" on their own, not information we impart as if our aims and rationale were self-evident. So, just as in teaching students for understanding, leaders must treat staff as respected learners aiming at understanding, not just workers to be informed or managed.

Note that we are not saying that leaders cannot lead or have the key vision. Nor are we saying the opposite: let the vision emerge from faculty consensus (so that there are no administrative leaders, only managers). Both views are flawed; neither approach can work because it presumes that the politics of the process matter more than the vision. We are saying that *regardless* of who offers a vision and a call for change, a consensus has to emerge, based on understanding, that this proposed direction makes sense, and that having such a vision (regardless of its author) is the only way to minimize political infighting because we are rallying around a worthy result, not just seeking political allies—as we noted in talking about the importance of objective learning principles that depersonalize the discussion.

The Six Facets of Understanding

Given that a deeper understanding of mission, vision, and goals by staff is critical for lasting reform, leaders are encouraged to consider the six facets of understanding discussed at length in *Understanding by Design* (Wiggins & McTighe, 2005). Indeed, the language of the facets immediately suggests useful directions about how change must be construed:

- What should staff be able to *explain* about the mission, the vision, and the reform goals?
- What information and data should staff be able to *interpret* to identify gaps between vision and current reality?
- What kinds of *application* to their work with students will make staff more effective coaches of learning?
- What *shifts in perspective* are necessary for staff to better understand and embrace needed changes?
- What *empathy* do we need to have—for each other, for learners, for parents, for board members—if we are to better honor the mission?
- What *self-understanding* is critical to overcoming comfortable habits and blind spots that may inhibit change?

These questions have direct implications for professional development: What approach to staff learning is required to achieve these kinds of understandings? How might we ensure that our professional development is results focused, not just informational or oriented toward techniques?

Predicting Misunderstandings

Experienced teachers are mindful of the fact that students often harbor predictable misconceptions about certain topics (for example, the belief that when you divide with a fraction you'll always get a smaller number). This awareness enables them to confront such misunderstandings—by design. Failure to address such misunderstandings when teaching can result in knowledge gaps and future learning problems, because new knowledge builds on prior knowledge.

Likewise, experienced leaders are aware that staff and others, such as parents and board members, may, in fact, misunderstand the learning principles (for example, "How can students be expected to apply learning until they have mastered all of the basics?") or have misunderstandings about proposed reforms (for example, "If we don't grade on a curve, how can we maintain rigor?"). Figure 9.2 shows a few examples of potential staff misunderstandings.

Failure by reformers to anticipate and confront such misunderstandings can result in staff's lack of commitment, or outright resistance, to needed reforms. (We discuss a practical strategy for confronting predictable misunderstandings and concerns of staff and others in the following chapters.)

Figure 9.2

Examples of Potential Staff Misunderstandings

Learning Principle	Potential Misunderstanding
Understandings cannot be given; they have to be engineered so that learners see the power for themselves.	*So I guess that means that students have to "discover" everything for themselves and that teachers should never lecture.*
Instruction is most effective when it is personalized.	*So now you expect me to individualize for every one of my students, including those who are ELL, special ed, and gifted?*
School Reforms	**Potential Misunderstanding**
Curriculum teams will "unpack" state standards to identify the big ideas and essential questions to be addressed in each course.	*There goes my academic freedom. I will no longer be able to respond to the teachable moments.*
Teachers within departments and grade-level teams will agree to use a set of core performance (transfer) tasks and common rubrics as part of their assessment.	*The state test uses mostly multiple-choice items, so why don't we just use the same format to assess our students?*

Making Connections

One important aspect of such understanding in today's world of "overloaded plates" involves helping staff see from the start and repeatedly how various initiatives and programs are connected. The superintendent and the curriculum director in New Hope, Pennsylvania, recognized this need when they were hired several years ago. They wanted to use Understanding by Design as a framework for curriculum reform in order to address the prevalence of "activity-" and "coverage-oriented" teaching in the district. At the same time, they wanted to acknowledge other effective programs and initiatives in the district (including ones that preceded their arrival) and show how these linked to UbD.

As a means of communicating the connections (and attempting to minimize the "Here comes one more new thing" lament), they constructed and presented a visual to the entire district staff (see Figure 9.3). The visual depicts Understanding by Design as a foundational element that supports five major district initiatives: curriculum mapping, Marzano's "Instructional Strategies to Improve Student Achievement" (Marzano et al., 2001), the data-driven school improvement planning process from the National Study of School Evaluation, Charlotte Danielson's Framework for Teaching as a basis for teacher observations (Danielson, 1996, 2007), and the Responsive Classroom, a popular and successful program in the district. This visual signaled three important things to the entire staff and to the board of education:

- These are the major initiatives in this district for the long term.
- These initiatives are connected, mutually supportive, and pointed toward our overall goal of enhancing meaningful learning.
- We will not be jumping on every new educational bandwagon that comes down the pike.

The third point is particularly relevant for schools and districts that have experienced "flavor of the month" professional development or TYNT ("this year's new thing") reforms that are not adequately supported or are dropped for NYNT ("next year's new thing").

Regardless of whether you resonate with this particular visual representation (or even the identified reform elements), we ask you to consider the larger strategy of overtly signaling program priorities and how they connect toward a larger purpose. Of course, a variation on this strategy would involve staff in coming up with their own representation of how various programs and initiatives fit together.

Essential Questions

An important way to cultivate staff understanding of needed reform lies in framing the reform in terms of questions. Consider this: if a particular reform initiative or

Figure 9.3

Connections Between Programs and Initiatives

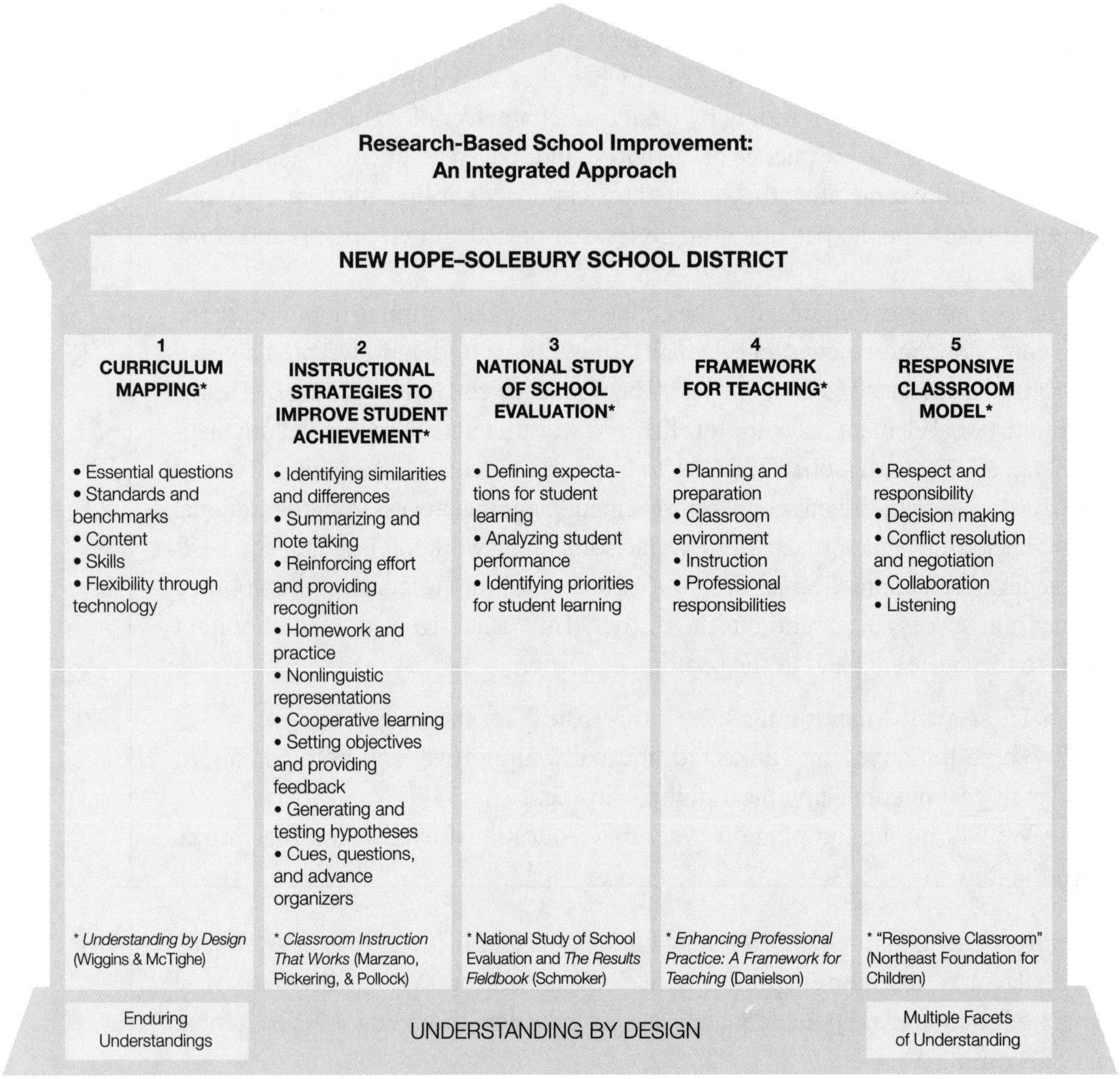

Research-Based School Improvement: An Integrated Approach

NEW HOPE–SOLEBURY SCHOOL DISTRICT

1 CURRICULUM MAPPING*	**2 INSTRUCTIONAL STRATEGIES TO IMPROVE STUDENT ACHIEVEMENT***	**3 NATIONAL STUDY OF SCHOOL EVALUATION***	**4 FRAMEWORK FOR TEACHING***	**5 RESPONSIVE CLASSROOM MODEL***
• Essential questions • Standards and benchmarks • Content • Skills • Flexibility through technology	• Identifying similarities and differences • Summarizing and note taking • Reinforcing effort and providing recognition • Homework and practice • Nonlinguistic representations • Cooperative learning • Setting objectives and providing feedback • Generating and testing hypotheses • Cues, questions, and advance organizers	• Defining expectations for student learning • Analyzing student performance • Identifying priorities for student learning	• Planning and preparation • Classroom environment • Instruction • Professional responsibilities	• Respect and responsibility • Decision making • Conflict resolution and negotiation • Collaboration • Listening
* *Understanding by Design* (Wiggins & McTighe)	* *Classroom Instruction That Works* (Marzano, Pickering, & Pollock)	* National Study of School Evaluation and *The Results Fieldbook* (Schmoker)	* *Enhancing Professional Practice: A Framework for Teaching* (Danielson)	* "Responsive Classroom" (Northeast Foundation for Children)

Enduring Understandings | UNDERSTANDING BY DESIGN | Multiple Facets of Understanding

Source: From New Hope–Solebury School District, New Hope, Pennsylvania. Adapted with permission.

program represents an "answer" or a "solution," then what question does it answer or what problem does it solve? When applied to curriculum design, essential questions are meant to "uncover" the content—that is, to stimulate student thinking and reflection on important ideas. In schooling by design, such questions have a similar intent—to engage *staff* in thinking about the need for change and to prompt reflection on prevailing habitual practices and unexamined norms.

Here's an example of an effective use of essential questions by an elementary school principal.

For several years, the principal had encouraged the school staff to incorporate essential questions in their teaching. As a result, essential questions were posted in most classrooms to focus thinking and learning around important ideas. He then decided that it would be beneficial to "walk the talk" and use essential questions with the professional staff as well as with students. To that end, he began the new school year by posing the following essential question at the initial back-to-school faculty meeting: "How would people know that we are truly a standards-based school?" The question sparked lively discussion and led to several specific ideas. One idea that was implemented involved printing the important content standards on card stock and posting these in the hallways. Thus, when people walked throughout the school, they would notice the standards prominently displayed. It then becomes both logical and accepted to have a public conversation about the extent to which current curricula and assessment adequately address the standards.

One characteristic of an essential question is that it can (and should) be revisited. Indeed, the principal asked the staff to return to the question as part of a professional development day later in the year. He prompted their thinking as follows: "OK, we've posted the key standards in the hallways, and people can see them when they visit the school. But how would people know that we are *teaching* to the standards or that our students are actually *learning* them?" This provocative extension of the original question led to new ideas, including one that was agreed to. During the next month, each grade-level team and the "specials" teachers would select several examples of student work that illustrated the learning of one or more of the standards. These would be collaboratively selected by team members and presented at an upcoming staff meeting.

Several weeks later, the staff shared their collected examples of student work, accompanied by spirited staff conversations. Several important questions emerged from that meeting: "Do we agree within and across teams as to what constitutes learning the various standards? How good does the work have to be? For example, how good is 'good enough' for 3rd grade reading and 5th grade writing?" These questions fueled further conversations regarding the meaning of the standards, the kinds of evidence needed to demonstrate learning them, and the appropriate performance standards for various grade levels.

The story illustrates the potential of using essential questions with staff. In this case, a single question ("How would people know that we are truly a standards-based school?") sparked an entire year's worth of teachers' reflections about the effectiveness of their work and the adjustments needed to improve the results. Isn't that the essence of professionalism in education?

For reformers interested in a similar use of essential questions, we offer additional examples related to various aspects of educational reform (Figure 9.4). Leaders' use of such questions with staff reflects an understanding of a key principle of learning:

An understanding is a learner realization about the power of an idea. Understandings cannot be given; they have to be engineered so that learners see the power for themselves.

This principle reminds us that leaders cannot simply inform staff of desired reforms or prescribe actions; they must take the time to cultivate *understanding* of the need for educational change if meaningful and lasting reform is to be realized.

Knowledge and Skills

The knowledge and skills section of Stage 1 specifies what staff will need to *know* and *be able to do* to effectively implement a targeted reform or program. Determining these needs often requires some type of diagnostic assessment of staff as a basis for planning appropriate professional development. Notice that this backward-design way of thinking represents a qualitatively different approach to planning professional development than what we have seen over the years—a school or district committee decides on a "theme," a central office person attends a conference and chooses the topic based on something she liked, an acclaimed speaker is available on a designated date.

In this chapter, we have explored key aspects of Stage 1—identifying school or district *goals* based on a gap analysis between a vision of desired results and present realities, determining the *understandings* needed by staff and others to address the gap, formulating related *essential questions* about reform, and specifying the requisite *knowledge and skills*. By attending to these Stage 1 elements, leaders establish the clarity and purpose needed to focus actions and realize desired results. We now turn, in Chapter 10, to the key stage in backward design, in which we consider the kinds of assessments needed for yielding evidence of Stage 1 desired results.

Ideas for Action

- Identify a broad goal or performance problem for your district, school, or team. Use the Stage 1 portion of the school reform template (Figure 8.1) to more sharply identify desired results, staff understandings sought, essential questions, and needed knowledge and skills related to the proposed reform.

Figure 9.4

Essential Questions for Educators

VISION AND BELIEFS
- To what extent do we (our team, school, district, community) share a common vision?
- What educational beliefs about teaching and learning do we all hold, if any? What do the answers imply?
- What assumptions about learning guide our instructional and assessment practices? To what extent do our policies, priorities, and actions reflect these beliefs?
- How might we better actualize our beliefs?

STANDARDS
- How would people know that we are a “standards-based” school/district? A learning organization? Honoring our mission well?
- What are observable indicators in the classroom? School? District?
- To what extent are we “walking the talk” and using mission-related standards and criteria to guide our work (in, for example, curriculum, assessment, instruction, professional development, staff appraisal)?

CURRICULUM
- How should curriculum be planned to better achieve the mission and overcome bad habits of coverage? To what extent do textbooks function as a resource (rather than as the syllabus)?
- To what extent is our curriculum coherent and aligned?
- To what extent does our curriculum highlight and elicit understanding and to what extent does it unwittingly impede learning for understanding?

ASSESSMENT
- How are we doing? What evidence is needed to answer this question?
- How will we know that students really understand the “big ideas”?
- Are we assessing everything we value (or only those things that are most easily tested and graded)?
- Is anything important “falling through the cracks” because we are not assessing it?
- How might our assessments better promote learning, not simply measure it?

INSTRUCTION
- To what extent is our instruction engaging and effective?
- To what extent does current instruction reflect research and best practices?
- To what extent are we engaging students in “doing” the subject—what percent of the time?
- Are we effectively reaching *all* students? All *kinds* of students? Who isn’t learning and why?

PROFESSIONAL DEVELOPMENT
- To what extent do our professional development practices reflect the research on adult learning?
- How does our staff view professional development?
- To what extent are our professional development practices “results oriented”?
- Is our professional development appropriately differentiated?

CHANGE PROCESS
- What do we believe about educational change? To what extent are these shared beliefs?
- To what extent are various initiatives seen as connected and coherent (as opposed to being seen as separate things or add-ons)?
- How might we work smarter and more effectively?

POLICY, STRUCTURES, CULTURE
- To what extent do our policies, structures, and culture reflect our beliefs about learning?
- How might we restructure to enhance learning?
- What messages do our policies send?
- Is our staff appraisal process working?
- To what extent do we have a culture of continuous improvement?
- What existing factors support this reform? What factors resist change?
- How do our leaders receive the honest feedback they need to improve?
- To what extent does our grading and reporting system communicate clearly and honestly?
- Are resources (such as time, money, facilities, technology) being used optimally to advance learning?
- Would you want *your* child to attend *our* school? Why or why not?

• Review existing school or district goals against the five criteria presented in this chapter (see p. 214). Revise the goal statement(s) as needed to better meet the criteria.

• Identify a goal or performance problem for your district, school, or team. Formulate one or more essential questions related to the goal or problem to discuss with staff to help them clarify the need and generate ideas for addressing it.

• Develop a graphic representation of how current programs and major initiatives connect to support the larger mission. Alternatively, ask each staff member (both teachers and administrators) to develop *their* representation of how current programs and major initiatives connect to indicate how *they* see the connections (or lack thereof). Share and discuss the various representations and their implications.

10

What Evidence Should We Collect?

> Feedback is the breakfast of champions.
>
> —Ken Blanchard

> The non-profit institution is not merely delivering a service. It wants the end user to be not a user but a *doer*. It uses a service to bring about a change in a human being. In that sense, a school, for instance, is quite different from Proctor & Gamble. It creates habits, vision, commitment. . . . It attempts to become part of the recipient rather than merely a supplier. Until this has happened the non-profit institution has had no results; it has only good intentions.
>
> —Peter Drucker

In Stage 2 of backward design, we shift our focus from the desired results of schooling and the goals of reform to "thinking like an assessor." What evidence will we need to determine that the mission and particular aims have been attained? What will successful implementation of this initiative look like? How will we know that we have achieved the desired results? What guideposts will help us assess our progress along the way? These are the questions that leaders need to consider in Stage 2 *before* they become too invested in or detailed about planning actions (Stage 3).

Just as we caution teachers against rushing to develop lessons and learning activities before they have worked through a draft of the first two design stages, we similarly remind reformers to avoid the rush to action. Backward design is intended to slow our instinct to "fire!" before getting "ready" and making sure we "aim" at the right target. Like effective problem solvers who take time up front to carefully define the problem before considering solutions, effective reformers take time to clarify not just their goals but also the needed assessment evidence and initial data *before* they generate a detailed action plan. This measured approach is especially important because the initial plan will inevitably change en route, so developing up front a process for self-assessment and self-adjustment is a vital element in successful reform of any kind.

Why should we take time to "think like assessors"—especially before there is much reform work to assess? Working through the Stage 2 assessment questions offers two benefits. First, determining the necessary evidence helps sharpen and clarify our goals. It's one thing to develop a general outcome statement (for example, "We want to make instruction more engaging") and quite another to specify exactly what "engaging teaching" is expected to look like and how we will measure levels of engagement in ways that are credible and useful. The rubber meets the road with assessment. Abstract or broad goals come to life when we agree on the observable indicators we hope to see or the quantifiable measures that will enable us to gauge success. A second benefit, as just noted, relates to the importance of regularly checking our progress and adjusting our plans as results dictate. Thus, clearly identified assessment evidence supports more than just summative evaluation; it guides initial and ongoing assessment of our actions. Just as effective coaches adjust their practices and game plans according to the players they have at the start of the season and, later, based on what's working and what isn't, skilled leaders continually self-assess, monitor, and modify their action plans—always with the end in mind.

Consider the goal of staff understanding. What will ongoing and specific feedback tell us if we are on the right path toward deep understanding of the learning principles? Phrases like "right path" suggest why this way of thinking is important: if you are trying to reach a far-off destination while hiking in the woods, a plan alone cannot get you where you want to go. You need constant feedback from a compass and topographical maps to tell you where you are versus where you wish to end up. What are your maps and compass when you are aiming for staff understanding? Where exactly is the trek beginning? What are the indicators and signs that you will constantly check to make sure you are making progress toward the destination? That's what must be carefully thought through in Stage 2.

Consider these guidelines from the Center for What Works, a not-for-profit organization that helps other not-for-profit organizations improve their performance (see www.whatworks.org). The first three steps of change are all assessment based:

> 1. Prepare
>
> *Assess organizational readiness:* Your organization should be *ready for* and *committed* to improvement.
>
> *Identify your mandate to improve:* To determine what is driving the need for change within your organization, look internally and externally.
>
> *Commit to quality:* A continuous commitment to benchmarking must come from the board, staff, community.
>
> *Create a benchmarking team:* If possible, assemble a team of staff members to manage the benchmarking process.
>
> *Write a benchmarking plan:* Include a purpose, scope, logistics, and deliverables.

2. Analyze What to Improve
Determine what needs improvement: Choose to improve things that will define success within your organization. To begin, focus within the four main impact areas: *management effectiveness, sustainability, community engagement, and program performance*. Select an impact area and form a specific goal, called an *impact goal*, for that area.
Identify key outcomes: Key outcomes enable an organization to achieve its *impact goal*. Together, the *impact goal* and the *key outcomes* form a success equation.
Attach performance measures: Performance measures are generally quantitative and indicate how far you are from achieving your goals.

3. Measure Performance
Measure the right thing: Strive for *specific, measurable, accountable, results-oriented, and time-bound* measurements (adapted from the American Strategic Management Institute).
Collect baseline data: Identify what information your organization already tracks as well as the reliability of that information. Use the information to set a baseline. (emphasis added)

A key reason to think through your feedback-gathering approaches *at the outset* is that we often do not quite know what the point of our "hike" really is. Although it may seem logical to identify our goals before the assessments and actions, in reality we often must clarify our purposes as we go. The architect's blueprint is typically adjusted, based on immediate feedback from clients and contractors, even before the concrete foundation has been poured. And once construction is under way, the blueprint changes again, sometimes frequently, as physical obstacles and unanticipated situations emerge. In education this is especially true: some of our initiatives may turn out to be inappropriate in retrospect as we get a clearer picture of what mission demands of us. So there must *always* be a plan to adjust (in Stage 3) based on the deliberate seeking of timely and frequent feedback (Stage 2)—the vision bumping up against (sometimes unfortunate) facts and unanticipated difficulties.

Mission-Critical Evidence

As Peters and Waterman (1982) noted more than 20 years ago in *In Search of Excellence,* "A long time ago, the organization theorist Mason Haire said, 'What gets measured gets done.' He argued that the simple act of putting a measure on something is tantamount to getting it done. It focuses management attention on that area" (p. 268).

We agree wholeheartedly, especially given the disconnect between conventional student assessment and what mission demands. Until and unless we assess for mission-based goals and in-depth student understanding, school won't change much. This is true *regardless* of how the external authorities audit performance annually via the state test or the provincial exam. As we have repeatedly argued, educators make a grave error when they confuse the state's audit function with the organization's need for more direct, powerful, and credible measures of its purposes. Rather than merely mimicking the government's superficial approach to accountability, we must design local assessment systems that *measure what matters* most!

Think Photo Album, Not Snapshot

Thinking like an assessor also means considering an *array* of evidence that will show that our efforts have succeeded. Indeed, effective assessment involves a synthesis of valid information from a variety of sources—a photo album, not a single snapshot. Because every assessment contains inherent measurement errors, the use of multiple measures will help moderate these inaccuracies.

As an example of such a "photo album" of multiple measures, look at the components of the district assessment system developed by the St. Charles Community Schools in Illinois (Figure 10.1). With the recognition that annual standardized tests provided only a snapshot of *some* of the learning occurring in the district, leaders presented to their board of education a plan to collect additional evidence to give a more complete picture of student performance based on district goals. Notice that their *local assessments* component features program (cornerstone) performance

Figure 10.1

Indicators of Student Learning

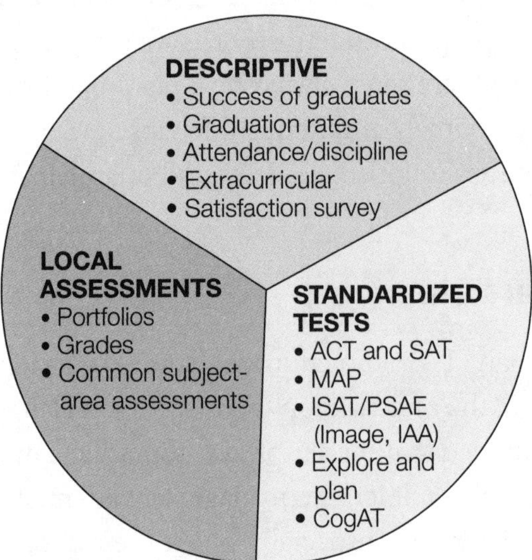

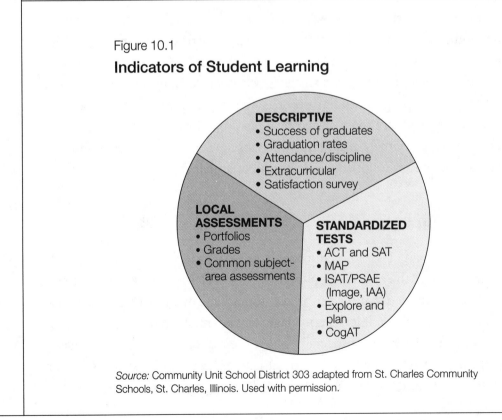

Source: Community Unit School District 303 adapted from St. Charles Community Schools, St. Charles, Illinois. Used with permission.

assessments and portfolios of student work to reveal evidence of understanding, transfer, and habits of mind—evidence that is unobtainable from the *standardized test* component alone.

Effective assessment matches the measures with the goals so that we can draw *valid* inferences. When knowledge of certain factual information is a desired result, objective quizzes and tests will provide appropriate measures. However, when our mission and program goals call for meaning making and the capacity to effectively apply learning in novel situations, a multiple-choice test of recall just will not suffice. We won't go into detail here about evidence of understanding and transfer, except to note that these goals demand the kind of evidence revealed through the six facets of understanding: explain, interpret, apply, see from different points of view, empathize, and demonstrate self-understanding. (For further information about various assessment approaches for gathering valid and reliable evidence, see *Understanding by Design,* Wiggins & McTighe, 2005).

Caution: Assessing What's Easy to Measure Instead of What's Vital

We advise caution when considering multiple measures, because both educational organizations and individual educators can fall victim to the unwitting problem of measuring what is easiest to measure instead of what is vital. Here is an illustration of this problem from the world of environmental issues:

> For 50 years, the Nature Conservancy had a clear mission: "to preserve the diversity of plants and animals by protecting the habitats of rare species around the world." For most of the Conservancy's history, its focus was on "protecting habitats." Each year, the Conservancy would add up the amount of annual charitable donations it received and the number of acres it was protecting. These measurements were commonly known as "bucks and acres." The measures were clear and easy to track. Year after year, the number of acres protected grew exponentially—they guarded 66 million acres in 1999—as did money raised—annual revenues were $775 million in 1999.
>
> Despite this apparent success, Conservancy managers began to realize that bucks and acres didn't adequately measure the progress of the organization toward achieving its mission. The Conservancy's goal, after all, wasn't to buy land or raise money; it was to preserve the diversity of life on earth. And by that standard, the Conservancy had been falling short every year of its existence. In fact, species were declining in the Conservancy's protected areas, while the species extinction rate was as high as it was during the great extinction that wiped out the dinosaurs 65 million years ago. (Adapted from Sawhill & Williamson, 2001, pp. 100–101)

The situation in school is arguably worse. The measures most in use at the school and district levels are too indirect (such as attendance rates) or too untimely and insensitive to small gains in performance (such as state test scores). Neither adequately addresses the key aspects of the long-term mission of school or provides us with robust feedback related to goals. Many individual teachers make the same mistake: they design simple quizzes, total up the scores, average them, and give grades accordingly—despite the facts that transfer, not recalled knowledge and skill, is the course goal, and that calculating the "average" does not tell them if there is consistent progress toward a long-term goal.

Clarifying the Goals by Clarifying the Measures

As we have noted, it is vital to think like an assessor to clarify (and perhaps change) the goals in Stage 1. How does this work in practice? Let's consider again the example of overeager curriculum mapping described in Chapter 9. In this case, the principal jumped to a solution—mapping the curriculum—before analyzing the problem by collecting relevant information about student performance and teacher use of the developed curriculum. She merely noted as a result of her various class visits that teachers did not seem to have shared curricular goals or timetables. How might a better pre-assessment have improved her goals and ultimately the reform results?

The first move might have been to develop a pilot curriculum map for a short period of time—say, the month of October—to see if the problem was as bad as the principal feared. (This is, indeed, a strategy recommended by Heidi Hayes Jacobs and other mapping proponents.) Second, a quick survey of staff, students, and parents could have revealed any concerns about redundancies and gaps in the program. Based on the results of both analyses, the principal and key staff would then have been in a much better position to assess the value of a full-scale mapping effort. Indeed, it is possible that the survey might well have identified other, more pressing problems related to student performance.

One can go further back in the analysis to ask: What exactly is the "problem"? How should the *diagnosis* be most clearly and thoroughly framed in terms of long-term learning goals? Consider these alternative problem statements:

- Problem: Teachers emphasize different things in how they teach the "same" units, so student performance may well vary far too much across teachers.
- Problem: Teachers plan in such a way as to miss out on cross-disciplinary integration and connections (for example, readings in language arts do not match social studies content), so student performance is needlessly weaker in terms of transfer.
- Problem: Teachers are unfamiliar with the curriculum framework, so lesson plans and assessments are frequently off target.
- Problem: The curriculum as currently written does not sufficiently focus everyone's work on learning priorities, so long-term goals are not sufficiently addressed in unit plans.

Notice that these statements not only reflect very different problems but also demand different pre-assessments in order to check assumptions and direct the focus on any action planning. A few weeks of information gathering and goal clarifying would have led to far more effective results by year's end.

The Value of Feedback from Clients and Staff

In the example, we propose surveying staff, students, and parents as part of the assessment. We remain puzzled as to why so few reform efforts seek, analyze, and act on survey results from clients. Here is a simple example from a former colleague of one of the authors. Each Friday he asked his high school students to answer the following question on a four-by-six-inch index card: "What worked for you this week? Why?" On the other side, the question was "What didn't work for you this week? Why?" He quickly noted the answers, reported the general patterns on Monday, and made whatever changes seemed wisest in his syllabus or methods, given the feedback from learners.

Here is a set of answers provided to us by a middle school math teacher who asked for the same kind of feedback from her students:

- **What works:** When you give an example after teaching a concept.
- **What doesn't:** When you give us two ways to solve the same problem—confusing!
- **What works:** When you give an example on the board and take the time to explain things.
- **What doesn't:** When you don't have time to explain, and when we can't ask anyone else questions if we are stuck on something.
- **What works:** When the teacher gives an example on the board and makes helpful drawings.
- **What doesn't:** Doing math in my head because I always have to draw pictures or write out a problem to get it and solve it.
- **What works:** When we check our answers on problems in class and go over them.
- **What doesn't:** When you get upset about our talking, but it's often about math!
- **What works:** When you give good examples and answer our questions.
- **What doesn't:** The textbook. Instructions are not clear, too many of same kind of problems, answers in the back are not very helpful sometimes.

Now imagine if there were a similar ongoing survey of staff by supervisors concerning the curriculum, professional development, and staff meetings. We predict that the information obtained could lead to positive changes.

In Figure 10.2, we present a more comprehensive set of possible sources of evidence categorized by type. Of course, leaders should identify those measures appropriate to the mission and their particular reform goals.

Notice on the school reform template (Figure 8.1 in Chapter 8) that Stage 2 is divided into two sections, *direct* and *indirect* evidence. By "direct" evidence we mean measures of long-term learning and student achievement—the ultimate goal of school improvement. The "indirect" section refers to evidence of related goals, such as changes in staff practices. For example, we may want to increase the use of differentiated instruction (DI) in order to address student diversity in learning styles, interests, and background experiences. Evidence of this goal might include staff surveys of the use of DI strategies and classroom observations. Such evidence would be listed as indirect because it focuses on *means* (teacher actions) as opposed to *ends* (enhanced learning by more students).

Contemporary school reform efforts and the related assessments typically focus too much on various means: structures (such as block scheduling), programs (such as Success for All), professional development (such as book study), curriculum (such as mapping), and instructional practices (such as cooperative learning). Certainly, such reforms serve as the fuel for the school improvement engine, but they must not be mistaken for the destination. If we are not careful, these actions can take on a life of their own and actually distract from the larger mission. Having 90 percent

Figure 10.2
Considering Multiple Sources of Data

	Quantitative	Qualitative
External	• State achievement tests ________________ ________________ • National standardized tests ________________ ________________	• Surveys of constituent groups (e.g., parents, business leaders, community members) • School accreditations • Structured observations by visitors (e.g., critical friend, university partner)
Internal	• Local achievement tests (e.g., common exams) • Cornerstone performance tasks • Student work • Grade distributions • Graduation/dropout rates • Other: ________________	• Surveys of students • Surveys of teachers • Surveys of administrators • Surveys of community • Structured observations (e.g., classroom visits) • Other: ________________

of the staff participate in a book study on *What Works in Classrooms* is an impressive accomplishment—as long as ideas about "what works" are actually applied in ways that enhance student achievement and that we collect evidence to show it. Today's educational leaders must remain vigilant about the confusion between means and ends by constantly reminding staff of the desired results: improved learning.

Observable Indicators of Success

In addition to quantifiable achievement data, certain mission-related and reform goals call for evidence of a more qualitative nature. One straightforward method involves the identification of "observable indicators." In other words, what do we expect to see and hear when we visit classrooms, schools, and districts where our reform ideas are successfully enacted? Figure 10.3 provides a useful format for identifying and using such indicators. This particular example was developed for a school seeking to use the Understanding by Design framework to support teacher planning (that is, using backward design around state standards), and teaching and assessing for understanding of the big ideas contained in the standards.

Notice the format of the figure. In the column on the left we identify specific, observable indicators based on our desired results from Stage 1. In the column on the right we list the indicators of opposite practices (or the current status quo) that we wish to change. The center of the chart contains a continuum to enable us to pre-assess where we are presently and to guide the development of our action plan (Stage 3). We can then use the same continuum to monitor our progress along the way.

The continuum can be more detailed. Indeed, some schools and districts have created a finer-grained developmental rubric or innovation configuration to support more consistent assessments by staff. Although the example highlights a particular curriculum reform (UbD), the format and process can be applied to any school or district initiative.

Assessing the Context for Reform

Before rushing to action, savvy leaders recognize the importance of assessing existing factors that are likely to influence their school reform efforts. In the following sections, we present three practical tools for assessing staff, assessing the contextual factors, and anticipating predictable concerns.

Assessing Staff

Clarifying desired results (Stage 1) and identifying evidence of success (Stage 2) are required "front-end" pieces of school reform planning. But educational leaders must also consider those involved in implementing the resulting action plan. As previously

Figure 10.3

Continuum of Observable Indicators

Understanding by Design Elements: Assessing Your School		
Use the continuum to analyze the classroom practices in your school according to the following UbD reform elements.		
1. Learning activities clearly address established content standards.	■ ■ ■ ■ ■ ■ ■ ■ ■ ■ ■ ■	1. Learning activities do not typically address established content standards.
2. The textbook is one resource among many used in teaching to the standards.	■ ■ ■ ■ ■ ■ ■ ■ ■ ■ ■ ■	2. Textbooks serve as the primary teaching resource. (The textbook functions as the syllabus.)
3. Instruction and assessment are focused on exploring big ideas and essential questions.	■ ■ ■ ■ ■ ■ ■ ■ ■ ■ ■ ■	3. Instruction consists primarily of content coverage, doing activities, and/or preparation for high-stakes standardized tests.
4. Student understanding of the big ideas in content standards is assessed through complex performance tasks using the six facets.	■ ■ ■ ■ ■ ■ ■ ■ ■ ■ ■ ■	4. Assessment consists primarily of quizzes and tests of factual knowledge and discrete skills.
5. Teacher evaluations of student products/performances are based upon known criteria, performance standards, and models.	■ ■ ■ ■ ■ ■ ■ ■ ■ ■ ■ ■	5. The students do not know (cannot explain) how their work will be evaluated. They are typically not shown models of exemplary work.
6. The students regularly self-assess their work based on the established criteria.	■ ■ ■ ■ ■ ■ ■ ■ ■ ■ ■ ■	6. Students do not regularly self-assess their work according to established criteria.
7. Teachers regularly pose open-ended questions with no obvious right answer. The questions are designed to direct and deepen inquiry and understanding.	■ ■ ■ ■ ■ ■ ■ ■ ■ ■ ■ ■	7. Most teacher questions are convergent, leading questions, pointing toward the knowledge students are expected to learn.
8. Students are given regular opportunities to rethink and revise their work based on feedback from ongoing (formative) assessments.	■ ■ ■ ■ ■ ■ ■ ■ ■ ■ ■ ■	8. Formative assessments are not routinely used. Students are rarely given opportunities to rethink and revise their work based on specific feedback.

noted, we recommend that all institutional change begin with a readiness assessment. To that end, we offer a framework that leaders can use to assess their staffs' *readiness* to instigate a reform, their *willingness* to undertake needed changes, and their *ability* to successfully implement the initiative. In practice, leaders estimate the percentage of staff who fall into the nine categories of the matrix (Figure 10.4).

These ratings may be determined through staff surveys, observations, or predictions based on previous behavior patterns. When the ratings are more subjective in nature, we recommend that, whenever possible, a leadership team (for example, the principal and the assistant principal) rather than an individual complete this staff assessment, thereby increasing the reliability of the estimates. Once the percentages are recorded in the matrix, leaders consider the implications and factor them into their planning. For example, a school that has the majority of staff *ready* and *able* but *unwilling* presents a very different leadership challenge than a school in which the majority of staff are *ready* and *willing* but *not yet able*. In the first case, we might proceed with a small group of open-minded volunteers rather than trying to confront a majority of resisters at the onset. In the second case, we would focus on professional development to support the willing staff with the necessary knowledge and skills.

We trust that readers will recognize another benefit of using the matrix for staff assessment—it provides a basis for planning *differentiated* staff development, by design. Just as successful teachers differentiate their instruction in response to the diversity of learners they face, strategic leaders understand that the tradition of one-size-fits-all staff development can be counterproductive to results-oriented school improvement. By tailoring training to the *needs* of staff (based on desired results and performance deficits), professional development resources can be used most efficiently and effectively.

Figure 10.4

Assessing Staff

Directions: *Insert percentage of staff who fall into each of the nine categories.*

	Ready	**Willing**	**Able**
Very			
Not Yet			
Not Likely			

And just as we advocated for longitudinal rubrics related to curricular goals, we advocate similar rubrics related to school change. Fortunately, we don't have to reinvent the wheel here. Again, we recommend the Concerns-Based Adoption Model (CBAM), a well-known long-term measurement system, validated by research, for assessing progress toward reform in terms of both attitude and competence (see Hord, Rutherford, Huling-Austin, & Hall, 1987).

Assessing Contextual Factors

School reform does not occur in a vacuum. Indeed, many existing factors can influence the course of our actions. A familiar and helpful analytic tool of organizational change, the Force-Field Analysis, can be used to assess the extent to which various factors may assist planned changes, as well as to identify those forces that may resist. Figure 10.5 presents a Force-Field Analysis frame containing several categories for education. Of course, the row labels can be customized to fit particular situations at the school, district, or institutional level. Figure 10.6 contains examples of both support and resistance factors related to a school district's intention to incorporate Understanding by Design as a framework for curriculum reform.

Strategic leaders trim their reform sails to ride the winds of assisting forces, while identifying those forces of resistance that must be confronted to avoid capsizing. This practice helps staff see viable connections among past and present initiatives and programs. On the resistance side of the ledger, wise leaders are careful to

Figure 10.5

Assessing Conditions for Reform: Force-Field Analysis

Directions: *Use this matrix to assess those forces that support planned reforms and those that resist.*

	Assist (+)	**Resist (–)**
Curriculum		
Assessment		
Instruction		
Professional Development		
Resources		
Policy		
Other: ____________		

Figure 10.6

Example of a Completed Force-Field Analysis Form

	Assist (+)	Resist (–)
Curriculum	• Curriculum mapping has been completed in all content areas. • Adoption of new "problem-based" mathematics series emphasizing conceptual understanding.	• No "quality control" process in place for local curriculum. • No experience with peer review.
Assessment	• Some teachers have experience using performance tasks and rubrics. • The use of portfolios in elementary language arts and secondary visual arts.	• Board of education and community fixate on state test scores. (Other evidence isn't valued.) • "Scantron-type" testing is predominant in our high school.
Instruction	• Widespread use of the writing process with peer editing and revision. • The use of the five Es as an instructional framework for science teaching.	• Many cases of "activity-based" teaching at the elementary level. • A "coverage" orientation at the secondary level.
Professional Development	• Several teachers involved in a pilot "action research" project through RESA. • Voluntary study group being formed at one elementary school.	• History of "one shot" events on inservice days. • A "this too shall pass" attitude on the part of too many staff members.
Resources	• Several sources of available grants to support reform activities (e.g., Goals 2000). • Installation of Internet-ready computers in every school.	• No budget allocation for summer design work. • Teacher appraisal process is not "results focused."
Policy	• State requires districts to develop "multiple measures" to assess content standards at the local level.	• No incentives for individuals and teams to experiment, share ideas, and critique work collaboratively. • No demands that designs be public.
Other: ____________		

distinguish those forces that are beyond their control (such as state accountability requirements) versus those that they can directly affect (such as instructional grouping practices), and they target their energies and resources accordingly.

Anticipating Concerns (and Misunderstandings)

Experienced teachers are able to anticipate areas of the curriculum that will prove difficult for learners (such as dividing fractions). For certain concepts, they know that some students will enter the classroom harboring predictable misconceptions (such as "the heavier object will land first"). When armed with this predictive knowledge, teachers can proactively confront these problem areas. Experienced educational leaders have a similar capacity—the ability to identify predictable misconceptions (such as "We can't do that; we have to prepare for the state tests") or staff concerns (such as "This takes too much time") related to a new program or initiative. Thus, it makes sense for leaders to try to forecast likely misunderstandings about, or objections to, needed reforms and be prepared to respond to the "Yes, buts . . ." that they are likely to encounter.

For example, here are the kinds of concerns that leaders are likely to hear when two prominent initiatives—Understanding by Design and differentiated instruction—are introduced:

- This takes too much time. I have too much content to cover.
- I have too many students to be able to individualize.
- We can't differentiate now that we have the same standards for all.
- This is too demanding. I couldn't possibly do this for everything I teach.
- It's not my job to develop curriculum. Besides, we already have a textbook.
- We are being held accountable for student performance on state tests. Some kids just can't pass them.
- I was not trained in gifted or special education.
- I already do all this. (In other words, "Leave me alone.")
- This year's new thing. (In other words, "Wait a while and this, too, shall pass.")

The implications are straightforward: because nearly every educational change is likely to elicit concerns from staff, parents, and policymakers, leaders will do well to try to anticipate those concerns and prepare thoughtful responses. Failure to anticipate potential objections can lead to awkward moments, such as when staff or board of education members ask tough questions for which the leaders have no convincing answers. Such a strategy is yet another example of the value of "thinking like an assessor"—by design.

Ideas for Action

- Develop a set of specific, observable indicators related to a vision for reform (such as students applying critical thinking in various subjects). Use the list to assess the current level of actualization and then to make plans to increase the occurrence of the indicators.

- Work with a grade-level, department, or school improvement team to analyze assessment results from two or more measures (such as state test scores and student performance on cornerstone assessments) and identify specific areas needing improvement.
- Have teachers try the "What Worked and What Didn't" technique with their students for identified topics and skills. Then, meet in grade-level and departmental groups to discuss the patterns discovered and their implications for instructional practice.
- Work with a leadership team of administrators and teachers to use the Concerns-Based Adoption Model with staff before full implementation of a program or reform initiative. Use the results to profile the staff and derive appropriate next steps for action. (For information about CBAM, see Hord et al., 1987.)
- Develop and conduct a survey of students, parents, and staff to obtain qualitative data about their perceptions of the need for reform, the effectiveness of a program, priorities for allocating resources, or any effort related to improving student achievement. Discuss the survey results and the implications for action.
- Work with a leadership team of administrators and teachers to conduct an analysis of how ready, willing, and able staff members are before developing plans to implement a specific program or reform initiative (see Figure 10.4). Discuss the results in terms of their implications for the implementation plan.
- Conduct a midstream assessment of the progress of an ongoing reform initiative. Identify specific midcourse corrections called for by the results.
- Work with a leadership team of administrators and teachers to conduct a Force-Field Analysis (see Figure 10.5) before developing plans to implement a specific program or reform initiative. Discuss the results in terms of their implications for action planning.
- Develop and distribute a FAQ document to address predictable concerns and misconceptions at the start of a reform effort.

11

What Actions Should We Plan?

> As long as I can conceive something better . . . I cannot be easy unless I am striving to bring it into existence or clearing the way for it.
>
> —George Bernard Shaw

In previous chapters we have outlined key ideas related to school mission, curriculum reform, learning principles, and new job-related policies and structures. We have summarized a planning process for closing the gap between current reality and the vision embodying the mission and principles of learning. And we have discussed how goal clarification and assessment frame the reform process to ensure fidelity to long-term goals and the greater likelihood of success at reform. The remaining question, then, is this: how should we approach the planning of particular actions to make success most likely?

What follows for curriculum design also follows for reform. In curriculum design, Stage 3 is devoted to planning for the learning activities and instruction students will need in order to develop the targeted knowledge, skills, and understandings (identified in Stage 1) and to give evidence of their learning (determined in Stage 2), including transferring it to new situations. The same logic applies to schooling by design—clarity about desired results (Stage 1) and required assessment evidence (Stage 2) guide the focused action planning needed to bring about targeted reforms (Stage 3).

Clearly, the particular actions undertaken locally will be highly contextualized—specific to *your* goals, needs, analysis, and culture. Nonetheless, we can offer a set of eight general tactical guidelines for planning school reform actions.

Guidelines for Planning School Reform Actions

1. Diagnose before prescribing. Any proposed action (new policy, structure, program) must be seen as a natural and appropriate response to current results and long-term goals. As we have said, far too many reformers jump to solutions before the problems are well understood and owned by staff. It follows that the decision to buy a program or adopt someone else's approach should be the last decision.

Thus, don't simply adopt Understanding by Design or the curriculum framework presented in this book before committing to a more general focus on understanding the issues. And don't commit to a particular diagnosis until you can justify such a focus by credible information related to current performance and needs. In short, don't prescribe until the diagnosis is conducted and its implications understood.

2. Go with talent and interest. As your pre-assessment will no doubt reveal, not every staff member is ready, willing, and able to undertake the major changes to familiar routines and comfortable habits called for by school reform. To invoke a pioneering metaphor, some staff members are excited and courageous trailblazers, whereas others are timid and reluctant settlers.

Thus, heed Jim Collins's sage advice from his highly acclaimed book, *Good to Great* (2001), and get the right people on the bus and in the right seats. Target and promote talented and eager colleagues who have the capacity and drive to enact needed reforms. If necessary, invent new roles and structures to place the right people in the right roles.

Here's a related understanding about leading school renovation: every organization includes a small set of influential individuals who hold sway over their colleagues. (Recall the famous ad: "When E. F. Hutton speaks, people listen.")

Thus, ensure that leadership of the change process is in the hands of respected staff members (the "E. F. Huttons" of the school or district), not merely the willing or those with "position power."

3. Plan carefully for the inevitable "Yes, but . . ." responses. Consider predictable misconceptions about, or objections to, the proposed reforms. Many initiatives have been derailed by a failure to anticipate concerns (be they legitimate issues or unfounded worries) and an incapacity to respond to objections.

Thus, meet with a leadership team to identify the likely "Yes, but . . ." responses and formulate credible and consistent replies. Publish a manufactured dialogue of common and predictable questions and responses, and develop and expand a FAQ section on the school or district Web site as an initiative unfolds.

4. Get the incentives right. Reforming schools is harder than maintaining the status quo, though rewarding when it succeeds. Therefore, the work of reform must be supported by both intrinsic and extrinsic rewards. The reform effort's intrinsic stimulation might come from participants' feelings about being a part of or being selected as part of an innovative team and receiving the resources to successfully initiate and sustain needed changes. Extrinsic rewards include freed-up time, secretarial support, a stipend, and supported travel to a professional conference. Regardless of the types of incentives provided, ensure that they are *results focused.* Too often reform initiatives provide too much support for initial effort and enthusiasm and inadequate support for what's needed to bring needed initiatives to fruition.

Thus, follow Deming's advice: Drive out fear as a motivator. ("Drive out fear" is a cardinal axiom in Deming's 14-point list of quality control principles [Deming, 1982, p. 24*ff.*]. Ensure that the majority of the rewards provided come due upon final delivery of quality work, judged against product/performance standards—not just for "hours spent" or staff "seat time."

5. Minimize disruptions while working toward change. First of all, make the "home" livable during "renovation." A common analogy heard in the midst of educational reform is that "we are trying to rebuild the plane while flying it." The analogy aptly describes the stress and seeming impossibility of keeping school while changing school. But we think that a more appropriate analogy for describing the optimal balance of change and stability involves the idea of remodeling a home, to once again invoke the architectural metaphor. Day-to-day living routines must continue while renovators do their work. So our plan must strive to minimize disruptions even while change happens all around. The key to managing the tension is to ensure that there is a prior plan for the disruption, not just a plan for the vision. Planners need to not only "think like an architect," they also need to "think like a contractor," because the contractor has to make the whole change process work for the clients living in the house.

Thus, make the change as livable as possible. School leaders have to be careful not to disrupt the effective operation of school in the zeal to renovate and rebuild. Indeed, successful reform requires a strategy for minimizing disruptions while working on the envisioned changes and for quickly adjusting the formal plans as unexpected events occur (as they surely will).

6. Practice and model what you preach. Effective leaders model the desired change for staff. For example, a principal who asks her faculty to use the three stages of backward design when planning units of study for their students can use the same method when planning staff meetings or committee work. People will be better able to focus their energies when what you are asking them to do is crystal clear. (Recall the adage "Your actions speak so loudly that they can't hear what you say.") The more people see reform leaders practicing what they preach, the more they perceive the reform to be credible and serious.

In addition to modeling *process,* leaders should provide tangible examples of the *products* of reform—understanding-based unit designs, curriculum maps, cornerstone assessments, common scoring rubrics, grading protocols, report cards. Adults, as well as younger learners, need to know what is expected and what quality looks like. Along with models, we recommend that a self-assessment and peer-review process be put in place to provide feedback toward achieving the models.

Thus, model the learning you seek staff to engage in, provide tangible examples of desired results, and deliberately seek feedback to improve both process and products.

7. Think big, start small, and go for an early win. We call this our "Iowa and New Hampshire primary tactic." Like the would-be U.S. presidential candidates, you need an early win in the primaries if you are going to gather momentum and succeed over the long haul. An early win breeds confidence as well as competence. Conversely, it is very difficult to regain momentum following an initial misstep or false start.

This idea can also be viewed as the "engineering prototype" tactic. Think about the manufacture of a highly successful product, such as the Apple iPod. Apple did not just build a million iPods and then wait for the feedback. They built a few different prototypes and perfected them through small-scale testing and feedback from consumer focus groups. Similarly, spending an initial year engaging a small team of willing teachers to design 5 exemplary UbD units will likely pay better long-term dividends than pushing an entire staff (including many hesitant or unwilling members) to crank out 95 weak units and 5 good ones.

Thus, begin a major reform by initiating small-scale pilots, using your best and most motivated people. Start with a group that is already on its way. Focus on a performance area that everyone acknowledges is badly in need of improvement. Use the insights gained from the pilot to help make the case and inform subsequent actions. Don't go to scale until staff have reached consensus about the value of the larger goal and direction from the small-scale pilots.

Note: In light of this recommendation, leaders are cautioned to avoid fixating on the pilot and losing sight of the end result of full-scale implementation. Once again, think of the pilot group as akin to the trailblazers of pioneer times—forging ahead into unfamiliar territory, taking risks, and smoothing the way for the settlers to follow. Although we celebrate the courage and tenacity of our educational trailblazers, our long-term goal is to bring the entire staff to "settle" the new territory of a reformed school.

8. Help everyone work smarter, not harder. Heed the aphorism "All of us are smarter than any one of us." Establish study groups and design teams to plan, lead, and implement needed reforms. Encourage teachers to work in teams when designing units, reviewing student performance results, and planning improvement actions. Enact structures (such as revised schedules) to buttress collaborative teamwork, and allocate support personnel to provide extra help for teams when needed.

Make sure that tools, resources, and a supportive infrastructure are built *before* large-scale change gets under way. As we argued in Chapter 3 on reframing the curriculum, you should develop a troubleshooting guide and support system alongside the reform "curriculum." Analogously, think of the support that accompanies a new software program—users are provided with tutorials, help manuals, FAQ materials, and predeveloped templates.

Consider ways to use technology to help staff "work smarter" on targeted reforms. For example, provide curriculum teams with a membership to Understanding by

Design Exchange (http://ubdexchange.org), a Web site containing thousands of units developed in the UbD format. Establish an online database of "good ideas" to share effective strategies and resources. Post change-related trainings online for 24/7 access. Such actions communicate to staff that you genuinely wish to support them along the reform journey.

Thus, ensure that a plan is put in place that fosters collaboration, uses time-saving technologies, and provides all participants with helpful supports as they embark on changes that may challenge comfortable habits and routines.

WHERETO as a Planning Organizer and Checklist

In *Understanding by Design,* we suggest an organizer for developing the learning plan in Stage 3, based on the acronym WHERETO (see Wiggins & McTighe, 2005, pp. 197–198, and McTighe & Wiggins, 2004, p. 214). Each letter refers to an important element of effective instruction for understanding and should therefore be considered by teachers and curriculum committees in their planning. WHERETO also functions as a checklist for reviewing instructional plans to ensure that they include important elements.

Because we are using the same backward-design process in *Schooling by Design* as in UbD, it makes sense to frame key activities around the same WHERETO elements. Here are considerations for each element of the acronym, applied to planning school reform:

Where are we headed? **W**here are we now? **W**here have we come from? **W**hat's next? Help staff understand.

Hook staff and others (for example, the board of education) by making the initial work stimulating and otherwise appealing to intrinsic as well as extrinsic motivation.

Explore new ideas and equip staff with appropriate knowledge and skills.

Rethink old habits and ways of looking at issues and problems.

Evaluate constantly, so that self-assessment (and adjustment) become the norm.

Tailor the work to the strengths, needs, and interests of staff (for example, differentiate staff development).

Organize the work in a sequence most likely to achieve desired results.

Where are we going and why? School reform initiatives sometimes appear to rank-and-file staff as disconnected puzzle pieces. Unless leaders make a concerted effort to show the linkage, few staff members have a sense of how this year's initiative relates to other ongoing efforts (even when the relationships seem obvious to the change agents). So do not assume that the connections are obvious and that because "we informed them, now they get it." Take the time to develop a fact sheet, with a vivid graphic, to show how recent, present, and proposed future work all fit together conceptually; the "building" graphic shown in Figure 9.3 in Chapter 9 is a good example. Frame the work under an essential question that makes clear how two or more projects are really responding to the same need in complementary ways. In short, treat this as a problem of understanding, not merely as a problem of information.

Hook and hold staff through thought-provoking and professionally inspiring activities. When was the last time you saw a staff truly stimulated and excited by a new school project? Over the years we have generally seen the opposite: staff are usually "handed" a reform rather than being "hooked" by a proposed change and an interesting and appealing role they might play in it. Consequently, staff expectations are typically very low—eye rolling is more common than excitement when any new venture is introduced. So there is little to lose and much to gain by trying an introduction that is stirring and thought provoking, appealing to the deeper interests, ambitions, and beliefs of staff. By taking the time to thoughtfully hook the staff *before* launching into a project's action plan, savvy reform leaders make it crystal clear that *this* initiative is different, that "this, too, will *not* pass."

Note: We caution leaders to realize that when we refer to "hooking" staff, we do not mean through an extravagant opening event. Far too many reform initiatives kick off with a whiz-bang initial day that costs lots of money, leads nowhere, and results in nothing but cynicism. By "hook," we mean stimulate and then *hold* their professional interest over time.

Here's an example. We regularly begin training by using an exercise designed to hook staff into the ideas of Understanding by Design by making them analyze their own experiences as learners. The exercise has three parts:

1. First, we ask participants to recall a *well-designed* learning experience that they had as a learner and to jot down thoughts on what made the situation/tasks/activities so effective and engaging.
2. We ask participants to share their answers in small groups. After everyone has shared, we ask that they draw generalizations. Regardless of content, what do the best-designed learning experiences have in common?
3. The group answers are shared and recorded for all to see. Then we show responses from other groups and note common patterns. The most frequent answers include mention of clear goals, interesting challenges, variety of methods used, hands-on work, ongoing assessment and feedback, and a focus on a genuine accomplishment or performance.

As a result of this engaging exercise, participants end up "discovering" that UbD just embodies common sense. Because the answers are theirs, not ours or yours, they are much more likely to "own" the vision. We then show how UbD tries to honor that vision.

This exercise is easily generalized and transferred by, for example, substituting "best teacher" or "best assessment" (whatever issue you want to focus on) for "best-designed learning experience." We characterize such exercises as "vision" hooks.

An alternative type of hook may be labeled "gap related." As an example, we might ask staff to look at carefully selected samples of student work in order to identify deficits in understanding and transfer performance. Again, the resultant analysis is theirs, not an outsider's. It is direct evidence of a need, not someone's harangue.

So take the time to find vivid samples, cases studies, and data sets that reflect an inescapable reality related to the vision (about, for example, discipline, misconceptions of key ideas, failure to do homework), and develop follow-up plans for staff to explore the extent of the problem and possible solutions. Such approaches are key to not only hooking staff but also holding their interest over time. Of course, the unspoken message is clear: we're serious that this issue needs to be owned and solved by staff.

Explore new ideas and equip staff with the skills and resources needed for the desired reform. This sounds obvious—of course, people will need new skills to advance the reform in question. However, it is rare for a school or a district to commit funds, time, and staff to thoroughly train people in a way that *truly* equips them to confidently and competently apply the new skills in *their* situation—that is, to transfer. Too often, professional development stops at the "awareness" level or relies on a "train the trainers" model that typically waters down the experience, like an overly copied photocopy. Indeed, many reforms die not because the ideas are poor but because no one ever acquires sufficient skill to successfully implement the required changes.

Any reform has to be designed backward from the following question: what will it take to make every teacher competent and comfortable doing this? As we have said throughout the book, conventional staff development cannot hope to address this question because the training must become ongoing and job embedded. In practice, that means ensuring a safe space for lots of practice and feedback, team support for the new approach, and ongoing opportunities and incentives to improve the skills in question.

Rethink and revise. Arguably the most important part of teaching for understanding, whether we are talking about children or adults, is the need to *rethink what we thought we understood*. We mean this in two ways. The planning of the reform must assume, from the start, that rethinking and adjusting will occur throughout—and that therefore a feedback-gathering and adjustment process is built into the plan from the start. But we also stress the importance of "rethinking" in the deeper cognitive and affective sense suggested by the discussion on habits in Chapter 12. Any significant reform should be designed to cause educators to realize that we must constantly and deeply question our habits if we are to become great, not merely good, teachers.

So any plan for change should build in regular opportunities for conscious self-reflection and honest self-assessment—the kind of deliberate staff "metacognition" that rarely occurs *by design* in formal school settings. We have seen teachers visibly shaken by a careful reading and discussion of Plato's "Allegory of the Cave" and Andersen's "The Emperor's New Clothes" (texts that we use in long-term UbD training) when they realize how blind they have been to some dysfunctional habits. We have seen similar soul-searching when teachers are confronted with videotaped conversations with current and former students describing what did not work for them at their school. In sum, by confronting the brutal facts, we are prompted to ask the hard questions and consider blunt answers that school typically keeps from us all.

But "rethink and revise" also has a gentler meaning. After all, we constantly tell students that "writing is revision," and we introduce the writing process so that they experience the power of this idea. Similarly, we must make clear in reform that we want, expect, and value "rough drafts." No one expects perfection right out of the box—excellence is achieved through successive approximations, via constant incremental improvements. So in UbD reforms we make clear that the first three units should be considered practice drafts, and that the measure of our success comes in the second or third year, when we look back on our initial drafts to see how far we have come. But such a process requires supportive structures, policies, and incentives, as well as patient leaders who always keep the end in mind.

Evaluate our individual and team work, as we go, against the vision for reform. It is rare to ask staff to self-assess on a regular basis against goals and visions of success, but it is vital to do so. Self-assessment and self-adjustment are really the only way that adults will truly own and understand the issues, diagnoses, and solutions in question. As a result, we think it important for leaders to routinely ask staff for formal written and oral self-assessments and action plans—by individual teachers, by teams, by departments, and by staff as a whole—as a key part of the job in a learning organization.

Tailor (personalize) the work of reform to suit the interests, experience, talents, and readiness levels of staff. Too often, reform efforts involve sweeping mandates that wrongly presume that everyone should be viewed as equally ready, willing, and able. Most educators acknowledge that students differ markedly in their prior knowledge, interests, and preferred approaches to learning. Consequently, differentiated instruction is increasingly seen as a "basic" pedagogical skill for helping all students maximize their learning. Ironically, in some schools and districts that preach differentiation in the classroom, we often witness the failure to apply the same thinking to the adults—whether it be in the normal job or a proposed reform effort.

Reformers are encouraged to carefully assess staff readiness, interest, and ability based on a careful look at the various tasks associated with needed change. Informed with pre-assessment information, leaders can then appropriately tailor professional development, committee assignments, incentives, and other aspects of school reform to address the diversity of the staff and make the most effective use of available resources.

Organize (sequence) the work wisely. Change agents, like teachers slavishly marching through a textbook, sometimes march through an action plan, assuming that there is no need to revisit the assumptions and essential questions that the reform is built upon. We recommend a more deliberate organization and sequencing of reform actions to honor the points made throughout the book—use backward design, build in opportunities for feedback, plan to adjust, and encourage deliberate reflection by staff.

The graphic in Figure 11.1 sums up the kind of sequence we have in mind. Note that a feedback loop is prominently featured in the figure. Indeed, as we have argued, it is crucial that leaders establish a procedure and a structure for ensuring that useful feedback is collected and analyzed in order to make timely adjustments. Throughout the planning process, it makes sense to build in opportunities to rethink the current assumptions about vision, goals, and strategy. Such an analytic role might be undertaken by a leadership team or a representative steering committee. Regardless of who is involved, feedback collection and analysis must be an explicit part of a carefully organized action plan.

Notice that the smaller *act-feedback-adjust* loop at the bottom of the graphic illustrates the need for another, more fundamental, kind of adjustment. In addition to modifying our plan as we go based on feedback, we may need to revisit our fundamental assumptions about the vision and how best to realize it once we become immersed in the work. Effective reformers typically discover that some of the most basic assumptions they began with—about where to head, what works, what doesn't, what learning is and isn't, what leadership is and isn't—have to be changed if the mission is to be achieved.

In other words, the sequence that looks "logical" in the Excel spreadsheet is only "logical" in the same way the naive college freshman's four-year course-enrollment plan is logical: it is orderly, but uninformed. It assumes that we understand everything we need to know and might want to accomplish and become before we start a brand-new journey.

So ensure that a reform steering committee or its equivalent is constantly on the lookout for what needs to be changed in the process and direction to suit the aims of the project, mindful of current reality.

Figure 11.1
Sequence for Organizing the Work of Reform

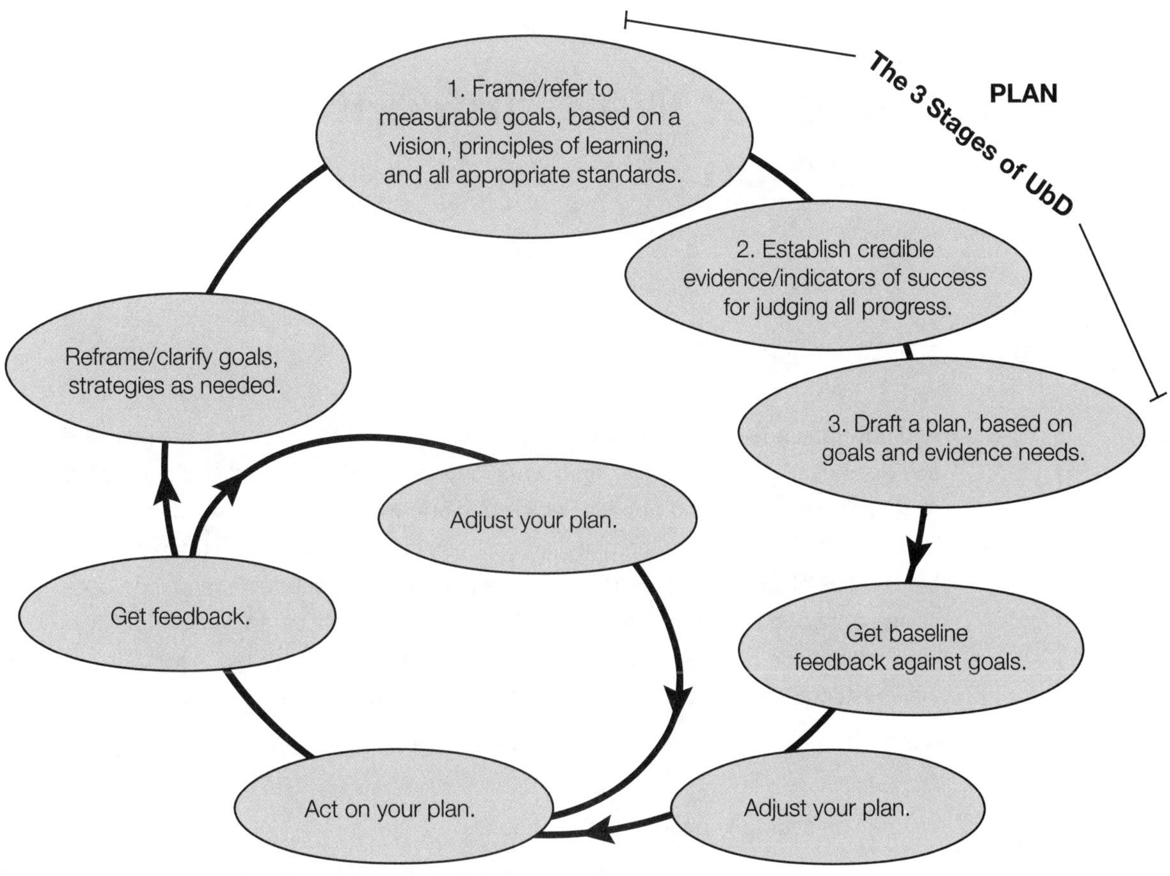

As we said at the outset, the details of reform are site-specific. We have tried to highlight more general tactical considerations for planning purposes that tend to be overlooked in many reform efforts. It all comes down to being disciplined about the logic of the three stages: resist the temptation to plan events that have not been developed and tested against the implicit demands of Stage 1, your desired results. It also comes down to resisting a plan cast in typical professional development terms. Instead, use the learning principles in Chapter 4 to develop and test your approach to staff learning. The ultimate goal of any particular reform is to have a faculty that so understands the mission and their role in it that future reforms evolve naturally from continual staff learning about learning. Then, we will have not only schooling but also school reform *by design*.

12

What Habits Must We Confront? A Closing Caution

> And now look again, and see what will naturally follow if the prisoners are released and disabused of their error. At first, when any of them is liberated and compelled suddenly to stand up and turn his neck round and walk and look towards the light, he will suffer sharp pains; the glare will distress him, and he will be unable to see the realities of which in his former state he had seen the shadows; and then conceive some one saying to him, that what he saw before was an illusion, but that now, when he is approaching nearer to being and his eye is turned towards more real existence, he has a clearer vision. What will be his reply?
>
> —From Plato's "Allegory of the Cave," *Republic*

> We may be said to know how by our habits.
>
> —John Dewey, *Human Nature and Conduct*

Is there a good reason why, despite the fact that many teachers *say* they aim for deep understanding, our schools rarely produce it? We have pondered this question for decades, yet in some ways it remains a mystery to us. And until we understand why the reform of conventional teaching has *perpetually* failed, we cannot hope to improve schooling, no matter how well a plan is designed on paper.

So, even with our "logical" approach to planning for school change, we need to take a long, hard, and realistic look at how reform should be conceived strategically in light of the discrepancy between what we say and what we do. In charting reform, it is not enough to say we seek understanding (whether in students or teachers) and plan for it. Our failure to achieve understanding with regularity (despite our claim that we value it) suggests that perhaps we misunderstand the psychology of change.

As we said in the first part of the book, our most often stated educational aims frequently fall through the cracks of day-to-day teaching and learning as a result of the key structures of school—curriculum, assessment, grading practices, and job descriptions. These important organizational elements are often directed not toward understanding but to low-level recall and skill. In a very real sense, we unwittingly work in a world that undercuts our aims.

But that doesn't fully explain how we fail to honor our ideals. Why isn't teaching more effective than it often is, in spite of difficult conditions? Why don't schools get progressively better, since everyone supposedly wants them to do so? Conventional wisdom asks us to consider the weak preparation of teachers, the growing diversity of student populations, inflexible administrative requirements, the harmful influence of textbooks and tests, and the dysfunctional governance structures of school. And almost everyone points to the lack of time!

In our view, those answers don't hold up to scrutiny as key, however. The problem of aimless and ineffective teaching is found in excellent private schools where class numbers are low, external impediments don't exist, teachers are well educated, and plenty of time exists for discussion; it is found in some of the best colleges, where professors have complete freedom to teach as they wish and have few hours in class, leaving plenty of preparation time; it is found in schools where models of good teaching can be found down every corridor, yet the good practices don't spread—and often aren't helped to. It is found in schools where teacher loads are light and every day has free periods of time for use by faculty.

Researchers who study organizations (Argyris, Senge, and others) have proposed that long-standing "disabilities" within an institution prevent us from reacting in helpful ways to our problems. For example, Senge (1990) identifies seven "learning disabilities" in an organization (here summarized with page references to *The Fifth Discipline*):

1. I Am My Position: This happens when we confuse our jobs with our identities. Then we end up seeing our responsibilities "as limited to the boundaries of the position." Fourth grade teachers never see how unprepared 6th graders are; science teachers take no responsibility for assigning and evaluating the quality of student writing. Mission is lost: "When people in organizations focus only on their position, they have little sense of responsibility for the results produced when all positions interact" (pp. 18–19).

2. The Enemy Is Out There: "There is in each of us a propensity to find someone or something outside ourselves to blame when things go wrong. . . . Some organizations elevate this propensity to a commandment: 'Thou shalt always find an external agent to blame' " (p. 19), whether it is students, board members, parents, state or federal agencies, television, or video games. Locked in our narrow role and removed from feedback, we end up blind to the fact that many unhappy results have schooling-based causes.

3. The Illusion of Taking Charge: Sometimes being "proactive" creates more problems than it solves. What this does is favor "taking action" over analyzing the situation thoroughly. Senge states, "All too often, proactiveness is reactiveness in disguise . . . if we simply become more aggressive fighting the 'enemy out there,' we are reacting. *True proactiveness comes from seeing how we contribute to our own problems*" (p. 21), emphasis in the original.

4. The Fixation on Events: "We are conditioned to see life as a series of events, and for every event, we think there is one obvious cause" (p. 21). However, the actual causes of problems are not directly linked with events and usually come from slow, gradual processes that are too complex to explain with one event. "If we focus on events, the best we can ever do is predict an event before it happens so that we can react optimally. But we cannot learn to create" solutions to address issues of long standing (p. 22).

5. The Parable of the Boiled Frog: Senge uses an extended metaphor to further the point: if you place a frog in boiling water, it will immediately try to scramble out. But if the frog is put into cool water that is gradually heated, the frog will stay in the water and get increasingly groggier from the heat until it is unable to climb out of the pot. "Why? Because the frog's internal apparatus for sensing threats to survival is geared to sudden changes in his environment, not to slow, gradual changes where effects play out over a long time" (p. 22). We are far less likely to recognize potential effects and causal links that occur over long periods of time, as we are identifying more dramatic occurrences. This is especially true in schools where the effects of teachers and learning occur over longer periods of time than most teachers are ever scheduled to perceive. It would be similar to multiple coaches facilitating an individual drill all season, but never seeing the whole team play a game.

6. The Delusion of Learning from Experience: Senge states that the "most powerful learning comes from direct experience," but "we each have a 'learning horizon,' a breadth of vision in time and space within which we assess our effectiveness. When our actions have consequences beyond our learning horizon, it becomes impossible to learn from direct experience" (p. 23). Since most of our important decisions involve factors beyond our direct experience, our focus cannot provide insight into those factors. The traditional way to get around this is by breaking the problem into components and delegating those parts, but the whole becomes lost because the factors are "addressed" in isolation from each other. So we say that kids need more "cooperative learning" in the current curriculum, when the real trouble is the curriculum.

7. The Myth of the Management Team: Instead of working collectively, leadership teams largely fight for turf but give the "appearance of a cohesive team" that hides the underlying differences that are never dealt with. "To keep up the image, they try to squelch disagreement; people with serious reservations avoid stating them publicly, and joint decisions are watered-down compromises . . . or else one person's view [is] foisted upon the group." If there should be any genuine disagreement, it quickly becomes personalized, "expressed in a manner that lays blame, polarizes opinion, and fails to reveal the underlying differences in assumptions and experiences in a way that the team as a whole could learn from." The unfortunate consequence is organizational failure to learn, "what Argyris calls 'skilled incompetence'—teams full of people who are incredibly proficient at keeping themselves from learning" (p. 25).

Senge's larger point is that "systems thinking" is needed to see all these inevitable yet typically hidden forces at play. Otherwise, we are doomed to repeat them without quite understanding why. To use our language from this and previous books, we have to anticipate misunderstandings and performance weaknesses in ourselves just as we need to do in students—and plan for it. That's why we have to change job descriptions, develop new policies, design troubleshooting guides, and "plan to adjust."

In terms of the first disability, we noted in an earlier chapter that a key need is for education to become far more depersonalized than it now is—our learning principles, curriculum reviews against established design standards, attention to learning results, and action research strategies are meant to help overcome this pressing problem. Otherwise, the second disability—blaming people and forces outside us—may be worse than in business. And, indeed, the blame game is endemic in schools, especially in high school staffs: "If only students would . . . if parents would just . . . if those middle school teachers had only . . ." The third disability has often been called "Ready, fire, aim" in education because we are often so unwilling or unable to carefully diagnose a problem before proposing solutions. The fourth, fifth, and sixth disabilities are particularly relevant to schooling, given the fact that few educators ever see the long-term effects of their work manifested in later performance and conduct of learners. The seventh describes the failure of academic subject areas to own and honor a mission larger than sharing their subject knowledge, and the concomitant failure of academic leaders to make the job of "causing understanding" central to everyone's concerns. Any fundamental reform of school will need to address the disabilities that Senge and others have highlighted.

Habits, Bad and Good

But calling these important problems "disabilities" hides something that we think it is crucial to face. Calling them "disabilities" is really a euphemism for what they seem to us to be. What we are talking about are just as well explained as bad habits.

We think it is time to consider an alternative hypothesis about institutional and personal professional change. We must face the fact that many people *say* they want to be better but unwittingly keep themselves from taking the habit-breaking actions necessary to make the needed changes. Though there is clear merit in thinking about the "system" and its invisible causes and effects, we think far too little attention has been given to what is quite visible: the bad habits of teaching, testing, grading, and discussing of school-related problems that are solvable by some old-fashioned soul-searching, commitment to change, and the hard work of breaking habits.

The problem related to the reform of teaching and schooling may thus be better conceived as finding ways to *face our own resistance* to improving teaching and schooling. "We have met the enemy and he is us," Pogo famously said. What if he was right? At the very least, we need to face our problems without the naïveté, posturing, constant blaming of forces outside school, and romanticism about the "good old days" that have bedeviled prior attempts at reform over the centuries.

Yes, *centuries*. Purposeless teaching and our unwillingness to face the long-term effects of our actions predate standardized schooling, testing, and textbooks—they even predate the Industrial Revolution and the problem of the so-called factory model of school. Here is Comenius, writing in 1632:

> We promise that the education given shall be not false but real, not superficial but thorough; that is to say, that man shall be guided, not by the intellects of others, but by his own; shall not merely read the opinions of others or commit them to memory and repeat them, but shall himself penetrate to the root of things and acquire the habit of genuinely understanding and making use of what he learns. (Comenius, 1632/1910, p. 82)

Here is Spencer (1861)—more than 140 years ago:

> The remark is trite that in his shop, or his office, in managing his estate or his family, in playing his part as director of a bank or a railway, he is very little aided by this knowledge he took so many years to acquire—so little, that generally the greater part of it drops out of his memory. . . . That which our school-courses leave almost entirely out, we thus find to be that which most nearly concerns the business of life. (p. 2)
>
> [P]ervading the whole is the vicious system of rote learning—a system of sacrificing the spirit to the letter. See the results. . . . Examinations being once passed, books are laid aside; the greater part of what has been acquired . . . soon drops out of recollection; what remains is mostly inert—the art of applying knowledge not having been cultivated; and there is but little power either of accurate observation or independent thinking. (p. 30)

Here is Goodlad (1984), more than 20 years ago, in the most exhaustive study of schooling ever conducted, describing what we all know, but deny, about what engages and disengages in school:

> The only subjects getting ratings of "very interesting" from *more than a third* of junior and senior high school students taking them were the arts, vocational education, physical education and foreign languages. (p. 232) (emphasis added)
>
> It was especially distressing to see that the kinds of classroom practices found most often in school were liked by small percentages of students. (p. 233)
>
> What do students perceive themselves to be learning? We asked [them] to write down the most important thing learned in school subjects. . . . Most commonly students listed a fact or topic. . . . Noticeably absent were responses implying the realization of having acquired some intellectual power. (pp. 233–234)

Our own workshop participants have shown a blind spot about their answers to questions about what works to cause real learning. We have more than 8,000 responses to this question: "What are the characteristics of the best-designed learning you have ever experienced?" The same answers appear over and over again: clear performance goals, safe conditions for risk taking, provocative challenges and questions, variety and choice, lots of opportunities for feedback and adjustment. Yet when we look at teaching and learning in the respondents' schools, we do not regularly see such practice or get a sense of *urgency* from teachers or administrators about the profound inconsistency between ideal and reality, stated beliefs and actions to be addressed.

In other words, though it is eminently logical and commonsensical to look at the gap between vision and reality as a motivator to drive local reforms, it turns out that it is profoundly difficult to see and act on the gap—and any school reform plan must take account of this dynamic. You cannot just "look" at the gap between vision and reality, because most of us will not "see" such a gap. Even if we do, we resist seeing any inconsistency between what we say we value and what we actually do; we find ways to turn away from it, to deny its existence. Denying the inconsistency seems like a way to avoid chaos, a worse state, or a foolish demand.

In psychological terms, then, we are in denial. We don't "resist" change in the sense of self-consciously fighting a change to teaching routines (though that is sometimes true). We "resist" change in the deep psychological sense: we do not even *realize* we are resisting because we do not easily see the lengths we go to in explaining away problems in our views, and we rationalize the status quo. We are blind to the need to change and blind to our resistance.

What impedes reform, then, may not be a lack of knowledge and skill in how to do things better, but an inability to see the unthinking routines that imprison us and make us defensive. What if we redefined the problem of ineffective schooling as something grounded in strong habits instead of as something reflecting a lack of knowledge and skill? What if *all* long-term successful learning—whether aimed toward a school mission or lifelong professional development—were as much about attaining new habits of behavior and mind as it is about acquiring new information and techniques?

We propose that the reform of schooling rarely happens because *our habits and our fears trump our ideals*. We may desire change in theory but lack the insight to see how our habits impede it, lack the will to examine deep-seated habits, and lack plans for supporting a change of habits. And school change agents rarely propose a plan capable of altering habits, overcoming fear of change, and providing everyone with a safe environment for confronting our embarrassing inability to honor how learning really occurs.

Teachers, like everyone else, are typically blind to the power of unthinking routines—a situation made worse by our isolation from other adults and trusted critical friends and a firm belief in our noble intentions. As Argyris and Schön (1974) said,

> When someone is asked how he would behave under certain circumstances, the answer he usually gives is his espoused theory of action for that situation. This is the theory of action to which he gives allegiance, and which, upon request, he communicates to others. However, the theory that actually governs his actions is this theory-in-use. (pp. 6–7)

Therefore, it is perhaps better to think about the planning of school reform in the same way we tackle difficult personal changes—as the struggle to develop new habits to replace bad habits. It seems to us that the familiar structures of school and "teaching as coverage" are, in fact, institutional and personal habits, causing us to respond in routine and unthinking ways much of the time, regardless of our ideals. The essence of institutional reform is to ferret out the bad habits and to confront what Collins (2001) calls the "brutal facts of reality," as discussed in Chapter 7.

Coverage as a Bad Habit

Think of "coverage" as a bad habit, then, like eating junk food, smoking cigarettes, or always being sarcastic in conversation. Giving endless quizzes on nitpicky facts is a bad habit; so is grading on a curve; so is relying on textbook pagination instead of working from a purposeful and coherent syllabus—the list goes on and on.

We would go so far as to say that "coverage" is not merely a bad habit; it is for many teachers an addiction. We persist in it despite its poor results; we aggressively defend it despite the fact that it makes teaching *and* learning unrewarding for all parties. "Oh, c'mon! After all, that's how *we* learned!" Reader, stay with us for a bit.

Doesn't just seeing that defensive reaction in print strike you as a weak bit of reasoning? Look at the fit, for example, when we slightly alter a familiar 12-step program for addressing an addiction to consider unproductive habits in teaching:

- We admit there is a problem: we are addicted to marching through the textbook, page by page, without external purpose.
- We find a "higher power" in our mission.
- We commit publicly to those goals.
- We conduct a "fearless inventory" against those goals.
- We admit to other educators and to students the nature of our past errors.
- We have a "spiritual awakening" about the true nature of our job: to cause learning, not just to "teach."

There is no moral blame here; recall our mantra: "Nothing personal, but . . ." It is easy for each of us to rationalize actions that have no real justification. (Recall the amusing line in the movie *The Big Chill,* stating that rationalization is more important than sex because we cannot go a day without rationalization.) Every educator tries very hard—that's not at issue! But as Winston Churchill once said, "It's no use saying, 'We are doing our best.' You have got to succeed in doing what is necessary." In our desire to glorify the noble craft of teaching, we may have to first confront the brutal fact that the emperor often has no clothes on but marches proudly on anyway.

Countless school practices have continued through the decades *despite the fact that these practices obviously impede learning*—a fact we would recognize if we would only take off the blinders or be tactfully helped to do so in our job. Consider the following:

- Treating the textbook as the syllabus, approached at a single "pace," regardless of whether students have failed to learn essential preceding material.
- Failure to pre-test to better understand learners' prior knowledge and readiness before teaching.
- "Secure" (that is, secret and "gotcha") tests of our goals (making it unlikely that we achieve our goals).
- Predictably boring and passivity-inducing pedagogical approaches (such as endless worksheets and end-of-chapter, low-level questions).
- Courses determined by a fixed semester or yearly schedule instead of by the time needed for learners to meet learning goals.
- Penalizing students' risk taking in early attempts to perform by recording all their grades on formative assessments and figuring them into the final grade.
- Fixation on letter grades calculated by the mathematical mean instead of based on more recent performance, resulting in the penalizing of growth.
- Rigid pacing guides that disregard inevitable variabilities of learning.

We nod agreement—yet we turn away. We acknowledge the problem in general—but we cannot attribute these brutal facts to *our* own classroom or school. As with all bad habits, in other words, we are in denial. For centuries we have known what engaged and effective learning for understanding looks like, but we don't confront the timeless routines that prevent us from heading there.

Perhaps a wiser approach to dealing with the perpetual failure of teaching to change much over the centuries is to say that teachers are in the grip of blind, strong, and unfortunate habits—made so much worse by the power of isolation, the need for control of a large group of youngsters, the lack of ongoing feedback, and the weight of tradition.

The Textbook as Enabler of Bad Habits

The textbook is a strong enabler of many of these bad habits. Its physical heft signals intellectual weight. Yet a typical textbook provides no more than an aimless compendium of information and exercises out of context. It merely parcels out content exhaustively in "logical" order, like an encyclopedia, a dictionary, a cookbook, or a baseball rulebook. Common sense tells us that it would be foolish to work through the dictionary page by page to learn the English language or to memorize the rulebook to learn how to play baseball. Reviewing a compendium of recipes doesn't make you a good cook, just as marching through an orderly list of content and exercises without formulating your own hypotheses and testing them doesn't make you an emerging scientist. A purpose (and, therefore, a purposeful use of the text) has to be supplied by the user and the instructor. The text is *consulted,* in other words, to learn how to achieve performance goals. Yet day in and day out, many educators remain blind to this common sense.

Making the matter seem even more unfortunate when we view things this way is the fact that few national textbooks are written to address *particular* state standards, not to mention the unique mission and local goals of *our* school or district. If our school seeks to stress "productive citizenship" and "critical thinking" in learning history, there are no national textbooks to serve us. Furthermore, most textbooks are written to capture a *national* market and be accepted in the three large states (California, Texas, and Florida) with state-adoption policies. It thus makes even less sense to teach the entire textbook when it strives to cover the waterfront of those states' copious standards—never mind the silliness of relying exclusively on that text if you live in one of the 47 other states.

In short, *the textbook is not and can never be the syllabus*. Common sense tells us it is a resource, like the phone book or the computer manual—and a very limited resource at that, because it rarely is designed to cause integrated performance and transfer of learning to new situations. Yet teachers everywhere fall into the habit of teaching the book; the majority of local curricula (including those with "pacing guides") are perversely designed to fit the textbook; few local adoption processes examine texts in light of clear mission-related aims related to transfer; and few academic departments or programs issue guidelines on which chapters to stress and which to ignore in light of local goals. So it is not a stretch to say that we are addicted to the textbook. Any vital and robust reform plan will confront this brutal reality by making us self-conscious about how we *should* use the textbook versus how we *do* use the textbook, and it will provide us with countless opportunities to become more conscious of our passive reliance on the book.

Real reform depends upon confronting this reality—with tact, empathetic support, and a plan for changing habits. More to the point of schooling, as we have said in earlier chapters, we will require a different kind of job description and a workplace that constantly demands the new habits and provides supporting structures and incentives to attain them. Looking at the problem in this way may finally explain the puzzle mentioned earlier—namely, how it is possible that we can *know* there is a better way to teach and to school but perpetually fail to do it.

How People Learn—and Paradoxically *Resist* Learning

Our provocative slant is actually supported by research. The modern literature on learning, on student misconception, on cognitive therapy, on habit formation and breaking, and on attribution theory all point toward a similar conclusion. Habits of thought and action notoriously resist easy change. Institutions are defensive and blind to dysfunctional interaction and practice.

Thinkers as diverse as Freud, Piaget, and Gardner recognize that the "bad" side of our active meaning making is that we are prone to resist new understandings and persist in old meanings—particularly when the new meanings cast doubt on cherished beliefs. We cannot help thinking of our current habits of mind and actions as being the result of rational decision making, and we hang onto unproductive meanings even when they are shown to be "unreasonable" by trusted others, texts, or revealing experience.

Yet such modern theory is just a variant of Plato's theory from more than 2,000 years ago. We, too, easily feel "blinded" by the new and for a while eagerly seek to return to the comfort of the familiar. Note that the "liberated" thinker has to be "dragged" against his will up the "rough ascent" to the light. Understanding takes not only time, but also the ability to persist in the face of severe doubt and uncertainty. Socrates, the speaker in the allegory, concludes by reminding his listeners that the story is a fable about the true nature of education:

> But then, if I am right, certain professors of education must be wrong when they say that they can put a knowledge into the soul which was not there before, like sight into blind eyes.
>
> They undoubtedly say this, he replied.

> Whereas, our argument shows that the power and capacity of learning exists in the soul already; and that just as the eye was unable to turn from darkness to light without the whole body, so too the instrument of knowledge can only by the movement of the whole soul be turned. (Plato's *Republic*)

All learners settle too easily for familiarity. Recall the famous scene in the movie *Teachers,* when "Ditto" dies in class, but it doesn't matter: students repeat the routine of picking up the daily worksheets, compliantly completing them, and returning them to his desk on the way out. Or recall a central message in *The Shopping Mall High School* (Powell, Farrar, & Cohen, 1985): teachers and students have a tacit agreement, a "treaty" not to challenge each other, even at the expense of learning.

It is not stretching the point too much to suggest that when one adult is embedded all year in a room away from other adults, the classroom can be thought of as an "intellectual cave." Teachers, like Socrates' cave dwellers, understandably resist seeing that textbook coverage, endless worksheets, or purposeless (albeit engaging) activities are just the educational versions of shadow naming—not because they are "dumb" or "close-minded," but because when the very conception of their job is challenged, the initial pain, confusion, loss of bearing, and loss of control are very difficult to handle (especially if we are on our own). Indeed, what is the alternative, if we take away textbooks and typical curriculum frameworks, but seeming chaos? That's how all change of habit feels: the new, "better" habit feels awkward, unfamiliar, not useful; our older habits feel right, comfortable. So initially we really have reason to say (as in the allegory) that the new habit is worse: we are "blinded by the light" and see less well and act less effectively than before.

Making Changes

Ask yourself, then, the following questions: Which habits have you broken, and what did you do to break them? Which personal habits have you wanted to break but been unable to? What made it so difficult? How have others broken such habits? How should we describe the difference between successful and unsuccessful habit change, and what does the research on habits teach us?

Let's consider a summary of the research on habits, written especially for mature adults, found in the AARP newsletter (Wadman, 2005):

> **How to Make the Change**
>
> How should you go about giving up a well-worn habit? Behavioral change experts generally agree on several tips for habit-changers from 18 to 88. Below, we've refined them where appropriate for those over 50.
>
> • *Figure out why you want to change.* An internal motivation (I want to be around to dance at my granddaughter's wedding) is preferable to an external one (my doctor told me to lose weight). But to start with, even cosmetic goals will do.

• *Use your life experience to your advantage.* Catalog the attempts you've made at change and why they've failed. Then apply what you've learned. Don't plan to work out at six each morning if you haven't risen before eight for the last five decades.

• *Develop a written plan for quitting that includes a start date.* The more detailed it is, the better. Don't say, "I want to lose weight." Instead, say, "I want to lose two pounds a month for six months beginning on February 1." Behavioral change expert Charles Stuart Platkin says that planning for a habit change should be undertaken with all the time and attention to detail that we put into planning our daughters' weddings.

• *Substitute a new behavior for the old one.* Exercise is a great replacement for smoking or eating. And even a less-than-virtuous substitute is better than a plainly bad habit. When Dena Jansen quit smoking, she was living in Las Vegas. She didn't know what to do with her hands. So she spent the next several weeks in casinos. "I figured if I was saving that much money, I might as well put it in the machines," she says.

• *Don't let the perfect be the enemy of the good.* If the prospect of trying to lose 20 pounds paralyzes you, start small. Walking for 20 minutes a day and consuming just 100 fewer calories daily—that's one tablespoon of mayonnaise—adds up to a 20-pound weight loss over the course of a year for an average-size person, according to Baylor's John Foreyt.

• *Get support.* Having friends and family on board is critical for most successful behavior change. Let those close to you know what you're planning to do and how it might affect your behavior. Conversely, stay away from people (including spouses!) who have an interest in undermining your efforts.

• *Anticipate obstacles.* Develop a plan for what you're going to do when the bread basket arrives at the restaurant table. Take a walk, order a veggie plate, or ask the waiter to take it away once others have been served.

• *Expect setbacks, and don't be undone by them.* Have a plan for the day after you slip.

• *Don't set yourself up for failure.* Late November may not be the best time to embark on a 1,200-calorie diet.

• *Don't quit trying.* Most people don't succeed in changing on their first try, says Wilkins of Cedars-Sinai. "You never want to give up because you don't know if it's the third time, the fourth time, or the fifth time where you will succeed."

We can adapt this article to our school reform needs quite easily:

• *Figure out why you want to change.* An internal motivation (I want to experience the joy of watching kids achieve an "Aha!") is preferable to an external one (my planning team is reading *Understanding by Design*). But to start, even an extrinsic goal will do.

• *Use your life experience to your advantage.* Catalog all your successful and unsuccessful lessons and changes of method as a teacher. Then apply what you've learned in small doses. Don't plan to change six units if you haven't rewritten a unit in years.

• *Develop a written plan for quitting that includes a start date.* The more detailed it is, the better. Don't say, "I want to stop aimless covering." Instead, say, "I want my unit on electrical circuits to culminate in a transfer task reflective of understanding."

• *Substitute a new behavior for the old one.* Organizing a lesson around an essential question or a provocative problem is a great replacement for aimless coverage. And even a less-than-virtuous substitute is better than a plainly bad habit: use a highly engaging game or video at the start of a unit, even if it is only tangentially related to the big idea.

• *Don't let the perfect be the enemy of the good.* If the prospect of trying to change *all* your units paralyzes you, start small. Making one lesson within each unit focus on an essential question will add up to a different classroom by year's end.

• *Get support.* Having friends and family on board is critical for most successful behavior change. Let those close to you know what you're planning to do and how it might affect your behavior. Conversely, stay away from people (including colleagues with whom you hang out!) who may intentionally or unwittingly undermine your efforts.

• *Anticipate obstacles.* Develop a plan for what you're going to do when you feel like you are falling behind in marching through the pages of the book. For example, prepare a summary or an outline of the chapter, skip an unimportant subsection of the text, or summarize the readings in a podcast for student download.

• *Expect setbacks, and don't be undone by them.* Have a backup plan for the day that doesn't go as planned.

• *Don't set yourself up for failure.* Late February may not be the best time to embark on a completely new course.

• *Don't quit trying.* Most teachers don't succeed in changing their teaching approach on their first try. "You never want to give up because you don't know if it's the third time, the fourth time, or the fifth time where you will succeed."

In *Changing for Good,* a book on altering habits in one's life, Prochaska, Norcross, and DiClemente (1994) argue (with lots of data from controlled medical studies) that if we are aware of the stage we are in during the change process and we respond appropriately to that stage (based on careful studies of successful self-changers and the stages they went through), our chance of success is greatly increased. Their approach is now considered best practice in national work in the areas of obesity and drug addiction. Their research identifies six stages of habit change that one must spiral through repeatedly:

- Precontemplation
- Contemplation
- Preparation
- Action
- Maintenance
- Termination

The key to the success of their approach is to be patient as the stages unfold and to realize that techniques are stage-sensitive: "Efficient self-change depends upon doing the right things at the right times . . . treatments that are quite effective in one stage may be ineffective or detrimental at another stage" (p. 59).

For example, when people in the preparation stage are encouraged to jump into significant actions before they are ready to do so, their chance of success is lowered and their willingness to continue is jeopardized. (This is a common problem in professional development.)

> Although those in the preparation stage are committed to action, and may appear ready for action, they have not necessarily resolved their ambivalence. They may still need to convince themselves that taking action is what's best for them. . . . This last-minute resolution is necessary and appropriate. (p. 43)

> Professionals who equate change with action design terrific action-oriented change programs and are bitterly disappointed when sign-up rates are minuscule, or when a large number of participants drop out after a brief stay. (p. 44)

More generally, the authors cite two frequent mismatches: self-changers (and therapists) who assume that self-awareness must precede all growth ("They try to modify behaviors by becoming more aware of them") and those who assume that jumping into action is all that is needed ("They try to modify behavior without awareness") (p. 59).

Conversely, the key action for people in the precontemplation stage is to help them recognize their defensive reaction to any suggestions of doing things differently and for the better. Because we have claimed that many teachers are not even aware that their approach to teaching is problematic, it is instructive to see what the experts advise for those in the precontemplation stage. They offer a simple three-question test to help people decide if they have a problem and begin to bring it to awareness, or if they have made a conscious, rational choice to act the way they do:

> Do you discuss your behavior pattern? Precontemplators are usually defensive about their problem behaviors. Do you tell people to mind their own business, or do you appreciate their concern?
>
> Are you well informed about your behavior? Precontemplators avoid learning about their [behavior as teachers and the problems that arise with their methods]. Do you turn the page . . . when you see an article about your behavior? Or do you read it with interest? . . .
>
> Are you willing to take responsibility for the consequences of your behavior [as it plays out in the classroom and in achievement results]? Precontemplators are uncomfortable with vividly imagining these consequences. Are you aware of the short-term and long-term results of your behavior [as reflected in levels of student engagement and achievement]? . . . Precontemplators rarely take responsibility for the negative consequences of their actions. . . .
>
> Your responses to these three questions will give you a good sense of whether a particular behavior is a problem or preference. If you can honestly say you are not defensive but well-informed, aware of the consequences of and responsible for the long-term effects [on students] of your behavior, then perhaps it is a preference. If, however—like most of us—you answered no to one or more of these questions, you are probably in the precontemplation stage. (pp. 78–79, bracketed phrases added)

Interestingly, this research parallels key ideas of the well-known Concerns-Based Adoption Model of school change (see, for example, Hord et al., 1987). By stressing the need to get at teacher concerns from the start, by separating out the assessment of innovation use from the attitudes of those who are expected to change, and by making clear in longitudinal rubrics and case studies the fact that change is long term and complex, Hord and colleagues have argued tirelessly for three decades for a more psychologically sophisticated view of the change process. They have suggested innumerable ways to promote as well as assess long-term change in education. We highly recommend that readers review this important research, validated over many years of experience.

We think this kind of analysis has to go even further, though. We need to address the personal and especially the *institutional* bad habits that make lasting change even more difficult to achieve.

Toward Breaking Institutional Bad Habits

Too often, educational reform has been viewed in terms of the imposition of new programs or instructional practices. We propose an alternative perspective: think of school reform as the challenge of breaking deep-seated and sometimes unconscious organizational habits that aren't working, as reflected in job descriptions, uses of time, governance procedures, and policies. We need to invent new school structures that provide very different incentives, opportunities, routines, and rewards than the current system. We need to invent a learning organization to replace the compliance and habit-bound culture that we have all inhabited.

We can start the process of change, then, by self-consciously and continually asking essential questions about discrepancies. "Why do we do *that*?" is such a question—one asked far too infrequently in staff and team meetings. As we have suggested, many timeless institutional as well as personal counterproductive practices are habits we never stop and consider. A learning organization, by contrast, is devoted to a conscious self-examination of any inconsistency between action and ideal. As Argyris and Schön (1978) put it, "Learning occurs when we detect and correct error . . . error is a mismatch between intentions and results." Argyris (1993) also notes that educational research rarely looks at such errors and how to address them (p. 28*ff*).

Barr and Tagg (1995) wrote in a now-famous paper on the need for reforms in higher education to move from what they term the "instruction paradigm" to the "learning paradigm," referring to Argyris's ideas and the need to "put our minds where our hearts are":

> That such a restructuring is needed is beyond question: the gap between what we say we want of higher education and what its structures *provide* has never been wider. To use a distinction made by Chris Argyris and Donald Schön, the difference between our espoused theory and our theory-in-use is becoming distressingly noticeable. An "espoused theory," readers will recall, is the set of principles people offer to explain their behavior; the principles we can infer from how people or their organizations actually behave is their "theory-in-use." Right now, the Instruction Paradigm is our theory-in-use, yet the *espoused* theories of most educators more closely resemble components of the Learning Paradigm. The more we discover about how the mind works and how students learn, the greater the disparity between what we say and what we do. Thus so many of us feel increasingly constrained by a system increasingly at variance with what we believe. To build the colleges we need for the 21st century—to put our minds where our hearts are, and rejoin acts with beliefs—we must consciously reject the Instruction Paradigm and restructure what we do on the basis of the Learning Paradigm. (p. 16)

So leaders must work with staff to look for the most promising examples of internal inconsistency that have the biggest potential impact in signaling the need for and value of change, with the least likelihood of arousing defensiveness. We would propose the reform of professional development as such an area.

The Reform of Professional Development

Typical inservice training, like typical teaching, assumes that exposure to new ways and new information changes learners. Worse, it is tacitly assumed that a little "exposure" to new practices is sufficient to cause transfer! To cap it off, little attempt is made to confront the bad habits that the new practice is meant to improve. It is considered extremely bad form to suggest to staff that some of our practices might be flawed. But what habit was ever changed by tiptoeing around it? Looking at reform as the challenge of breaking deep-seated and sometimes unconscious habits that aren't working helps us see why professional development (or preservice training) has often been ineffective *and is likely to remain so*. And no one should be surprised or offended by such a claim—it is a familiar lament in our profession.

We can start afresh, then, with a blameless critique: regardless of all past good efforts, professional development must model the change we seek in school. The brutal fact we must face is that many conventional approaches to training and change are bound to fail if they presume that the problem is merely a lack of information and skill. Ingrained habits are *never* broken by such "training." If it were so, schools would have changed long ago—just as no one would any longer smoke cigarettes or strike a child in anger.

As we have argued in earlier chapters, professional development must become more habit focused, hence job embedded, not simply a series of events and scheduled offerings. It must become clear that learning about learning is an expected and evaluated part of the job, rewarded in the workplace. Time must be allotted for slowly and repeatedly trying out new practices in safe increments, in teams, with coaching and moral support.

Two decades ago, Schön (1983) and others asserted that healthy modern organizations *had* to be designed for the encouragement of learning because continuous learning is the key to organizational vitality and success:

> We must, in other words, become adept at learning. We must become able not only to transform our institutions, in response to changing situations and requirements; we must invent and develop institutions which are "learning systems," that is to say, systems capable of bringing about their own continuing transformation. (p. 28)

According to Peter Senge (1990), learning organizations are places where

> people continually expand their capacity to create the results they truly desire, where new and expansive patterns of thinking are nurtured, where collective aspiration is set free, and where people are continually learning to see the whole together. (p. 3)

"Leader as teacher" is not about you "teaching" people how to achieve your vision. It is about fostering learning, for everyone. Such leaders help people throughout the organization develop systemic understandings and shared vision (Senge, 2003). Accepting this responsibility of common sense may be the only antidote to a common downfall of otherwise gifted teachers—losing their commitment to the truth. "Commitment to the truth . . . means a relentless willingness to root out ways we limit or deceive ourselves from seeing what is" (p. 148). But when teachers are isolated, insulated from disinterested feedback, harried, and working in an organization that does not reward group inquiry and self-assessment, why should such unfortunate behavior surprise us?

This commitment to shared inquiry is at the heart of the modern literature on professional learning communities as articulated by Darling-Hammond, the DuFours, and others in recent years (see the Web site for the National Staff Development Council at www.nsdc.org/standards/learningcommunities.cfm, and the site for the Southwest Educational Development Laboratory (1997) at www.sedl.org/change/issues/issues61.html). It harkens back to our focus on nonteaching action research responsibilities in Chapter 6. But we cannot be psychologically naive. Not only must we heed Senge's warnings about system-related blind spots, but we too easily overlook Schaefer's (1967) caution from more than 40 years ago:

> Crucial to any change would be school administrators of sufficient security of tenure, or perhaps simply of sufficient courage, to admit publicly that the school is ordinarily only modestly successful. . . . To cease behaving as if all that was required was more of the same—more [facilities, learning materials, funds, time]—would provide a notable beginning. . . . The first obstacle to overcome, then, if any school is to become a center of inquiry [into teaching and learning], is the fear of admitting how little we know. (p. 60)

More recently, Argyris (1993) cautioned that the defensive routines of the individuals in the organization are very strong, go unnoticed, and are typically unaddressed—worse, they are treated as *undiscussable* (like any addiction, we might add):

> Advice in the literature about how to correct educational ineffectiveness is abstract and distant. Almost no advice is given on how to engage the defensive activities and consequences just described. They are ignored, and the fact that they are ignored is also ignored. . . . As Brodsky documents, teachers are often unaware of how skillfully they create defensive routines, how skillfully they compound them when they try to reduce them, how skillfully they blame others, and how skillfully they deny all of the above. (pp. 30–32)

We have seen this phenomenon repeatedly over the past 25 years. More tellingly, even when educators acknowledge inadequacies in student performance, too many express lack of confidence that they have the power or capacity to make a difference. Experience abets the fatalism that many teachers feel: given the way schools are run, few people do actually change much. So the very real fear of embarrassment or failure is often too strong for us to publicly acknowledge. But such fatalism is the antithesis of habit change.

In short, most schools have, ironically, been *poor* examples of learning organizations, afraid as they typically are of taking that first crucial step of admitting ignorance about how to cause more and deeper learning, and stuck as they typically are in unexamined and self-perpetuating routines in which defensiveness about any critique of comfortable practice is the norm. And the typical job conditions abet the problem: individual teachers are often weak models of *learners* in action because they are asked only to "teach" instead of continually being asked by job requirements and norms to show a commitment to continual questioning and openness to change.

So it won't do for school leaders and professional development programs to demand something of individuals that schools do not model. Professional development must be based on truly essential questions and puzzles about learning: What would it take to get more learners to learn well? When is the problem theirs and when is it ours? Which practices work and which don't? Who is having the most success and why? Professional development can then emerge around the action research and training that follow from such inquiries.

It is therefore incumbent on change agents to be the kind of questioners—that is, habit challengers and habit breakers—we are describing, and to work with staff to develop structures and situations in which exploring our most important questions and needs is safe and supported. That will require leaders to charge not only the professional developers but also every staff member to make a commitment to root out institutional inconsistency between mission and practice as a central job responsibility.

This was, after all, Covey's (1989) initial message in *The Seven Habits of Highly Effective People:* the first habit is to overcome passivity and a culture of blame—to become proactive. The key to becoming increasingly proactive and effective is to

> make a promise—and keep it. Or we can set a goal—and achieve it. As we make and keep commitments, even small commitments, we begin to establish an inner integrity that gives us awareness of self-control and the courage and strength to accept more responsibility. . . . The power to make and keep commitments to ourselves is the essence of developing the basic habits of effectiveness. (p. 92)

The only solution to the passivity and fatalism that we see in so many schools is the commitment to change what isn't working and the feeling of efficacy that will come from tackling a real problem well (no matter how small the problem).

So one key antidote to poor professional development, ironically, is to expect every teacher to develop, act on, and report back on a yearly action research plan in which the teacher targets a weakness in performance related to student achievement. Initially, the work could be done with a buddy or in small teams if we felt that such a grouping would be more supportive. But over time, the message would be simple: we *must* learn, we *can* learn, we *can* change, and we *can* actually change schooling for the better. Unless we experience that sense of efficacy in our work, school will never achieve its aim.

Fortunately, in recent years, a number of successful approaches, such as Japanese lesson study, administrative walkabouts, child study teams, professional learning communities, and the use of "tuning protocols," have helped school staffs break ineffective habits—both personal and institutional—to become more effective. Although different in substance and process, each of these approaches embodies several commonalities: an *explicit goal* related to learning about learning and improving performance, a *structured process* to guide action, professional *collaboration,* and a *long-term* orientation. Changing habits and transforming a school culture demand such proactive measures.

Ideas for Action

The following ideas are organized under four broad steps for challenging the status quo and developing new institutional habits.

1. Come to an awareness of the problem.
   - Set up disequilibrium: find practices and policies clearly at odds with mission and beliefs (such as a mismatch with grading approaches and report cards).
   - Confront the safest "brutal facts" (such as unsatisfactory public results).
   - Use data (such as achievement results, student surveys) to reveal inadequacies.
2. Offer a compelling alternative.
   - Collect, disseminate, and discuss exemplary lessons or units, student work, and instructional practices.
   - Engage staff in visioning exercises (such as Picture the Graduate, Best Design).
   - Write position papers, based on research and data, summarizing faculty visions for the school based on mission (for example, have subject-area committees develop a statement and plan for explicitly addressing the overall mission within their program).
   - Develop clear and compelling responses to FAQs and the many "Yes, buts . . ." that easily impede reform (such as "Yes, but we have to teach to the state test").

- Tug at both head and heart (for example, refer to heartfelt letters from former students).
- Show how the proposed vision connects with current initiatives (rather than being just another add-on).

3. Create a supportive and collaborative culture to support the needed changes.
   - Proactively address (by design)
     - Predictable discomfort (internal resistance) by endlessly communicating (by words and deed) "Nothing personal, but . . . ."
     - Pushback—from staff, students, parents ("Yes, but . . .").
     - Implementation dip.
   - Develop a plan that places everyone in study teams to investigate and report on persistent achievement problems or other identified needs.
4. Establish structures, roles, and resources to support the needed changes.
   - Draft new job descriptions (see Chapter 6).
   - Develop differentiated professional development based on needs analysis, personal interests, and staff feedback.
   - Create new templates for the design of courses, units, and lessons in keeping with mission and program goals.
   - Explicitly allocate available resources to the goals.
   - Identify and provide tools and resources for working smarter (such as subscriptions to the Understanding by Design Exchange; see http://ubdexchange.org/).

References

Adler, M. J. (1982). *The Paideia proposal: An educational manifesto.* New York: Macmillan.

Adler, M. J. (1984). *The Paideia program: An educational syllabus.* New York: Macmillan.

Alverno College. (2001a). *Ability-based learning program: The biology major.* Milwaukee, WI: Publisher.

Alverno College. (2001b). *Ability-based learning program: The history major.* Milwaukee, WI: Publisher.

American Council on the Teaching of Foreign Languages. (1998). *ACTFL performance guidelines for K–12 learners.* Available: www.actfl.org/

American Council on the Teaching of Foreign Languages. (2003). *ACTFL integrated performance assessment manual.* Available: www.actfl.org/

American Psychological Association. (1995). *Learner-centered psychological principles: A framework for school redesign and reform.* Washington, D.C.: APA.

Argyris, C. (1993). *Knowledge for action: A guide to overcoming barriers to organizational change.* San Francisco: Jossey-Bass.

Argyris, C., & Schön, D. (1974). *Theory in practice: Increasing professional effectiveness.* San Francisco: Jossey-Bass.

Argyris, C., & Schön, D. (1978). *Organizational learning: A theory of action perspective.* Reading, MA: Addison-Wesley.

Arter, J., & McTighe, J. (2001). *Scoring rubrics in the classroom: Using performance criteria for assessing and improving student performance.* Thousand Oaks, CA: Corwin Press.

Aseltine, J., Faryniarz, J., & Rigazio-DiGilio, A. (2006). *Supervision for learning: A performance-based approach to teacher development and school improvement.* Alexandria, VA: Association for Supervision and Curriculum Development.

Barendsen, R. D., et al. (Comps.). (1976). *The American Revolution: Selections from secondary school history books of other nations.* Washington, DC: U.S. Department of Health, Education, and Welfare.

Barr, R., & Tagg, J. (1995, November/December). From teaching to learning—A new paradigm for undergraduate education. *Change,* 13–25.

Black, P., Harrison, C., Lee, C., Marshall, B., & Wiliam, D. (2004, September). Working inside the black box: Assessment for learning in the classroom. *Phi Delta Kappan, 86*(1), 9–21.

Black, P., & Wiliam, D. (1998, October). Inside the black box: Raising standards through classroom assessment. *Phi Delta Kappan, 80*(2), 139–148.

Bloom, B. S., Englehart, M. D., Furst, E. J., Hill, W. H., & Krathwohl, R. R. (Eds.). (1956). *Taxonomy of educational objectives: The classification of educational goals: Handbook I, cognitive domain.* New York: David McKay.

Blythe, T., Allen, D., & Powell, B. (1999). *Looking together at student work.* New York: Teachers College Press.

Bounds, H. M., Rucker, S. M., Kaase, K., Couey, J. M., Chapman, C., & Guy, M. (2007). *Mississippi mathematics framework 2007.* Mississippi Department of Education. Available: www.mde.k12.ms.us/ACAD/ID/Curriculum/Math/pdfs/MF07(finalcorrections).pdf

Brandt, Ronald S. (1998). *Powerful learning.* Alexandria, VA: ASCD.

Bransford, J. D., Brown, A. L., & Cocking, R. R. (Eds.). (1999). *How people learn: Brain, mind, experience, and school*. Washington, DC: National Academy Press.
Bransford, J. D., Brown, A. L., & Cocking, R. R. (Eds.). (2000). *How people learn: Brain, mind, experience, and school* (expanded ed.). Washington, DC: National Academy Press.
Bruner, J. S. (1971). *The relevance of education*. New York: Norton.
Buckingham, M., & Coffman, C. (1999). *First, break all the rules: What the world's greatest managers do differently.* New York: Simon & Schuster.
Burton, G. M., Maletsky, E. M., Bright, G. W., Helton, S. M., Hollis, L. Y., Johnson, H. C., et al. (1998). *Math advantage I*. New York: Harcourt Brace.
Clark, R. (2003). *Building expertise: Cognitive methods for training and performance improvement* (2nd ed.). Washington, DC: International Society for Performance Improvement.
Collins, J. C. (2001). *Good to great: Why some companies make the leap—and others don't*. New York: HarperBusiness.
Collins, J. C. (2005). *Good to great and the social sectors: A monograph to accompany Good to Great.* Boulder, CO: Author.
Comenius, A. (1910). "Great didactic." In Kessinger reprint of M. W. Keating Oxford edition. Chapter XII, 2, 82. (Original work published 1632)
Commission on Public Secondary Schools. (2005). Standards for accreditation for high schools, middle/high schools, and K–12 schools. *New England Association of Schools and Colleges*. Available: www.neasc.org/cpss/standards_2005.pdf
Cooper, J., & Robinson, P. (2000). Getting started: Informal small-group strategies in large classes. In *New directions for teaching and learning, no. 81* (pp. 17–24). San Francisco: Jossey-Bass.
Costa, A. L., & Kallick, B. (2000). *Discovering and exploring habis of mind.* Alexandria, VA: Association for Supervision and Curriculum Development.
Covey, S. R. (1989). *The seven habits of highly effective people: Restoring the character ethic*. New York: Simon & Schuster.
Danielson, C. (1996). *Enhancing professional practice: A framework for teaching*. Alexandria, VA: Association for Supervision and Curriculum Development.
Danielson, C. (2007). *Enhancing professional practice: A framework for teaching* (2nd ed.). Alexandria, VA: Association for Supervision and Curriculum Development.
Darling-Hammond, L. (1997). *The right to learn: A blueprint for creating schools that work.* San Francisco: Jossey-Bass.
Deal, T. E., & Peterson, K. D. (1999). *Shaping school culture: The heart of school leadership.* San Francisco: Jossey-Bass.
Deming, W. E. (1982). *Out of the crisis.* Cambridge, MA: MIT Press.
Detterman, D., & Sternberg, R. (Eds.). (1993). *Transfer on trial: Intelligence, cognition and instruction.* Norwood, NJ: Ablex.
Dewey, J. (1916). *Democracy and education: An introduction to the philosophy of education.* New York: Macmillan.
Drucker, P. (1990). *Managing the non-profit organization.* New York: Harper.
DuFour, R., & Eaker, R. (1998). *Professional learning communities at work: Best practices for enhancing student achievement.* Bloomington, IN: National Educational Service/ASCD.
Elmore, R. F. (2002, January–February). The limits of "change." *Harvard Education Letter.* Available: www.edletter.org/past/issues/2002-jf/limitsofchange.shtml
Elmore, R. F. (2004). *School reform from the inside out: Policy, practice, and performance.* Cambridge, MA: Harvard University Press.
Erickson, L. (2002). *Toward concept-based curriculum and instruction: Teaching beyond the facts.* Thousand Oaks, CA: Corwin Press.
Erickson, L. (2007). *Concept-based curriculum and instruction for the thinking classroom.* Thousand Oaks, CA: Corwin Press.
Fullan, M. (2001). *Leading in a culture of change.* San Francisco: Jossey-Bass.
Gardner, H. (1991). *The unschooled mind.* New York: Basic Books.
Gardner, H. (1999). *The disciplined mind: What all students should understand.* New York: Simon & Schuster.
Georgia Department of Education. (2007a). Curriculum frequently asked questions. Retrieved May 12, 2007, from www.georgiastandards.org/faqs.aspx#q4
Georgia Department of Education. (2007b). English language arts standards. Retrieved May 12, 2007, from www.georgiastandards.org/english.aspx

Gilbert, T. F. (1978). *Human competence: Engineering worthy performance.* New York: McGraw-Hill.
Goodlad, J. (1984). *A place called school.* New York: McGraw-Hill.
Gragg, C. I. (1954). Because wisdom can't be told. In M. P. McNair (Ed.), *The case method at the Harvard Business School: Papers by present and past members of the faculty and staff.* New York: McGraw-Hill.
Hirsch, E. D., Kett, J., & Trefil, J. (1988). *Cultural literacy: What every American needs to know.* New York: Vintage Books.
History–Social Science Curriculum Framework and Criteria Committee. (2005). *History–social science framework for California public schools kindergarten through grade twelve.* California Department of Education. Available: www.cde.ca.gov/re/pn/fd/documents/hist-social-sci-frame.pdf
Hord, S. M., Rutherford, W. L., Huling-Austin, L., & Hall, G. E. (1987). *Taking charge of change.* Alexandria, VA: Association for Supervision and Curriculum Development.
Howe, B. (Ed.). (1999). *Soccer: How to play the game: The official playing and coaching manual of the United States Soccer Federation.* New York: Universe Publishing.
Hunter, M. (1971). *Teach for transfer.* El Segundo, CA: TIP Publications.
Lewis, C. (2002). *Lesson study: A handbook of teacher-led instructional change.* Philadelphia: Research for Better Schools.
Light, R. (1990). *The Harvard assessment seminar: Explorations with students and faculty about teaching, learning, and student life* (vol. 1). Cambridge, MA: Harvard University.
Light, R. J. (2001). *Making the most of college: Students speak their minds.* Cambridge, MA: Harvard University Press.
Marshall, K. (2005, June). It's time to rethink teacher supervision and evaluation. *Phi Delta Kappan, 86*(10), 727–735.
Martin, M., Mullis, I., Gregory, K., Hoyle, C., & Shen, C. (2000). *Effective schools in science and mathematics: IEA's Third International Mathematics and Science Study.* Boston: International Study Center, Lynch School of Education. Boston College. http://nces.ed.gov/timss/
Marzano, R. J. (2003). *What works in schools: Translating research into action.* Alexandria, VA: Association for Supervision and Curriculum Development.
Marzano, R. J., Pickering, D. J., & Pollock, J. E. (2001). *Classroom instruction that works: Research-based strategies for improving student achievement.* Alexandria, VA: Association for Supervision and Curriculum Development.
Massoud, M. R. F. (n.d.). Advances in quality improvement: Principles and framework. *QA Brief.* Quality Assurance Project. Available: www.reproline.jhu.edu/english/6read/6pi/pi_advances/pdf/pi_advances.pdf
Mazur, E. (1997). *Peer instruction: A user's manual.* Upper Saddle River, NJ: Prentice Hall.
McKeough, A., Lupart, J., & Marini, A. (1995). *Teaching for transfer: Fostering generalization in learning.* Mahwah, NJ: Erlbaum.
McTighe, J., & Emberger, M. (2006, Winter). Teamwork on assessments creates powerful professional development. *Journal of Staff Development, 27*(1), 44.
McTighe, J., & Thomas, R. (2003, February). Backward design for forward action. *Educational Leadership, 60*(5), 52–55.
McTighe, J., & Wiggins, G. (2004). *Understanding by design: Professional development workbook.* Alexandria, VA: Association for Supervision and Curriculum Development.
Mursell, J. (1954). *Successful teaching: Its psychological principles* (2nd ed.). New York: McGraw-Hill.
Nater, S., & Gallimore, R. (2005). *You haven't taught until they have learned: John Wooden's teaching principles and practices.* Morgantown, WV: Fitness Information Technology.
New Jersey Department of Education. (2004a). Introduction. In New Jersey core curriculum content standards. Available: http://education.state.nj.us/cccs/?_intro
New Jersey Department of Education. (2004b). *New Jersey core curriculum content standards for social studies.* Available: www.nj.gov/njded/cccs/s6_ss.htm
New Jersey Mathematics Coalition. (1994, September). *Mathematics to prepare our children for the 21st century: A guide for New Jersey parents.* Available: http://dimacs.rutgers.edu/nj_math_coalition/framework/standards/std_vision.html
Newmann, F. M., Bryk, A. S., & Nagaoka, J. K. (2001). *Authentic intellectual work and standardized tests: Conflict or coexistence?* Chicago: Consortium on Chicago School Research.
Perkins, D. (1992). *Smart schools: Better thinking and learning for every child.* New York: Free Press.
Perkins, D. (1993, Fall). An apple for education: Teaching and learning for understanding. *American Educator, 17*(3), 8, 28–35.

Peters, T. J., & Waterman, R. H. (1982). *In search of excellence: Lessons from America's best-run companies.* New York: Harper & Row.

Powell, A. G., Farrar, E., & Cohen, D. K. (1985). *The shopping mall high school: Winners and losers in the educational marketplace.* Boston: Houghton Mifflin.

Prochaska, J. O., Norcross, J. C., & DiClemente, C. C. (1994). *Changing for good: The revolutionary program that explains the six stages of change and teaches you how to free yourself from bad habits.* New York: Morrow.

Reeves, D. (2003). *Making standards work.* Englewood, CO: Advanced Learning Press.

Reeves, D. (2004). *Accountability in action: A blueprint for learning organizations* (2nd ed.). Englewood, CO: Advanced Learning Press.

Reeves, D. (2006). *The learning leader: How to focus school improvement for better results.* Alexandria, VA: Association for Supervision and Curriculum Development.

Resnick, L., Hall, M. W., & Fellows of the Institute for Learning. (2001). *The principles of learning: Study tools for educators* [CD]. Pittsburgh, PA: Institute for Learning, Learning Research and Development Center, University of Pittsburgh.

Rosenstein, J. G., Caldwell, J. H., & Crown, W. D. (1996, December). *New Jersey mathematics curriculum framework.* New Jersey Mathematics Coalition and the New Jersey Department of Education. Available: www.state.nj.us/njded/frameworks/math/math.pdf

Russell, J. (2003, September 13). On campuses, handhelds replacing raised hands. *Boston Globe.* Available: www.boston.com/news/nation/articles/2003/09/13/on_campuses_handhelds_replacing_raised_hands/

Sagor, R. (2000). *Guiding school improvement with action research.* Alexandria, VA: Association for Supervision and Curriculum Development.

Sawhill, J., & Williamson, D. (2001). Measuring what matters in nonprofits. *McKinsey Quarterly, 2.* Available: www.mckinseyquarterly.com/article_abstract_visitor.aspx?ar=1053

SCANS (Secretary's Commission on Achieving Necessary Skills). (1991). *What work requires of schools.* Washington, DC: U.S. Department of Labor.

Scarsdale High School. (n.d.). *Philosophy and goals of social studies department.* Available: http://scarsdale schools.k12.ny.us/hs/social/social.html

Schaefer, R. J. (1967). *The school as a center of inquiry.* New York: Harper & Row.

Schlechty, P. (1997). *Inventing better schools: An action plan for educational reform.* San Francisco: Jossey-Bass.

Schlechty, P. (2001). *Shaking up the schoolhouse: How to support and sustain educational innovation.* San Francisco: Jossey-Bass.

Schlechty, P. (2002). *Working on the work: An action plan for teachers, principals, and superintendents.* San Francisco: Jossey-Bass.

Schmoker, M. (1996). *Results: The key to continuous school improvement.* Alexandria, VA: Association for Supervision and Curriculum Development.

Schmoker, M. (2003, February). First things first: Demystifying data analysis. *Educational Leadership, 60*(5), 22–24.

Schmoker, M. (2006). *Results now: How we can achieve unprecedented improvements in teaching and learning.* Alexandria, VA: ASCD.

Schön, D. A. (1983). *The reflective practitioner: How professionals think in action.* New York: Basic Books.

Senge, P. (1990). *The fifth discipline: The art and practice of the learning organization.* New York: Doubleday/Currency.

Senge, P. (2006). *The fifth discipline: The art and practice of the learning organization* (rev. & updated ed.). New York: Doubleday/Currency.

Senge, P., Cambron-McCabe, N., Lucas, T., Smith, B., Dutton, J., & Kleiner, A. (2000). *Schools that learn: A fifth discipline fieldbook for educators, parents, and everyone who cares about education.* New York: Doubleday.

Shepard, L. A. (1989, April). Why we need better assessments. *Educational Leadership, 46*(7), 4–9.

Shewhart, W. (1934). *The economic control of quality of manufactured products.* New York: Van Nostrand. Cited in Massoud, M. R. F. (n.d.), Advances in quality improvement: Principles and framework. *QA Brief.* Bethesda, MD: Quality Assurance Project.

Sizer, T. (1984). *Horace's compromise: The dilemma of the American high school.* Boston: Houghton Mifflin.

Southwest Educational Development Laboratory. (1997). Professional learning communities: What are they and why are they important? *Issues . . . About Change*, 6(1). Available: www.sedl.org/change/issues/issues61.html

Spencer, H. (1861). What knowledge is of most worth. In *Education: Intellectual, moral, and physical.* New York: Appleton. Reprinted by Adamant Media, 2006.

Tomlinson, C. A. (1999). *The differentiated classroom: Responding to the needs of all learners.* Alexandria, VA: Association for Supervision and Curriculum Development.

Tomlinson, C. A., & Eidson, C. C. (2003). *Differentiation in practice: A resource guide for differentiating curriculum, grades 5–9.* Alexandria, VA: Association for Supervision and Curriculum Development.

Tyler, R. W. (1950). *Basic principles of curriculum and instruction: Syllabus for Education 360.* Chicago: University of Chicago.

Wadman, M. (2005, January and February). Breaking free: Dropping bad habits after 50. *AARP: The Magazine*. Available: www.aarpmagazine.org/health/Articles/a2004-11-17-mag-breaking free.html

Weimer, M. (2002). *Learner-centered teaching.* San Francisco: Jossey-Bass.

Wiggins, G., & McTighe, J. (2005). *Understanding by design* (2nd ed.). Alexandria, VA: Association for Supervision and Curriculum Development.

Index

Note: page numbers followed by *f* refer to figures

AARP newsletter, 262–263
academic freedom, 27–28
accomplishments or performance. *See also* cornerstone performances
  curricular frameworks and core subject areas, 61–66, 64*f*, 65*f*
  curriculum based on, 41–46
  learning activities vs., 50*f*
  mission and, 17
accountability tests. *See* testing, standardized
action plans
  in curriculum design, 242
  guidelines for reform planning, 242–246
  in strategic planning, 205
  WHERETO model, 246–251, 251*f*
action research, 168–170, 180, 190
activity-oriented instruction
  accomplishments vs., 50*f*
  backward design and, 205–206
  cornerstone assessments and, 97
  curricular frameworks and, 62
  as teacher misunderstanding, 147–150
adaptation, 68*f*
adjustment
  coaching and, 140–141
  in curriculum design, 53–57
  feedback and, 119
  self-adjustment, 114, 119
  strategic planning and, 203, 208–209
Adler, Mortimer, 129, 136, 143
Advanced Placement (AP) program, 95, 97
agendas, personalized, 104
"Allegory of the Cave" (Plato), 249, 252, 261–262
Alverno College, Milwaukee, 32–33, 191
American Council on the Teaching of Foreign Languages, 79, 91
American Educational Research Association, 46
analytic rubrics, 87–90, 88*f*–89*f*, 90*f*
anchors, 95–97, 96*f*, 118, 164–165
Andersen, Hans Christian, 249
Annual Yearly Progress (AYP) requirements, 150
application. *See* transfer
appraisal of teacher performance, 186–188, 187*f*
architectural analogy, 1–2, 3, 38–40, 74–75
Argyris, Chris, 23, 255, 258, 267, 269
Arter, J., 165
arts, 49, 65, 72–73, 86*f*
Aseltine, J., 168
assessment(s). *See also* cornerstone performances; standards; testing, standardized
  content-focused, 79
  curricular frameworks and, 62
  curriculum blueprint and, 41
  curriculum mapping and, 217
  diagnostic, 101–102, 104
  essential questions for, 225*f*
  feedback and, 56–57
  Force-Field Analysis of, 239*f*
  formative, 102–103
  goal clarification and, 232–233
  hiring process and, 182
  learning principles and, 117, 118
  multiple measures, 230–233, 230*f*, 234*f*
  review of, 176
assessment(s) *(continued)*
  self-assessment, 102, 114, 119, 141, 249
  spiral curriculum and, 66
  of staff readiness, 235–238, 237*f*
  standards and goals in relation to, 211
  strategic planning and, 204–205
  transfer and, 213
  transparency in, 84–85
  understanding focus and, 16
assessment frameworks, 41
assignments, classroom, 123
authentic performance, 82–85, 187*f*
autonomy, 135, 141

backward design
  coaching and, 137–138
  curriculum and, 36, 42–44
  data analysis and, 160–161
  driving example, 25–26
  knowledge and skills in, 224
  longitudinal rubrics and, 91
  mission and, 10, 19, 34
  multilevel use of, 207
  order of stages of, 227
  reform and, 3
  strategic planning and, 202–203, 204–207, 206*f*
  teacher roles and, 129, 153
  template for school reform, 206*f*
Baltimore County Public Schools, Maryland, 86*f*
Barendsen, R., 143
Barr, R., 267
behaviorism, 52
benchmarks, 90, 90*f*, 94
best practices, 167, 169. *See also* learning principles

Big Chill, The (film), 259
big ideas. *See* essential questions (big ideas)
biology, 32
Black, P., 54
blaming, 253, 255
Blanchard, Ken, 227
Bloom's Taxonomy, 45, 79
blueprint for curriculum, 38–42
Boston Globe, 133
brainstorming, 15
Bransford, J. D., 122–123, 140, 141, 146
Bruner, Jerome, 51, 52
Bryk, A. S., 123
Buckingham, M., 181
Burton, G. M., 14–15

California standards, 17–18, 30
Candlewood Middle School, New York, 181–182
CBAM (Concerns-Based Adoption Model), 238, 266
Center for What Works, 228–229
Changing for Good (Prochaska, Norcross, & DiClemente), 263–264
Christmas Carol, A, 147
Churchill, Winston, 259
civics, 84*f*
classroom assignments, 123
classroom observations, 186, 187*f*
"climbing-the-ladder" model of cognition, 45–46
coaching role, 130–131, 130*f*, 135–143, 186, 187*f*
Coalition of Essential Schools, 42
Coffman, C., 181
Cohen, D. K., 262
collaboration, 157, 160–165. *See also* teams
Collins, Jim, 160, 172, 177–179, 181, 243, 258
Comenius, A., 256
committees, cross-disciplinary, 191
common sense, 115, 116, 122, 269
compacting, 104
comparison process poster, 99*f*
computerized student-response system, 133
concept attainment protocol, 100–101
Concerns-Based Adoption Model (CBAM), 238, 266
constructivist learning experiences, 118, 140
content-mastery approach
  assessments and, 79
  context, loss of, 3–4, 38–39
  curriculum writing and, 37, 45–46
content-mastery approach *(continued)*
  facilitation and, 134–135
  feedback, failure to use, 103
  mission and, 17–19
  teacher roles and, 144–146, 146*f*
  Tyler rationale and, 20–21
content standards, 71–75, 144–146, 146*f*
context for reform, assessing, 235–240, 237*f*, 238*f*, 239*f*
continuous learning, 166–170, 183, 185*f*. *See also* professional development
contracts, learning, 104
Cooper, J., 133
cornerstone performances
  as collections of evidence, 85–87, 86*f*, 87*f*
  as curriculum component, 79–85, 83*f*, 84*f*
  curriculum design and, 42–43, 48–51
  curriculum maps and, 75–76
  learning activities and, 97
course-level maps, 79, 80*f*–81*f*
"coverage" mode of instruction, 145–146, 206, 258–260. *See also* content-mastery approach
Covey, Steven, 25, 34, 190, 210, 270
critical friend review, 158, 176
critical thinking
  coaching about content, 142–143
  curricular frameworks and, 61–63, 64*f*
  vision and, 41
cross-disciplinary departments or committees, 191
culture, 192–193, 225*f*
curricular philosophy, 66, 67*f*
curriculum components
  overview, 58–60, 60*f*
  accomplishments in core subject areas, 61–66, 64*f*, 65*f*
  anchor work samples, 95–97, 96*f*
  cornerstone assessments and collections of evidence, 79–87, 83*f*, 84*f*, 86*f*, 87*f*
  curricular philosophy, 66, 67*f*
  curriculum mapping, 75–79, 76*f*, 77*f*–78*f*, 80*f*–81*f*, 82*f*
  diagnostic assessments, 101–102
  differentiation, 104–105, 105*f*
  formative assessments, 102–103
  learning strategies, 97–98
  mission-related goals and, 59*f*
  rubrics, analytic and longitudinal, 87–94, 88*f*–89*f*, 90*f*, 92*f*–93*f*
curriculum components *(continued)*
  strategy-imbedded tools, 98, 99*f*, 100*f*
  teaching protocols, 98–101
  troubleshooting guides, 105–107, 106*f*
  understandings and essential questions, 66–75, 68*f*
curriculum development and design
  overview, 36–38
  action plans, 242
  activity-oriented, 147–150
  athletic drills analogy, 46–47
  backwards design, 42–44
  blueprint for, 38–42
  cornerstone performance challenges, 42–43, 48–51
  discipline and, 47–48, 50*f*
  essential questions for, 225*f*
  feedback and adjustment in, 53–57, 54*f*, 158, 159
  field testing, 158–159
  Force-Field Analysis of, 239*f*
  ideas for action, 57, 107–110
  leadership and, 175–177
  learning principles and, 116, 117
  monitoring progress, 109*f*
  peer reviews, 158
  performance goals, framing curriculum around, 44–46
  process cycle, 107, 108*f*
  spiral of key questions and performances throughout, 52–53, 66
  strategic planning and, 204
  teacher role in contributing to, 155–160
  typical approach to, 37, 38–39, 45–46, 51, 52–53
  vision and, 24*f*
curriculum guides, 97, 99–101
curriculum maps
  as curriculum component, 75–79, 76*f*, 77*f*–78*f*, 80*f*–81*f*, 82*f*
  goal clarification and, 232–233
  mission and, 216–218
  understandings and, 221, 222*f*

Danielson, Charlotte, 181, 221
Dansereau, Donald, 133
Darling-Hammond, L., 194, 269
data analysis, 160–165, 163*f*, 164*f*. *See also* assessment(s); evidence collection; feedback
data-driven approach, 160, 164*f*
Deal, T. E., 192–193
decision-making process, site-based, 207

Delaware standards, 68–71
Deming, W. E., 244
departments
  cross-disciplinary, 191
  goals, departmental, 32–34
  results-based, 188–192
  transfer and, 213
depersonalization, 111–113, 115, 255
design, defined, 9
desired results stage of school reform
  essential questions, 221–224, 225*f*
  goals, 213–218, 214*f*
  ideas for action, 224–226
  knowledge and skills, 224
  mission-related goals, 210–211
  understanding, 218–221, 220*f*
  vision, 212–213
developmental rubrics, 91
Dewey, John, 52, 58, 252
diagnostic assessments (pre-assessments), 101–102, 104, 119
Dichter, Alan, 207
Dickens, Charles, 147–148
DiClemente, C. C., 263–264
didactic instruction role, 129, 130*f*
differentiated instruction
  coaching and, 139
  concerns about, 240
  as curriculum component, 104–105, 105*f*
  hiring process and, 182
  learning principles and, 121
differentiated staff development, 237, 249
direct and indirect evidence, 234
direct instruction models, 97–98, 129, 130*f*
disciplines, 47–48
disruptions, minimizing, 244
Donne, John, 155
drills, 46–47, 85
Drucker, Peter, 172, 180, 199, 200, 201, 227
DuFour, R., 194, 269

Eaker, R., 194
efficacy, sense of, 113, 117
efficiency vs. effectiveness, 25–26
ELLs (English language Learners), 105, 105*f*
Emberger, M., 165
"Emperor's New Clothes, The" (Andersen), 249
ends vs. means, 215
engagement
  activity-oriented curriculum and, 149–150
engagement *(continued)*
  evidence collection and, 228
  learning principles and, 117, 118
"engineering prototype" tactic, 245
English and language arts
  anchor work samples, 95, 96*f*
  cornerstone performance challenges, 49
  curricular frameworks, 63
  Delaware essential questions, 70–71
  Georgia standards, 30–31
  portfolio options, 87*f*
  program-level accomplishments, 65
  understandings and essential questions, 68*f*
  Victorian Tea unit, 147–148
English language Learners (ELLs), 105, 105*f*
environment, safe and supportive, 114, 120
Erickson, Lynn, 67
essential questions (big ideas)
  content standards and, 72
  in course-level framework for history, 80*f*–81*f*
  curricular frameworks and, 62
  as curriculum component, 66–71, 68*f*
  curriculum mapping and, 77*f*–78*f*
  hiring and, 181–182
  learning principles and, 113, 117, 120
  mathematics example, 15
  reform framed by, 221–224, 225*f*
  spiral of, 52
  strategic planning and, 204
  understanding focus and, 16
  in unit-level map for math, 82*f*
evaluation of staff, learning principles and, 119
events, fixation on, 254
evidence collection. *See also* assessment(s); feedback
  overview, 227–229
  context for reform, assessing, 235–240, 237*f*, 238*f*, 239*f*
  cornerstone assessments and, 85–87, 86*f*, 87*f*
  determining acceptable evidence, 204–205
  direct and indirect evidence, 234
  ideas for action, 240–241
  mission-critical evidence, 229–235, 230*f*, 234*f*, 236*f*
  qualitative evidence, 235, 236*f*
exemplars
  annotated, 96*f*
  coaching and, 137
  collaborative evaluation of student work and, 164–165
  defined, 95
  learning principles and, 118
experience, delusion of learning from, 254
expert review, 157
extrinsic rewards, 243

face validity, 152
facilitative teaching, 130, 130*f*, 131–135
faculty meetings. *See* staff meetings
Fairfax County, Virginia, 96–97
fairness, 15
Farrar, E., 262
Faryniarz, J., 168
fatalism, 270
feedback. *See also* assessment(s); evidence collection
  coaching and, 139–140
  computerized student-response system, 133
  curriculum design and, 53–57, 54*f*, 158, 159
  formative assessments, 102–103
  gap analysis and, 178–180
  against goals, 209
  learning principles and, 114, 117, 119
  longitudinal rubrics and, 94
  mission and, 28
  reform planning and, 250, 251*f*
  staff understanding and, 228
  on standards, 211
  strategic planning and, 203, 205
  understanding-based schooling and, 126
  value of, 233–235
field testing, 158–159
Fifth Discipline, The (Senge), 253–255
fine arts. *See* arts
"5 by 5" commitment, 186–188
flexible grouping, 104
Force-Field Analysis, 238–239, 238*f*, 239*f*
foreign (world) languages, 49, 77*f*–78*f*, 83*f*
Foreyt, John, 263
formative assessments, 102–103
Framework for Teaching (Danielson), 181
Framework for Teaching model, 221, 222*f*

France, Anatole, 1
freedom, academic, 27–28
Freud, S., 261
friendship, 68*f*
frog in boiling water parable, 254
Fullan, M., 178, 181

gap analysis
desired results of reform and, 212
failure to see the gap, 257
goals and, 213
leadership and, 177–180
Gardner, H., 19, 261
Georgia standards, 30–31
Gilbert, Thomas, 53–54
goals. *See also* accomplishments or performance
action planning and, 242–243
coaching and, 137, 138
content standards and, 71–75
defined, 213
departmental and grade-level, 32–34
effective vs. problematic, 214–215, 214*f*
framing curriculum around, 44–46, 47
learning principles and, 114, 118–119
map of, 76*f*
measure clarification and, 232–233
mission and need, goals closest to, 216–218
mission-related reform goals, 210–211
product-oriented, 191
standards and, 211, 213
test scores and, 152–153
tips on goal setting, 215–216
Tyler rationale and, 20–21
"Goldilocks" problem, 72, 215
Goodlad, John, 51, 141, 256–257
Good to Great (Collins), 178–179, 243
grade-level objectives, longitudinal rubrics and, 94
grading and reporting systems, transfer-focused, 213
Gragg, C. I., 132
graphic organizers, 101
Greece Central School District, New York, 76*f*, 95, 96*f*
Greene, Andy, 181–182, 183–185, 185*f*

habits of mind and action
overview, 252–253
as barriers to reform, 255–258
habits of mind and action *(continued)*
breaking institutional bad habits, 266–267
change process, 262–266
coverage as bad habit, 258–260
curricular frameworks and, 62
discipline and, 48
facilitation and, 135
focus on, 13–14
ideas for action, 271–272
learning principles and, 114, 120
reform of professional development, 268–271
resistance to learning, 261–262
Senge's organizational "learning disabilities," 253–255
textbooks as enablers of bad habits, 260–261
Haire, Mason, 229
Harvard Assessment Seminar, 103
highest-leverage actions, 216–217
hiring and placement, 119, 181–183
Hirsch, E. D., 20
history
coaching critical thinking about content, 142–143
cornerstone performance challenges, 49
course-level framework for, 80*f*–81*f*
curricular frameworks, 61–63, 64*f*
essential questions, 68–70
mission statements on, 30, 32
performance assessment tasks, 84*f*
program-level accomplishments, 65
hooks, 118, 247–248
Hord, S. M., 266
Howe, B., 138
How People Learn (Bransford, Brown, & Cocking), 46, 122–123, 127
Human Nature and Conduct (Dewey), 252
Hunter, Madeline, 20

if/then questioning, 23–25
improvement planning, data analysis for, 160–165, 163*f*, 164*f*
incentives, 243–244
independent studies, 104
Indian Hill Schools, Ohio, 179
induction programs, 183, 184*f*
influential individuals, 243
information analysis, 160. *See also* feedback
innovation and mission, 28
In Search of Excellence (Peters and Waterman), 229
inservice training, 268
instruction. *See also* teacher job functions; *entries at* curriculum
classroom assignments and standardized tests, 123
essential questions for, 225*f*
Force-Field Analysis of, 239*f*
teaching to the test, 150–153
instructional principles. *See* learning principles
"Instructional Strategies to Improve Student Achievement," 221, 222*f*
instruction paradigm, 267
Internet, 180
intrinsic rewards, 243
"Iowa and New Hampshire primary tactic," 245

Jacobs, Heidi Hayes, 232
Japan, 169
journal articles, discussion of, 183–185, 185*f*
"just-in-time" instruction, 140

Kentucky Department of Education, 102
key assessment tasks. *See* cornerstone performances
knowledge and skills for reform, 224

language arts. *See* English and language arts
languages, world, 49, 77*f*–78*f*, 83*f*
leader job functions
overview, 172–173
curriculum and, 175–177
gap analysis, 177–180
learning organizations and, 179, 193–195
mission and learning principles and, 173–174
personnel, 180–187, 184*f*, 185*f*, 187*f*
school culture and, 192–193
structures, policies, and resources, 188–192
leadership, defined, 172
learning
continuous, 166–170
defined, 113
resistance to, 261–262
learning contracts, 104
learning disabilities, organizational, 253–255
learning goals. *See* goals
learning organizations, 179, 193–195, 267, 268–270

learning paradigm, 267
learning principles
depersonalization of teaching, 111–113, 115
ideas for action, 126–127
implications of, 116–121
leadership and, 174
particularity of, 121–122
set of, 113–115
staff misunderstandings of, 220*f*
standardized testing and, 122–126, 124*f*, 125*f*
understanding-based schooling and, 126
vision and, 212–213
learning strategies, 97–98
lesson study, 169
Levy, Marv, 54–55
Lewis, C., 194
lifelong learning, 166–170
Light, Richard, 103
Lincoln, Abraham, 199
literature, world, 68*f*
Littleton High School, Colorado, 84*f*
longitudinal rubrics, 91–94, 92*f*–93*f*
lower-achieving students, 45

management team, myth of, 254–255
management vs. leadership, 173
maps, curriculum, 75–79, 76*f*, 77*f*–78*f*, 80*f*–81*f*, 82*f*
marketing, 43–44
Marshall, Kim, 186–188
Marzano, Robert, 40, 54, 98, 221
mathematics
adjusting algebra curriculum, 55–56
cornerstone performance challenges, 49
curricular frameworks, 63
data-driven improvement planning, 164*f*
as "discipline," 48
portfolio options, 87*f*
program-level accomplishments, 65
Pythagorean theorem problems, 124–125, 124*f*, 125*f*
supported inclusion students, ideas for, 105*f*
understanding-focused approach to measures of central tendency, 14–16
unit-level map for, 82*f*
Mazur, Eric, 134–135
McLuhan, Marshall, 191
meaning making. *See also* understanding(s)
cornerstone performances and, 43
meaning making *(continued)*
curriculum blueprint and, 41
facilitation and, 134
mission and, 14
resistance to new understandings, 261
teaching protocols and, 98–101
means vs. ends, 215
measures of central tendency, 14–16
meetings. *See* staff meetings
Meisels, Samuel, 91
metacognitive strategies, 119, 141
mission
collective commitment to, 27–28
content vs. transfer focus and, 16–20
correction of conduct at odds with, 179
curriculum blueprint and, 40–42
curriculum framework and mission-related goals, 59*f*
definition and purpose of, 9–11
departmental and grade-level goals and, 32–34
evidence, mission-critical, 229–235, 230*f*, 234*f*, 236*f*
gap analysis and, 177
goals and, 216–218
ideas for action, 34–35
if/then questioning and, 23–25
importance of, 21–22
leadership and, 173–174
learning principles and, 117
long-term commitment to, 12–13
mathematics example, understanding-focused, 14–16
mission-related reform goals, 210–211
point of schooling and, 11–13
purpose and, 25–27
school culture and, 193
standards and, 28–31, 213
strategic principles for accomplishing, 202–203
student as achiever of, 217
test scores and, 152–153
understanding, transfer, and habits of mind, focus on, 13–14
mission statements
accomplishments and, 26
"critical thinking" in, 41
New England Association of Schools and Colleges, 10
point of schooling and, 11–12
standards and, 29–30
subject-matter content and, 16–17
Mississippi curriculum framework, 74
mistakes, learning from, 120
misunderstandings and misconceptions
by staff, 220, 220*f*, 255
by students, 101–102
of teacher job functions, 144–153, 146*f*
Mursell, J., 153

Nagoaka, J. K., 123
Nater, Sven, 128
National Assessment of Education Progress, 91
national curriculum materials for England, 91, 92*f*–93*f*
National Research Council, 46, 122
National Staff Development Council, 168
National Study of School Evaluation, 221, 222*f*
"Nation's Report Card," 91
Nature Conservancy, 231
NCLB (No Child Left Behind), 94
NEASC Accreditation Standards, 36
New England Association of Schools and Colleges (NEASC), 10, 36
New Hope–Solebury School District, Pennsylvania, 186, 187*f*, 221, 222*f*
New Jersey Core Curriculum Content Standards, 17, 29, 49–51
New Jersey curriculum framework, 74
Newman, F. M., 123
new teacher induction programs, 183, 184*f*
New York City Board of Education, 207
New York curriculum map for world languages, 77*f*–78*f*
New York Department of Education, 95, 124*f*
No Child Left Behind (NCLB), 94
Norcross, J. C., 263–264

observable indicators, 235, 236*f*
observations in the classroom, 186, 187*f*
Omnibus system for literacy development, 91
openness, modeling, 120
ownership of curriculum, 156

Paideia Proposal, The (Adler), 129
parent feedback, 179–180
PDSA cycle (Plan, Do, Study, Act), 208
peer reviews, 158, 176
performance goals. *See* goals

performance indicators, 30–31, 90. *See also* observable indicators
performances. *See* accomplishments or performance; cornerstone performances
performing arts. *See* arts
personal improvement plans, 118
personalization of teaching, 111–112
personalized agendas, 104
personalized learning, 114, 121, 139
personnel responsibilities
  overview, 180–181
  feedback and appraisal, 186–188, 187*f*
  hiring and placement, 181–183
  professional development, 183–185, 184*f*, 185*f*
Peters, T. J., 229
Peterson, K. D., 192–193
philosophy, curricular, 66, 67*f*
Piaget, J., 261
Pickering, D. J., 54
"Picture the Graduate" exercise, 173–174
Place Called School, A (Goodlad), 51, 141
placement decisions, 182–183
Plan, Do, Study, Act (PDSA) cycle, 208
planning, strategic. *See* strategic planning for school reform
Platkin, Charles Stuart, 263
Plato, 249, 252, 261–262
Pogo, 256
policy
  essential questions for, 225*f*
  Force-Field Analysis of, 239*f*
  leadership and, 188–192
Pollock, J. E., 54
portfolios, 85–87, 86*f*, 87*f*
position focus, 253
Powell, A. G., 262
pre-assessments, 101–102, 104, 119
precontemplation stage of change, 265–266
preparation stage of change, 265
principles of learning. *See* learning principles
priorities and learning principles, 114, 118–119
proactiveness, 253–254, 270
problem-solving strategies wheel, 100*f*
process, confusion between results and, 207
process modeling, 244
Prochaska, J. O., 263–264
product modeling, 244
product-oriented goals, 191
professional development
  continuous learning and, 167–168
  curriculum design and, 157
  differentiated, 237
  essential questions for, 225*f*
  Force-Field Analysis of, 239*f*
  leadership and, 183–185, 184*f*, 185*f*
  learning principles and, 116, 117, 120, 121
  reform of, 268–271
  transfer-focused, 213
professionalism
  continuous learning and, 166
  depersonalization and, 112
  mission and, 27
  peer reviews and, 158
program-level curriculum maps, 76–79, 76*f*, 77*f*–78*f*
progress, measurement of, 91
protocols, teaching, 98–101
purpose and mission, 25–27
Pythagorean theorem, 124–125, 124*f*, 125*f*

qualitative evidence, 235, 236*f*
quotas, arbitrary, 215

RateMyTeachers.com, 180
readiness assessment, 235–238, 237*f*
recurring performances, 82–83, 83*f*, 84*f*
Reeves, Douglas, 67, 207
reflection. *See* self-assessment and self-adjustment
reform planning. *See* strategic planning for school reform
Republic (Plato), 252, 261–262
research, in-school, 169–170
resources, 188–192, 239*f*
Responsive Classroom model, 221, 222*f*
results-based teams and departments, 188–192
rethinking
  learning principles and, 114, 120
  reform planning and, 248–249
rewards, intrinsic and extrinsic, 243
Rigazio-DiGilio, A., 168
risk taking, 120
Robinson, P., 133
Rogers, Richard, 133
rubrics
  analytic, 87–90, 88*f*–89*f*, 90*f*
  common, 94
  defined, 87
  holistic, 87
rubrics *(continued)*
  learning principles and, 118
  longitudinal, 91–94, 92*f*–93*f*
Russell, J., 133

San Jose State University, California, 63
Sawhill, J., 231
SCANS report, 18–19, 42
Scarsdale High School, New York, 33
Schaefer, Robert, 169–170, 193–194, 269
Schlechty, P., 42
Schön, Donald A., 194–195, 258, 267, 268
School as a Center of Inquiry, The (Schaeffer), 169–170
school culture, 192–193
schooling by design, defined, 2
science
  cornerstone performance challenges, 49
  as "discipline," 48
  longitudinal rubric for scientific inquiry, 92*f*–93*f*
  performance assessment tasks, 84*f*
  program-level accomplishments, 65
  supported inclusion students, ideas for, 105*f*
Scoring Rubrics in the Classroom (Arter and McTighe), 165
self-assessment and self-adjustment
  coaching and, 141
  learning principles and, 114, 119
  misconceptions and, 102
  reform planning and, 249
self-changers, 265
seminar format, 131
Senge, Peter, 47, 156, 194, 253–255, 268–269
sequencing of reform work, 250–251, 251*f*
Seven Habits of Highly Effective People, The (Covey), 25, 190, 210, 270
Shanker, Albert, 42
Shaw, George Bernard, 242
Shepard, Lori, 45–46
Shewhart, Walter, 208
Shewhart Cycle, 208, 208*f*
Shopping Mall High School, The (Powell, Farrar, & Cohen), 262
Sizer, Ted, 42, 138
small-group activities, 104
social studies
  mission statements, 30, 33
  New Jersey standards, 49–51
  performance assessment tasks, 84*f*
  program-level accomplishments, 65

Socrates, 261–262
South-Orange Maplewood, New Jersey, 84*f*
speaking and listening, 90*f*
special education (SPED), 105, 105*f*
Spencer, H., 256
spiral curriculum, 52–53, 66
St. Charles Community Schools, Illinois, 230–231, 230*f*
staff meetings
  backward design of, 160–162
  discussion of journal articles in, 183–185, 185*f*
  results-focused, 190–191, 213
standards
  analysis and "unpacking" of, 175–176, 192
  architectural analogy, 3
  content focus of, 17–18
  content standards, 71–75, 144–146, 146*f*
  cornerstone performances and, 49–51
  curriculum and, 36
  essential questions for, 225*f*
  goals and, 211, 213
  "Goldilocks" problem and, 215
  mission and, 28–31
  performance indicators, framing by, 90
Standards for Professional Development (National Staff Development Council), 168
State College Area School District, Pennsylvania, 23, 24*f*
statement of objectives, 20
state standards. *See* standards
statistics, 68*f*
strategic planning for school reform
  definitions and overview, 199–203
  adjustment and, 203, 208–209
  backward design and, 202–203, 204–207, 206*f*
  problems in implementation of, 205–207
  tactics and, 200–202
  vision-reality gap, closing, 203, 208
strategies
  defined, 200–201
  differentiated instruction, strategies and tactics for, 104
  learning strategies, 97–98
strategy-imbedded tools, 98, 99*f*, 100*f*
structures, 188–192, 225*f*
student choice, 104
student-response system, computerized, 133
successful learning, 114
supervision
  learning-focused, 186, 187*f*
  learning principles and, 116, 117, 119, 120, 121
Supervision for Learning (Aseltine, Faryniarz, & Rigazio-DiGilio), 168
supported inclusion students, 105*f*
surveys, 117, 121, 233
sustainability, 195
syllabi
  big ideas and, 120
  differentiation and, 121
  feedback and, 119
  textbooks and, 145, 260
  transfer and, 116, 118
systems thinking, 255

tactics, 104, 200–203, 245
Tagg, J., 267
taking charge, illusion of, 253–254
teacher job functions
  overview, 128–129, 155
  activity-oriented approach, 147–150
  backward design and, 153
  categories of instructional roles, 129–131, 130*f*
  coaching, 130–131, 130*f*, 135–143
  content-coverage approach, 144–146, 146*f*
  continuous learning, 166–170
  curriculum, contribution to, 155–160
  data analysis, 160–165, 163*f*, 164*f*
  facilitation of understanding, 130, 130*f*, 131–135
  ideas for action, 153–154, 170–171
  matching approach to situation, 143–144
  teaching to the test, 150–153
Teachers (film), 262
teaching protocols, 98–101
teams
  analyzing student work in, 162–163
  curriculum design in, 156–157
  learning principles and, 118, 119
  results-based, 188–192
  transfer and, 213
technology, 133
testing, standardized
  analysis of, 162
  learning principles and, 122–126, 124*f*, 125*f*
testing, standardized *(continued)*
  medical exam analogy, 151–152
  teaching to the test, 150–153
textbooks, 63, 144–145, 146*f*, 260–261
tiered activities, 104
time resources, 188–191
TIMSS (Trends in International Mathematics and Science Study), 123
Tomlinson, Carol Ann, 139
tour director task, 83*f*
Towson University, Maryland, 63
training. *See* professional development
transfer. *See also* backward design
  accomplishment-based curriculum and, 43–44
  curricular frameworks and, 61, 62
  curriculum design and, 41, 45
  discipline and, 48
  expert review of ideas on, 157
  focus on, 13–14
  importance of, 2–4
  instructional roles and, 131
  learning principles and, 113, 116–117
  mission and, 18–20
  recurring performances and, 82–83, 83*f*, 84*f*
  standardized testing and, 123–126, 124*f*, 125*f*
  understanding focus and, 16
  vision and, 212–213
transfer goals. *See* goals
transparency in assessment, 84–85
Trends in International Mathematics and Science Study (TIMSS), 123
troubleshooting, 159–160, 176–177
troubleshooting guides, 105–106, 106*f*
Tyler, Ralph, 9, 20–21
Tyler rationale, 20–21

"uncoverage," 118
understanding(s)
  accomplishment-based curriculum and, 43–44
  common diagnosis based on, 194–195
  connections between programs and initiatives, 221, 222*f*
  as curriculum component, 66–71, 68*f*
  curriculum mapping and, 77*f*–78*f*
  essential questions and, 224
  evidence collection and, 228
  importance of, 2–4
  instructional roles and, 131, 134

understanding(s) *(continued)*
  learning principles and, 113, 118, 126
  mission and focus on, 13–16
  resistance to change in, 261
  six facets of, 219
  staff misunderstandings, 220, 220*f*, 240
  strategic planning and, 204
  in unit-level map for math, 82*f*
  vision for reform and, 218–219
Understanding by Design Exchange, 245–246
unit-level maps, 79, 82*f*
"urgent" vs. "important," 190
U.S. Soccer Federation (USSF) guidelines, 137–138

value, recognition of, 113, 117
Victorian Tea unit, 147–148
vision
  curriculum blueprint and, 41
  desired results of reform and, 212–213
  essential questions for, 225*f*
  learning principles and, 116, 121
  mission and, 23
  strategic planning and, 203
  understandings and, 218–219
visual arts. *See* arts

Wadman, M., 262–263
Waterman, R. H., 229
"What We Believe About Learning" exercise, 126–127
WHERETO model, 246–251, 251*f*
Wiliam, D., 54
Williamson, D., 231
Wooden, John, 46, 128, 138
world languages, 49, 77*f*–78*f*, 83*f*
writing, 76*f*, 88*f*–89*f*, 95, 96*f*

"Yes, but . . ." responses, 243

About the Authors

Grant Wiggins is the president of Authentic Education in Hopewell, New Jersey, a consulting, research, and publishing organization. He earned an Ed.D. from Harvard University and a B.A. from St. John's College in Annapolis, Maryland. Wiggins consults with schools, districts, and state education departments on a variety of reform matters; organizes conferences and workshops; and develops print materials and Web resources on curricular change. He is perhaps best known for being the coauthor, with Jay McTighe, of *Understanding by Design,* the award-winning and highly successful series of materials on curriculum published by ASCD. His work has been supported by the Pew Charitable Trusts, the Geraldine R. Dodge Foundation, and the National Science Foundation.

For 20 years, Wiggins has worked on some of the most influential reform initiatives in the country, including Vermont's portfolio system and Ted Sizer's Coalition of Essential Schools. He has established statewide consortia devoted to assessment reform for North Carolina, and headed standards clarification work for the state education departments in Delaware, New Jersey, and Mississippi. Wiggins is the author of *Educative Assessment* and *Assessing Student Performance,* both published by Jossey-Bass. His many articles have appeared in such journals as *Educational Leadership* and *Phi Delta Kappan*.

Wiggins's work is grounded in 14 years of secondary school teaching and coaching. He has taught English and electives in philosophy; coached soccer, cross country, baseball, and track and field; and has coached his own children in soccer and baseball. Wiggins plays guitar and sings in the Hazbins, a rock band. He can be reached at grant@authenticeducation.org. Resources in support of *Understanding by Design* and *Schooling by Design* can be found at www.bigideas.org.

Jay McTighe has a wealth of experience developed during a rich and varied career in education. He served as director of the Maryland Assessment Consortium, a state collaboration of school districts working together to develop and share formative performance assessments. Prior to this position, McTighe was involved with school improvement projects at Maryland State Department of Education. He is well known for work with "thinking skills," having coordinated statewide efforts to develop instructional strategies, curriculum models, and assessment procedures for improving the quality of student thinking. McTighe also directed the development of the Instructional Framework, a multimedia database on teaching. In addition to his work at the state level, McTighe has experience at the district level in Prince George's County, Maryland, as a classroom teacher, resource specialist, and program coordinator. He also served as director of the Maryland Summer Center for Gifted and Talented Students, a statewide residential enrichment program held at St. Mary's College.

McTighe has published articles in a number of leading journals and books, including *Educational Leadership, Developing Minds, Thinking Skills: Concepts and Techniques,* and *The Developer*. He has coauthored three books on assessment: *Assessing Learning in the Classroom, Assessing Outcomes: Performance Assessment Using the Dimensions of Learning Model,* and *Evaluation Tools to Improve as Well as Evaluate Student Performance*. He is coauthor, with Grant Wiggins, of the best-selling *Understanding by Design* series and the newly released *Connecting Content and Kids: Integrating Differentiation and Understanding by Design*, coauthored with Carol Ann Tomlinson.

McTighe has an extensive background in staff development and is a regular speaker at national, state, and district conferences and workshops. He is also a featured presenter in four videotape programs, *Performance Assessment in the Classroom, Developing Performance Assessments, Understanding Understanding,* and *Using Backward Design.*

McTighe earned an undergraduate degree from the College of William and Mary and a master's degree from the University of Maryland, and has completed post-graduate studies at Johns Hopkins University. He was selected to participate in the Educational Policy Fellowship Program through the Institute for Educational Leadership in Washington, D.C. McTighe served as a member of the National Assessment Forum, a coalition of education and civil rights organizations advocating reforms in national, state, and local assessment policies and practices. He served a three-year term on the ASCD Publications Committee, serving as committee chair from 1994 to 1995. McTighe may be reached at 6581 River Run, Columbia, MD 21044-6066. Phone: (410) 531-1610. E-mail: jmctighe@comcast.net.

Related ASCD Resources: Understanding by Design

At the time of publication, the following ASCD resources were available; for the most up-to-date information about ASCD resources, go to www.ascd.org. ASCD stock numbers are noted in parentheses.

Audiotapes

Applying Understanding by Design to School Improvement Planning by Jay McTighe and Ronald S. Thomas (#202143)

Structures That Support Understanding by Design by Fran Prolman and Grant Wiggins (#299321)

Understanding by Design: Structures and Strategies for Designing School Reform by Jay McTighe and Grant Wiggins: (#202189)

Walking the Talk: Applying Standards to Our Own Work by Jay McTighe and Grant Wiggins (#200334)

What Does Understanding by Design Have to Do with Professional Development by Harolyn Katherman and others (#202137)

Working Smarter in Curriculum Design by Jay McTighe and Grant Wiggins (#20114)

Networks

Visit the ASCD Web site (www.ascd.org) and click on About ASCD. Under the header of Your Partnership with ASCD, click on Networks for information about professional educators who have formed groups around topics, including "Arts in Education," "Authentic Assessment," and "Brain-Based Compatible Learning." Look in the Network Directory for current facilitators' addresses and phone numbers.

Online Courses

Understanding by Design: An Introduction (register for these online or by calling ASCD)

Understanding by Design: Six Facets of Understanding

Understanding by Design: The Backward Design Process

Print Products

Integrating Differentiated Instruction & Understanding by Design: Connecting Content and Kids by Carol Ann Tomlinson and Jay McTighe (#105004)

Understanding by Design Expanded 2nd Edition by Grant Wiggins and Jay McTighe (#103055)

The Understanding by Design Handbook by Jay McTighe and Grant Wiggins (#199030)

Understanding by Design Professional Development Workbook by Jay McTighe and Grant Wiggins (#103056)

Understanding by Design Study Guide (#100246)

Understanding by Design Bundle for Study Groups, includes 10 copies of *Understanding by Design* and 1 copy of the *Study Guide* (#100245)

Training

The ASCD Understanding by Design Faculty: ASCD will arrange for a UBD expert to deliver onsite training tailored to the needs of your school, district, or regional service agency. Call (703) 578-9600, ext. 5677

Videotapes

The Understanding by Design Video Series, three tapes (#400241)

Web Products

Professional Development Online, at http://pdonline.ascd.org, features several UbD-related online study courses.

The UbD Exchange, at http://www.ubdexchange.org/, features a database of units designed using the Understanding by Design framework. It contains short tutorials and self-checks to guide designers through the electronic unit template as they build units and assessments to store in the database. Users of the Exchange can interact with others by giving and receiving feedback on curriculum units using the design standards.

Exemplars of essential questions, enduring understandings, performance tasks, rubrics, and learning activities are highlighted with blue ribbons and trophies awarded by the authors and other expert UbD trainers.

For additional resources, visit us on the World Wide Web (http://www.ascd.org), send an e-mail message to member@ascd.org, call the ASCD Service Center (1-800-933-ASCD or 703-578-9600, then press 2), send a fax to 703-575-5400, or write to Information Services, ASCD, 1703 N. Beauregard St., Alexandria, VA 22311-1714 USA.